P9-AGA-463

Internet and Intranet Security

Second Edition

For quite a long time, computer security was a rather narrow field of study that was populated mainly by theoretical computer scientists, electrical engineers, and applied mathematicians. With the proliferation of open systems in general, and the Internet and the World Wide Web (WWW) in particular, this situation has changed fundamentally. Today, computer and network practitioners are equally interested in computer security, since they require technologies and solutions that can be used to secure applications related to electronic commerce (e-commerce). Against this background, the field of computer security has become very broad and includes many topics of interest. The aim of this series is to publish state-of-the-art, high standard technical books on topics related to computer security. Further information about the series can be found on the WWW at the following URL:

http://www.esecurity.ch/serieseditor.html

Also, if you'd like to contribute to the series by writing a book about a topic related to computer security, feel free to contact either the Commissioning Editor or the Series Editor at Artech House.

Recent Titles in the Artech House Computer Security Series

Rolf Oppliger, Series Editor

Computer Foresnsics and Privacy, Michael A. Caloyannides
Demystifying the IPsec Puzzle, Sheila Frankel
Electronic Payment Systems for E-Commerce, Second Edition,
    Donal O'Mahony, Michael Peirce, and Hitesh Tewari
Information Hiding Techniques for Steganography and Digital Watermarking,
    Stefan Katzenbeisser and Fabien A. P. Petitcolas
Java Card for E-Payment Applications, VesnaHassler, et al.
Non-repudiation in Electronic Commerce, Jianying Zhou
Secure Messaging with PGP and S/MIME, Rolf Oppliger
Security Fundamentals for E-Commerce, Vesna Hassler
Security Technologies for the World Wide Web, Rolf Oppliger

For a complete listing of the *Artech House Computing Library,*
turn to the back of this book.

Internet and Intranet Security

Second Edition

Rolf Oppliger

Artech House
Boston • London
www.artechhouse.com

Library of Congress Cataloging-in-Publication Data
Oppliger, Rolf.
    Internet and Intranet security / Rolf Oppliger.—2nd ed.
        p. cm. — (Artech House computer security series)
    Includes bibliographical references and index.
    ISBN 1-58053-166-0 (alk. paper)
        1. Internet—Security measures. 2. Intranets (Computer networks)—Security measures.
    3. Computers—Access control. 4. TCP/IP (Computer network protocol). I. Title.
    II. Series.

    TK5105.875.I57 O67 2001
    005.8—dc21   2001045752

British Library Cataloguing in Publication Data
Oppliger, Rolf
    Internet and intranet security.—2nd ed. — (Artech House
    computer security series)
        1. Internet—Security measures 2. Internet—Access control
        3. Intranets (Computer networks)—Security measures
        4. Intranets (Computer networks)—Access control
        I. Title
        005.8

    ISBN 1-58053-166-0

Cover design by Igor Valdman

© 2002 ARTECH HOUSE, INC.
685 Canton Street
Norwood, MA 02062

International Standard Book Number: 1-58053-166-0
Library of Congress Catalog Card Number: 2001045752

10 9 8 7 6 5 4 3 2 1

To Isabelle and Marc

Contents

Preface

In general parlance, the term TCP/IP refers to an entire suite of communications protocols that center around the Transmission Control Protocol (TCP) and the Internet Protocol (IP). The emerging use of TCP/IP networking has led to a global system of interconnected hosts and networks that is commonly referred to as the Internet.[1] The Internet was created initially to help foster communications among government-sponsored research groups and grew steadily to include most educational institutions, commercial organizations, and government agencies.

During the last decade, the Internet has experienced a triumphant advance. Today, it is the world's largest computer network and has been doubling in size each year.[2] With this phenomenal growth rate, the Internet's size is increasing faster than any other network ever created, including even the public-switched telephone network (PSTN).[3] As such, the Internet is commonly seen as the basis and first incarnation of an information superhighway, or national information infrastructure (NII) as, for example, promoted by the U.S. government.

But in spite of this exacting role, the initial, research-oriented Internet and its communications protocols were designed for a more benign environment than now

---

[1]Note the definite article and the capital letter "I" in the term "Internet." More generally, the term "internet" is used to refer to any TCP/IP-based internetwork.

[2]K. G. Coffman and A. M. Odlyzko, "Internet Growth: Is There a 'Moore's Law' for Data Traffic?" to be published.

[3]Only mobile networks experience similar growth rates.

exists. It could, perhaps, best be described as a collegial environment, where the users were mutually trusting each other and were interested in a free and open exchange of information. In this environment, the people on the Internet were the people who actually built the Internet. Later, when the Internet became more useful and reliable, these people were joined by others. With fewer common goals and more people, the Internet steadily twisted away from its original intent.

Today, the Internet environment is much less collegial and trustworthy. It contains all the dangerous situations, nasty people, and risks that one can find in society as a whole. Along with the well-intentioned and honest users of the Internet, there are always people who intentionally try to break into computer systems and networks connected to it. Consequently, the Internet is plagued with the kind of delinquents who enjoy the electronic equivalent of writing on other people's walls with spray paint, tearing off mailboxes, or sitting in the street honking their car horns. In this new environment, the openness of the Internet has turned out to be a double-edged sword. Since its very beginning, but especially since its opening in the late 1990s and its ongoing commercialization in the new millenium, the Internet has become a popular target to attack. The number of security breaches has in fact escalated more than in proportion to the growth of the Internet as a whole.

Many security problems with networks in general and the Internet in particular have received public attention, and the media have carried stories of high-profile malicious attacks by way of the Internet against government, business, and academic sites. Perhaps the first and most significant incident was the Internet Worm, launched by Robert T. Morris, Jr., on November 2, 1988 [1, 2]. The Internet Worm flooded thousands of hosts interconnected to the Internet and woke up the Internet community accordingly. Since then, reports of network-based attacks, such as password sniffing, IP spoofing and sequence number guessing, session hijacking, flooding, and other distributed denial of service attacks, as well as exploitations of well-known design limitations and software bugs, have grown dramatically [3–5]. In addition, the use and wide deployment of executable content, such as that provided by Java applets and ActiveX controls, for example, have provided new possibilities to attack hosts and entire sites.[4]

The Internet Worm gained a lot of publicity and led to increased awareness of security issues on the Internet. In fact, the Computer Emergency Response Team (CERT)[5] that is operated by the Software Engineering Institute at Carnegie Mellon University was created in the aftermath of the Internet Worm, and other

---

[4]Visit the home page of DigiCrime at URL http://www.digicrime.com to convince yourself that executable content is, in fact, dangerous.

[5]http://www.cert.org

CERTs have been founded in many countries around the world.[6] Today, the CERT at Carnegie Mellon University serves as CERT coordination center (CERT/CC). The CERT/CC receives an average of three to four new computer security incident reports each day (and this number is not likely to decrease in the future). Taking further into account that many security incidents go unnoticed and unreported, the situation is scary, to say the least.

Many Internet breaches are publicized and attract the attention of the Internet community. For example, early in 1994, thousands of passwords were captured by sniffer programs that had been remotely installed on compromised hosts on various university networks connected to the Internet. At the end of the same year, IP spoofing, sequence number guessing, and TCP SYN flooding attacks were successfully combined by Kevin Mitnick to attack several computer centers, including, for example, the San Diego Center for Supercomputing [6]. This story actually shocked the world when it became *The New York Times* headline news on January 23, 1995. In the second half of the 1990s, several forms of denial of service (DoS) attacks were launched, such as e-mail bombing and TCP SYN flooding. In February 2000, some distributed denial of service (DDoS) attacks were successfully launched against some of the largest and most widely known Internet sites, such as Yahoo!, Amazon, eTrade, eBay, CNN, and ZDNet. A few months later, the ILOVEYOU virus and a series of imitators shocked the world by successfully attacking the messaging infrastructures and intranet environments of leading companies and organizations throughout the world. The incidents showed that executable content and configuring computer systems in a way that such content is automatically executed is one of the most dangerous things one can do from a security point of view.

Despite the fact that unscrupulous people make press headlines with various types of attacks, the vulnerabilities they exploit are usually well known. For example, security experts have warned against passwords transmitted in the clear since the very beginning of internetworking, and Robert T. Morris, Jr., described IP spoofing and sequence number attacks for BSD UNIX version 4.2 when he was with AT&T Bell Laboratories in 1985 [7, 8]. Also, the vulnerabilities that are exploited by DoS and DDoS attacks and the threats related to executable content are known and particularly well documented.

Today, individuals, commercial organizations, and government agencies depend on the Internet for communications and research, and thus have much more to lose if their sites are successfully attacked. As a matter of fact, virtually everyone on

---

[6]Most of these CERTs are members of the Forum of Incident Response and Security Teams (FIRST).

the Internet is vulnerable, and the Internet's security problems are the center of attention, generating much fear throughout both the computer and communications industries. Concerns about security problems have already begun to chill the overheated expectations about the Internet's readiness for full commercial activity, possibly delaying or preventing it from becoming a mass medium for the NII, or even the global information infrastructure (GII).

Several studies have independently shown that many individuals and companies are abstaining from joining the Internet simply because of security concerns. At the same time, analysts are warning companies about the dangers of not being connected to the Internet. In this conflicting situation, almost everyone agrees that the Internet needs more and better security. In a workshop held by the Internet Architecture Board (IAB) in 1994, scaling and security were nominated as the two most important problem areas for the Internet architecture as a whole [9]. This has not changed and it is not likely that it will change in the foreseeable future. For example, in November and December 1996, Dan Farmer conducted a security survey of approximately 2,200 computing systems on the Internet.[7] What he found was indeed surprising: Almost two-thirds of the more interesting sites had some serious security problems that could have been exploited by determined attackers. Meanwhile, these numbers have been confirmed by many independent investigations about the security status of the Internet.

But security in general and Internet security in particular are vague terms that may mean various things to different people. Security is a property that is not provable by nature. The best we can show is resistance against a certain set of attacks we know and with which we are familiar. There is nothing in the world that can protect us against new types of attack. For example, timing attacks, differential fault analysis (DFA), differential power analysis (DPA), and other side-channel attacks against hardware devices that are designed to securely store cryptographic keys have gained a lot of attention in the recent past. In this book, we are not going to give a formal definition of what exactly is security. Instead, we focus on technologies that are available today and that can be used to provide network security in terms of access control and communication security services. The assumption is that if a network is able to provide these services, there are at least some obstacles to overcome in order to successfully launch an attack. If the security services are well designed, properly implemented, and strictly enforced, the resulting obstacles are too big to be overcome by occasional intruders (they may still be negligibly small for professional hackers and intelligence agencies).

---

[7]http://www.fish.com/survey/

Obviously, the same technologies that are used to secure the Internet as a whole can also be used to secure parts of it. As the term "intranet" refers to a TCP/IP-based corporate or enterprise network, any book that focuses on TCP/IP and Internet security automatically addresses intranet security as well. As a matter of fact, the title "intranet security" better reflects the scope of any book on TCP/IP and Internet security, since it is usually not the Internet as a whole that must be protected, but only well-defined parts of it (these parts are usually an intranet or a set of interconnected but logically separated intranets). Consequently, *Internet and Intranet Security* has been chosen as a title for this book. This title reflects our interest in both standardized security technologies for the entire Internet, as well as security technologies that can be used and deployed within intranet environments. This title has remained valid for the second edition of the book.

In addition to *Internet and Intranet Security*, I have written several companion books for Artech House, including *Authentication Systems for Secure Networks* (1996), *Security Technologies for the World Wide Web* (2000), and *Secure Messaging with PGP and S/MIME* (2001). The latter two books have been published—along with this book—in Artech House's Computer Security Series.[8]

Internet and Intranet Security has been written to serve the needs of computer and network professionals that have interest in understanding, establishing, and supporting secure TCP/IP-based networks. I also hope that this book provides sufficient background to help security professionals propose approaches to secure commercial applications for the Internet.

The book is tutorial in nature but still requires familiarity with the fundamentals of computer networks and distributed systems, as well as cryptography and the use of cryptographic protocols in networked and distributed systems. Many of the references cited throughout the book are tutorial and may be used to obtain additional background information. In particular, I recommend [10–13] for an introduction to computer networks and distributed systems. In regard to cryptography, I recommend [14–16], and in regard to the use of cryptographic protocols in networked and distributed environments, I recommend [17–20]. Historical notes can be found in [21–23]. A good source for contemporary information are various information pages offered on the World Wide Web (WWW) by companies actively working in the field, as well as the frequently asked questions (FAQs) periodically posted to the corresponding USENET newsgroups. Finally, [24] and [25] provide interesting considerations about computer and Internet security in general.

---

[8]Refer to `http://www.esecurity.ch/serieseditor` for an overview about the Artech House Computer Security Series and the scheduled and available books published in the series.

In short, *Internet and Intranet Security* introduces and discusses security technologies that are available today to provide Internet and intranet security in terms of access control and communication security services. As such, it does not cover issues related to the security of the underlying operating systems. There are many books, mainly on computer security and hacking, that address issues related to (network) operating system security. Consequently, we do not review this area in the book.

Internet and Intranet Security is organized into four parts:

- Part I, *Fundamentals*, introduces and briefly elaborates on the fundamentals that are necessary to read and understand the book.

- Part II, *Access Control*, addresses technologies that can be used to provide access control services to corporate intranets connected either to other intranets or extranets, or to the Internet as a whole.

- Part III, *Communication Security*, addresses technologies and security protocols that have been proposed, specified, implemented, and deployed for the network access, Internet, transport, and application layer of the Internet model.

- Part IV, *Discussion*, concludes with final remarks and some selected topics.

Contrary to the first edition of this book, this second edition of *Internet and Intranet Security* no longer includes a glossary. This is because in May 2000, an *Internet Security Glossary* was published as informational RFC 2828 (or FYI 36, respectively) [26]. This document can be used as a reference for anyone working in the field. However, the second edition of *Internet and Intranet Security* still includes a list of abbreviations and acronyms. References are included at the end of each chapter. At the end of the book, an About the Author section is included to tell you a little bit about me. Finally, there is an index to help you find particular terms.

Internet and intranet security is such a fast-moving field that I have to reserve the right to be out of date or simply wrong. While time brings new technologies and outdates current technologies, I have attempted to focus on the fundamentals and conceptual approaches to provide Internet and intranet security. By the time this book is published, several of my comments will probably have moved from the future to the present, and from the present to the past.

Because of the nature of this book, it is also necessary to mention some company, product, and service names. It is, however, only fair to mention that the presence or absence of a specific name neither implies any criticism or endorsement, nor does it imply that the corresponding company, product, or service is necessarily the best one available. For a more comprehensive product overview, I recommend the annually published *Computer Security Products Buyers Guide* from the Computer Security Institute (CSI).[9] It provides a good and very comprehensive source for information about products that are commercially available.

Whenever possible, I have added uniform resource locators (URLs) as footnotes to the text. The URLs point to corresponding information pages provided in the WWW. While care has been taken to ensure that the URLs are valid now, unfortunately, due to the dynamic nature of the Web, I cannot guarantee that these URLs and their contents remain valid forever. In regard to these URLs, I apologize for any information page that may have been removed or replaced since the writing and publishing of this book. To make the problem less severe, I have not included very specific URLs that are likely to be removed or replaced soon.

I would like to take the opportunity to invite you as a reader of this book to let me know your opinions and thoughts. If you have something to correct or add, please let me know. If I have not expressed myself clearly, please let me know. I appreciate and sincerely welcome any comment or suggestion in order to update the book in the next edition. The best way to reach me is to send electronic mail to `rolf.oppliger@esecurity.ch`. You can also visit the book's Web home page at `http://www.esecurity.ch/Books/iis2e.html`. In the future, I will use this page to periodically post additional information and materials regarding the topic of the book (e.g., slides that can be used to teach courses or lectures with the book).

REFERENCES

[1] E. H. Spafford, "The Internet Worm: Crisis and Aftermath," *Communications of the ACM*, Vol. 32, 1989, pp. 678–688.

[2] J. A. Rochlis and M. W. Eichin, "With Microscope and Tweezers: The Worm from MIT's Perspective," *Communications of the ACM*, Vol. 32, 1989, pp. 689–703.

[3] P. J. Denning, *Computers Under Attack: Intruders, Worms, and Viruses*, ACM Press/ Addison-Wesley, New York, 1990.

[4] P. G. Neumann, *Computer-Related Risks*, ACM Press/Addison-Wesley, New York, 1995.

[5] J. D. Howard, *An Analysis of Security Incidents on the Internet 1989–1995*, Ph.D. thesis, Carnegie Mellon University, April 1997.

---

[9]`http://www.gocsi.com`

[6] T. Shimomura with J. Markoff, *Takedown*, Hyperion, New York, 1996.

[7] R. T. Morris, *A Weakness in the 4.2BSD UNIX TCP/IP Software*, Computer Science Technical Report No. 117, AT&T Bell Laboratories, Murray Hill, NJ, February 1985.

[8] S. M. Bellovin, "Security Problems in the TCP/IP Protocol Suite," *ACM Computer Communication Review*, Vol. 19, No. 2, 1989, pp. 32–48.

[9] R. Braden, et al., "Report of the IAB Workshop on Security in the Internet Architecture (February 8–10, 1994)," Request for Comments 1636, June 1994.

[10] F. Halsall, *Data Communications, Computer Networks and Open Systems*, 4th Edition, Addison-Wesley, Reading, MA, 1996.

[11] A. S. Tanenbaum, *Computer Networks*, 3rd Edition, Prentice-Hall, Englewood Cliffs, NJ, 1998.

[12] D. E. Comer and R. E. Droms, *Computer Networks and Internets*, 2nd Edition, Prentice-Hall, Englewood Cliffs, NJ, 1998.

[13] D. Comer, *Internetworking with TCP/IP: Vol. I: Principles, Protocols, and Architecture*, 4th Edition, Prentice-Hall, Englewood Cliffs, NJ, 2000.

[14] D. Stinson, *Cryptography Theory and Practice*, CRC Press, Boca Raton, FL, 1995.

[15] B. Schneier, *Applied Cryptography: Protocols, Algorithms, and Source Code in C*, 2nd Edition, John Wiley & Sons, New York, 1996.

[16] A. Menezes, P. van Oorschot, and S. Vanstone, *Handbook of Applied Cryptography*, CRC Press, Boca Raton, FL, 1996.

[17] M. Purser, *Secure Data Networking*, Artech House, Norwood, MA, 1993.

[18] W. Ford, *Computer Communications Security: Principles, Standard Protocols and Techniques*, Prentice Hall, Englewood Cliffs, NJ, 1994.

[19] C. Kaufman, R. Perlman, and M. Speciner, *Network Security: Private Communication in a Public World*, Prentice Hall, Englewood Cliffs, NJ, 1995.

[20] W. Stallings, *Cryptography and Network Security*, 2nd Edition, Prentice-Hall, Englewood Cliffs, NJ, 1998.

[21] D. Kahn, *Sezing the Enigma*, Houghton Mifflin, Boston, MA, 1991.

[22] D. Kahn, *The Codebreakers*, Revised Edition, Scribner, New York, 1996.

[23] S. Singh, *The Code Book: The Secret History of Codes and Codebreaking*, Fourth Estate, London, UK, 1999.

[24] B. Schneier, *Secrets and Lies: Digital Security in a Networked World*, John Wiley & Sons, New York, 2000.

[25] R. Power, *Tangled Web: Tales of Digital Crime from the Shadows of Cyberspace*, Que, Indianapolis, IN, 2000.

[26] R. Shirey, "Internet Security Glossary," Request for Comments 2828, May 2000.

Acknowledgments

First, I want to express my thanks to all people who contributed to and were involved in the writing, publishing, and selling of the first edition of this book. Among these people, I am particularly grateful for the interest and support of Kurt Bauknecht, Dieter Hogrefe, Hansjürg Mey, and Günther Pernul. Also, I want to thank all buyers of the first edition; they have made it possible for me to update the book and to develop a second edition. Since the publication of the first edition in 1997, many security professionals, colleagues, customers, and students have provided valuable comments, suggestions, and pointers for further material to me. I hope that this input is taken into proper consideration. Again, the staff at Artech House was enormously helpful in producing the second edition of this book. Among these people, I'd like to thank Rebecca Allendorf, Ruth Harris, Tim Pitts, Judi Stone, Susanna Taggart, and Igor Valdman. Above all, I want to thank my family (i.e., my wife, Isabelle, and my son, Marc) for their encouragement, support, and patience during the writing of the book. The result is dedicated to them.

Rolf Oppliger, Ph.D.
Muri b. Bern, Switzerland
October 2001

Part I

FUNDAMENTALS

Chapter 1

Terminology

The field of computer science is filled with ill-defined terminology used by different persons in conflicting and sometimes even contradictory ways. This is especially true in the field of computer and communication security. Hence, we sacrifice the first chapter of this book to work against this tradition and to introduce and define some basic terms that are used in the rest of the book. As already mentioned in the preface, many terms related to Internet and intranet security are defined in RFC 2828 [1]. You may refer to this document to get a more comprehensive compilation of terms, definitions, and corresponding acronyms.

According to *Webster's Dictionary*, the term *information* refers to "knowledge communicated or received concerning a particular fact or circumstance" in general, and "data that can be coded for processing by a computer or similar device" in computer science. Also, according to RFC 2828, information refers to "facts and ideas, which can be represented (encoded) as various forms or data." Despite the fact these definitions are fairly broad and not too precise in a mathematically strong sense, they are sufficient for the purpose of this book. Anybody who is interested in a more precise and formal definition and treatment of information is referred to Claude E. Shannon's communication or information theory [2, 3].

In accordance with the definition for information, the term *information technology* (IT) is used to refer to any kind of technology that can be used to manage information. In particular, IT focuses on the questions of how to effectively and efficiently store, process, and transmit electronic data that encodes information.

Similarly, the term *IT security* is used to refer to the special field of IT that deals with security-related issues. In fact, IT security comprises both computer and communication security:

- The aim of *computer security* is to preserve resources (e.g., data that encodes information) against unauthorized use and abuse, as well as to protect data from accidental or deliberate damage, disclosure, and modification. More specifically, computer security is to protect data during its storage and processing in computer systems that may or may not be networked.

- The aim of *communication security* is to protect data that encodes information during its transmission in and between computer systems and networks.

In addition to these technically oriented aspects (e.g., computer and communication security), IT security must also take into account organizational and legal issues. These issues, however, are not further addressed in this book. There are many complementary books that focus entirely on organizational and legal issues related to IT security.

According to Andrew S. Tanenbaum, the term *computer network* refers to an interconnected collection of autonomous computer systems [4].

- The systems are *interconnected* if they are able to directly exchange data (i.e., without using external storage media, such as floppy disks or tapes). In the past, this form of interconnection typically required a physical cable between the systems. Today and in the future, however, the use of wireless technologies will become more and more important and predominant to interconnect systems.

- The systems are *autonomous* if there does not exist a clear master-slave relationship between them. For example, a system with one control unit and several slaves is not a network, nor is a large computer with remote card readers, printers, and terminals.

There is considerable confusion in the literature about what exactly distinguishes a distributed system from a computer network. Referring to Leslie Lamport, a *distributed system* consists of a collection of distinct processes that are spatially separated and that communicate with one another by exchanging messages.[1] In

---

[1] In a more humorous note, Lamport has also defined a distributed system as a "system that stops you from getting work done when a machine you've never seen crashes."

addition to that, Lamport refers to a system as a distributed system if the message transmission delay is not negligible compared with the time between events in a single process [5]. Note that this definition is particularly well suited to discuss time, clocks, and temporal ordering of events in distributed environments.

Again referring to Tanenbaum, the key distinction between a computer network and a distributed system is that in a distributed system, the existence of multiple autonomous computer systems is transparent and not necessarily visible to the user. In principle, the user can type a command to run a program, and it runs. It is up to the operating system to select the best processor available for the program to run, to find and transport all input data to that processor, and to put the results as output data in the appropriate place. In other words, the user of a distributed system should not necessarily be aware that there are multiple processors involved; to the user, the distributed system looks like a virtual uniprocessor. Note that in this example, a distributed system can be seen as a special case of a computer network, namely, one whose software gives it a very high degree of cohesiveness and transparency. Thus, the distinction between a computer network and a distributed system lies within the software in general and the operating system in particular, rather than within the hardware.

In accordance with the security frameworks developed by the Joint Technical Committee 1 (JTC1) of the International Organization for Standardization (ISO) and the International Electrotechnical Committee (IEC) [6], we use the term *principal* to refer to a human or system entity that is registered in and authenticatable to a computer network or distributed system. Users, hosts, and processes are commonly considered as principals:

- A *user* is an entity made accountable and ultimately responsible for his or her activities within a computer network or distributed system.

- A *host* is an addressable entity within a computer network or distributed system. The entity is typically addressed either by a name or a network address.

- A *process* is an instantiation of a program running on a particular host. It is common to use the *client-server model* to distinguish between client and server processes:

  - A *client* is a process that requests (and eventually also obtains and uses) a network service.

  - A *server* is a process that provides a network service. In this terminology, a *service* refers to a coherent set of abstract functionality, and a server is typically a continuously running background program (a so-called *daemon*) that is specialized in providing the functionality.

Note that sometimes a process can act either as client or server. For example, in a UNIX system a print server is usually created by and associated with a superuser. The print server acts as a server for printing requests by clients; however, the print server may also act as a client when it requests files to print from the file server. Also note that the client and server typically use a specific (set of) protocol(s) to communicate with each other. In fact, there should be made a strong distinction between a service and a protocol: A *service* refers to something an application program or a higher-layer protocol can use, whereas a *protocol* refers to a set of rules and messages to actually provide the service.

The client-server model provides an attractive paradigm for designing and implementing applications and application protocols for computer networks and distributed systems. In the simplest case, a service is implemented by just one server. But sometimes it is more convenient to have two or even more servers working collectively and cooperatively to provide a specific service. One point is that a single server may become overloaded or may not be sufficiently close to all users in a networked or distributed environment. Another point is availability. If a service is replicated, it does not matter if some of the replicas are down or unavailable. Often, the fact that a service is replicated is transparent to the user, meaning that the user does not know whether there is a single copy of the service or there are replicas. The development and analysis of technologies that can be used to securely replicate services is an interesting and very challenging area of research.

The ISO/IEC JTC1 uses the term *standard* to refer to a documented agreement containing technical specifications or other precise criteria to be used consistently as rules, guidelines, or definitions of characteristics to ensure that materials, products, processes, and services are fit for their purpose. Consequently, an *open system standard* is a standard that specifies an open system and allows manufacturers to build corresponding interoperable products, whereas an *open system* is a system that conforms to open system standards.

A computer network in general, and a distributed system in particular, is a complex collection of cooperating software and hardware. To aid in the understanding of these systems, network practitioners have developed some standard ways to model networked and distributed systems and to break them down into simpler pieces. A reference model is a model used to explain how the various components of a system fit together and what the common interface specifications are among the various components. A basic feature of a reference model is the division of the overall functionality into layers, done in an attempt to reduce complexity.

Table 1.1
Layers of the OSI Reference Model

Layer 7	Application layer
Layer 6	Presentation layer
Layer 5	Session layer
Layer 4	Transport layer
Layer 3	Network layer
Layer 2	Data link layer
Layer 1	Physical layer

In 1978 the ISO/IEC JTC1 proposed a *Reference Model for Open Systems Interconnection* (OSI-RM) as a preeminent model for structuring and understanding communications functions within open systems. The OSI-RM follows the widely accepted structuring technique of layering, and the communication functions are partitioned into a hierarchical set of layers accordingly. More precisely, the OSI-RM specifies seven layers of communications system functionality, from the physical layer at the bottom to the application layer at the top. The layers are overviewed in Table 1.1. Refer to the books cited in the preface for a more comprehensive description of the OSI-RM and its seven layers.

The OSI-RM is useful because it provides a commonly used terminology and defines a structure for data communication standards. It was approved as an international standard (IS) in 1982 [7]. Two years later, the Telecommunication Standardization Sector of the International Telecommunication Union (ITU-T)[2] adopted the OSI-RM in its recommendation X.200.

The use of open system standards and open systems that conform to these standards has many advantages, and we are not going to discuss them in this book. However, we want to point out that open systems may also negatively influence security. For example, if an attacker knows the communications protocols that are used between a client and a server, it is much simpler for him or her to eavesdrop on the communications and to actually understand what is actually going on. Consequently, security is a vital concern in open systems, and the apparent contradiction between openness and security is deceptive. In fact, it has often seduced people to buy proprietary systems instead of open systems. The assumption that has led to this purchase behavior is our strong belief in "security through obscurity." We think that to hide information about the design of a system is the best way to prevent

---

[2]The ITU-T was formerly known as Consultative Committee on International Telegraphy and Telephony (CCITT).

potential attackers from learning something about the system's own vulnerabilities. Network security technologies, if well designed and properly implemented, can be used to solve the contradiction between openness and security, and it is one of the main goals of this book to provide a basic understanding for the proper design and implementation of such technologies.

A *protocol suite* is a set of protocols that work together and fit into a common protocol model. However, there might be more protocols in a protocol suite than are practical for use with a particular application. Therefore, a *protocol stack* is a selection of protocols from a protocol suite that is selected to support a particular application or class of applications. In the OSI world, various national and international standarization bodies specify profiles for stacks of OSI protocols. In the rest of this book we will see many protocol stacks to address specific security requirements of the Internet.

This book is entitled *Internet and Intranet Security*. As such, it focuses on the security of special computer networks and distributed systems, namely the ones that are based on the TCP/IP communications protocol suite. The fundamentals of TCP/IP networking are introduced in numerous books and briefly summarized in Chapter 2. However, we still want to point out that many things that are said in this book are equally true for other data networks as well, especially if they use packet switching (e.g., X.25-based networks).

According to RFC 2828, a *vulnerability* refers to "a flaw or weakness in a system's design, implementation, or operation and management that could be exploited to violate the system's security policy" [1]. In a computer network or distributed system, passwords transmitted in the clear often represent a major vulnerability. The passwords are exposed to passive eavesdropping and sniffing attacks. Similarly, the ability of a network host to boot with a network address that has originally been assigned to another host refers to another vulnerability that can be used to spoof that particular host and to masquerade the host accordingly.

There are at least three reasons why networked computer systems are generally much more vulnerable than their standalone counterparts:

1. More points exist from which an attack can be launched. Someone who is not able to physically access or connect to a computer system cannot attack it. Consequently, by adding more network connections for legitimate users, more vulnerabilities are added as well.

2. The physical perimeter of a system is artificially extended by having it connect to a computer network. This extension usually leads beyond what is controllable by a system administrator.

3. Networked computer systems typically run software that is inherently more complex and error-prone. There are many network software packages that are known to be "buggy," and more often than not, intruders learn about these bugs before system administrators do. To make things even worse, intruders must know and be able to exploit just one single bug, whereas system administrators usually must know and be able to fix each of them.

Again according to RFC 2828, a *threat* refers to "a potential for violation of security, which exists when there is a circumstance, capability, action, or event that could breach security and cause harm" [1]. Computer networks and distributed systems are susceptible to a wide variety of possible threats that may be mounted either by legitimate users or intruders.[3] As a matter of fact, legitimate users are generally much more powerful adversaries, because they possess internal information that is not usually available to intruders. Unfortunately, protection against legitimate users is also much more difficult to achieve than protection against intruders. In fact, perimeter security (e.g., firewalls) does not affect and does not protect against legitimate users acting maliciously.

With respect to possible threats in computer networks and distributed systems, it is common to distinguish between host and communication compromises. A *host compromise* is the result of a subversion of an individual host within a computer network or distributed system. Various degrees of subversion are possible, ranging from the relatively benign case of corrupting process state information to the extreme case of assuming total control of the host. Web servers are heavily exposed to attackers trying to compromise the corresponding hosts.[4] A *communication compromise* is the result of a subversion of a communication line within a computer network or distributed system.

Last, a *countermeasure* refers to "an action, device, procedure, or technique that reduces a threat, a vulnerability, or an attack by eliminating or preventing it, by minimizing the harm it can cause, or by discovering and reporting it so that corrective action can be taken" [1]. For example, the use of strong authentication techniques (as discussed in many points throughout this book) reduces the vulnerability of passwords transmitted in the clear. Similarly, the use of cryptographic authentication at the network layer effectively eliminates attacks based on machines spoofing other machines' IP addresses.

---

[3] The term *hacker* is often used to describe computer vandals who break into computer systems. These vandals call themselves hackers, and that is how they got the name, but in my opinion, they do not deserve it. In this book, we use the terms *intruder* and *attacker* instead.

[4] For example, refer to `http://www.onething.com/archive/` for an archive of "hacked" Web sites.

Against this background, it is fair to say that this book is about security technologies and countermeasures that can be used and deployed in TCP/IP-based networks (e.g., intranets) to provide security services.

REFERENCES

[1] R. Shirey, "Internet Security Glossary," Request for Comments 2828, May 2000.

[2] C. E. Shannon, "A Mathematical Theory of Communication," *Bell System Technical Journal*, Vol. 27, No. 3/4, July/October 1948, pp. 379–423/623–656.

[3] C. E. Shannon, "Communication Theory of Secrecy Systems," *The Bell System Technical Journal*, Vol. 28, No. 4, October 1949, pp. 656–715.

[4] A. S. Tanenbaum, *Computer Networks*, 3rd Edition, Prentice-Hall, Englewood Cliffs, NJ, 1998.

[5] L. Lamport, "Time, Clocks, and the Ordering of Events in a Distributed System," *Communications of the ACM*, Vol. 21, 1978, pp. 558–565.

[6] ISO/IEC 10181, Information Technology—Security Frameworks in Open Systems, 1993.

[7] ISO/IEC 7498, Information Processing Systems—Open Systems Interconnection Reference Model, 1982.

Chapter 2

TCP/IP Networking

In general parlance, the term *TCP/IP* is used to refer to an entire suite of data communications protocols[1] that derives its name from two of its core protocols, namely the Transmission Control Protocol (TCP) and the Internet Protocol (IP). In short, IP provides a connectionless and unreliable datagram or packet delivery service, whereas TCP provides a connection-oriented and reliable data transport service on top of IP.

In this chapter, we overview and briefly discuss the fundamentals of TCP/IP networking. More specifically, we elaborate on the history and development of the TCP/IP communications protocol suite in Section 2.1,[2] overview the current and future status of the Internet in Section 2.2, explain how Internet standardization works in Section 2.3, and introduce the Internet model with its four layers in Section 2.4. Some relevant attacks against TCP/IP-based networks are discussed later in Chapter 3.

---

[1]Some people dispute whether the TCP/IP protocols should be referred to as *protocols* or *services*. It could be argued, for example, that Telnet is a protocol, a service, or even a command. Where it makes obvious sense, this book follows the protocol view.

[2]More information about the history of the Internet can be found in a paper entitled "A Brief History of the Internet." The paper is authored by a group of Internet pioneers and is electronically available at http://www.isoc.org/internet/history/brief.html (at the time of this writing, a Spanish translation also is available).

2.1 HISTORY AND DEVELOPMENT

In the early 1960s, the Defense Advanced Research Projects Agency (DARPA)[3] of the U.S. Department of Defense (DoD) sponsored some research and development projects that were asked to develop and come up with network technologies and topologies that provide maximal reliability even in the case of node and circuit failures. Packet switching was considered to be a possible answer to this problem [1–4]. Consequently, some DARPA-sponsored organizations and research laboratories started to think about interconnecting hosts using packet switching in the late 1960s. The resulting network was called the *ARPANET*, and the ARPANET was the predecessor of the Internet. In fact, the Internet has evolved from the ARPANET and sometimes people still confuse the ARPANET with the Internet. This confusion mainly results because the ARPANET was the first backbone network of the early Internet and remained a part of it until it was finally retired in 1990.

In 1969, the ARPANET interconnected four hosts located at the University of California at Los Angeles (UCLA), the Stanford Research Institute (SRI), the University of California at Santa Barbara (UCSB), and the University of Utah. After this initial phase, more hosts were added to the ARPANET, and work proceeded on specifying and implementing a functionally complete host-to-host protocol and other networking software. In 1970, the first ARPANET host-to-host protocol, called Network Control Protocol (NCP), was specified and deployed. In the following years, the NCP became the protocol of choice for ARPANET researchers and developers (there were not many users at this time).

In 1972, the ARPANET was demonstrated to the general public, and the first application, namely, electronic mail (e-mail), was introduced to be used on the ARPANET. Afterward, the name of the original ARPANET changed, from ARPA Internet to the Federal Research Internet to TCP/IP Internet and finally to its current name of just the Internet. The Internet, in turn, was (and still is) based on the idea that there would be multiple independent networks of rather arbitrary design, beginning with the ARPANET as the pioneering packet switching network, but soon to include packet satellite networks, packet radio networks, and some other networks.

Fairly soon it was realized that the NCP did not sufficiently meet the needs and requirements of the evolving Internet. Consequently, it was decided to develop a new version of the protocol. The development effort was mainly driven by Robert

---

[3]The Advanced Research Projects Agency (ARPA) changed its name to Defense Advanced Research Projects Agency (DARPA) in 1971, then back to ARPA in 1993, and back to DARPA in 1996. In this book, we use the term DARPA to refer to either of the two acronyms.

E. Kahn at Bolt Beranek and Newman (BBN), Inc., and Vinton G. Cerf at Stanford University. In the early 1970s, the resulting approach was publicly announced and the corresponding protocol was named Transmission Control Protocol (TCP). TCP was originally intended to support a range of transport services, ranging from totally reliable sequenced data delivery (following the virtual circuit model) to a datagram delivery service in which the application made direct use of the underlying network service, which might imply occasional lost, corrupted, or reordered packets.

However, the initial effort to implement TCP resulted in a version that was considerably simpler and only provided support for the virtual circuit model. This simpler version of TCP worked fine for file transfer and remote terminal access, but some of the early work on advanced network applications, in particular voice transmission over packet switched networks, made clear that in some cases packet losses should not be corrected by TCP, but should be left to the application to deal with. This led to a reorganization of TCP into two protocols:

- The Internet Protocol (IP), which provided only for the addressing and forwarding of individual packets;
- The new TCP, which was concerned with more sophisticated service features, such as flow control and recovery from packet losses.

For those applications that did not need the services provided by TCP, an alternative transport protocol was added to provide direct access to the basic packet delivery service provided by IP. This protocol was called and further referred to as the User Datagram Protocol (UDP). UDP is primarily used in situations where applications can live with packet losses (e.g., real-time communications), or in situations where the establishment of TCP connections is simply too inefficient or costly (e.g., multicast applications).

After this design effort, DARPA had three contractors at Stanford, BBN, and UCLA implement TCP/IP. The Stanford team produced the detailed specification and within about a year there were three independent and interoperable implementations of TCP. This was the beginning of long-term experimentation and development to evolve and mature the Internet concepts and technology. Since the first three networks (ARPANET, Packet Radio, and Packet Satellite) and their initial research communities began, the experimental environment has grown to incorporate essentially every form of network and a very broad research and development community.

In 1980, TCP/IP was adopted as a DoD standard, and on January 1, 1983, the ARPANET host protocol was officially changed from NCP to TCP/IP. This transition was carefully planned within the Internet community for several years before it actually took place and went surprisingly smoothly (in fact, it resulted in a distribution of buttons saying "I survived the TCP/IP transition"). The transition of ARPANET from NCP to TCP/IP also permitted it to be split into a MILNET supporting operational requirements for the military and an ARPANET supporting research needs. Thus, by 1985, the Internet was already well established as a technology supporting a broad community of researchers and developers, and was beginning to be used by other communities for daily computer communications. E-mail was being used broadly across several communities, often with different systems, but interconnection among different e-mail systems was demonstrating the utility of broad-based electronic communications among people.

Much of the early popularity of the TCP/IP protocols was due to their implementation in version 4.2 of the BSD UNIX operating system. The BSD UNIX was developed at the University of California at Berkeley (UCB) by the Computer Systems Research Group (CSRG). Again, the development was partly funded by DARPA. Because of the source of its funding, BSD UNIX version 4.2 was made publicly available at the cost of its distribution and so its use spread quickly. Coincidentally, BSD UNIX version 4.2 became available at the same time as some inexpensive microprocessors, such as the Motorola 680x0 and the Intel 80x86 chip series. Both startup and established companies took advantage of the combination to build computer systems, mainly workstations, incorporating both the newly available microprocessors and the BSD UNIX operating system. Notably the most prominent startup company of this kind is Sun Microsystems. Since then, the development of the UNIX operating system and the TCP/IP protocols became intimately intertwined. Nevertheless, it is important to say that the Internet is not a UNIX network and that the TCP/IP protocols have been implemented on most other operating systems, including, for example, Microsoft Windows NT and Windows 2000.

At the same time that the Internet technology was being experimentally validated and widely used among computer science researchers, other networks and networking technologies were being pursued. The usefulness of computer networking demonstrated by DARPA and the DoD contractors on the ARPANET was not lost on other communities and disciplines, so that by the mid-1970s, computer networks began to spring up wherever funding could be found for the purpose. For example, the U.S. Department of Energy (DoE) established MFENet for its researchers in Magnetic Fusion Energy, whereupon DoE's High Energy Physicists responded by building HEPNet. The National Aeronautics and Space Agency (NASA) followed with SPAN, and some researchers established CSNET for the (academic and industrial) computer science community with an initial grant from the U.S. National

Science Foundation (NSF). AT&T's free-wheeling dissemination of the UNIX operating system spawned USENET, based on UNIX's built-in UUCP communication protocols, and in 1981 BITNET was initiated to interconnect academic mainframe computers.

With the exception of BITNET and USENET, these early networks (including the ARPANET) were purpose-built, meaning that they were intended for, and largely restricted to, closed user communities. Consequently, there was little pressure for the individual networks to be compatible and, indeed, they largely were not. In addition, alternate technologies were being pursued in the commercial sector, including, for example, XNS from Xerox, DECNet from DEC, and SNA from IBM. It remained for the British JANET and the U.S. NSFNET programs to explicitly announce their intent to serve the entire higher education community, regardless of discipline.

During the 1980s and 1990s, the roles of DARPA and NSF fundamentally changed, and NSF's privatization policy culminated in 1995 with the defunding of the NSFNET Backbone. Today, the Internet is mainly funded by private companies, collectively referred to as *Internet Service Providers* (ISPs). ISPs can operate in the backbone of the Internet or at the edges. Big telecommunications companies typically operate in the backbone, whereas most smaller ISPs only operate at the edges and provide local Internet connectivity to their subscribers.

Today, the Internet is growing exponentially and diversifying rapidly, hence the exact form of its future is unpredictable. Beginning about 1988, the size of the Internet has been more than doubling every year and promises to continue doing so. The current and future status of the Internet is overviewed next.

2.2   INTERNET

In October 1995, the U.S. Federal Networking Council (FNC) unanimously passed a resolution defining the term *Internet*.[4] According to this resolution, the term refers to the global information system that:

- Is logically linked together by a globally unique address space based on IP or its subsequent extensions or follow-ons;

- Is able to support communications using the TCP/IP protocol suite or its subsequent extensions, follow-ons, and other IP-compatible protocols;

- Provides, uses, or makes accessible, either publicly or privately, high-level services layered on the communications and related infrastructure.

---

[4]http://www.fnc.gov/Internet_res.html

As this definition is neither sufficiently simple nor very precise, we are not going to use it in this book. Instead, we use the term *Internet* to refer to the global internet(work) based on the TCP/IP communications protocol suite, and the term *intranet* to refer to a TCP/IP-based corporate or enterprise network. We have already discussed in the preface that the Internet is seen as the basis and first incarnation of an information superhighway, NII, or GII as promoted, for example, by the U.S. government. We have also seen that virtually everyone on the Internet is vulnerable, and that the Internet's security problems are the center of attention, generating much fear throughout both the computer and the communication industries.

As mentioned, packet switching works by dividing messages to be sent over the network into discrete parts, each of which is called a *packet*. Each packet is routed from one computer to the next across the network until it reaches its final destination. Dedicated computers, called *routers*, are used to route the packets through the network. Routers are connected to each other by physical data connections that are also called *links*. Each networked computer is called a *host*. A host is connected to a network in the same way as a router. The main difference between a host and a router is that a host usually has a single link to one network, whereas a router may have several links typically to more than one network (i.e., it routes packets between these networks).

The Internet is heavily supported by the research community that elaborates on data networks. Consequently, the Internet also provides a testbed and experimental environment for upcoming and leading-edge network technologies and applications. For example, the *Internet2 consortium* provides a platform for the development of the next generation Internet. In fact, the Internet2 consortium is being led by more than 180 universities working in partnership with industry and government to develop and deploy advanced network applications and technologies, accelerating the creation of tomorrow's Internet. According to the Internet2 consortium's home page,[5] the primary goals of Internet2 are to:

- Create a leading-edge network capability for the national research community;
- Enable revolutionary Internet applications;
- Ensure the rapid transfer of new network services and applications to the broader Internet community.

Refer to the Internet2 consortium's home page to find more information about the Internet2 consortium and its current work.

---

[5]`http://www.internet2.org`

2.3   INTERNET STANDARDIZATION

In this section, we focus on Internet standardization. More specifically, we overview the technical bodies that are engaged in Internet standardization, elaborate on the documentation series that are officially published by these bodies, and discuss the standardization process. You may refer to the indicated URLs or [5] for a more complete discussion of Internet standardization and governance.

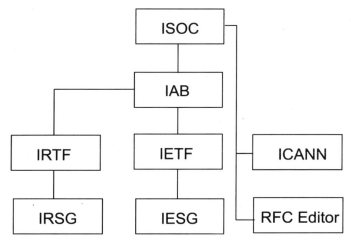

Figure 2.1   The organizations and technical bodies that are engaged in Internet standardization.

2.3.1   Technical Bodies

There are many organizations and technical bodies engaged in Internet standardization. The most important ones are overviewed in Figure 2.1 and further explained next.

ISOC

On the top level of Figure 2.1, the *Internet Society* (ISOC) is an organization whose task is to promote the use of the Internet for research and scholarly communication and collaboration. According to the ISOC's home page,[6] the mission is "to assure

---

[6]http://www.isoc.org

the open development, evolution, and use of the Internet for the benefit of all people throughout the world." As such, the ISOC is the organizational home of all technical bodies illustrated in Figure 2.1 and further addressed next. Also, an ever-increasing number of issues, such as censorship and freedom of expression, taxation, governance, and intellectual property protection, are discussed within the ISOC.

The ISOC was formed in 1992 as an international nonprofit membership organization. ISOC members can either be individuals (i.e., individual members) or organizations (i.e., organizational members). The ISOC holds an annual meeting, hosts several conferences,[7] and periodically publishes a newsletter. Also, a newsletter entitled *OnTheInternet* is available in electronic form.[8]

IAB

The *Internet Architecture Board* (IAB) is an appointed group that assists in the management of the Internet standards process operating under the auspices of the ISOC.[9] As such, the IAB is the technical advisory group of the ISOC and acts as a source of advice and guidance to the board of trustees and officers of the ISOC concerning technical, architectural, procedural, and (where appropriate) policy matters pertaining to the Internet and its enabling technologies. Also, the IAB is responsible for editorial management and publication of the Request for Comments (RFC) series of documents, and for the administration of the various Internet assigned numbers. More information about the IAB is available at its home page.[10] The IAB has two task forces:

- The *Internet Engineering Task Force* (IETF);

- The *Internet Research Task Force* (IRTF).

Both the IETF and the IRTF have steering groups associated with them. They are called *Internet Engineering Steering Group* (IESG) and *Internet Research Steering Group* (IRSG), respectively. The task forces and their appropriate steering groups are addressed next.

---

[7]The largest and most important conference of the ISOC is the INET conference, which is held annually at various locations around the globe.

[8]http://www.isoc.org/oti/

[9]Until June 1992, the acronym IAB was used to refer to "Internet Activities Board."

[10]http://www.iab.org

IETF and IESG

The IETF is the task force of the IAB that elaborates on engineering and operational issues related to TCP/IP networking in general, and the Internet in particular. According to the IETF home page,[11] the IETF "is a large, open international community of network designers, operators, vendors, and researchers concerned with the evolution of the Internet architecture and the smooth operation of the Internet. It is open to any interested individual." The IETF organizes and holds a meeting three times a year in various places throughout the world.[12]

Table 2.1
IETF Technical Areas (March 2001)

Application Area
General Area
Internet Area
Operational Requirements Area
Routing Area
Security Area
Transport Area
User Services Area

The technical work of the IETF is done in working groups (WGs) that are organized by topic into several areas. Table 2.1 overviews the IETF technical areas as of March 2001 (in alphabetical order). Every technical area has a director who is ultimatively responsible for coordinating the activities in this area. Note that this book addresses Internet and intranet security, and as such it primarily focuses on the work that is done within the IETF Security Area.[13] Further information about the IETF Security Area is available from a special home page hosted at Massachusetts Institute of Technology (MIT).[14]

Each IETF technical area has WGs that handle specific design and specification projects according to its charter, which includes, for example, projected milestones.

---

[11]http://www.ietf.org

[12]For example, the 51th and 52th IETF Meetings were scheduled to take place in August 2001 (in London) and December 2001 (in Salt Lake City, Utah), respectively.

[13]Some work is done in working groups that jointly belong to more than one technical area. For example, the Transport Layer Security (TLS) WG is jointly chartered by the Security and Transport Areas.

[14]http://web.mit.edu/network/ietf/sa/

In theory, participation in these WGs is by individuals and not by representatives of organizations and companies. In practice, however, the WGs are populated mostly by individuals representing organizations and companies that are interested in having specific technologies and protocols be submitted to and forwarded on the Internet standards track. Participants of IETF WGs can either meet during the IETF meetings or outside these meetings. In addition, they regularly discuss draft documents and other issues using mailing lists.

Table 2.2
Active IETF Security Area WGs (as of March 2001)

Name	Acronym
An Open Specification for Pretty Good Privacy	OPENPGP
Authenticated Firewall Traversal	AFT
Common Authentication Technology	CAT
IP Security Policy	IPSP
IP Security Protocol	IPSEC
IP Security Remote Access	IPSRA
Intrusion Detection Exchange Format	IDWG
Kerberized Internet Negotiation of Keys	KINK
Kerberos WG	KRB-WG
Multicast Security	MSEC
One Time Password Authentication	OTP
Public-Key Infrastructure (X.509)	PKIX
S/MIME Mail Security	SMIME
Secure Network Time Protocol	STIME
Secure Shell	SECSH
Securely Available Credentials	SACRED
Security Issues in Network Event Logging	SYSLOG
Transport Layer Security	TLS
Web Transaction Security	WTS
XML Digital Signatures	XMLDSIG

Table 2.2 overviews the IETF Security Area WGs as of March 2001 (again in alphabetical order). Note that new WGs are dynamically created and old ones become obsolete. Consequently, the current set of active IETF Security Area WGs may look different by the time you read this book. Refer to the IETF home page to get a more accurate and up-to-date picture. Also note that uppercase letters are used to refer to the WGs' acronyms in this book (in contrast to the acronyms used on the relevant IETF Web pages).

In the remaining parts of this book, we summarize and briefly discuss some of the major results that have been achieved in some of the IETF Security Area WGs mentioned in Table 2.2:

- The OPENPGP WG and the SMIME WG specify open standards for secure messaging on the Internet (i.e., OpenPGP and S/MIME). We briefly introduce and elaborate on these evolving standards in Chapter 17 when we talk about message security protocols.

- The AFT WG specifies a protocol that can be used to securely traverse a firewall system (i.e., the SOCKS protocol). We address the SOCKS protocol in Chapter 9 about circuit-level gateway.

- The CAT WG specifies a common generic security services application programming interface (GSS-API) for authentication and key distribution systems, such as the Kerberos systems. This book does not primarily address software developers, so we do not delve into the technical details of the GSS-API in this book. Nevertheless, we address the Kerberos authentication system and some extensions thereof in Chapter 16 which focuses on application layer security protocols.

- The IPSP, IPSEC, and IPSRA WGs all address aspects related to Internet layer security protocols (i.e., the IPsec protocols). As such, we address the results and the current status of these WGs in Chapter 14.

- The IDWG WG specifies a standardized exchange format for data collected by *intrusion detection systems* (IDS). This book mainly focuses on security technologies to provide access control and communication security services. As such, it only briefly addresses IDS at the end of the book.

- The KINK and KRB-WG WGs both address aspects of using the Kerberos authentication system on the global Internet. As mentioned, we address the Kerberos system and some extensions thereof in Chapter 16 when we talk about application layer security protocols.

- The MSEC WG addresses issues related to multicast security. Multicast security is a relatively new topic and field of study. It is only briefly addressed in Chapter 14, when we discuss Internet layer security protocols.

- The OTP WG specifies and standardizes a one-time password authentication scheme for the Internet. We elaborate on one-time passwords in Chapter 6 about authentication and key distribution.

- The PKIX WG focuses on X.509 certificates and their use to establish a public key infrastructure (PKI) for the global Internet. We address the results of this WG in Chapter 19 when we examine PKIs.

- The STIME WG specifies a protocol that can be used to securely determine the time on the Internet. As this book will demonstrate, many security technologies depend on accurate time settings and synchronized clocks (e.g., the Kerberos system). Consequently, having a protocol to securely determine the time on the Internet is very important. However, we do not address the protocol in this book.

- The SECSH WG provides an open specification for the Secure Shell (SSH) protocol that is widely deployed on the Internet. We address the results of this WG in Chapter 16 about application layer security protocols.

- The SACRED WG elaborates on possibilities to use and secure credentials (e.g., public key certificates) on the Internet. This WG was chartered only recently and has not provided any results thus far.

- The SYSLOG WG documents and tries to improve the security of the syslog mechanism used in the UNIX operating system. Similar to the SACRED WG, this WG was chartered only recently and has not provided any results yet.

- The TLS WG specifies a standardized transport layer security protocol for the Internet. We address the results of this WG in Chapter 15 when we examine transport layer security protocols for the Internet.

- The WTS WG focuses on the requirements for secure transactions on the Web. As such, we briefly address some results of this WG in Chapter 16 about application layer security protocols.

- The XMLDSIG elaborates on using XML to digitally sign documents. The results of this WG are not addressed in this book (they are only briefly mentioned in Chapter 17 when we discuss message security and message security protocols).

The IESG is the steering group of the IETF. It recommends actions on standardization to the IAB (most actions are recommended by the IESG and approved by the IAB). The IESG consists of a group of people that basically includes all directors of the IETF technical areas. As of this writing, the director of the General Area serves as chair of the IESG (and also chairs the IETF and is a member of the IAB). The IAB appoints a new IETF chair and all IESG candidates from a list provided by the IETF nominating committee.

IRTF and IRSG

As its name suggests, the IRTF is the task force of the IAB that is responsible for topics that are oriented toward research (rather than operational engineering). According to its home page,[15] the mission of the IRTF is "to promote research of importance to the evolution of the future Internet by creating focused, long-term, and small research groups working on topics related to Internet protocols, applications, architecture and technology." As such, the IRTF has chartered a number of research groups that are enumerated in Table 2.3. Furthermore, both a privacy and security research group, and an information infrastructure architecture research group were chartered almost two decades ago, but have ceased operation. As such, they are of historical interest only.

Table 2.3
IRTF Research Groups (as of March 2001)

Authentication Authorisation Accounting Architecture
Building Differentiated Services
End-to-End
Internet Resource Discovery
Interplanetary Internet
Network Management
NameSpace
Reliable Multicast
Routing
Secure Multicast
Services Management

The IRTF research groups guidelines and procedures are described and fully explained in RFC 2014 [6]. The IRTF is managed by the IRTF chair in consultation with the IRSG. The IRSG, in turn, is the steering group of the IRTF. Its membership includes the IRTF chair, the chairs of the various research groups, and other individuals from the research community. Furthermore, the IRTF chair is appointed by the IAB, the research group chairs are appointed as part of the formation of research groups, and all other IRSG members are chosen by the IRTF chair in consultation with the rest of the IRSG and on approval of the IAB. In addition to managing the research groups, the IRSG may hold topical workshops focusing

---

[15]http://www.irtf.org

on research areas of importance to the evolution of the Internet, or more general workshops, for example, to discuss research priorities from an Internet perspective.

ICANN

The *Internet Corporation for Assigned Names and Numbers* (ICANN) is the non-profit corporation that was formed to assume responsibility for the IP address space allocation, protocol parameter assignment, domain name system management, and root server system management functions previously performed under U.S. government contract by the *Internet Assigned Numbers Authority* (IANA) and some other entities.

Further information about ICANN and its mission is available from its home page.[16]   Furthermore, the numbers assigned by the IANA are available at ftp://ftp.isi.edu/in-notes/iana/assignments/.

RFC Editor

The *RFC Editor* is responsible for the final editorial review of the documentation series described in Section 2.3.2. The ISOC funds the RFC Editor function. More information is available from the RFC Editor home page.[17]

2.3.2   Documentation Series

A key to the rapid growth of the Internet has been the free and open access to basic documents, especially the specifications of the protocols that collectively constitute the TCP/IP communications protocol suite. There are two major series of documents related to Internet standardization: Internet-Drafts and RFC documents.

Internet-Drafts

Internet-Drafts are working documents of the IETF and its technical areas' WGs. During the development of a protocol specification, Internet-Drafts are made publicly available for informal review and comment by placing them in a specific IETF Internet-Drafts' directory.[18] The directory is replicated on a number of mirror sites

---

[16]http://www.icann.org
[17]http://www.rfc-editor.org
[18]http://www.ietf.org/ID.html

to make the evolving Internet-Drafts readily available to a wide audience, facilitating the process of public review and revision considerably.[19]

Internet-Drafts are valid for a maximum of 6 months and may be updated, replaced, and made obsolete by other documents at any time. An Internet-Draft that is published as an RFC, or that has remained unchanged in the Internet-Drafts directory for more than 6 months without being recommended by the IESG for publication as an RFC, is silently discarded and removed from the IETF Internet-Drafts' directory. The list of current Internet-Drafts can be accessed at `http://www.ietf.org/ietf/1id-abstracts.txt`.

Because of their transient nature, it is inappropriate to use Internet-Drafts as reference material or to cite them as anything other than "work in progress." Following this commonly agreed convention, Internet-Drafts are not referenced in this book. Where necessary and appropriate, Internet-Drafts are appended as footnotes to the text.

RFC Documents

The beginnings of the ARPANET and the Internet were characterized by a university research community that promoted and celebrated the academic tradition of open publication of ideas and results. The normal cycle of academic publication, however, turned out to be too formal and slow for the dynamic exchange of ideas essential for the design and implementation of computer networks and distributed systems. Consequently, a new series of documents was established in 1969. The documents were called RFCs and were intended to be an informal fast-distribution way to share ideas with other researchers. As such, the series of RFC documents steadily increased its importance in the research community. Today, it is the official publication channel for the IETF. In addition to protocol specifications that are submitted to the Internet standards track, the RFC documents cover a wide range of topics, such as early discussion of new research topics, concepts, and status memos about the Internet as a whole.

RFC publication is the direct responsibility of the RFC Editor, under the general direction of the IAB. RFC documents are numbered and usually referred to by their appropriate numbers. They can be obtained from the IETF RFC home page[20] or any other Internet site that serves as an RFC archive.[21]

---

[19] As of this writing, a list of currently available IETF mirror sites for Internet-Drafts is available at `http://www.ietf.org/shadow.html`.

[20] `http://www.ietf.org/rfc.html`.

[21] A well-designed archive is available at `http://www.faqs.org/rfcs/`.

The rules for formatting and submitting RFC documents are defined in RFC 1543 [7]. In short, every RFC must be available in ASCII text format and may additionally be available in other formats. In this case, the other versions of the RFC may contain additional material such as diagrams, figures, and illustrations not present in the ASCII text version, and it may be formatted differently. For protocol specifications that are submitted to the Internet standards track, however, the ASCII text version is considered as the definitive reference. As such, it must be a complete and accurate specification of the standard, including all necessary diagrams, figures, and illustrations.

There are several subseries within the series of RFC documents. These subseries are briefly overviewed next. A good archive for RFC documents and its various subseries is available at http://www.faqs.org/rfcs/.

STD Subseries. Some RFC documents specify protocols that are submitted to the Internet standards track, and some of these protocol specifications also reach the status of an Internet Standard. These RFC documents form the STD subseries. Each document within the STD subseries is labeled with an STD number (in addition to the RFC document number). For example, when the Post Office Protocol version 3 (POP3) specified in RFC 1939 [8] became an Internet Standard, it was officially assigned the STD number 53. Consequently, RFC 1939 and STD 53 refer to the same protocol specification (i.e., POP3). Note that the STD number of a protocol always refers to the latest specification of the protocol, and that there may be several RFC documents specifying various versions of a protocol. For example, RFC 1725 specifies an elder version of POP3 and RFC 1939 has made this version obsolete. Nevertheless, STD 53 still refers to both RFC 1725 and RFC 1939. Because of the incremental nature of the RFC document numbering scheme, this ambiguity does not pose any problem. STD 1 (currently RFC document 2700) [9] describes the state of standardization of protocols used in the Internet. This document is the authoritative source for references on Internet Standards. In addition, an STD document index is available at http://www.faqs.org/rfcs/std/std-index.html.

BCP Subseries. In the past, Internet Standards were mainly concerned with the technical specifications for the protocols that collectively form the TCP/IP communications protocol stack. Because the Internet itself is composed of networks operated by a great variety of companies and organizations with diverse goals and rules, good user service also requires that the operators and administrators of these networks follow some common guidelines for policy and operation. While these guidelines are usually different in scope and style from protocol standards, their establishment needs a similar process for consensus building. Therefore, some RFC documents elaborate on the results of community deliberations about statements of principle or conclusions about what is the best way to perform some specific operations or IETF process function. These RFC documents form the best current practice (BCP) subseries. Similar to the STD subseries, the RFC documents published in the BCP subseries are assigned additional BCP numbers. A BCP document index is available at `http://www.faqs.org/rfcs/bcp/bcp-index.html`.

FYI Subseries. Finally, not all specifications of protocols or services should or will become part of the STD or BCP subseries [10]. Such nonstandard track specifications are not subject to the rules for Internet standardization. Nonstandard track specifications may be published as experimental or informational RFCs at the discretion of the RFC Editor in consultation with the IESG [8]. Some of these RFC documents form the FYI subseries, with FYI meaning "for your information." An FYI document index is available at `http://www.faqs.org/rfcs/fyi/fyi-index.html`.

2.3.3 Internet Standards Process

In the past, TCP/IP protocols were often specified and implemented ad hoc with little formality; this informality was considered to be a major factor in their success. This situation has changed. Today, there are many people involved in specifying TCP/IP protocols and even more people involved in implementing, testing, and using them. In this new environment, a more formal, or at least more codified, Internet standards process is urgently needed.

In short, an Internet Standard refers to a protocol specification that is stable and well understood; is technically competent; has multiple, independent, and interoperable implementations with substantial operational experience; enjoys significant public support; and is recognizably useful in some or all parts of the Internet. In theory, the process of creating Internet Standards is simple and straightforward. A protocol specification undergoes a period of development and several iterations of review by the Internet community and revision based upon experience, is adopted as an Internet Standard by the appropriate body, and is finally published in an appropriate format. In practice, however, the process is more complicated, due to the difficulty of creating specifications of high technical quality, the need to consider the interests of all affected parties, the importance of establishing widespread community consensus, and the difficulty of evaluating the utility of a particular specification for the Internet community.

According to RFC 2026 and BCP 9 [11], the Internet standards process is an activity of the ISOC that is organized and managed on behalf of the Internet community by the IAB and IESG. It is concerned with all protocols, procedures, and conventions that are used in or by the Internet, whether or not they are part of the TCP/IP communications protocol suite. As such, it resembles many other standards processes, including, for example, the one employed by the ISO.[22]

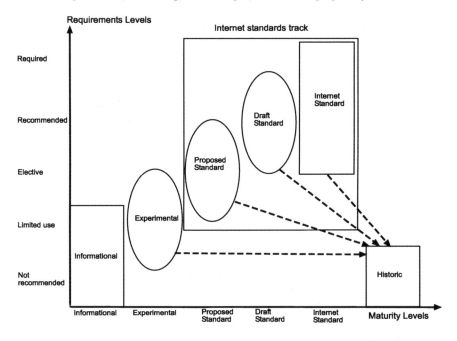

Figure 2.2   The two-dimensional classification scheme for Internet specifications.

In theory, the Internet standards process distinguishes between technical specifications and applicability statements:

- A *technical specification* is a description of a protocol, service, procedure, convention, or format that either completely describes all of its relevant aspects or leaves one or more parameters or options unspecified. Consequently, a technical

---

[22]In the ISO standards process, a specification first becomes a committee draft (CD), before it moves forward to become a draft international standard (DIS) and international standard (IS).

specification may be completely self-contained, or it may incorporate material from other specifications by reference to other documents. A technical specification must include a statement of its scope and the general intent for its use. Thus, a technical specification that is inherently specific to a particular context will contain a statement to that effect. However, a technical specification does not specify requirements for its use within the Internet; these requirements, which depend on the particular context in which the technical specification is incorporated by different system configurations, are defined by a corresponding applicability statement.

- An *applicability statement* specifies how, and under what circumstances, one or more technical specifications may be applied to support a particular Internet capability. An applicability statement identifies the relevant technical specifications and the specific way in which they are to be combined, and may also specify particular values or ranges of technical specification parameters or subfunctions of a technical specification protocol that must be implemented.

Although technical specifications and applicability statements are conceptually separate, in practice an Internet standards track document may combine an applicability statement and one or more related technical specifications. For example, technical specifications that are developed specifically and exclusively for some particular domain of applicability, such as for e-mail servers, often contain within a single specification all of the relevant applicability statement and technical specification information. In such cases, no useful purpose would be served by deliberately distributing the information among several documents just to preserve the formal distinction between technical specifications and applicability statements. However, a technical specification that is likely to apply to more than one domain of applicability should be developed in a modular fashion to facilitate its incorporation by multiple applicability statements.

In the Internet standards process, each specification (i.e., a technical specification or an applicability statement) is assigned a *requirement level* (sometimes also called an *applicability status*) and a *maturity level*. As illustrated in Figure 2.2, this leads to a two-dimensional classification scheme for Internet specifications. Requirement and maturity levels are overviewed and briefly discussed next.

Requirement Levels

The Internet standards process distinguishes among five requirement levels that may be assigned to technical specifications and/or applicability statements (the levels are indicated on the vertical axis in Figure 2.2):

- *Required:* Implementation is required to achieve minimal conformance.

- *Recommended:* Implementation is not required for minimal conformance, but experience or generally accepted technical wisdom suggest its desirability in the domain of applicability. Vendors are strongly encouraged to include the functions, features, and protocols of recommended specifications in their products, and should omit them only if the omission is justified by some special circumstance.

- *Elective:* Implementation is optional within the domain of applicability. However, a particular vendor may still decide to implement it, or a particular user may decide that it is a necessity in a given environment.

- *Limited use:* Implementation is considered to be appropriate for use only in limited or unique environments.

- *Not recommended:* Implementation is considered to be inappropriate for general use. This may be because of its limited functionality, specialized nature, or historic status.

The first three requirement levels (i.e., required, recommended, and elective) may be assigned to specifications that are submitted to the Internet standards track. For example, IP and ICMP are required and must be implemented by all Internet hosts using the TCP/IP protocols. In addition, the Telnet protocol is recommended and should be implemented by all hosts that would benefit from remote terminal access, whereas the DECnet management information base (MIB) is elective and could be seen as valuable only in environments where DECnet protocols are still in use (certainly a rare species today). The other two requirement levels (i.e., limited use and not recommended) may be assigned to specifications that are not submitted to the Internet standards track or have been retired from it.

Maturity Levels

In addition to the five requirement levels, the Internet standards process distinguishes among six maturity levels that may be assigned to technical specifications or applicability statements (the maturity levels are indicated on the horizontal axis in Figure 2.2). Three maturity levels (i.e., Proposed Standard, Draft Standard, and Internet Standard) may be assigned to specifications that are submitted to the Internet standards track. The three other maturity levels (i.e., informational, experimental, and historic) may be assigned to specifications that are not submitted to the Internet standards track (in the case of informational and experimental) or have been retired from it (in the case of historic).

- *Proposed Standard:* A specification that is generally stable, has resolved known design choices, is believed to be well understood, has received significant community review, and appears to enjoy enough community interest to be considered valuable. Nevertheless, further experience might result in a change or retraction of the specification before it advances on the Internet standards track. Usually, neither implementation nor operational experience is required for the designation of a specification as a Proposed Standard. However, such experience is highly desirable and will usually represent a strong argument in favor of a Proposed Standard designation. As a matter of fact, the IESG may require implementation or operational experience prior to granting Proposed Standard status to a specification that materially affects the core Internet protocols or that specifies behavior that may have significant operational impact on the Internet. Implementors should treat Proposed Standards as immature specifications. It is desirable to implement them to gain experience and to validate, test, and clarify the specification. However, because the content of Proposed Standards may be changed if problems are found or better solutions are identified, deploying implementations of such standards into a disruption-sensitive environment is not recommended. A specification must remain at the Proposed Standard level for at least 6 months.

- *Draft Standard:* A specification from which at least two independent and interoperable implementations from different code bases have been developed, and for which sufficient successful operational experience has been obtained, may be elevated to the Draft Standard level. The corresponding WG chair is responsible for documenting the specific implementations that qualify the specification for Draft or Internet Standard status along with documentation about testing of the interoperation of these implementations. The documentation must include information about the support of each of the individual options and features. This documentation should be submitted to the responsible IETF area director with the protocol action request. In general, elevation to Draft Standard is a major advance in status, indicating a strong belief that the specification is mature and will be useful. A Draft Standard is normally considered to be a final specification, and changes are likely to be made only to solve specific problems encountered. In most circumstances, it is reasonable for vendors to deploy implementations of Draft Standards into a disruption-sensitive environment. A specification must remain at the Draft Standard level for at least 4 months, or until at least one IETF meeting has occurred, whichever comes later.

- *Internet Standard:* A specification for which significant implementation and successful operational experience has been obtained may be elevated to the Internet Standard level. An Internet Standard is characterized by a high degree of technical maturity and by a generally held belief that the specified protocol or service provides significant benefit to the Internet community. A specification that reaches the status of an Internet Standard is assigned a number in the STD subseries while retaining its RFC number.

- *Informational:* A specification that is published for the general information of the Internet community and does not represent an Internet community consensus or recommendation.

- *Experimental:* A specification that is part of some research or development effort. Such a specification is published for the general information of the Internet community and as an archival record of the work, subject only to editorial considerations and to verification that there has been adequate coordination with the standards process.

- *Historic:* A specification that has been superseded by a more recent specification or is for any other reason considered to be obsolete.[23]

The informational, Internet Standard, and historic states are permanent, or at least there is no limit on how long a protocol may stay in one of those states. That is the reason why they are shown as rectangles in Figure 2.2. The other states are all temporary and transient. As such, they are shown as ellipses.

Standardization Process

The Internet standardization process requires decisions of the IESG concerning the elevation of a specification onto the Internet standards track or the movement of a standards track specification from one maturity level to another (e.g., from a Proposed Standard to a Draft Standard or from a Draft Standard to an Internet Standard). Although a number of reasonably objective criteria are available to guide the IESG in making a decision to move a protocol specification onto, along, or off the standards track, there is no guarantee of elevation to or progression along the standards track for any specification. The experienced collective judgment of the IESG concerning the technical quality of a specification is an essential component of the decision-making process.

---

[23]Some people have suggested that the correct word for "historic" should be "historical"; however, the use of "historic" is historical.

A specification that is intended to enter or advance in the Internet standards track must be posted as an Internet-Draft unless it has not changed since publication in an RFC document. It shall remain as an Internet-Draft for a period of time, not less than 2 weeks, that permits useful community review, after which a recommendation for action may be initiated. A standards action is initiated by a recommendation by the IETF WG responsible for the specification to its area director, copied to the IETF secretariat, or, in the case of a specification not associated with a WG, a recommendation by an individual to the IESG. The IESG then determines whether or not the specification satisfies the applicable criteria for the recommended action and must also determine whether or not the technical quality and clarity of the specification is consistent with that expected for the maturity level to which the specification is recommended. The IESG sends notice to the IETF of the pending IESG consideration of the documents to permit a final review by the Internet community. This last-call notification will be through e-mail to the IETF announce mailing list. Comments will be accepted from anyone, and should be sent as directed in the last-call announcement. The last-call period will be no shorter than 2 weeks except in those cases where the Proposed Standards action was not initiated by an IETF WG, in which case the last-call period will be no shorter than 4 weeks. If the IESG believes that the community interest would be served by allowing more time for comment, it may decide on a longer last-call period or to explicitly lengthen a period. In a timely fashion after the expiration of the last-call period, the IESG shall make its final determination of whether or not to approve the standards action and will notify the IETF of its decision again through e-mail to the IETF announce mailing list. If a standards action is approved, notification is sent to the RFC editor and copied to the IETF with instructions to publish the specification as an RFC. The specification will at that point be removed from the Internet-Draft directory.

Note that the minimum time for a protocol specification to reach Internet Standard status is 10 months (6 months for Proposed Standard and another 4 months for Draft Standard). These minimum periods are intended to ensure adequate opportunity for community review without severely impacting timeliness. When a standards track specification has not reached the Internet Standard level but has remained at the same maturity level for at least 2 years, and every year thereafter until the status is changed, the IESG shall review the viability of the standardization effort responsible for that specification and the usefulness of the technology. Following each such review, the IESG will approve termination or continuation of the development effort. At the same time the IESG will also decide to maintain the specification at the same maturity level or to move it to historic status. This provision is not intended to threaten a legitimate and active WG effort, but to provide an administrative mechanism for terminating a moribund effort.

A new version of an established Internet Standard must progress through the full Internet standardization process as if it were a completely new specification. As technology changes and matures, it is possible and even likely that the new Internet Standard specification is so clearly technically superior that one or more existing standards track specifications for the same function should be retired. In this case, or when it is felt for some other reason that an existing standards track specification should be retired, the IESG will approve a change of status of the old specifications to historic. This recommendation will be issued with the same last-call and notification procedures used for any other standards action. A request to retire an existing standard can originate from a WG, an area director, or some other interested party. In other cases, both versions may remain Internet Standards to honor the requirements of an installed base. In this situation, the relationship between the previous and the new versions must be explicitly stated in the text of the new version or in another appropriate document.

Disputes are possible and likely to appear at various stages during the Internet standards process. As much as possible, the process is designed so that compromises can be made and genuine consensus achieved. However, there are times when even the most reasonable and knowledgeable people are unable to agree. Such conflict must be resolved by a process of open review and discussion. RFC 2026 specifies the procedures that shall be followed to deal with Internet Standards issues that cannot be resolved through the normal processes whereby IETF WGs and other Internet standards process participants ordinarily reach consensus [11].

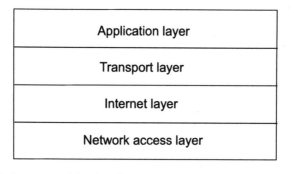

Figure 2.3   The Internet model and its four layers.

2.4   INTERNET MODEL

In this section, we introduce and briefly overview the Internet model that is used for TCP/IP networking. As illustrated in Figure 2.3, the Internet model consists of four layers, namely the network access layer, the Internet layer, the transport layer, and the application layer. This is somehow contradictory to the OSI-RM in which the Internet application layer is further divided into three distinct OSI layers (i.e., the application layer, the presentation layer, and the session layer), and the Internet network access layer is further divided into two OSI layers (i.e., the data link layer and the physical layer). The fact that the Internet model uses another layering structure than the OSI-RM should not be overemphasized and is mainly due to the fact that the Internet model was designed before the OSI-RM.

In the sections that follow, we overview and briefly discuss the four layers of the Internet model. Keep in mind that the explanations are fairly short and that you may refer to one of the references mentioned in the preface to get a more comprehensive picture about TCP/IP networking.

2.4.1   Network Access Layer

Part of the popularity of the TCP/IP communications protocol suite is due to its ability to be implemented on top of various local area network (LAN) technologies and corresponding network access layer protocols. Most of these protocols are specified by the Institute of Electrical and Electronic Engineers (IEEE) in its 802 series. Examples include IEEE 802.3 (mainly for Ethernet), IEEE 802.4 (mainly for Token Bus), and IEEE 802.5 (mainly for Token Ring). Following the terminology of the IEEE, these protocols are generally referred to as *media access layer protocols*. In addition, there are high-speed technologies and corresponding network access layer protocols, such as Fast Ethernet, Fiber Distributed Data Interface (FDDI), and Asynchronous Transfer Mode (ATM), as well as protocols to dial up and connect to TCP/IP networks, such as the Point-to-Point Protocol (PPP).

The predominant strategy today is to use Ethernet for local area networking, and to connect the Ethernet through a leased line (e.g., a T1 line) to an ISP that interconnects to the Internet. This is also the strategy that an organization new to TCP/IP networking is likely to use, if for no other reason than because many vendors of personal computers and workstations sell their systems with built-in Ethernet interfaces.

2.4.2 Internet Layer

In this section, we overview and briefly discuss the Internet Protocol (IP) and some of its routing and support protocols.

Internet Protocol

IP, as specified in RFC 791 [12] and STD 5, is by far the most important protocol in the entire TCP/IP communications protocol stack. In fact, the Internet layer is the only layer in the Internet model that is dominated by a single protocol (i.e., IP). Underneath and above the Internet layer, there are many protocols that coexist on each layer. The current version of IP is IP version 4, or *IPv4*. In this book, we use the term IP to refer to IPv4. If we refer to another version of IP, we usually append the corresponding version number.

In essence, IP provides a connectionless and unreliable datagram delivery service. What this basically means is that messages and application-specific data segments are split into datagrams (i.e., IP packets)[24] and that these IP packets are routed individually through the (inter)network. To allow each IP packet to be routed individually, it must include some source and destination address information in a unique address space. This address space allows us to construct large internetworks concatenated from many different physical networks. Each of these networks may use its own network access layer protocol and its own addressing scheme. IP provides a logical address space and a corresponding addressing scheme on top of them.

In practice, each host network interface must be configured with an IP address. As discussed later, this IP address must either be globally unique or private. If a host has more than one network interface, each interface must have a separate IP address. Network practitioners often refer to a host address when they really mean the host's network interface address. But keep in mind that hosts do not have IP addresses; network interfaces do. Unfortunately, the protocols specified in various RFC documents often use the term host address instead of network interface address, so, this nomenclature is followed in this book, although it is somehow misleading.

An IP (source or destination) address is 32 bits wide, resulting in a total address space of 2^{32}. The corresponding IP addresses are usually written in dotted-decimal notation, where each byte appears as a decimal number separated by periods, arranged from high-order byte to low-order byte. Primarily to simplify routing, an IP address is divided into two parts:

---

[24]In this book, we use the term *IP packet* instead of the more accurate term *datagram*.

- A network number;
- A host number.

For all machines to communicate successfully, every network interface on the same physical network segment must have the same network number and a unique host number. Originally, IP used the high-order byte as the network number and the low-order 3 bytes as the host number. But soon after IP was specified, it became obvious that there would be more than $2^8 - 2 = 254$ interconnected networks (the network numbers 0x00 and 0xFF are reserved). A specific encoding of the high-order bits in the high-order byte of the IP address lets the network number be 1, 2, or 3 bytes long, with the remaining byte(s) used for the host number. This encoding scheme divides the IP address space into five classes of IP addresses (i.e., class A through class E). Table 2.4 summarizes the five classes and their corresponding bit encodings. Class A through class C are the most commonly used classes of IP addresses today. Class D is reserved for multicast communications, and class E is still unused and reserved for future use except for one address. This address (i.e., the address 255.255.255.255) refers to "any host on this network." It can be used only as a destination address, and an IP packet with this destination address is broadcasted to the hosts on the same network segment as the sender of the IP packet.

Table 2.4
IP Address Classes

Class	Bit Encoding	Network Range	Host Range
A	0	0.0.0.0 to 127.0.0.0	0.0.0 to 255.255.255
B	10	128.0.0.0 to 191.255.0.0	0.0 to 255.255
C	110	192.0.0.0 to 223.255.255.0	0 to 255
D	1110	224.0.0.0 to 239.255.255.255	—
E	11110	240.0.0.0 to 255.255.255.255	—

When an IP address is written in dotted-decimal notation, it is fairly simple and straightforward to determine the class of the address from the bit encoding simply by referring to the value of the highest-order byte. Addresses in each class are numerically contiguous. IP allows the host number to be further subdivided by using subnets. More specifically, IP subnetting makes it possible to logically partition an IP address space, and to use each partition as if it belonged to a distinct IP network number. IP uses a network mask to determine which bits in the host number are to be used as a subnet number.

IP packetizes a message by creating an IP packet for each message or data segment it receives from transport layer. Each packet consists of an IP header, followed by a payload that may be used to encapsulate and hold a transport layer protocol data unit. As far as IP is concerned, the payload is just a sequence of arbitrary data bytes.

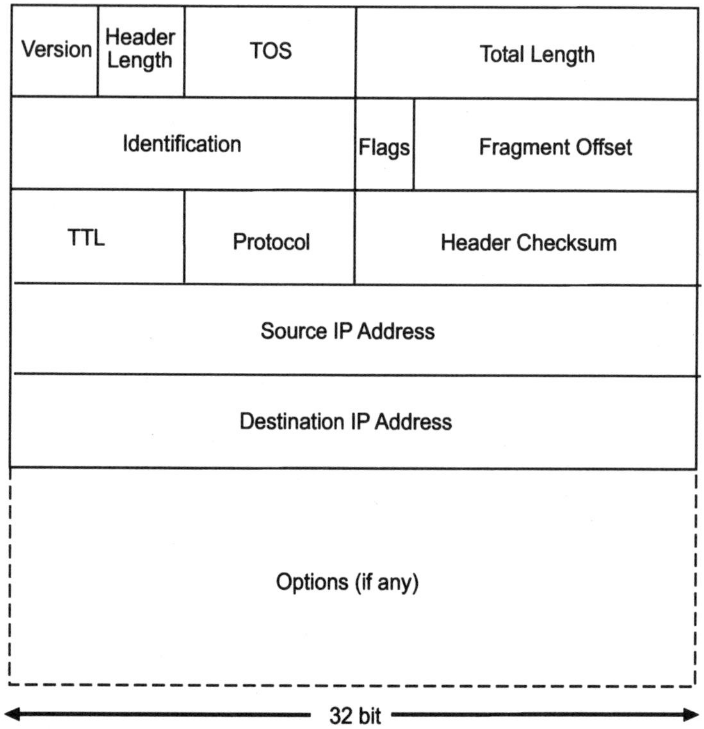

Version	Header Length	TOS	Total Length	
Identification			Flags	Fragment Offset
TTL		Protocol	Header Checksum	
Source IP Address				
Destination IP Address				
Options (if any)				

◄──────────────── 32 bit ────────────────►

Figure 2.4   The format of an IP header (IPv4).

There are many books that cover IP networking in detail. For the purpose of this book, we are mainly interested in the IP header. As illustrated in Figure 2.4, an IP (i.e., IPv4) header consists of the following fields:

- The 4-bit *version* field is used to indicate the number of the IP version. As mentioned earlier, the current version is 4, although the next version of IP (i.e., IP version 6) is already specified and being deployed.

- The 4-bit *header length* field is used to indicate the length of the IP header. The minimum, and typical, size of an IP header is 20 bytes. Because the header length is always indicated in 32-bit words, the header length field is initialized with the number 5 in this case.

- The 8-bit *TOS* field is used to indicate a type of service (TOS) or priority for the IP packet. Type of service processing is seldom used today, so this field is almost always set to the default value of zero.[25]

- The 16-bit *total length* field is used to indicate the total length of the IP packet (including the header) in bytes.

- The 16-bit *identification,* 3-bit *flags,* and 13-bit *fragment offset* fields are used to fragment and properly reassemble IP packets. Refer to any book on IP networking to learn about IP fragmentation and reassembly.

- The 8-bit *TTL* field is used to indicate a time to live (TTL). The TTL value specifies the time in seconds that an IP packet may exist. The value is decremented by at least 1 each time the IP header is processed by a router or host. Unless the packet is queued in a buffer for a long period of time, the TTL value actually indicates the maximum number of intermediate routers a packet may cross before it is dropped. Whenever the TTL reaches 0, IP must drop the packet unconditionally. This feature prevents a packet from looping around an internetwork forever because of a routing error.

- The 8-bit *protocol* field is used to indicate the protocol data that is encapsulated and carried in the payload of the IP packet. For example, the value 1 is used for ICMP, 6 for TCP, and 17 for UDP. Other values have been assigned to various protocols.[26]

- The 16-bit *header checksum* field is used for error detection. It carries the 16-bit 1's complement sum of all 16-bit words in the IP header, and checks for transmission errors that may have occured accordingly. It is important to note that the header checksum covers the IP header only, and that the upper-layer protocols must handle error control for the encapsulated data themselves. For example, a packet can be lost on its route to the destination because of transmission errors or a router might deliberately drop a packet because of buffer space shortage. Also, IP may deliver a packet more than once. It is up

---

[25]This is beginning to change and some legitimate uses of the TOS field are being discussed today. For example, the basic idea of differentiated services for the Internet is to label IP packets according to their quality of service (QOS) requirements, and to use the labels to optimize the routing. In this area, the TOS field can be used to carry the label for each IP packet.

[26]ftp://ftp.isi.edu/in-notes/iana/assignments/protocol-numbers

to the protocols that compose the encapsulated payload to be aware of these problems and to take appropriate steps. IP simply moves packets through the internetwork using a best-effort algorithm.

- The 32-bit *source IP address* field is used to carry the IP address of the host or network interface from which the packet originated.

- The 32-bit *destination IP address* field is used to carry the IP address of the packet's final destination host or network interface, regardless of the number of intermediate routers the packet may pass through. Note that because each IP packet header contains a source and destination IP address, it is self-contained and may be routed independently to its destination.

- The *options* field can be used to indicate the following options:

  - Source routing (enables an IP packet's route to be explicitly controlled);
  - Route recording (records the route of the packet);
  - Timestamping (adds a time stamp by each intermediate router);
  - Security (includes security options);
  - Padding (pads the IP packet header to an even 4-byte boundary).

From a security point of view, the IP source routing and security options are of primary interest. In short, IP source routing can be used to specify a direct route to a destination and return path back to the origin. The route could involve the use of other routers or hosts that normally would not be used to forward the packet to its destination. As source routing can be used to launch sophisticated attacks, it should be normally disabled on a security gateway. The IP security options are mainly used in environments that provide support for multilevel security, such as military applications [13]. IP security options can also be used to constrain routing decisions or to control cryptographic transformations.

IP is not finished when it creates a packet. It also has to determine which network interface to use and then pass enough information to the network access layer protocol output module so it can properly encapsulate the IP packet in a corresponding frame. Frame formats are specific to each network access layer protocol. For example, when sending a packet on an Ethernet, IP passes to the output module the Ethernet destination address, the Ethernet-type field value that indicates that the encapsulated packet is an IP packet, and the IP packet itself. The Ethernet output module, in turn, sets the source Ethernet address to the Ethernet address of the network interface it uses to transmit the frame, calculates an Ethernet checksum, and generates a corresponding frame with header and trailer.

Because different transport protocols layered on top of IP can send messages that are larger than the frame size of the underlying network hardware, IP also does fragmentation of packets when they are transmitted on a network that cannot accomodate the original packet size or reassembly of the pieces of a previously fragmented packet.

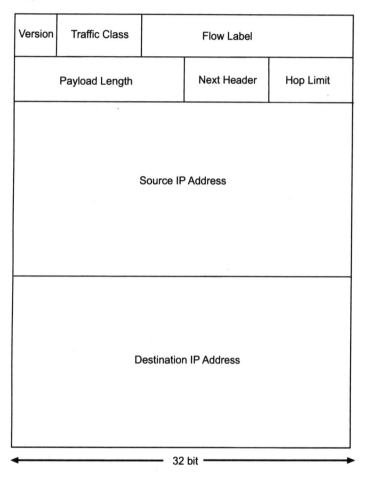

Figure 2.5 The IPv6 header format.

The process of packetizing, framing, fragmenting, and reassembling are fundamental IP operations. They give IP the flexibility to operate with many different physical network media and transport layer protocols. As mentioned, IP fragmentation and reassembly are beyond the scope of this book and you may refer to any book on IP networking to learn about it.

IP next generation (IPng) is a name often used to refer to the next version of IP. This new version has been given the number 6.[27] IP version 6, or IPv6, builds on the architecture that made IPv4 successful, but is a complete redesign. The original claim was to address and substantially improve addressing and routing and to deal with long-term growth issues such as security, autoconfiguration, real-time services, and transition. The development of IPv6 is briefly overviewed in [14] and fully described in [15, 16]. The current IPv6 specification [17] has been approved by the IESG as a Draft Standard.

The major change from IPv4 to IPv6 is the increase in IP address size from 32 to 128 bits. In addition, some IPv4 header fields have been dropped or made optional to reduce the common-case processing cost of packet handling and to limit the bandwidth cost of the IPv6 header accordingly. Figure 2.5 illustrates the format of a basic IPv6 header. It consists of the following fields:

- The 4-bit *version* field has remained unchanged from IPv4. It is still used to indicate the version number of IP. For IPv6 the value must be set to 6.

- The 8-bit *traffic class* field is used to indicate the traffic requirements of the packet and is similar to the TOS field in the IPv4 header (in principle, it specifies a priority for the packet relative to other packets traveling across the network).

- The 20-bit *flow label* field remains somehow experimental for IPv6. The flow label value, together with the source IP address, identifies a particular traffic flow in the network. Establishing flow labels is the responsibility of protocols other than IP such as, for example, the resource reservation protocol (RSVP).

- The 16-bit *payload length* field is used to indicate the length of the IP packet payload data in bytes (i.e., the rest of the packet following the IPv6 header). Because this field is 16 bits in size, it normally limits IP packets to 65,535 bytes or less.

- The 8-bit *next header* field identifies the type of header immediately following the basic IPv6 header. This field uses the same values as the IPv4 protocol field.

---

[27]The number 5 could not be used for IPng because it had been allocated to ST, an experimental "stream" protocol designed to carry real-time services in parallel with IP.

- The 8-bit *hop limit* field is used to indicate a hop limit value. The value is decremented by 1 each node that forwards the IP packet. The packet is discarded if the value is decremented to zero. In short, the hop limit value determines how far a datagram will travel and is conceptually similar to the TTL field in IPv4.

- The 128-bit *source address* field identifies the IP address of the originator of the IP packet.

- The 128-bit *destination address* field identifies the IP address of the intended receiver of the IP packet.

In IPv6, optional Internet layer information may be encoded in separate extension headers that are placed between the IPv6 basic header and the upper-layer protocol header. There is a relatively small number of extension headers, each identified by a distinct next header value. There are extension headers defined for hop-by-hop options, routing, fragment, destination options, authentication, and encapsulating security payload. With the exception of the last two, we are not going to further address IPv6 extension headers in this book.

Routing Protocols

The purpose of a routing protocol is to enable routing decisions to be made at the Internet layer. As such, the routing protocol must manage and periodically update the routing tables that are stored at each router. An Internet router may be part of an autonomous system, which is basically a collection of routers that are under a single administration. These routers run the same routing protocol, usually called an interior gateway protocol (IGP). There are several IGPs in use today, but all routers within an autonomous system normally run the same one. To communicate with another autonomous system, however, a router usually uses an exterior gateway protocol (EGP). The EGP does not know details of routing within another domain. To make an analogy, an IGP is like a local telephone exchange, whereas an EGP is more like a long-distance operator.

Today, a wide variety of routing protocols are used on the Internet. These routing protocols generally fall into two categories: reachability and distance vector protocols. A reachability protocol tells whether a path exists to a distant network. A distance vector protocol calculates a distance metric to this network. The distance metric can be just the number of routers between the source and destination network, or it can include more information about each link, such as bandwidth and load. In general, IGPs are distance vector protocols and EGPs are reachability protocols.

Internet routing an increasingly important and complex field of study. In fact, there are many books that entirely address Internet routing and corresponding protocols [18].

Support Protocols

There are several support protocols for IP to handle specific tasks, such as routing redirects, error messages, and mappings between IP addresses and physical network access layer addresses. These protocols do not make routing decisions at the Internet layer, although they can be used by protocols that do make such decisions.

- The *Address Resolution Protocol* (ARP) as specified in RFC 826 (and STD 37) [19] can be used to find the network access layer address for a given IP address.
- Contrary to ARP, the *Reverse Address Resolution Protocol* (RARP) as specified in RFC 903 (and STD 38) [20] can be used to find the IP address for a given network access layer address.
- The *Internet Control Message Protocol* (ICMP) as specified in RFC 792 [21] is a required protocol that must be implemented in conjunction with IP (it is part of STD 5). It is used to send and receive control information between hosts.
- The *Internet Group Management Protocol* (IGMP) as specified in RFC 1112 [22] is a protocol that can be used in an IP multicast environment to control host group memberships (it also is part of STD 5).

Support protocols are essential for the overall security of a TCP/IP implementation. For example, ICMP redirect messages can be used to fake routes and hosts acting as routers into using false routes. These false routes would aid in directing traffic to an attacker's system instead of a legitimate trusted system.

2.4.3   Transport Layer

The transport layer protocols make use of the packet delivery service provided by IP to provide transport layer services to applications. In short, there are two transport layer protocols: TCP and UDP. TCP provides a connection-oriented and reliable transport layer service, whereas UDP provides a connectionless and unreliable transport layer service.

Transmission Control Protocol

TCP as specified in RFC 793 and STD 7 [23] provides a connection-oriented and reliable transport layer service (i.e., a virtual circuit) to the communicating peers. More specifically, the sending TCP module processes a byte stream from an application process and divides it into distinct TCP segments that are sent to the receiving module on the other side of the TCP connection. The receiving TCP module, in turn, collects the TCP segments, recreates the original byte stream and passes it on to the corresponding application process.

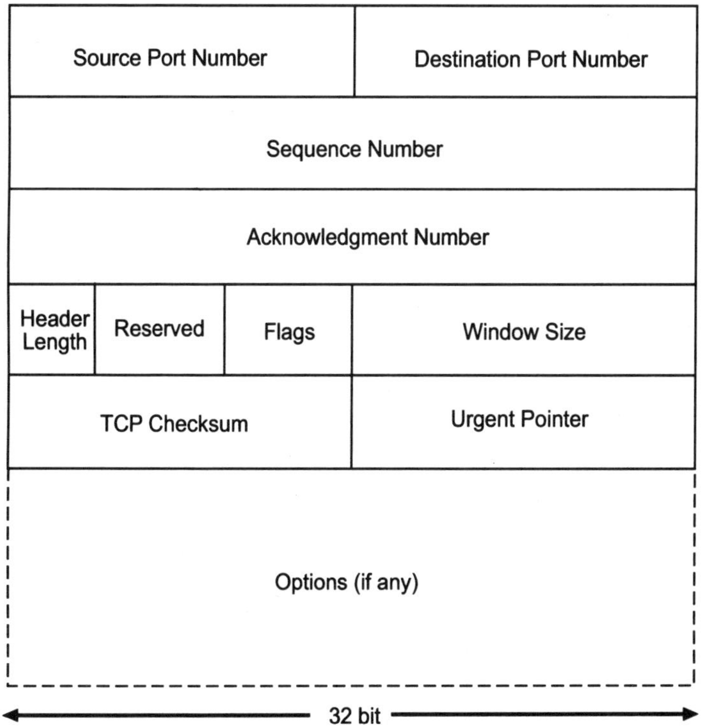

Figure 2.6   The TCP header format.

Figure 2.6 illustrates the format of a TCP header. The header is put in front of the TCP segment.

- Along with the source and destination IP addresses found in a packet's IP header, the 16-bit *source port number* and the 16-bit *destination port number* uniquely identify the two application processes associated with the TCP/IP connection.

- The 32-bit *sequence number* field is used to indicate the relative byte offset of the first byte in the current message. The sequence number starts at an arbitrary 32-bit number that is negotiated when a TCP/IP connection is established. The field is examined only when the SYN bit is set (see the following discussion of the flags).

- The 32-bit *acknowledgment number* field is used to acknowledge received data. In particular, its value indicates the relative byte position of the last byte successfully acknowledged. The field is examined only when the ACK bit is set (again see the following discussion of the flags).

- The 4-bit *header length* field is used to indicate the number of 32-bit words in the TCP header, or the offset to the beginning of the *Data* field from the beginning of the header, respectively.

- The 6-bit *reserved* field is reserved for future use. It is always set to zero.

- The 6-bit *flags* field is used to indicate 1-bit values for the flags summarized in Table 2.5.

- The 16-bit *window size* field is used to indicate the number of data bytes that the sender of a message is willing to accept. TCP uses this field for flow control and buffer management, which is very important in an internetwork with links of varying speed.

- The 16-bit *TCP checksum* field is used for error detection. It usually carries the 16-bit 1's complement sum of each 16 bits in the header and data part of the message.

- The 16-bit *urgent pointer* field is used to indicate the byte position of data in the message that should be processed first.

- The *options* field may be used to specify various TCP options. These options, however, are very seldom used today.

- Finally, the *data* field contains the payload data of the TCP message up to a maximum of 65,535 bytes.

It should be noted at this point that the source and destination port numbers uniquely identify the application processes that send and receive messages. Port numbers are assigned to each client process running on a host; therefore, no two clients on the same host use the same port number for a TCP/IP connection. Client port assignments are enforced by the local host operating system. On the

Table 2.5
TCP Flags

Flag	Description
URG	This flag is used to send out data without waiting for the receiver to process data already in the stream. When the flag is set, the urgent pointer field is valid.
ACK	When the flag is set, the acknowledgment number field is valid.
PSH	The flag tells the TCP module to deliver data for this message immediately.
RST	When the flag is set, the connection is reset because of unrecoverable errors.
SYN	When the flag is set, the sequence number field is valid.
FIN	This flag is used to terminate a connection.

other side, well-known port numbers are assigned to server processes depending on the service they provide. For example, an SMTP server usually uses TCP port 25, a Telnet server TCP port 23, and an FTP server TCP port 21 for the control connection and TCP port 20 for the data connection. A server port number must be well known because it, along with the destination IP address, needs to be used when initiating a TCP/IP connection to a particular host and service. There is a general rule that only privileged server processes (i.e., those processes that operate with UNIX superuser privileges) can use port numbers less than 1,024. These port numbers are referred to as privileged ports. Servers mostly use privileged ports, whereas clients generally request unprivileged port numbers from the local operating system. Although this rule is not firm and is not required in the TCP/IP specifications, BSD-based UNIX systems generally adhere to it. Because client port assignments are unique for each host and servers use well-known ports, a unique address for each connection is the concatenation of the server IP address, the server port number, the client IP address, the client port number, and the transport layer protocol in use, such as TCP or UDP.

TCP uses a three-way handshake protocol to establish a connection, and to set the initial sequence numbers for each side of the connection accordingly. Referring to Figure 2.7, we assume the client on the left side wishes to establish a TCP connection to the server on the right side. Therefore, the client begins by sending a SYN message to the server. The SYN message is basically a TCP connection establishment request message with the SYN flag set and the client's initial sequence number X contained in the sequence number field. The server acknowledges the SYN message by sending a SYN-ACK message back to the client. The SYN-ACK message is a TCP message with both the SYN and ACK flags set, and containing the client's sequence number X in the acknowledgment number field and the server's sequence number Y in the sequence number field.[28] The client finishes establishing the TCP/IP connection by responding with an ACK message. This is a TCP message with the ACK flag set and the server's sequence number Y contained in the acknowledgment number field. From that moment on, the TCP/IP connection between the client and server is established and can be used for data transmission. None of the three messages contains any data; all information passed is conveyed in the TCP headers. Also note that the closing of the connection is handled by a two-way handshake protocol. When one side of the connection has finished sending data, it sends a message with the FIN flag set. Because the connection is full duplex, the other side can continue to send data until it also sends a message with the FIN flag set. In either case, a message with the RST flag set can be used to ultimately reset the connection.

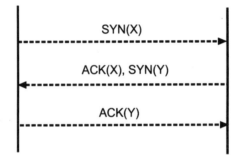

Figure 2.7   The TCP/IP three-way handshake connection establishment protocol.

User Datagram Protocol

UDP as specified in RFC 768 and STD 6 [24] provides a connectionless and unreliable transport layer service to communicating peers. Because of the connectionless nature of UDP, there may be more than two peers involved in a UDP-based communication (e.g., multicast communications). Because UDP data units are delivered individually, they are also called datagrams. Each UDP datagram is encapsulated in an IP packet and UDP has the same notion of ports as TCP. Consequently, the *destination port number* and the *source port number* fields serve the same purposes as they do for TCP. Furthermore, a UDP message also includes a *UDP length* field

---

[28]For simplicity, we omit the fact that the server acknowledges X+1 instead of X at this point.

that indicates the length of the message, as well as a *checksum* field that contains a checksum for the entire UDP header and message. Figure 2.8 illustrates the format of a UDP header.

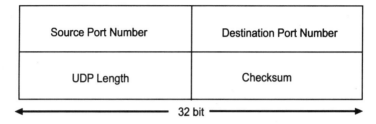

Figure 2.8   The UDP header format.

UDP is a connectionless protocol, and as such it does not have a connection setup procedure. Because sequence numbers and window sizes need not be exchanged, neither the initial three-way handshake nor the closing two-way handshake are needed. A server process using UDP can simply receive datagrams from any client that sends the message to the server's port address. A UDP-based server's ability to receive UDP datagrams from any number of clients contrasts sharply with the TCP paradigm of having each server only receive messages from a single client. In general, there is a higher risk associated with UDP-based services than with TCP-based services. The reason for that is due to the fact that it is much easier to spoof UDP packets than TCP packets, since there are no handshakes or sequence numbers. Extreme caution is therefore indicated when using the IP source address from any such packet. Concerned applications must make their own arrangements with regard to proper message authentication.

From an application developer's point of view, it would be inconvenient for every application to deal directly with TCP or UDP. The construction of TCP messages, as well as the details of TCP flow control, need not and should not be a part of an application program. To facilitate dealings with TCP and UDP, several programming interfaces have been developed for programming at the transport layer. Examples are the Berkeley sockets and the Transport Layer Interface (TLI) found on System V UNIX systems. Most commonly, IP applications that run under UNIX are written for one of these interfaces.

2.4.4   Application Layer

There are a wide variety of application protocols and services layered on top of TCP and UDP. The aim of this section is to briefly overview this variety without going into detail with each of these protocols and services. Probably the most important and most commonly used applications are:

- Remote terminal access, implemented by the Telnet remote login protocol as specified in RFC 854 and STD 8 [25];

- File transfer, implemented by the File Transfer Protocol (FTP) as specified in RFC 959 and STD 9 [26];

- Electronic mail (e-mail), implemented by the SMTP as specified in RFC 821 and STD 10 [27], and some message store access protocols, such as the Post Office Protocol (POP) as specified in RFC 1939 or STD 53 [28] and the Internet Message Access Protocol (IMAP) [29];

- Web transactions, implemented by the Hypertext Transfer Protocol (HTTP) [30].

Among these protocols, FTP is special, as it requires two TCP connections to be estabished between the client and server (a control connection and a data connection). Beyond that, there are some other application protocols that are layered on top of TCP:

- The Network News Transfer Protocol (NNTP) can be used to deliver and access USENET news over the Internet.

- The Network Time Protocol (NTP) can be used to arrange for hosts to keep the same time of day.

- The Simple Network Management Protocol (SNMP) can be used to manage diverse components in an intranet or Internet environment.

- The X11 protocol can be used to manage X Windows sessions between X servers and clients.

In addition to these TCP-based application protocols, there also are several protocols that are layered on UDP:

- The Remote Procedure Call (RPC) protocol can be used to have procedures executed on remote hosts. Secure RPC extends RPC to support cryptographic authentication. All RPC calls are authenticated using a shared secret key that is distributed using the Diffie-Hellman key exchange. Unfortunately, Sun's version of Secure RPC is not strong enough to resist more sophisticated cryptanalytical attacks.

- The Network File System (NFS) uses RPC to provide transparent file access over a network. To the extent that it is available, NFS can also make use of Secure RPC.

- Similarly, the Network Information System (NIS) uses RPC to allow multiple systems to share data (e.g., the password file) for centralized management. NIS$^+$ is an enhancement made to NIS primarily to handle large system configurations and to secure exchange of critical information.

Most TCP/IP services and corresponding application protocols require some form of mapping between logical names (i.e., host names) and physical addresses (i.e., IP addresses). The mapping of logical names to physical addresses is called forward mapping, whereas the mapping of physical addresses to logical names is called reverse mapping. For example, when a user points a browser at `www.esecurity.ch`, the browser must use forward mapping to get the IP address of the corresponding Web server. It must then establish a TCP connection to port 80 (i.e., the default port for HTTP) of this server and use HTTP to actually retrieve the requested resources (e.g., HTML files).

In the early days of the Internet, the mapping between logical names and physical addresses was provided by a static file that was periodically updated and distributed to the hosts that were connected to the Internet. In the meantime, however, this static approach has been replaced with a distributed service called the Domain Name System (DNS). The DNS is provided by a hierarchical and highly distributed database containing resource records (RR). There is one RR type for each different type of information. Some examples of RR types include the A record that identifies an IP address for a given DNS name (e.g., a Web server), the NS record that identifies a name server for a given domain name, and the MX record that identifies a mail exchange for a given DNS name.

The hierarchical ordering of the DNS provides a globally unique namespace. It takes the form of a tree with a single root node (`.`). The first level under the root is divided into large groupings, such as commercial (`com`), organization (`org`), educational (`edu`), and so on. Outside the United States, this level is structured according to country information (e.g., `de` for Germany and `ch` for Switzerland). The level following this typically represents a specific organization or company, such as `esecurity.ch`. As the tree is traversed from leaf to root, a fully qualified domain name (FQDN) is formed. Note that an FQDN always ends with a dot (representing the root of the tree). In the DNS, every FQDN is unique. An FQDN query results in the tree being traversed from root to leaf in order to find the appropriate IP address. A similar tree exists for reverse mappings. In this case, an IP address query results in an FQDN. The distributed database resides in DNS servers that connect to the Internet and corporate intranets. The most commonly used DNS server is provided by the Berkeley Internet Name Daemon (BIND), which is part of most operating systems today.

REFERENCES

[1] L. Kleinrock, *Information Flow in Large Communication Nets*, RLE Quarterly Progress Report, July 1961.

[2] L. Kleinrock, *Communication Nets: Stochastic Message Flow and Delay*, McGraw-Hill, New York, 1964.

[3] R. E. Kahn, "Communications Principles for Operating Systems," Internal BBN memorandum, January 1972.

[4] V. G. Cerf and R. E. Kahn, "A Protocol for Packet Network Interconnection," *IEEE Trans. Comm. Tech.*, May 1974, pp. 627–641.

[5] W. A. Foster, A. M. Rutkowski, and S. E. Goodman, "Who Governs the Internet?" *Communications of the ACM*, Vol. 40, No. 8, August 1997, pp. 15–20.

[6] A. Weinrib and J. Postel, "IRTF Research Group Guidelines and Procedures," Request for Comments 2014, October 1996.

[7] J. Postel, "Instructions to RFCs Authors," Request for Comments 1543, October 1993.

[8] J. Myers and M. Rose, "Post Office Protocol—Version 3," Request for Comments 1939 (STD 53), May 1996.

[9] J. Reynolds and R. Braden, "Internet Official Protocol Standards," Request for Comments 2700 (STD 1), August 2000.

[10] C. Huitema, J. Postel, and S. Crocker, "Not All RFCs Are Standards," Request for Comments 1796, April 1995.

[11] S. Bradner, "The Internet Standards Process—Revision 3," Request for Comments 2026, October 1996.

[12] J. Postel, "Internet Protocol," Request for Comments 791, September 1981.

[13] S. Kent, "Security Options for the Internet Protocol," Request for Comments 1108, November 1991.

[14] R. M. Hinden, "IP Next Generation Overview," *Communications of the ACM*, Vol. 39, No. 6, June 1996, pp. 61–71.

[15] C. Huitema, *IPv6: The New Internet Protocol*, Prentice Hall, Englewood Cliffs, NJ, 1996.

[16] S. A. Thomas, *IPng and the TCP/IP Protocols: Implementing the Next Generation Internet*, John Wiley & Sons, New York, 1996.

[17] S. Deering and R. M. Hinden, "Internet Protocol, Version 6 (IPv6) Specification," Request for Comments 2460, December 1998.

[18] U. D. Black, *IP Routing Protocols: RIP, OSPF, BGP, PNNI and Cisco Routing Protocols*, Prentice Hall, Englewood Cliffs, NJ, 2000.

[19] D. C. Plummer, "An Ethernet Address Resolution Protocol," Request for Comments 826 (STD 37), November 1982.

[20] R. Finlayson, et al., "A Reverse Address Resolution Protocol," Request for Comments 903 (STD 38), June 1984.

[21] J. Postel, "Internet Control Message Protocol," Request for Comments 792 (part of STD 5), September 1981.

[22] S. Deering, "Host Extensions for IP Multicasting," Request for Comments 1112 (part of STD 5), August 1989.

[23] J. Postel, "Transmission Control Protocol," Request for Comments 793 (STD 7), September 1981.

[24] J. Postel, "User Datagram Protocol," Request for Comments 768 (STD 6), August 1980.

[25] J. Postel and J. Reynolds, "Telnet Protocol Specification," Request for Comments 854 (STD 8), May 1983.

[26] J. Postel and J. Reynolds, "File Transfer Protocol (FTP)," Request for Comments 959 (STD 9), October 1985.

[27] J. B. Postel, "Simple Mail Transfer Protocol," Request for Comments 821 (part of STD 10), August 1982.

[28] J. Myers and M. Rose, "Post Office Protocol—Version 3," Request for Comments 1939 (STD 53), May 1996.

[29] M. Crispin, "Internet Message Access Protocol—Version 4rev1," Request for Comments 2060, December 1996.

[30] R. Fielding, et al., "Hypertext Transfer Protocol—HTTP/1.1," Request for Comments 2068, January 1997.

Chapter 3

Attacks

According to RFC 2828 [1], an attack refers to "an assault on system security that derives from an intelligent threat, i.e., an intelligent act that is a deliberate attempt (especially in the sense of a method or technique) to evade security services and violate the security policy of a system." As such, there are many attacks that can be launched against the security of a system interconnected to the Internet. Most of these attacks are due to vulnerabilities in the underlying network operating systems. In fact, the complexity of contemporary network operating systems makes it possible and very likely that we will see an increasingly large number of such attacks in the future. You may refer to a book about hacking (e.g., [2]) or a hacker Web site for an overview about the vulnerabilities of contemporary network operating systems and tools that can be used to exploit them.

In this chapter, we overview and briefly discuss some exemplary passive and active attacks that can be launched against TCP/IP-based networks (i.e., intranets or the Internet). Roughly speaking, a passive attack "attempts to learn or make use of information from the system but does not affect system resources," whereas an active attack "attempts to alter system resources or affect their operation" [1]. Obviously, passive and active attacks can also be combined to effectively invade a computing or networking environment. For example, a passive wiretapping attack can be used to eavesdrop on authentication information that is transmitted in the clear (e.g., username and password), and this information can later be used to masquerade another user and to actively attack a system accordingly.

3.1 PASSIVE ATTACKS

As mentioned earlier, a passive attack "attempts to learn or make use of information from the system but does not affect system resources" [1]. As such, it primarily threatens the confidentiality of data being transmitted. The situation is illustrated in Figure 3.1. The data transmitted from the originator (on the right side) to the recipient (on the left side) may be observed by the intruder (in the middle).[1] This data may include anything, including, for example, confidential e-mail messages or usernames and passwords transmitted in the clear. In fact, the cleartext transmission of authentication information, such as usernames and passwords, is the single most important vulnerability in computer networks and distributed systems today.

Figure 3.1   A passive attack threatens the confidentiality of data being transmitted.

In regard to the intruder's opportunities to interpret and extract the information that the transmitted data encodes, passive wiretapping and traffic analysis attacks are usually distinguished:

- In a *passive wiretapping attack*, the intruder is able to interpret and extract the information that the transmitted data encodes. For example, if two parties communicate unencrypted, a passive wiretapper is trivially able to extract all information that is encoded in the data.

- In a *traffic analysis attack*, the intruder is not able to interpret and extract the information that the transmitted data encodes. Instead, traffic analysis

---

[1]Note that many publications on network security use names, such as "Alice" and "Bob," to refer to the sending and receiving network entities, and other names, such as "Eve," to refer to a possible intruder. This is a convenient way of making things unambiguous with relatively few words, because the pronoun "she" can be used for Alice, and "he" can be used for Bob. However, the advantages and disadvantages of this naming scheme are controversial, and we are not going to use it in this book.

refers to the inference of information from the observation of external traffic characteristics. For example, if an attacker observes that two companies—one financially strong, the other financially weak—begin to trade a large number of messages, he or she may infer that they are discussing a merger. Other examples occur in military environments.

The feasibility of a passive attack primarily depends on the physical transmission medium in use and its physical accessibility for an intruder. For example, mobile communications is by its very nature easy to tap, whereas metallic transmission media at least require some sort of physical access. Lightwave conductors also can be tapped, but this is quite expensive. Also note that the use of concentrating and multiplexing techniques, in general, makes it more difficult to passively attack data in transmission.

It is important to note that a passive attacker does not necessarily have to tap a physical communications line. Most network interfaces can operate in a so-called "promiscuous mode." In this mode, they are able to capture all frames transmitted on the local area network segment they are connected to, rather than just the frames addressed to the machine of which they are part. This capability has useful purposes for network analysis, testing, and debugging (e.g., by utilities such as `etherfind` and `tcpdump` in the case of the UNIX or Linux operating system). Unfortunately, this capability also can be used by attackers to snoop on all traffic on a particular network segment. Several software packages are available for monitoring network traffic, primarily for the purpose of network management (e.g., Sniffer Pro[2] from Network Associates, Inc.). These software packages are dual-use, meaning they can, for example, be effective in eavesdropping and capturing e-mail messages or usernames and passwords as they are transmitted over shared media and communications lines.

Given the availability and ease of use of contemporary sniffer tools, one may wonder whether there are technologies to protect against passive attacks. Fortunately, the use of switching technologies makes it more difficult for an attacker to passively attack and eavesdrop on a network segment, because network traffic is directed only to the intended network interfaces. Furthermore, a new family of tools is being developed and deployed. These tools try to reveal the mere existence of systems with network interfaces that operate in promiscuous mode. For example, AntiSniff is a tool developed by L0pht Heavy Industries, Inc., and commercially distributed by Security Software Technologies, Inc. The tool "allows tests to be run that determine, through a variety of fashions, whether a remote system is capturing and analyzing packets that are not destined to its hardware address." For example,

---

[2]`http://www.sniffer.com`

the tool may generate an Ethernet frame with a randomly chosen MAC address and a correct IP address for a remote system under consideration. The IP packet may encapsulate an ICMP request message. If the system responds with an ICMP message, one may argue that its network interface is operating in promiscuous mode. This is because the system has responded to a message it should not have been able to receive in the first place (because the MAC address is randomly chosen). Similarly, AntiSniff implements and is able to run a number of tests that are briefly explained in an unpublished technical paper.[3]

There are several technologies that can be used to protect against passive wiretapping attacks. For example, the use of data encryption is both effective and efficient. In fact, data encryption is still the technology of choice to protect against passive wiretapping attacks in today's computer networks and distributed systems. In Part III, we discuss many cryptographic security protocols that have been developed, implemented, and deployed to encrypt data as it is being transmitted in TCP/IP-based networks.

Contrary to passive wiretapping attacks and the use of data encryption, protection against traffic analysis attacks is much more complicated and requires more sophisticated security technologies. For example, the use of encryption techniques does not protect against traffic analysis. In fact, there are only a few technologies available today that can be used to protect against traffic analysis. Exemplary technologies include traffic padding and onion routing as proposed and developed by a group of researchers at the U.S. Naval Research Laboratory (NRL) [3–7].[4] Unfortunately, technologies to protect against traffic analysis generally do not meet the requirements and needs of packet-switched networks. In either case, these technologies are beyond the scope of this book. Keep in mind, however, that it is possible and very likely that privacy enhancing technologies (PETs) will become very important in the future, and that technologies to protect against traffic analysis also represent PETs.

3.2 ACTIVE ATTACKS

As mentioned in Section 3.1, an *active attack* "attempts to alter system resources or affect their operation" [1]. As such, it primarily threatens the integrity or availability of data being transmitted. The situation is illustrated in Figure 3.2. In this case, the data transmitted from the originator (on the right side) to the recipient (on the

---

[3]http://www.securitysoftwaretech.com/antisniff/tech-paper.html
[4]http://www.onion-router.net

left side) may not only be observed but also fully controlled by the intruder (in the middle). What this basically means is that the attacker can modify, extend, delete, or replay any data unit.

Figure 3.2   An active attack threatens the integrity or availability of data being transmitted.

As will become clear, the underlying reason why most active attacks are possible and fairly easy to launch is that the data units that are sent and received (e.g., Ethernet frames, IP packets, UDP datagrams, and TCP segments) are not protected in terms of authenticity and integrity. Consequently, it is simple to do such things as flooding a recipient to cause a denial of service, spoofing the identity of somebody else, or taking over and "hijacking" already-established TCP connections. Overviews of some of these attacks are discussed next. Keep in mind, however, that the attacks have been chosen randomly and arbitrarily, and that many other attacks are possible and likely to be discovered and published in the future.

3.2.1   Denial of Service

A denial of service (DoS) refers to the prevention of authorized access to resources or the delaying of time-critical operations. Consequently, a DoS attack prevents resources from functioning according to their intended purposes. It may range from a lack of available memory or disk space to a partial shutdown of an entire network segment. Typically, a DoS attack leaves one or more systems incapable of serving their original purposes.

In the past, many DoS attacks have been developed and deployed to crash the systems of a victim:

- In an *e-mail bombing attack* an attacker floods the mail store of a victim with large bogus messages. E-mail bombing is an increasingly popular DoS attack, and there are many tools publicly and freely available on the Internet that can be used to launch e-mail bombing attacks against arbitrary e-mail accounts.

- In a *smurf attack* an attacker multicasts or broadcasts an ICMP echo request (a "ping" message) with a spoofed IP address of the victim system. Each system that receives the request (because it listens, for example, to the multicast group) will send a response to the victim system. As a result, the victim system will be flooded and deny its services very rapidly.

Furthermore, any system connected to the Internet and providing TCP/IP network services is potentially subject to the TCP SYN flooding attack [8]. The potential for this attack arises at the point where the server has returned a SYN-ACK message to the client but has not yet received a corresponding ACK message in a TCP connection establishment process (refer to Figure 2.7 for an overview about the TCP three-way handshake connection establishment protocol). This situation refers to a half-open connection on the server side. As a matter of fact, the server has built in its own memory a data structure describing all parameters for pending half-open connections. If there was no limit to the number of half-open connections, a busy host could easily exhaust all its memory space trying to process connection requests. However, there is typically a small upper limit (e.g., 10) to the number of half-open TCP connections that can concurrently coexist in a system's *backlog queue*. When the queue limit is reached, any attempt to establish another TCP connection will fail until a backlogged connection becomes established, reset, or timed-out (typically after 75 seconds).

The TCP connection establishment process and the use of a backlog queue with a limited size can also be (mis)used to launch a simple but highly efficient DoS attack: The attacker only has to send a series of SYN messages to fill the victim system's backlog queue. If the attacker makes sure that the corresponding IP source addresses reference clients that are currently unable to respond to the SYN-ACK messages generated by the server, the SYN-ACK messages will be lost. Consequently, the final ACK messages will never be sent to the server and the server's backlog queue will eventually fill up. At that moment, however, the server will be unable to accept any new connection request until the backlog queue is (entirely or partially) emptied out. As mentioned, there is normally a time-out associated with each half-open connection, so the backlog queue will recover. However, the attacker can simply continue sending bogus SYN messages faster than the victim server expires half-open connections. In most cases, the victim of a TCP SYN flooding attack will have difficulty in accepting any new incoming network connection. The attack does not affect existing and open incoming connections nor the ability to originate outgoing connections. However, in some cases, the system may exhaust memory, crash, or be rendered otherwise inoperative.

In February 2000 some distributed denial of service (DDoS) attacks were successfully launched against commercial Internet sites, such as Yahoo!, Amazon, eTrade, eBay, CNN, and ZDNet.[5] In a DDoS attack, the intruder distributes and installs attack agents (sometimes also called "zombies") on some compromised systems on the Internet. At some later point in time, he or she signals the start of the DDoS attack by sending a specific message to the attack agents. Each attack agent that receives the message then launches a DoS attack against the victim system. Consequently, the victim system is simultaneously attacked and flooded from multiple locations, which is why the attack is distributed.

Similar to traffic analysis attacks, protection against DoS and DDoS attacks is generally hard to achieve. This is similar to the physical world: How can you protect, for example, your letter mailbox against somebody filling it up with advertisement flyers, useless paper, or any other physical material? Contrary to the physical world, however, there is at least a chance to provide protection against specific DoS attacks in the digital world (most DDoS attacks remain difficult to protect against). For example, some DoS attacks can be prevented by setting up and enforcing ingress filtering (i.e., configuring routers to block IP packets that arrive with illegitimate source addresses) [9]. Furthermore, current research and development activities address the Internet traceback problem (i.e., how to determine the source of an attack on the Internet). The traceback problem is surprisingly difficult due to the stateless nature of Internet routing. For example, in [10] a number of probabilistic packet marking mechanisms are introduced that may eventually be used to address the Internet traceback problem. Unfortunately, probabilistic packet marking and related mechanisms cannot be provided at the edge and require the cooperation of many ISPs. Finally, another approach to protect an implementation against the TCP SYN flooding attack is to avoid establishing the state after having received an initial SYN message in the first place [11]. Such an approach is employed, for example, by SYN cookies as used in some UNIX systems. Instead of establishing the state, the corresponding information is returned to the client in a form that is protected in terms of authenticity and integrity. Only if the state information is resubmitted by the client in a corresponding SYN-ACK message and this information is verifiable, does the server establish the state in its backlog queue. This approach

---

[5]There are many tools that can be used to launch DDoS attacks. Examples include Tribe Flood Network (TFN), Trin00, Stacheldraht (German for "barbed wire"), and TFN2K, an updated version of TFN. Most of these tools are publicly and freely available on the Internet. David Dittrich from the University of Washington has analyzed the tools. The corresponding reports are available at `http://staff.washington.edu/dittrich/misc/tfn.analysis` (for TFN), `http://staff.washington.edu/dittrich/misc/trinoo.analysis` (for Trin00), and `http://staff.washington.edu/dittrich/misc/stacheldraht.analysis` (for Stacheldraht). Also, a white paper entitled "Distributed Denial of Service Attack Tools" is available from Internet Security Systems at `http://documents.iss.net/whitepapers/ddos.pdf`.

is certainly the right way to go. Unfortunately, however, it also requires a major modification of TCP and its connection establishment process.

3.2.2   Degradation of Service

One of the charactersitics of DoS and DDoS attacks is that a victim recognizes very easily (and immediately) that he or she is under attack (this is because his or her systems no longer work properly). Note that a complete DoS may not necessarily occur and that it may make more sense from an attacker's point of view to simply degrade the quality of service. One reason to launch a corresponding degradation of service attack is to frustrate the customers of the service and to give them a good reason to change their service provider. For example, if the provider of search engine X manages to degrade the quality of service of search engine Y, it is possible and very likely that customers of Y will change their behavior and start using alternative search engines. Similarly, you may think of many scenarios in which a company has a commercial interest to degrade the quality of service of one or several of its competitors to attract their customers. The main advantage of a degradation of service attack, as compared to a DoS or DDoS attack, is that it is less likely to be recognized immediately.

3.2.3   Spoofing Attacks

In addition to the DoS and degradation of service attacks discussed so far, TCP/IP-based networks offer many possibilities to launch spoofing attacks. Some examples are described in [12].

IP Spoofing

As already mentioned in Chapter 2, each IP packet carries a source IP address in the corresponding field of its IP header (refer to Figure 2.4 for the format of an IPv4 header and Figure 2.5 for the format of an IPv6 header). This address, however, is not used to route the IP packet to its final destination. Consequently, it does not really matter what IP address is included in this field of the IP header. The term *IP spoofing* is used to refer to an attack in which the intruder puts a wrong IP address in the source IP address field of the packets he or she sends out. The wrong IP address may include any 32-bit number.

DNS Spoofing

The DNS as it is used today has many vulnerabilities and security problems. For example, a simple spoofing attack may use the fact that logical names (e.g., www.esecurity.ch) are translated to IP addresses (e.g., the IP address of the Web server that hosts www.esecurity.ch) using the DNS. Consequently, if an attacker is able to control this mapping, he or she can establish any system under a given logical address. More specifically, if the attacker is able to have the DNS map www.esecurity.ch to an IP address of his or her choice, he or she can establish a faked HTTP server under this address. An obvious possibility to control the forward mapping is to compromise the corresponding DNS server and to alter the relevant entries in the DNS database accordingly.

More worrisome, there are also applications that use the DNS for authorization purposes. When a remote client connects to such an application server, the server takes the IP address of the client and queries its DNS name. If the returned DNS name is what the server expects (and trusts), access is granted. Against this background, a malicious user can grab a small IP address space and register a DNS server for the reverse mapping of the corresponding IP addresses. Note that there is nothing that prevents an administrator for a given IP address space from mapping an IP address back to an FQDN for which he or she is not authorized. The administrator can then map an IP address to a host name, which the application server is configured to trust. Therefore, when the application server receives a request from a client it should not trust, but whose IP address maps back to an FQDN it trusts, the server will give access to the client. Some of the more common applications that once did this have been redesigned to make sure that the DNS name reverts to the same IP address, but there are still many applications that do not do this extra step. For example, older versions of the Berkeley r-tools (e.g., rlogin and rsh), NFS, X Windows, and HTTP may still be vulnerable to this form of attack.

The underlying problem that is common to DNS spoofing attacks is that there is no way to verify that a DNS response comes from an authentic server and contains authentic data. To solve this problem, the IETF has worked out security extensions to the DNS, and these security extensions are commonly referred to as DNS Security, or DNSSEC in short. We address DNSSEC in Chapter 16 when we discuss application layer security protocols.

Sequence Number Guessing

The TCP three-way handshake connection establishment protocol (refer to Figure 2.7 and the related explanations) lends itself to the so-called sequence number guess-

ing attack. We have already mentioned in the preface that Robert T. Morris, Jr.,
described the feasibility of this attack in a technical report in 1985 [13, 14].

The sequence number guessing attack basically exploits two weaknesses in most
TCP/IP implementations:

- A TCP/IP host, in general, does not verify the authenticity of the source IP
  address in packets it receives;

- Initial sequence numbers, in general, are not randomly generated.

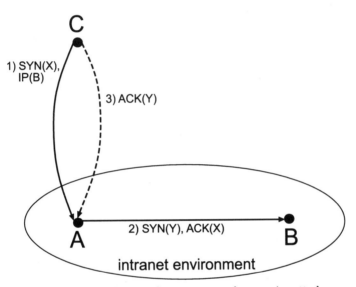

Figure 3.3   A configuration to illustrate the sequence number guessing attack.

The first weakness allows an attacking host to send packets on behalf of another
host (i.e., IP spoofing), whereas the second weakness allows the attacking host
to guess initial sequence numbers that must be known to successfully establish a
TCP/IP connection. In spite of the fact that initial sequence numbers are intended
to be more or less random, the TCP specification proposes to increment a 32-bit
counter by 1 in the low-order position about every 4 microseconds, and the BSD-
derived UNIX kernels increment it by a constant every second, and by another
constant for each new connection. In both cases, the resulting initial sequence

numbers are not randomly generated and can be guessed with a high degree of confidence.

Let us assume a configuration as illustrated in Figure 3.3. There is an intranet environment that includes two hosts (i.e., host A and host B). Furthermore, there is a trust relationship between host A and host B (not illustrated in Figure 3.3), meaning that host A trusts host B in the sense that users that have been locally authenticated by host B can have specific commands (e.g., `rlogin`, `rsh`, and `rcp`) be executed by host A without having to provide authentication information. The existence of such trust relationships is very common in contemporary networked and distributed systems. Finally, there is an attacker C who wants to use the trust relationship between host A and host B to spoof a legitimate user of host B. What this basically means is that C tries to establish a TCP connection to A for which A believes it is connected to a legitimate user of host B. If C manages to establish such a connection, C can execute malicious commands at host A without having to provide a valid username and password.

The sequence number guessing attack works in four steps:

1. C collects enough information to reliably predict the initial sequence numbers chosen by A. One possibility to collect this information is to establish a few TCP connections to A and to study the initial sequence numbers chosen by A for these connections.

2. C initiates a TCP connection establishment handshake protocol execution by sending a SYN message to A. This step is indicated with 1) in Figure 3.3. With regard to this protocol execution, C spoofs B, meaning that C uses B's IP address. After having received this SYN message, A would send a SYN-ACK message with its own initial sequence number Y to B (because A believes that B is trying to establish the TCP connection).

3. C sends an ACK message that establishes the TCP connection to A. Because C has collected enough information to reliably predict the initial sequence numbers chosen by A, C can guess the value Y. At this point, a TCP connection is established between A and C, and A thinks that A has connected to B.

4. C can execute an arbitrary command at host A.

What happens if B receives the SYN-ACK message that A sends out in step two of the three-way handshake? In this case, B would send an RST packet back to A and finish the handshake accordingly. Thus, to successfully launch a sequence number attack, C has to make sure that B does not receive A's SYN-ACK message. C can therefore launch a TCP SYN flooding attack against B, before he starts the sequence number attack against A, or simply wait until B is out of service or taken off the intranet.

There are certain precautions to address sequence number and TCP SYN flooding attacks. With regard to sequence number attacks, cryptographical authentication is obviously the right long-term solution. As this requires each host to change its TCP/IP software, however, a more practical and short-term solution is to generate sequence numbers that are randomly selected [15]. In addition, a firewall configuration can be adapted to resist some attacks of this sort. This is because, in most cases, the attacking host will be from the Internet, but it will send packets on behalf of a system that claims to be inside the firewall. To resist such an attack, a firewall can be configured so that if an IP packet arrives from the Internet with the source address of an inside host, the firewall discards and drops the packet. With regard to TCP SYN flooding attacks, we discuss some countermeasures in Part II.

3.2.4   Session Hijacking

When a TCP connection is established between a client and server, all information that is relevant for this connection is transmitted in the clear. This allows an attacker to learn the initial sequence numbers chosen by the client and server and to (mis)use this information to disturb or even take over (i.e., "hijack") an already-established connection. For example, it is possible for an attacker to create a desynchronized state on both ends of a TCP connection (so that the two points cannot exchange data any longer) and to create valid TCP segments that are encapsulated in IP packets for both ends [16]. Consequently, the attacker is able to completely take over and hijack the TCP connection. Note that this attack is successful even if the client uses strong authentication mechanisms (e.g., one-time passwords) to authenticate to the server. In fact, the attack starts after the connection establishment and authentication steps have taken place.

One possibility to protect against session hijacking attacks is to combine the authentication step with the exchange of a shared secret (i.e., sesson key) and to use this key to cryptographically protect (i.e., authenticate or encrypt) all subsequent communications.

REFERENCES

[1] R. Shirey, "Internet Security Glossary," Request for Comments 2828, May 2000.

[2] J. Scambray, S. McClure, and G. Kurtz, *Hacking Exposed: Network Security Secrets and Solutions*, 2nd Edition, McGraw-Hill, New York, 2000.

[3] M. G. Reed, P. F. Syverson, and D. M. Goldschlag, "Proxies for Anonymous Routing," *Proceedings of Annual Computer Security Applications Conference (ACSAC '96)*, San Diego, CA, 1996, pp. 95–104.

[4] D. M. Goldschlag, M. G. Reed, and P. F. Syverson, "Privacy on the Internet," *Proceedings of INET '97*, June 1997.

[5] P. F. Syverson, D. M. Goldschlag, and M. G. Reed, "Anonymous Connections and Onion Routing," *Proceedings of IEEE Symposium on Security and Privacy*, Oakland, CA, May 1997, pp. 44–54.

[6] P. F. Syverson, M. G. Reed, and D. M. Goldschlag, "Private Web Browsing," *Journal of Computer Security*, Special Issue on Web Security, Vol. 5, No. 3, 1997, pp. 237–248.

[7] D. M. Goldschlag, M. G. Reed, and P. F. Syverson, "Onion Routing for Anonymous and Private Internet Connections," *Communications of the ACM*, Vol. 42, No. 2, 1999, pp. 39–41.

[8] C. L. Schuba, et al., "Analysis of a Denial of Service Attack on TCP," *Proceedings of IEEE Symposium on Security and Privacy*, Oakland, CA, May 1997.

[9] P. Ferguson and D. Senie, "Network Ingress Filtering: Defeating Denial of Service Attacks Which Employ IP Source Address Spoofing," Request for Comments 2267, January 1998.

[10] S. Savage, et al., *Practical Network Support for IP Traceback*, Department of Computer Science and Engineering, University of Washington, Seattle, Technical Report UW-CSE-00-02-01.

[11] R. Oppliger, "Protecting Key Exchange and Management Protocols Against Resource Clogging Attacks," *Proceedings of the IFIP TC6 and TC11 Joint Working Conference on Communications and Multimedia Security*, September 1999, pp. 163–175.

[12] E. W. Felten, et al.,"Web Spoofing: An Internet Con Game," *Proceedings of the National Information Systems Security Conference*, October 1997.

[13] R. T. Morris, *A Weakness in the 4.2BSD UNIX TCP/IP Software*, Computer Science Technical Report No. 117, AT&T Bell Laboratories, Murray Hill, NJ, February 1985.

[14] S. M. Bellovin, "Security Problems in the TCP/IP Protocol Suite," *ACM Computer Communication Review*, Vol. 19, No. 2, 1989, pp. 32–48.

[15] S. Bellovin, "Defending Against Sequence Number Attacks," Request for Comments 1948, May 1996.

[16] L. Joncheray,"A Simple Active Attack Against TCP," *Proceedings of the 5th USENIX UNIX Security Symposium*, June 1995.

Chapter 4

OSI Security Architecture

In this chapter, we introduce and briefly overview the security architecture that has been proposed and appended to the OSI-RM. More specifically, we introduce the topic in Section 4.1, enumerate the security services and security mechanisms that make up the OSI security architecture in Sections 4.2 and 4.3, and briefly address security management in Section 4.4.

4.1 INTRODUCTION

According to RFC 2828, a security architecture refers to "a plan and set of principles that describe (a) the security services that a system is required to provide to meet the needs of its users, (b) the system elements required to implement the services, and (c) the performance levels required in the elements to deal with the threat environment" [1]. As such, a security architecture is always the result of applying good principles of systems engineering and addresses issues related to physical security, computer security, communication security, organizational security (e.g., administrative and personnel security), and legal security. This is complicated but very important. More often than not, systems and applications are built and deployed without having an appropriate security architecture in mind.

To illustrate the importance of having an appropriate security architecture in mind, it is worthwhile to have a look at the real (i.e., physical) world. If we want to build a house, the first and sometimes most important person to whom we talk is the architect. We hardly know anything about architecture or the art of designing and building houses, so we feel pretty comfortable to have a professional deal with these issues on our behalf. One of the first things an architect typically does—either explicitly or implicitly—is risk analysis. For example, most of the time he or she would design a house with a front door that can be locked. Similarly, he or she would make sure that entering the house always requires either breaking the door's lock or breaking the glass of a window. In general, the architect would not design the house with unbreakable window glass. Unbreakable window glass is simply too expensive to be used for ordinary houses. If, however, our house is going to host a bank in the basement, broken windows are much more likely to occur and the architect would plan the use of unbreakable window glass (or no glass at all). Also, he or she would consult a security specialist to procure a burglar alarm system and a vault. This kind of risk analysis is simple and very common in daily life. It finally results in an architecture that is sufficiently secure for a given environment and its inherent risks.

Contrary to the real world, the importance of doing risk analysis and coming up with an appropriate security architecture is far less common and hardly understood in the digital world. Instead, many companies and organizations try to avoid the definition of a security architecture and jump directly to ad hoc testing (e.g., ethical hacking investigations) against the security of their computing and networking environment. The reasoning and rationale behind this procedure are too simple, and basically work as follows:

1. We do not know whether our systems and applications are secure.

2. Therefore, we hire some external forces that attempt to attack and break into our systems and applications from the outside world. If the forces are not able to break into the systems or applications, we assume them to be secure. If, however, the forces are able to break into the systems and applications, we assume them to not be secure. In this case, we patch the corresponding vulnerabilities and security holes and hope that we are complete (i.e., we have found and eliminated all vulnerabilities and security holes).

3. We periodically repeat the test.

Obviously, the decision whether we are secure or not is fairly arbitrary in this line of argumentation. It heavily depends on the capabilities of the external forces and the tools they are aware of and have at hand. The fact that the forces are not able to break the security of the systems and applications only means that at a given point a specific group of people has not been able to find a sufficiently large vulnerability or security hole. Does that mean we are secure? Not necessarily. Would it not be possible for another group of people equipped with another set of tools to find a vulnerability the first group simply did not know about? Of course. Also, if the group finds a vulnerability and patches it, does that mean that we are secure now? Again, not necessarily. The real world analog of an "ethical hacker" would be an "ethical burglar" and we do not see that in reality (note that the term "ethical burglar" does not even exist). In fact, ex-burglars are seldom hired to break windows or rob houses simply to show we are vulnerable. There is arguably no market for ex-burglars to ethically break into houses. In the real world, we neither trust them nor do we believe in the value of such investigations. Why should the digital world be different? Also, another point to keep in mind and consider with care when it comes to ethical hacking investigations is that such investigations mainly address threats from the outside world. This is not particularly useful, as most statistical investigations reveal that most IT systems and networks are attacked from the inside.

In the digital world we need a clear understanding of what we are going to design and implement, what adversaries we should keep in mind, what resources (in terms of time and computational power) these adversaries typically have, what attack strategies are most likely to occur, what the implications are if an adversary succeeds, what reactions are planned, and so on. All these considerations should be included in a corresponding security architecture.

To extend the field of application of the OSI-RM, the ISO/IEC JTC1 appended a security architecture as part two of ISO/IEC 7498 in 1989 [2]. Since its publication, the OSI security architecture has turned out to be a primary reference for network security professionals. In 1991, the ITU-T adopted the OSI security architecture in recommendation X.800 [3], and in the early 1990s the IRTF Privacy and Security Research Group (PSRG) adapted the OSI security architecture in a corresponding Internet security architecture published as an Internet-Draft.[1] In essence, ISO/IEC 7498-2, ITU-T X.800, and the Internet security architecture all describe the very same security architecture, and in this book we are going to use the term *OSI security architecture* to refer to all of them.

In short, the OSI security architecture provides a general description of security services and related security mechanisms and discusses their interrelationships. It

---

[1] This work has been abandoned.

also shows how the security services map onto a given network architecture and briefly discusses their appropriate placement within the OSI-RM. Having the definition of a security architecture in mind [1], it is obvious that the OSI security architecture as specified in [2] and [3] does not conform to it. In fact, the OSI security architecture rather refers to a terminological framework and a general description of security services and related security mechanisms than to a full-fledged security architecture. For convenience, however, we still use the term *OSI security architecture* in this book.

Table 4.1
Classes of OSI Security Services

1	Peer entity authentication service
	Data origin authentication service
2	Access control service
3	Connection confidentiality service
	Connectionless confidentiality service
	Selected field confidentiality service
	Traffic flow confidentiality service
4	Connection integrity service with recovery
	Connection integrity service without recovery
	Selected field connection integrity service
	Connectionless integrity service
	Selected field connectionless integrity service
5	Non-repudiation with proof of origin
	Non-repudiation with proof of delivery

4.2   SECURITY SERVICES

As shown in Table 4.1, the OSI security architecture distinguishes between five classes of security services. These classes comprise authentication, access control, data confidentiality, data integrity, and non-repudiation services. Just as layers define functionality in the OSI-RM, so do services in the OSI security architecture. The services may be placed at appropriate layers in the OSI-RM.

1. *Authentication services* are to provide for the authentication of communicating peer entities or for the authentication of data origins:

- A *peer entity authentication service* is to provide the ability to verify that a peer entity in an association is the one it claims to be. In particular, a peer entity authentication service provides assurance that an entity is not attempting to masquerade or perform an unauthorized replay of some previous association. Peer entity authentication is typically performed either during a connection establishment phase or, occasionally, during a data transfer phase.

- A *data origin authentication service* is to allow the sources of data received to be verified to be as claimed. A data origin authentication service, however, cannot provide protection against the duplication or modification of data units. In this case, a data integrity service must be used in conjunction with a data origin authentication service. Data origin authentication is typically provided during a data transfer phase.

Authentication services are important because they are a prerequisite for proper authorization, access control, and accountability. Authorization refers to the process of granting rights, which includes the granting of access based on access rights. Access control refers to the process of enforcing access rights, and accountability to the property that ensures that the actions of a principal may be traced uniquely to this particular principal.

2. *Access control services* are to provide for the protection of system resources against unauthorized use. As mentioned previously, access control services are closely tied to authentication services: A user or a process acting on a user's behalf must be properly authenticated before an access control service can effectively mediate access to system resources. In general, access control services are the most commonly thought of services in both computer and communication security.

3. *Data confidentiality* refers to the property that information is not made available or disclosed to unauthorized individuals, entities, or processes. Thus, *data confidentiality services* provide for the protection of data from unauthorized disclosure:

    - A *connection confidentiality service* provides confidentiality of all data transmitted in a connection.

    - A *connectionless confidentiality service* provides confidentiality of single data units.

    - A *selective field confidentiality service* provides confidentiality of only certain fields within the data during a connection or in a single data unit.

- A *traffic flow confidentiality service* provides protection of information that may otherwise be compromised or indirectly derived from a traffic analysis.

We will see later that the provision of a traffic flow confidentiality service requires fundamentally different security mechanisms than the other data confidentiality services mentioned.

4. *Data integrity* refers to the property that information is not altered or destroyed in an unauthorized way. Thus, *data integrity services* provide for the protection of data from unauthorized modifications:

- A *connection integrity service with recovery* provides integrity of data in a connection. The loss of integrity is recovered, if possible.

- A *connection integrity service without recovery* provides integrity of data in a connection. In this case, however, the loss of integrity is not recovered.

- A *selected field connection integrity service* provides integrity of specific fields within the data during a connection.

- A *connectionless integrity service* provides integrity of single data units.

- A *selected field connectionless integrity service* provides integrity of specific fields within single data units.

Note that on a connection, the use of a peer entity authentication service at the start of the connection and a connection integrity service during the connection can jointly provide for the corroboration of the source of all data units transferred on the connection, the integrity of those data units, and may additionally provide for the detection of duplication of data units, for example, by using sequence numbers.

5. *Non-repudiation services* prevent one of the entities involved in a communication from later denying having participated in all or part of the communication. Consequently, they have to provide some sort of protection against the originator of a message or action denying that he or she has originated the message or the action, as well as against the recipient of a message denying that he or she has received the message. Consequently, there are two non-repudiation services to be distinguished:

- A *non-repudiation service with proof of origin* provides the recipient of a message with a proof of origin.

- A *non-repudiation service with proof of delivery* provides the sender of a message with a proof of delivery.

Non-repudiation services are becoming increasingly important in the context of electronic commerce on the Internet. This importance can be best illustrated through an example. An investor decides to sell a large number of shares, and sends the request to a stockbroker who sells the stocks. Now the stock price rises sharply, and the investor denies ever sending the order to sell the stocks. Conversely, it is possible that under reverse circumstances, the stockbroker may deny receiving the order to sell the stock. In this type of situation, it is easy to see that non-repudiation services are essential and critical for transacting securely over the Internet [4].

4.3   SECURITY MECHANISMS

The OSI security architecture distinguishes between specific security mechanisms and pervasive security mechanisms, and we follow this distinction in this section.

4.3.1   Specific Security Mechanisms

Specific security mechanisms may be incorporated into an appropriate layer to provide some of the security services mentioned in Section 4.2. As shown in Table 4.2, the OSI security architecture enumerates eight specific security mechanisms.

Table 4.2
OSI Specific Security Mechanisms

1	Encipherment
2	Digital signature mechanisms
3	Access control mechanisms
4	Data integrity mechanisms
5	Authentication exchange mechanisms
6	Traffic padding mechanisms
7	Routing control mechanisms
8	Notarization mechanisms

1. *Encipherment* is used either to protect the confidentiality of data units and traffic flow information or to support or complement other security mechanisms. The cryptographic techniques that are used for encipherment are examined in Chapter 5.

2. *Digital signature mechanisms* are used to provide an electronic analog of hand-written signatures for electronic documents. Like handwritten signatures, digital signatures must not be forgeable; a recipient must be able to verify it, and the signer must not be able to repudiate it later. But unlike handwritten signatures, digital signatures incorporate the data (or the hash of the data) that are signed. Different data therefore result in different signatures even if the signatory is un-changed. Again, we postpone the discussion of digital signatures mechanisms to Chapter 5.

3. *Access control mechanisms* use the authenticated identities of principals, infor-mation about these principals, or capabilities to determine and enforce access rights. If a principal attempts to use an unauthorized resource, or an authorized resource with an improper type of access, the access control function rejects the attempt and may additionally report the incident for the purposes of generating an alarm and recording it as part of a security audit trail.

   Access control mechanisms and the distinction between discretionary access con-trol and mandatory access control have been extensively discussed in the com-puter security literature referenced in the preface. They are usually described in terms of subjects, objects, and access rights. A subject is an entity that can access objects. It can be a host, a user, or an application. As such, it is a syn-onym for principal. An object is a resource to which access should be controlled. An object can range from a single data field in a file to a large program. Access rights specify the level of authority for a subject to access an object, so access rights are defined for each subject-object-pair. Examples of UNIX access rights include read, write, and execute.

4. *Data integrity mechanisms* are used to protect the integrity of either single data units and fields within these data units or sequences of data units and fields within these sequences of data units. Note that data integrity mechanisms, in general, do not protect against replay attacks that work by recording and replaying previously sent valid messages. Also, protecting the integrity of a sequence of data units and fields within these data units generally requires some form of explicit ordering, such as sequence numbering, time-stamping, or cryptographic chaining.

5. *Authentication exchange mechanisms* are used to verify the claimed identities of principals. In accordance with ITU-T recommendation X.509 [5], we use the term *strong* to refer to an authentication exchange mechanism that uses cryptographic techniques to protect the messages that are exchanged, and *weak* to refer to an authentication exchange mechanism that does not do so. In general, weak authentication exchange mechanisms are vulnerable to passive wiretapping and replay attacks.

6. *Traffic padding mechanisms* are used to protect against traffic analysis attacks. Traffic padding refers to the generation of spurious instances of communication, spurious data units, and spurious data within data units. The aim is not to reveal if data that are being transmitted actually represent and encode information. Consequently, traffic padding mechanisms can only be effective if they are protected by some sort of a data confidentiality service.

7. *Routing control mechanisms* can be used to choose either dynamically or by pre-arrangement specific routes for data transmission. Communicating systems may, on detection of persistent passive or active attacks, wish to instruct the network service provider to establish a connection via a different route. Similarly, data carrying certain security labels may be forbidden by a security policy to pass through certain networks or links.

8. *Notarization mechanisms* can be used to assure certain properties of the data communicated between two or more entities, such as its integrity, origin, time, or destination. The assurance is provided by a trusted third party (TTP) in a testifiable manner.

Table 4.3
OSI Pervasive Security Mechanisms

1	Trusted functionality
2	Security labels
3	Event detection
4	Security audit trail
5	Security recovery

4.3.2 Pervasive Security Mechanisms

Pervasive security mechanisms are not specific to any particular security service and are in general directly related to the level of security required. Some of these mechanisms can also be regarded as aspects of security management. As shown in Table 4.3, the OSI security architecture enumerates five pervasive security mechanisms.

1. The general concept of *trusted functionality* can be used to either extend the scope or to establish the effectiveness of other security mechanisms. Any functionality that directly provides, or provides access to, security mechanisms should be trustworthy.

2. System resources may have *security labels* associated with them, for example, to indicate sensitivity levels. It is often necessary to convey the appropriate security label with data in transit. A security label may be additional data associated with the data transferred or may be implicit (e.g., implied by the use of a specific key to encipher data or implied by the context of the data such as the source address or route).

3. Security-relevant *event detection* can be used to detect apparent violations of security.

4. A security audit refers to an independent review and examination of system records and activities to test for adequacy of system controls, to ensure compliance with established policy and operational procedures, to detect breaches in security, and to recommend any indicated changes in control, policy, and procedures. Consequently, a *security audit trail* refers to data collected and potentially used to facilitate a security audit.

5. *Security recovery* deals with requests from mechanisms such as event handling and management functions, and takes recovery actions as the result of applying a set of rules.

4.4 SECURITY MANAGEMENT

Security of all system and network management functions and the communication of all management information is important. As shown in Table 4.4, the OSI security architecture enumerates three areas of security management:

Table 4.4
Areas of Security Management

1	System security management
2	Security service management
3	Security mechanism management

1. *System security management* addresses the management of the overall distributed computing environment.

2. *Security service management* addresses the management of security services. This service provides for the invocation of specific security mechanisms using appropriate security mechanism management functions.

3. *Security mechanism management* addresses the management of security mechanisms.

In short, a *network management station* is a system that supports a network management protocol and the applications necessary for it to process and access information from managed entities on the network. Examples of network management protocols include the Simple Network Management Protocol (SNMP) and the Common Management Information Protocol (CMIP). Today, SNMP is by far the most widely used network management protocol on the Internet.

Keep in mind that the OSI security architecture has not been developed to solve a particular network security problem, but to provide the network security community with a terminology that can be commonly used to describe and discuss security-related problems and corresponding solutions. We will use the terminology to further describe solutions for specific intranet and Internet security problems in the remainder of this book.

REFERENCES

[1] R. Shirey, "Internet Security Glossary," Request for Comments 2828, May 2000.

[2] ISO/IEC 7498-2, Information Processing Systems—Open Systems Interconnection Reference Model—Part 2: Security Architecture, 1989.

[3] ITU X.800, Security Architecture for Open Systems Interconnection for CCITT Applications, 1991.

[4] J. Zhou, *Non-repudiation in Electronic Commerce*, Artech House, Norwood, MA, 2001.

[5] ITU-T X.509, The Directory—Authentication Framework, November 1987.

Chapter 5

Cryptographic Techniques

In this chapter, we introduce some basic cryptographic techniques that are used in the rest of this book. More specifically, we introduce the topic in Section 5.1; address cryptographic hash functions, secret key cryptography, and public key cryptography in Sections 5.2, 5.3, and 5.4, respectively; address digital envelopes in Section 5.5; and elaborate on some techniques to protect private keys and generate pseudorandom bit sequences in Sections 5.6 and 5.7. Finally, we discuss some legal issues that surround the use of cryptography in Section 5.8, and introduce a notation that can be used to describe cryptographic protocols and applications in Section 5.9. Note that this chapter is far too short to provide a comprehensive overview about all cryptographic techniques that are relevant for Internet and intranet security. For this purpose, you must read one (or several) of the many books on cryptography that are available today. Among these books, I particularly recommend [1–3].

5.1 INTRODUCTION

According to [3], the term *cryptography* refers to the study of mathematical techniques related to various aspects of information security such as confidentiality, data integrity, entity authentication, and data origin authentication. It is commonly agreed that cryptography is a major enabling technology for network security, and that cryptographic algorithms and protocols are the essential building blocks:

- A *cryptographic algorithm* is an algorithm defined by a sequence of steps precisely specifying the actions required to achieve a specific security objective.

- A *cryptographic protocol* is a distributed algorithm defined by a sequence of steps precisely specifying the actions required of two or more entities to achieve a specific security objective.

Cryptographic algorithms and protocols are being studied in both theory and practice. The aim is to design and come up with algorithms and protocols that are both secure and practical. Note, however, that there are at least two basic approaches to discussing the security of cryptographic algorithms and protocols:

- *Computational security* measures the computational effort required to break a specific cryptographic algorithm or protocol. An algorithm or protocol is said to be computationally secure if the best method for breaking it requires at least n operations, where n is some specified, usually very large, number. The problem is that no known practical algorithm or protocol can be proven to be secure under this definition. In practice, an algorithm or protocol is called *computationally secure* if the best known method of breaking it requires an unreasonably large amount of computational resources (e.g., time or memory). Another approach is to provide evidence of computational security by reducing the security of an algorithm or protocol to some well-studied problem that is thought to be difficult. For example, it may be possible to prove that an algorithm or protocol is secure if a given integer cannot be factored or a discrete logarithm cannot be computed. Algorithms and protocols of this type are sometimes called provably secure, but it must be understood that this approach only provides a proof of security relative to the difficulty of solving another problem, not an absolute proof of security.

- *Unconditional security* measures the security of a cryptographic algorithm or protocol when there is no upper bound placed on the amount of computational resources for an adversary. Consequently, an algorithm or protocol is called unconditionally secure if it cannot be broken, even with infinite time and memory at hand.

The computational security of a cryptographic algorithm or protocol can be studied from the point of view of computational complexity, whereas the unconditional security cannot be studied from this point of view because computational resources are allowed to be infinite. The appropriate framework in which unconditional security must be studied is the probability theory, and the application thereof is the communication or information theory.

Obviously, unconditional security is preferable from a security point of view, because it protects against a potentially very powerful adversary. Unfortunately, unconditional security is generally hard and expensive to achieve in many cases, and sometimes impossible. For example, the theory shows that unconditionally secure encryption systems use very long keys, making them unsuitable for most practical applications. Similarly, there is no such thing as an unconditionally secure public key cryptosystem. The best we can achieve is provable security, in the sense that the problem of breaking the public key cryptosystem is arguably at least as difficult as solving a complex mathematical problem. Consequently, one is satisfied with computational security, given some reasonable assumptions about the computational power of a potential adversary. But keep in mind that the security that a computationally secure cryptographic algorithm or protocol may provide is, for the most part, based on the perceived difficulty of a mathematical problem, such as the factorization problem or the discrete logarithm problem in the case of public key cryptography. Confidence in the security of such systems may be high because the problems are public and many minds have attempted to attack them. However, the vulnerability remains that a new insight or computing technology may defeat this type of cryptography. There are at least two developments that provide some evidence for this intrinsic vulnerability:

- In 1994, Peter W. Shor proposed randomized polynomial-time algorithms for computing discrete logarithms and factoring integers on a quantum computer, a computational device based on quantum mechanical principles [4, 5]. Presently, it is not known how to actually build a quantum computer, or if this is even possible.

- Also in 1994, Len M. Adleman[1] demonstrated the feasibility of using tools from molecular biology to solve an instance of the directed Hamiltonian path problem, which is known to be hard[2] [6]. The problem instance was encoded in molecules of deoxyribonucleic acid (DNA), and the steps of the computation were performed with standard protocols and enzymes. Adleman notes that while the currently available fastest supercomputers can execute approximately 10^{12} operations per

---

[1]Len M. Adleman is a coinventor of the Rivest, Shamir, and Adleman (RSA) cryptosystem.

[2]According to theoretical computer science, the directed Hamiltonian path problem is NP-complete.

second, it is plausible for DNA computers to execute 10^{20} or even more operations per second. Moreover, a DNA computer would be far more energy efficient than existing supercomputers. Similar to the quantum computer, it is not clear at present whether it is feasible to actually build a DNA computer with such performance characteristics. Further information on DNA computing can be found in [7].

Should either quantum computers or DNA computers ever become practical, they would have a tremendous impact on cryptography. In fact, many cryptographic algorithms and protocols that are computationally secure today would be rendered worthless. This is particularly true for algorithms and protocols that use public key cryptography.

Cryptographic algorithms and protocols are used to establish secured channels (both in terms of authenticity and integrity, as well as confidentiality). Note the subtle difference between a *secure* channel and a *secured* channel. Certain channels are assumed to be secure, including trusted couriers and personal contacts between communicating parties, whereas other channels may be secured by physical or cryptographic techniques. Physical security may be established through physical means, such as dedicated communication links with corresponding access controls put in place, or the use of *quantum cryptography*. Contrary to conventional cryptography, the security of quantum cryptography does not rely upon any complexity-theoretic or probability-theoretic assumptions, but is based on the Heisenberg uncertainty principle of quantum physics [8]. As such, quantum cryptography is immune to advances in computing power and human cleverness. In the future, quantum cryptography may provide a physical alternative to unconditionally secure cryptographic algorithms and protocols. In the meantime, however, conventional and computationally secure cryptographic algorithms and protocols are much easier to use and deploy. Consequently, we are not going to delve into the details of quantum cryptography in this book.

5.2   CRYPTOGRAPHIC HASH FUNCTIONS

According to [3], a *hash function* is a function h that has, as a minimum, the following two properties:

- h maps an input x of arbitrary finite bit-length, to an output $h(x)$ of fixed bit-length (compression);

- Given h and x, $h(x)$ is easy to compute (ease of computation).

In addition, hash functions that are relevant for cryptographic applications (i.e., cryptographic hash functions) may fulfill one or several of the following requirements [3]:

- A hash function is *preimage resistant* (or *one-way*) if for essentially all prespecified outputs, it is computationally infeasible to find any input which hashes to that output, that is, to find any preimage x' such that $h(x') = y$ when given any y for which a corresponding input is not known.

- A hash function is *second-preimage resistant* (or *weak collision resistant*) if it is computationally infeasible to find any second input which has the same output as any specified input, that is, given x, to find a second preimage $x' \neq x$ such that $h(x) = h(x')$.

- A hash function is *collision resistant* (or *strong collision resistant*) if it is computationally infeasible to find any distinct inputs x, x' that has the same output, that is, such that $h(x) = h(x')$.

In the literature, the term *one-way hash function* (OWHF) or *weak one-way hash function* is often used to refer to a hash function that is both preimage resistant and second-preimage resistant, whereas the term *collision resistant hash function* (CRHF) or *strong one-way hash function* is often used to refer to a hash function that is collision resistant. Furthermore, the term *cryptographic hash function* is used to refer to either of them (i.e., OWHF or CRHF). Mainly because of their efficiency, *cryptographic hash functions* are of central importance for cryptographic algorithms and protocols. For example, OWHFs can be used to compute and verify digests for arbitrary messages. In this context, OWHFs may also be called *message digest algorithms*, and in this book we use both terms synonymously and interchangeably.

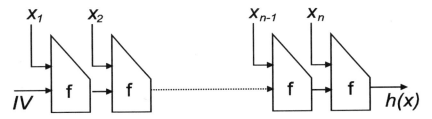

Figure 5.1   An iterative cryptographic hash function.

All definitions given above are not precise in a mathematically strong sense, because they do not resolve what the terms "easy" and "computationally infeasible" actually mean. Nevertheless, we want to use these definitions in this book. It is important to note that the existence of OWHF (or even CRHF) is still an unproven assumption and that, until today, no function has been shown to be preimage resistant (i.e., one-way) in a mathematically pure sense. Obviously, a sufficiently large domain prohibiting an exhaustive search is a necessary but not sufficient condition for a function to be preimage resistant.

Most cryptographic hash functions in use today are iterative. In short, a cryptographic hash function is iterative if data are hashed by iterating a basic compression function on subsequent blocks of data. The basic idea is illustrated in Figure 5.1. A message x is decomposed into n blocks of data $x_1, \ldots, x_n$. A basic compression function f is then applied to each block and the result of the compression function of the previous block. This continues until the result of the last compression step is interpreted as output $h(x)$. Examples of such cryptographic hash functions include MD2 [9], MD4 [10], MD5 [11], and the secure hash algorithm 1 (SHA-1) [12]. MD2, MD4, and MD5 produce 128-bit hash values, whereas SHA-1 produces 160-bit hash values. RIPEMD is another example of an iterative cryptographic hash function. It was developed as part of a European research project and is basically a variation of MD4. RIPEMD-160 is a strengthened version of RIPEMD producing another 160-bit hash value [13].

As of this writing, MD5 and SHA-1 are by far the most widely used and deployed cryptographic hash functions. MD5 takes as input a string of arbitrary length and produces as output a 128-bit hash value. In theory, we would need 2^{128} (in the worst case) or 2^{127} (in the average case) trials before finding a preimage, and hence a new message that results in the same MD5 hash value. Even if each trial only lasted a nanosecond, this would still require some billions of billions of centuries in computing time. However, recent results in cryptographic research show that it is possible to take advantage of the particularities of the cryptographic hash function algorithm to speed up the search process. According to Paul van Oorschot and Michael Wiener, you can actually build a machine able to find messages that hash to an arbitrary value [14]. What this means is that cryptanalysis is catching up and that a 128-bit hash value may soon be insufficient. In addition, Hans Dobbertin has shown that MD5 is vulnerable to specific collision search attacks [15]. Taking this into account, SHA-1 and RIPEMD-160 appear to be a cryptographically stronger cryptographic hash function than MD5. In any case, implementors and users of cryptographic hash functions should be aware of possible cryptanalytic developments regarding any of these functions, and the eventual need to replace them.

5.3   SECRET KEY CRYPTOGRAPHY

Secret key cryptography refers to traditional cryptography. In this kind of cryptography, a secret key is established and shared between communicating peers, and the key is used to encrypt and decrypt messages on either side. Because of its symmetry, secret key cryptography is often referred to as *symmetric cryptography.*

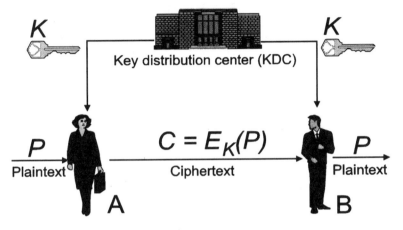

Figure 5.2   A secret key cryptosystem.

The use of a secret key cryptosystem is overviewed in Figure 5.2. We assume that A on the left side wants to send a confidential message to B on the right side. A therefore shares a secret key K with B. This key may be preconfigured manually or distributed by a trusted third party (TTP) or key distribution center (KDC). Note that during its distribution, K must be secured in terms of confidentiality, integrity, and authenticity. This is usually done by having the KDC encrypt K with secret keys that it shares with A and B, respectively. A encrypts a plaintext message P by applying an encryption function E and the key K, and sends the resulting ciphertext $C = E_K(P)$ to B. On the other side, B decrypts C by applying the decryption function D and the key K. B therefore computes $D_K(C) = D_K(E_K(P)) = P$, and recovers the plaintext P accordingly.

Secret key cryptography has been in use for many years in a variety of forms. Two basic categories of secret key cryptosystems are *block ciphers* and *stream ciphers*. As their names suggest, block ciphers operate on blocks of data (e.g., 64 bits), whereas stream ciphers usually operate on data one bit or byte at a time.

Examples of secret key cryptosystems that are in widespread use are summarized in Table 5.1 and overviewed next. Again, refer to [1–3] for a full description of the cryptosystems and corresponding encryption and decryption algorithms.

Table 5.1
Secret Key Cryptosystems

Algorithm Name	Main Mode	Effective Key Length
DES	Block cipher	56 bits
Triple-DES (3DES)	Block cipher	112 or 168 bits
IDEA	Block cipher	128 bits
SAFER	Block cipher	64 or 128 bits
Blowfish	Block cipher	Variable from 1 up to 448 bits
CAST-128	Block cipher	128 bits
RC2, RC5, and RC6	Block cipher	Variable from 1 up to 2,048 bits
RC4	Stream cipher	Variable from 1 up to 2,048 bits

5.3.1   DES

The Data Encryption Standard (DES) is (still) the most well-known and widely deployed secret key cryptosystem today. It was originally designed by a group of researchers at IBM and published as Federal Information Processing Standard (FIPS) 46 in 1977 [16]. As such, it has been used for the encryption of unclassified information by the U.S. National Institute of Standards and Technology (NIST) for almost a quarter of a century.

DES operates as a block cipher with 64-bit blocks, 16 rounds, and a variable key length up to 56 bits. In electronic code book (ECB) mode, DES encrypts data in discrete blocks of 64 bits. To improve its cryptographical strength, DES is often used in cipher block chaining (CBC) mode. In this mode, the encryption of each block depends on the contents of the previous one, preventing an interloper from tampering with the message by rearranging the encrypted blocks. Furthermore, there are two modes that can be used to turn DES into a stream cipher: cipher feedback (CFB) mode and output feedback (OFB) mode.

DES's 56-bit effective key length was sufficiently secure during its first two decades of operation, but it is far too short today.

5.3.2 Triple-DES

One way to improve the cryptographical strength of a secret key cryptosystem with limited key length (e.g., DES), is to apply the algorithm multiple times. Applying the algorithm twice does not improve the situation, because of the existence of a specific cryptanalytical attack (a so-called "meet-in-the-middle" attack). Consequently, at least three applications are necessary for a security improvement, and the threefold application of DES is called Triple-DES (3DES). It can be used with two or three different keys, and the resulting secret key cryptosystems are usually called two-key 3DES and three-key 3DES. Many contemporary applications use 3DES as a replacement for DES. Note, however, that the use of 3DES is not very efficient (in fact, it is approximately three times slower than DES), and that there are many real-time applications that require faster encryption algorithms.

5.3.3 IDEA

The International Data Encryption Algorithm (IDEA) was developed by Xuejia Lai and James Massey in the early 1990s at the ETH Zurich, Switzerland [17]. IDEA is a 64-bit block cipher that uses a 128-bit key. The algorithm is patented and may be licensed from the iT_SEC iT_Security AG.[3]

5.3.4 SAFER

After having developed IDEA, James Massey proposed SAFER K-64 and SAFER K-128. As their names suggest, SAFER K-64 uses a 64-bit key [18], whereas SAFER K-128 uses a proprietary key schedule algorithm that is able to accommodate 128-bit keys. Furthermore, SAFER K-64 uses 6 rounds, whereas SAFER K-128 recommends 10 rounds (12 maximum).

5.3.5 Blowfish

The Blowfish algorithm was developed by Bruce Schneier [19]. It is a DES-like encryption algorithm that can be used as a block cipher with 64-bit blocks, 16 rounds, and variable key lengths up to 448 bits.

---

[3]http://www.it-sec.ch/idea_lic.html

5.3.6   CAST-128

The term CAST refers to a design procedure for a family of DES-like encryption algorithms with variable key size and numbers of rounds. In RFC 2144, a 128-bit CAST encryption algorithm is specified [20]. This algorithm is called CAST-128 and is used and widely deployed for Internet applications.

5.3.7   RC2, RC4, RC5, and RC6

RC2, RC4, RC5, and RC6 are secret key cryptosystems with variable key lengths that were designed by Ronald L. Rivest for RSA Security, Inc.:

- RC2 is a block cipher (block size is 64 bits), designed as a replacement for DES.

- RC4 is a stream cipher.

- RC5 is a block cipher that is configurable with regard to word length and number of rounds (in addition to the ley length).

- RC6 is a recent proposal to improve RC5.

The RC2 and RC4 algorithms were originally protected by trade secrets, but were disassembled, reverse-engineered, and anonymously posted to a Usenet newsgroup in 1996 and 1994, respectively.

5.3.8   AES

More recently, the U.S. NIST standardized an Advanced Encryption Standard (AES) to replace DES in the future. The AES emerged from a proposal called Rijndael that originated from Belgium. You may refer to `http://www.esat.kuleuven.ac.be/~rijmen/rijndael/` for more information about the Rijndael algorithm.

5.4   PUBLIC KEY CRYPTOGRAPHY

The idea of using one-way functions, which can only be inverted if a certain secret (a so-called "trapdoor") is known, has led to the invention of *public key cryptography* or *asymmetric cryptography* [21]. Today, public key cryptography is a battlefield for mathematicians and theoretical computer scientists. We are not going to delve into the mathematical foundations of public key cryptography. Instead, we address public key cryptography from a more practical point of view. From this point of view, a public key cryptosystem is simply a cryptosystem in which a user has a pair of mathematically related keys:

- A *public key* that can be published without doing any harm to the system's overall security;

- A *private key* that is assumed to never leave the possession of its owner.

For both the public and the private keys, it is computationally infeasible for an outsider to derive one from the other. The use of a public key cryptosystem is overviewed in Figure 5.3. A and B each has a public key pair (k_A, k_A^{-1}) and (k_B, k_B^{-1}). The private keys k_A^{-1} and k_B^{-1} are kept secret, whereas the public keys k_A and k_B are publicly available in certified form (e.g., digitally signed by a certification authority as further addressed later).

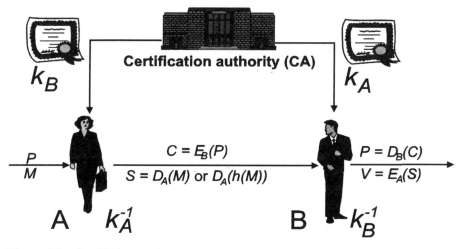

Figure 5.3 A public key cryptosystem.

If A wants to protect the confidentiality of a plaintext message P, she uses the public key of B, which is k_B, encrypts P with this key, and sends the resulting ciphertext $C = E_{k_B}(P)$ to B (the term $E_{k_B}(P)$ is abbreviated with $E_B(P)$ in Figure 5.3). On the other side, B uses his private key k_B^{-1} to successfully decrypt $P = D_{k_B^{-1}}(C) = D_{k_B^{-1}}(E_{k_B}(P))$. Note that the terms $D_{k_B^{-1}}(C)$ and $D_{k_B^{-1}}(E_{k_B}(P))$ are abbreviated with $D_B(C)$ and $D_B(E_B(P))$ in Figure 5.3.

A public key cryptosystem can not only be used to protect the confidentiality of a message, but also to protect its authenticity and integrity. If A wanted to protect the authenticity and integrity of a message M, she would compute a digital signature S for M. Digital signatures provide an electronic analog of handwritten signatures for electronic documents, and—similar to handwritten signatures—digital signatures must not be forgeable, recipients must be able to verify them, and the signers must not be able to repudiate them later. However, a major difference between a handwritten signature and a digital signature is that the digital signature cannot be constant, but must be a function of the entire document on which it appears. If this were not the case, a digital signature, because of its electronic nature, could be copied and attached to arbitrary documents.

Arbitrated digital signature schemes are based on secret key cryptography. In such a scheme, a TTP validates the signature and forwards it on the signer's behalf. True digital signature schemes, however, should come along without TTPs taking an active role. They usually require the use of public key cryptography: Signed messages are sent directly from signers to recipients. In essence, a *digital signature scheme* consists of:

- A key-generation algorithm that randomly selects a public key pair;

- A signature algorithm that takes as input a message and a private key and that generates as output a digital signature for the message;

- A signature verification algorithm that takes as input a digital signature and a public key and that generates as output a message and an information bit according to whether the signature is valid for the message.

A comprehensive overview and discussion of public key-based digital signature schemes are given in [22]. According to the OSI security architecture, a digital signature refers to data appended to, or a cryptographic transformation of, a data unit that allows a recipient of the data unit to prove the source and integrity of the data unit and protect against forgery (e.g., by the recipient). Consequently, there are two classes of digital signatures:

- A *digital signature giving message recovery* refers to the situation in which a cryptographic transformation is applied to a data unit. In this case, the data is automatically recovered if the recipient verifies the signature.

- In contrast, a *digital signature with appendix* refers to the situation in which some cryptographically protected data is appended to the data unit. In fact, the data represents a digital signature and can be decoupled from the data unit that it signs.

In the case of digital signatures with appendix, the bandwidth limitation of public key cryptography is unimportant because of the use of one-way hash functions as auxiliaries. Again referring to Figure 5.3, A can use her private key k_A^{-1} to compute a digital signature $S = D_A(M)$ or $S = D_A(h(M))$ for message M. In the second case, h refers to a collision-resistant one-way hash function that is applied to M before generating the digital signature. Anyone who knows the public key of A can verify the digital signature by decrypting it with k_A and comparing the result with another hash value that is recomputed for the same message with the same one-way hash function.

The use of public key cryptography simplifies the problem of key management considerably. Note that in Figure 5.3, instead of providing A and B with a unique session key that is protected in terms of confidentiality, integrity, and authenticity, the trusted third party, which is now called a *certification authority* (CA), has to provide A and B with the public key of the communicating peer. This key is public in nature and must not be protected in terms of confidentiality. Nevertheless, the use of public key cryptography requires an authentication framework that binds public keys to user identities. As further addressed in Chapter 19, a *public key certificate* is a certified proof of such binding vouched for by a TTP acting as a CA [23]. According to *Webster's Dictionary*, the term *certificate* refers to a document stating the truth. In the digital world we live in today, the term is mostly used to refer to a collection of information to which a digital signature has been affixed by some authority who is recognized and trusted by some community of certificate users. According to this definition, there exist various types of certificates that potentially serve many purposes. In either case, a certificate is a form of credentials. Examples of credentials used in daily life are drivers' licenses, Social Security cards, or birth certificates. Each of these credentials has some information on it identifying its owner and some authorization stating that someone else has confirmed the information. A public key (or digital) certificate consists of three things:

- A public key;

- Certificate information that refers to the certificate owner's identity, such as his or her name);

- One or more digital signatures.

The aim of the digital signature(s) on the certificate is to state that the certificate information has been attested to by some other person or entity.

A digital certificate can be one of a number of different formats, including, for example, PGP and X.509. PGP and X.509 certificates are identified in different ways. More specifically, PGP certificates are identified by user identifiers (IDs) that typically comprise a person's name followed by a bracketed e-mail address, whereas X.509 certificates are identified by X.500 distinguished names (DNs) or other naming schemes. Another major difference between the two certificate formats is that PGP allows many identities and signatures per certificate, whereas X.509 permits only one identity and one signature per certificate.

As their name suggests, X.509 certificates conform to the ITU-T recommendation X.509. In fact, X.509 specifies both a certificate format and a certificate distribution scheme [24]. It was first published in 1988 as part of the X.500 directory recommendations. The X.509 version 1 (X.509v1) format was extended in 1993 to incorporate two new fields to support directory access control, resulting in the X.509 version 2 (X.509v2) format. In addition, and as a result of attempting to deploy certificates within the global Internet, X.509v2 was revised to allow for additional extension fields. The resulting X.509 version 3 (X.509v3) specification was officially released in June 1996. Meanwhile, the ITU-T recommendation X.509 has been approved by the ISO/IEC Joint Technical Committee 1 (JTC1) [25]. The format of an X.509v3 certificate has originally been specified in a notation called Abstract Syntax Notation One (ASN.1). One can apply encoding rules to a certificate specified in ASN.1 format to produce a series of bits and bytes suitable for transmission in computer networks.

A *trust model* refers to the set of rules a system or application uses to decide whether a certificate is valid. There are (at least) three different trust models:

- In the *direct trust model*, a user trusts a key that is valid because he or she knows where it came from (e.g., the user gets the key directly from another user).

- In the *hierarchical trust model*, there are a number of "root" certificates from which trust extends. More specifically, in this model, certificates may certify public keys, or they may certify certificates that certify still other certificates down some chain.

- The *cumulative trust model* encompasses both the direct and hierarchical trust models but also adds the notion that trust is in the eye of the beholder and the idea that more information is better. In this model, a certificate might be trusted directly, trusted in some chain going back to a directly trusted root certificate, or trusted by some group of introducers.

Obviously, direct trust is the simplest trust model, and many systems that use cryptography depend on it. For example, in Web browsers root CA keys are directly trusted because they are shipped together with the software packages.

Contrary to that, the trust model often used in the context of ITU-T X.509 certificates is hierarchical [24, 25].[4] In this case, the simplest model one may think of is a certification hierarchy representing a tree with a single root CA. However, more general structures and graphs (including mutually certifying CAs, cross-certificates, and multiple root CAs) are also possible. In X.509 parlance, the term *public key infrastructure* (PKI) refers to an infrastructure that can be used to issue, validate, and revoke public keys and public key certificates. As such, a PKI comprises a set of agreed-upon standards, CAs, structures among multiple CAs, methods to discover and validate certification paths, operational and management protocols, interoperable tools, and supporting legislation. A PKI structure among multiple CAs generally provides one or more certification paths between a subscriber and a certificate-using application. A *certification path* (or *certification chain*) refers to a sequence of one or more connected nodes between the subscriber and a root CA. The root CA, in turn, is a CA that the certificate-using application trusts and has securely imported and stored its public key certificate.

In the following sections, we overview some public key cryptosystems that are in widespread use today. The notion of a PKI will be further addressed in Chapter 19.

5.4.1 RSA

The most widely used public key cryptosystem is RSA, invented by Ronald L. Rivest, Adi Shamir, and Len M. Adleman at MIT in 1977 [26]. The RSA cryptosystem gets its security from the difficulty and intractability of the integer factorization problem. What this means is that it is fairly simple to multiply two large prime numbers, but difficult to compute the prime factors of a large number. One of the nice properties of RSA is that the same algorithm can be used for both message

---

[4]Note that X.509 does *not* embody a hierarchic trust model. The existence of cross-certificates, as well as forward and reverse certificates, makes the X.509 model a mesh, analogous in some ways to PGP's web of trust. The X.509 model is often erroneously characterized as a hierarchic trust model because it is usually mapped to the directory information tree (DIT), which is hierarchic, more like name schemes.

encryption and decryption, as well as digital signature generation and verification. This is not the case for most other public key cryptosystems.

Mathematically spoken, the RSA public key cryptosystem requires two distinct large primes (p and q). Denote $n = pq$ and $\phi(n) = (p-1)(q-1)$, where ϕ refers to the Euler function. Each user chooses a large number $d > 1$ such that $(d, \phi(n)) = 1$ and computes the number e ($1 < e < \phi(n)$) that satisfies the congruence $ed \equiv 1$ (mod $\phi(n)$). The numbers n and e constitute the public key, whereas the remaining items p, q, $\phi(n)$, and d form the private information. More commonly, d is referred to as the private key. Against this background, message encryption and decryption work as follows:

- To encrypt, one raises the plaintext block P to the power of e and reduces modulo n: $C = P^e \pmod{\phi(n)}$;

- To decrypt, one raises the ciphertext block C to the power of d and reduces modulo n: $P = C^d \pmod{\phi(n)}$.

Digital signature generation and verification uses the same algorithms with different keys (the private key is used to digitally sign a message, whereas the public key is used to verify the signature).

The RSA public key cryptosystem was protected by U.S. Patent No. 4,405,829 "Cryptographic Communications System and Method," issued and granted to MIT on September 20, 1983. The patent expired on September 20, 2000.

5.4.2   Diffie-Hellman

In 1977, Whitfield Diffie and Martin Hellman proposed a key agreement protocol that allows participants to agree on a key over an insecure public channel [21]. The protocol gets its security from the difficulty and intractability of the discrete logarithm problem in a finite cyclic group, such as the multiplicative group of a finite field. What this basically means is that, in general, the inverse operation of the exponentiation function is the logarithm function. There are efficient algorithms for computing logarithms in many groups; however, one does not know a polynomial-time algorithm for computing discrete logarithms in cyclic groups. For example, for a very large prime number p and two smaller numbers y and a, it is computationally intractable to find an x that satisfies the equation $y = a^x \bmod p$.

Mathematically speaking, the Diffie-Hellman key agreement protocol requires a finite cyclic group G of order $\mid G \mid$ and generator a. To agree on a session key, A and B then secretly choose elements x_A and x_B in G. These elements represent A and B's private keys. A and B compute their public keys $y_A = a^{x_A}$ and $y_B = a^{x_B}$, and exchange these public keys over an unsecured public channel. Finally, A and B compute $K_{AB} = y_B^{x_A} = a^{x_B x_A}$ and $K_{BA} = y_A^{x_B} = a^{x_A x_B}$. Note that $K_{AB} = K_{BA}$, so this value can actually be used as a session key to secure communications between A and B.

The Diffie-Hellman key agreement protocol was protected by U.S. Patent No. 4,200,770, "Cryptographic Apparatus and Method," issued and granted to Stanford University on April 29, 1980. The patent expired in 1997.

5.4.3 ElGamal

In the early 1980s, Taher ElGamal adapted the Diffie-Hellman key agreement protocol and came up with a public key cryptosystem that can be used for data encryption and digital signatures [27, 28]. Contrary to RSA, however, the ElGamal algorithms for data encryption and decryption are different from the the ElGamal algorithms for digital signature generation and verification. This is no serious drawback but is not advantageous from an implementor's point of view.

Unlike many other public key cryptosystems, the ElGamal public key cryptosystem is not covered by any patents.

5.4.4 DSS

In the early 1990s, the U.S. NIST published the Digital Signature Standard (DSS) as a viable alternative to RSA signature schemes. The DSS refers to an optimized modification of the ElGamal cryptosystem that can be used only for digital signature generation and verification [29].

5.4.5 ECC

More recently, the use of elliptic curve cryptography (ECC) has attracted a lot of interest. ECC-based public key cryptosystems obtain their security from the difficulty and intractability of the elliptic curve discrete logarithm problem (that uses groups of points on elliptic curves). As illustrated in Table 5.2, a number of different types of cryptography have been defined over elliptic curves. The resulting ECC-based public key cryptosystems seem to be advantageous with regard to their security properties (meaning that smaller keys are required for a similar level of security). As such, they are particularly useful in situations where small keys are required (e.g., mobile and wireless applications).

Table 5.2
ECC-Based Public Key Cryptosystems

Acronym	Text
ECDH	Elliptic curve Diffie-Hellman key agreement
ECDSA	Elliptic curve digital signature algorithm
ECES	Elliptic curve encryption scheme
ECMQV	Elliptic curve MQV key agreement
ECNRA	Elliptic curve Nyberg-Rueppel signature scheme with appendix

Unlike RSA, the general category of ECC is not patented. Individual companies, however, have filed patents for specific efficiency or security algorithms that are related to ECC. Most important, the Certicom Corporation[5] holds several patents in this field.

5.5   DIGITAL ENVELOPES

There are advantages and disadvantages related to both secret and public key cryptography. For example, the use of secret key cryptography is efficient but does not scale well beyond a certain number of participants. Furthermore, secret key cryptography does not provide the possibility to digitally sign data. Conversely, public key cryptography solves the scalability and digital signature problems but is highly inefficient in terms of required computational resources.

In an attempt to combine the advantages of secret and public key cryptography, a hybrid scheme may be used. In short, a hybrid scheme combines secret and public key cryptography to produce a scheme that is as efficient and effective as possible. For example, the *digital envelope* is a hybrid scheme that is heavily used in various applications. The aim of a digital envelope is similar to a letter envelope: It must protect the confidentiality of a message. As such, the digital envelope provides a digital analog for the letter envelope in the physical world (with hopefully better security properties).

---

[5] http://www.certicom.com

When A wants to send a confidential message M to B, she can generate a digital envelope for M and send the envelope to B. On the sender's side the procedure is as follows:

1. A retrieves B's public key k_B from a directory service or from a local repository.

2. A randomly generates a transaction key K from a secret key cryptosystem.

3. A encrypts M with K (the result is $\{M\}K$).

4. A encrypts K with k_B (the result is $\{K\}k_B$).

5. A concatenates $\{M\}K$ with $\{K\}k_B$, and sends the result to B.

Upon receipt of $\{M\}K$ and $\{K\}k_B$, B uses his private key k_B^{-1} to decrypt the message. The two-step procedure is as follows:

1. B decrypts $\{K\}k_B$ with k_B^{-1} (the result is K).

2. B decrypts $\{M\}K$ with K (the result is M).

Obviously, an alternative procedure would be to directly encrypt the message M with B's public key k_B, and to send the result, $\{M\}k_B$, to B. However, the use of a digital envelope as discussed above has at least two advantages compared with this simple scheme:

1. The use of a digital envelope is more efficient. Remember from our previous discussions that public key cryptography is computationally expensive compared with secret key cryptography. Consequently, encrypting a message with a public key requires more computational resources than encrypting a message with a secret key. The longer the message, the more efficient and advantageous the use of secret key cryptography.

2. The use of a digital envelope is more appropriate for messages sent to multiple recipients. If A wanted to send a message M to recipients $B_1, B_2, \ldots, B_n$ $(n > 1)$, she would have to build $\{M\}k_{B_i}$ for each recipient B_i $(i = 1, \ldots, n)$ individually. The resulting message would grow in proportion to the number of recipients. For example, if A wanted to send a 1-MB file to $n = 4$ recipients $(B_1, \ldots, B_4)$, the resulting messages would fill 4 MB of data. Contrary to that, the use of digital envelopes considerably reduces this amount of data. If the public keys of the $n = 4$ recipients are 1,024 bits long each, the digitally enveloped message would

fill 1 MB + 4 ∗ 1 KB = 1.004 MB of data. The situation is illustrated in Figure 5.4 (without digital envelopes) and Figure 5.5 (with digital envelopes). Note, however, that in either case it is sufficient to break the security of one single recipient's private key if a message is sent to multiple recipients.

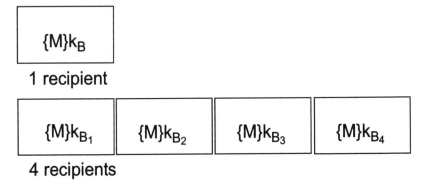

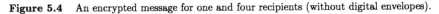

Figure 5.4   An encrypted message for one and four recipients (without digital envelopes).

Consequently, the use of digital envelopes is almost always advantageous, as compared with public key cryptography used for bulk data encryption.

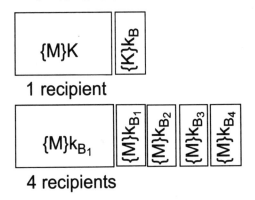

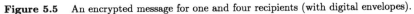

Figure 5.5   An encrypted message for one and four recipients (with digital envelopes).

5.6   PROTECTION OF CRYPTOGRAPHIC KEYS

Any system that uses cryptographic techniques has to deal with keys that must be protected against passive and active attacks. This is equally true for session keys that originate from a secret key cryptosystem and private keys that originate from a public key cryptosystem. If such a key is locally stored on a computer system, it is vulnerable to access and misuse by unauthorized users. In fact, file permissions alone are not adequate for protecting cryptographic keys on most computer systems, though they are part of an overall solution. Cryptographic keys protected only by file permissions are generally vulnerable to intruders and the accidental missetting of permissions.

Encryption is an accepted solution for protecting a cryptographic key stored on a removable media, such as a floppy disk. The use of encryption, however, also requires access to some other key that must be protected from disclosure. Consequently, the use of encryption to protect cryptographic keys leads to a recursion, and this recursion can only be stopped by making some key derivable from otherwise available information. The recommended advice is to make this information a passphrase selected by the user. A passphrase is different from a password in that no restrictions are usually placed on its length or value. This accomplishes two useful features:

1. The domain from which the passphrase is chosen is limited only by the input device of the user.

2. The user can select an easily remembered value, such as a favorite quotation or other concatenation of easily remembered words.

The key that is used to actually encrypt and protect another key (e.g., the user's private key) is derived from the user's passphrase. A preferred option is to use an OWHF to compute a random-looking hash value from the user's passphrase. Whenever the private key is needed (e.g., to decrypt an encryption key or to digitally sign a message), the user enters his or her passphrase, the cryptographic key is derived, the private key is decrypted, and then the private key is available for use. Typically, the file that is used to store the encrypted private key also includes a one-way hash value of the private key. Checking the hash value after decrypting the file contents provides a fast mechanism for determining if the correct passphrase was entered by the user. Without the hash value check, the only mechanism by which the private key's value can be checked would be to use it and see if it works. This may be computationally expensive.

If a user's private key is stored in encrypted form, the user must enter his or her passphrase to decrypt and locally use the key. From a security point of view, this is the optimal behavior. However, users quickly become irritated if they must send or receive more than a few messages during a session (because they have to reenter their passphrase multiple times). Consequently, many products include a feature that allows the passphrases to be kept in memory and users to choose usability over security. Needless to say, the very fact that the passphrases are kept in memory badly hurts the overall security properties.

In summary, the combination of file permissions and passphrase-derived encryption provides some nondisclosure protection for cryptographic keys (if the users choose appropriate passphrases). Better protection is provided if the file containing the encrypted cryptographic key is stored on a removable media, such as a floppy disk. Even better protection is provided if the key is stored in some tamper-resistant hardware device, such as a smart card, a PCMCI card, or a USB token. Recent research and development activities also focus on the use of alternative hardware devices, such as cellular phones, personal assistants (e.g., Palm Pilots), or any other device that implements the Wireless Application Protocol (WAP). There is arguably no single best hardware token to store cryptographic keys. Any device the user usually carries around with him or her is a potentially good hardware token and may serve this purpose (if properly modified).

5.7   GENERATION OF PSEUDORANDOM BIT SEQUENCES

Many cryptographic systems use sequences of random (or pseudorandomly generated) bits. For example, if an e-mail message is digitally enveloped, an encryption key sometimes also called *session key* must be randomly selected by the sender of the message. This key is used to encrypt and digitally envelope the message. Also, random or pseudorandom numbers are required to initially generate public key pairs.

Randomness is a statistical property of a sequence of values. In the case of bit values, the requirement is for an adversary to be unable to predict the next bit in a sequence even when all previously generated bits are known. The problem is that if it is possible to predict some of the sequence of bits used, it may be possible to reduce the size of the domain from which the key being generated is selected. If the domain is significantly reduced, an exhaustive key search may become feasible.

Locating a source of unpredictable bits presents a unique challenge on most computer systems (because a hardware source of unpredictable bits is usually not available). Consequently, a whole branch of cryptographic research is dedicated to the problem of how to generate pseudorandom bit sequences using only software. In fact, there are various approaches to address this problem. For example, one software-based approach is to use a cryptographically strong OWHF to hash a large amount of information with limited unpredictability available. Such information can, for example, be derived from the current status of the computer system (using corresponding system commands) or the mouse movements and position of keyboard strokes. Because a one-way hash function generates a fixed size quantity, the process is iterated as many times as are necessary to get the required number of bits.

In 1994, an informational RFC was published that addresses the problem of how to randomly or pseudorandomly generate bit sequences [30]. It recommends the use of hardware and shows that the existing hardware on many systems can be used for this purpose. Also, it provides suggestions to ameliorate the problem when a hardware solution is not available.

5.8   LEGAL ISSUES

There are some legal issues to keep in mind when using cryptographic techniques. In particular, there are patent claims; regulations for the import, export, and use of cryptography; and legislation for electronic and digital signatures. Some legal issues are briefly mentioned next. You may refer to [31, 32] for more information about the legal implications of using cryptographic techniques.

5.8.1   Patent Claims

Patents applied to computer programs are usually called *software patents*. In the U.S. computer industry, software patents are a subject of ongoing controversy. Some of the earliest and most important software patents granted by the U.S. Patent and Trademark Office were in the field of cryptography. These software patents go back to the late 1960s and early 1970s. Although computer algorithms were widely thought to be unpatentable at that time, cryptography patents were granted because they were written as patents on encryption devices built in hardware. Indeed, most early encryption devices were built in hardware because general-purpose computers simply could not execute the encryption algorithms fast enough in software. For example, IBM obtained several patents in the early 1970s on its Lucifer algorithm, which went on to become the DES [16]. Today, many secret key cryptosystems also are covered by patent claims. For example, DES is patented but royalty-free, whereas IDEA is patented and royalty-free for noncommercial use, but requires a license for commercial use. Later in the 1970s, many pioneers in the field of public key cryptography filed and obtained patents for their work. Consequently, the field of public key cryptography is largely governed by a couple of software patents. Some of them have already expired or are about to expire soon.

Outside the United States, the patent situation is quite different. For example, patent law in Europe and Japan differs from U.S. patent law in one very important aspect. In the United States, an inventor has a grace period of 1 year between the first public disclosure of an invention and the last day on which a patent application can be filed. In Europe and Japan, there is no grace period. Any public disclosure instantly forfeits all patent rights. Because the inventions contained in the original patents related to public key cryptography were publicly disclosed before patent applications were filed, these algorithms were never patentable in Europe and Japan.[6]

Under U.S. patent law, patent infringement is not a criminal offense, and the penalties and damages are the jurisdiction of the civil courts. It is the responsibility of the user of a particular cryptographic algorithm or technique to make sure that correct licenses have been obtained from the corresponding patent holders. If these licenses do not exist, the patent holders can sue the user in court. Therefore, most products that make use of cryptographic algorithms or techniques include the licenses required to use them.

Finally, it is important to note that the IETF has a special requirement with regard to the use of patented technology in Internet standards track protocols. In fact, before approving a protocol specification for the Internet standards track, a written statement from a patent holder is required that a license will be made available to applicants under reasonable terms and conditions.

5.8.2   Regulations

There are different regulations for the import, export, and use of cryptographic techniques. For example, the United States has been regulating the export of cryptographic systems and technical data regarding them for quite a long time. These regulations have gone far beyond the Wassenaar Arrangement on export controls for conventional arms and dual-use goods and technologies.[7] More specifically, U.S.

---

[6]As a consequence of the lack of patent claims, public key cryptography has been more widely adapted in European countries and in Japan.

[7]The Wassenaar Arrangement is a treaty originally negotiated in July 1996 and signed by 31 countries to restrict the export of dual-use goods and technologies to specific countries considered to be dangerous. The countries that have signed the Wassenaar Arrangement include the former Coordinating Committee for Multilateral Export Controls (COCOM) member and cooperating countries, as well as some new countries such as Russia. The COCOM was an international muni-

export controls on commercial encryption products are administered by the Bureau of Export Administration (BXA) in the Department of Commerce (DoC). Regulations governing exports of encryption are found in the Export Administration Regulations (EAR). Consequently, if a U.S. company wants to sell cryptographic systems and technical data overseas, it must have export approval by the BXA according to the EAR.

Unfortunately, the laws that drive the U.S. export controls are not too clear, and their interpretation changes over time. Sometimes vendors get so discouraged that they leave encryption out of their products altogether. Sometimes they generate products that, when sold overseas, have encryption mechanisms seriously weakened or removed. It is usually possible to get export approval for encryption if the key lengths are shortened. So, sometimes vendors intentionally use short keys or cryptosystems with varying key lengths. Probably the most widely deployed example of this kind is browser software (e.g., Netscape Navigator and Microsoft Internet Explorer) that comes in two versions: the U.S. domestic version that uses strong encryption with 128-bit RC4 session keys, and the international version of the same product that uses encryption with only 40-bit RC4 session keys. Because of some recent cryptanalytical attacks and breakthroughs, it seems that a lower bound for a key length that protects against a brute-force attack is 80 bits [33]. This value may still serve as a good rule of thumb.

On January 14, 2000, the BXA published a regulation implementing the White House's announcement of a new framework for U.S. export controls on encryption items (the announcement was made on September 16, 1999).[8] The policy is in response to the changing global market, advances in technology, and the need to give U.S. industry better access to these markets, while continuing to provide essential protections for national security. The regulation enlarges the use of license exceptions, implements the changes agreed to at the Wassenaar Arrangement in December 1998, and eliminates the deemed export rule for encryption technology. In addition, new license exception provisions are created for certain types of encryption, such as source code and toolkits. There are some countries exempted from the

---

tions control organization that also restricted the export of cryptography as a dual-use technology. It was formally dissolved in March 1994. More recently, the Wassenaar Arrangement was updated. The participating countries of the Wassenaar Arrangement are Argentina, Australia, Austria, Belgium, Bulgaria, Canada, Czech Republic, Denmark, Finland, France, Germany, Greece, Hungary, Ireland, Italy, Japan, Luxembourg, The Netherlands, New Zealand, Norway, Poland, Portugal, The Republic of Korea, Romania, Russian Federation, Slovak Republic, Spain, Sweden, Switzerland, Turkey, Ukraine, United Kingdom, and the United States. Further information on the Wassenaar Arrangement can be found on the Web by following the URL http://www.wassenaar.org.

[8]http://www.bxa.doc.gov/Encryption

regulation (i.e., Cuba, Iran, Iraq, Libya, North Korea, Sudan, and Syria). In these countries, some or all technologies and products mentioned in this book will not be available. In all other countries most technologies and products mentioned in this book will be available.

5.8.3   Electronic and Digital Signature Legislation

In the recent past, many countries have enacted electronic or digital signature laws in an effort to facilitate electronic commerce (e-commerce) and e-commerce applications:

- In the European Union (EU), the European Parliament and the Council of the European Union adopted Directive 1999/93/EC on a community framework for electronic signatures[9] on December 13, 1999. The purpose of the directive was (and still is) to facilitate the use of electronic signatures and to contribute to their legal recognition in Europe. According to the directive, EU "member states shall bring into force the laws, regulations and administrative provisions necessary to comply with this Directive before 19 July 2001." As of this writing, several EU member states already have an electronic signature law or are about to draft and enact one.

- In the United States, former president Bill Clinton signed the Electronic Signatures in Global and National Commerce Act (E-SIGN) on June 30, 2000. The E-SIGN Act implements a national uniform standard for all electronic transactions that encourages the use of electronic signatures, electronic contracts, and electronic records by providing legal certainty for these instruments when signatories comply with its standards. The E-SIGN Act became effective on October 1, 2000.

In addition, many countries outside the EU and the United States have enacted electronic or digital signature laws or are about to work out the legal details thereof.

Unfortunately, the formal specification of requirements for both certification service providers (i.e., CAs) and cryptographic devices that can be used to securely store private keys and generate digital signatures (e.g., smart cards or USB tokens) is very difficult and challenging in practice. For example, how do you measure and quantify the security and trustworthiness of a commercial certification service provider? What criteria are relevant? How do you take into account organizational

---

[9]http://europa.eu.int/comm/internal_market/en/media/sign/

criteria? Similarly, how do you measure and quantify the security of a cryptographic device that is used to store private keys and/or digitally sign documents? Does the device, for example, really sign what the user sees on the screen (i.e., "what you sign is what you see") or can it be spoofed with wrong input data? Keep in mind that the cryptographic device runs in a potentially hostile environment and that any kind of spoofing attack is possible there. The requirements for certification service providers and cryptographic devices tend to be either too strong or too weak:

- If the requirements are too strong, their implementation may become too expensive and prohibitive in practice. This is basically what happened in Germany when the first version of a signature law was put in place some years ago.

- If the requirements are too weak, their implementation—or the security thereof— may be challenged in court. Consequently, the legal value of the resulting electronic or digital signatures may not be very high.

Against this background, it will be interesting to see the requirements of future electronic and digital signature legislations. In either case, there is still a long way to go until we use electronic or digital signatures the same way we use handwritten signatures in daily life.

5.9   NOTATION

As mentioned before, a cryptographic protocol is a distributed algorithm defined by a sequence of steps precisely specifying the actions required of two or more entities to achieve a specific security objective. The following notation is used in this book to describe cryptographic protocols:

- Capital letters, such as A, B, C, ..., are used to refer to principals, whereas the same letters put in italics are used to refer to the corresponding principal identifiers. Note that many publications on cryptography and cryptographic protocols use names, such as Alice and Bob, to refer to principals. This is a convenient way of making things unambiguous with relatively few words, because the pronoun "she" can be used for Alice, and "he" can be used for Bob. However, the advantages and disadvantages of this naming scheme are controversial, and we are not going to use it in this book.

- K is used to refer to a secret key. A secret key is basically a key of a secret key cryptosystem.

- The pair (k, k^{-1}) is used to refer to a public key pair, whereas k is used to refer to the public key and k^{-1} is used to refer to the corresponding private key.

In either case, key subscripts are used to indicate principals. In general, capital letter subscripts are used for long-term keys, and small letter subscripts are used for short-term keys. For example, K_A is used to refer to A's long-term secret key, whereas k_b is used to refer to B's short-term public key.

- The term $\{M\}K$ is used to refer to a message M that is encrypted with the secret key K. Since the same key K is used for decryption, $\{\{M\}K\}K$ equals M. If K is used to compute and verify a message authentication code (MAC) for message M, then the term $\langle M \rangle K$ is used to refer to the MAC.

- Similarly, the term $\{M\}k$ is used to refer to a message M that is encrypted with the public key k. The message can only be decrypted with the corresponding private key k^{-1}. If a public key cryptosystem is used to digitally sign messages, the private key is used for signing, and the corresponding public key is used for verifying signatures. Referring to the terminology of the OSI security architecture, the term $\{M\}k^{-1}$ is used to refer to a digital signature giving message recovery, and $\langle M \rangle k^{-1}$ is used to refer to a digital signature with appendix. Note that in the second case, $\langle M \rangle k^{-1}$ in fact abbreviates $M, \{h(M)\}k^{-1}$, with h being an OWHF or CRHF.

Finally, the term $X \ll Y \gg$ is used to refer to an X.509 public key certificate that has been issued by X for Y's public key. It implies that X has verified Y's identity and certified the binding of Y's long-term public key k_Y with its identity. Unlike an X.509 certificate, a PGP certificate may include several identities that are assigned to a public key. Also, each identity may be signed multiple times (by different parties).

REFERENCES

[1] D. Stinson, *Cryptography Theory and Practice*, CRC Press, Boca Raton, FL, 1995.

[2] B. Schneier, *Applied Cryptography: Protocols, Algorithms, and Source Code in C*, 2nd Edition, John Wiley & Sons, New York, 1996.

[3] A. Menezes, P. van Oorschot, and S. Vanstone, *Handbook of Applied Cryptography*, CRC Press, Boca Raton, FL, 1996.

[4] P. W. Shor, "Algorithms for Quantum Computation: Discrete Logarithms and Factoring," *Proceedings of IEEE 35th Annual Symposium on Foundations of Computer Science*, 1994, pp. 124–134.

[5] P. W. Shor, "Polynomial-Time Algorithms for Prime Factorization and Discrete Logarithms on a Quantum Computer," *SIAM Journal of Computing,* October 1997, pp. 1484–1509.

[6] L. M. Adleman, "Molecular Computation of Solutions to Combinatorial Problems," *Science*, November 1994, pp. 1021–1024.

[7] G. Păun, G. Rozenberg, and A. Salomaa, *DNA Computing: New Computing Paradigms*, Springer-Verlag, New York, 1998.

[8] C. H. Bennett, G. Brassard, and A. K. Ekert, "Quantum Cryptography," *Scientific American*, October 1992, pp. 50–57.

[9] B. Kaliski, "The MD2 Message-Digest Algorithm," Request for Comments 1319, April 1992.

[10] R. L. Rivest, "The MD4 Message-Digest Algorithm," Request for Comments 1320, April 1992.

[11] R. L. Rivest and S. Dusse, "The MD5 Message-Digest Algorithm," Request for Comments 1321, April 1992.

[12] U.S. National Institute of Standards and Technology (NIST), "Secure Hash Standard (SHS)," FIPS PUB 180-1, April 1995.

[13] H. Dobbertin, A. Bosselaers, and B. Preneel, "RIPEMD-160: A Strengthened Version of RIPEMD," *Proceedings of Fast Software Encryption Workshop*, 1996, pp. 71–82.

[14] P. van Oorschot and M. Wiener, "Parallel Collision Search with Applications to Hash Functions and Discrete Logarithms," *Proceedings of ACM Conference on Computer and Communications Security*, November 1994.

[15] H. Dobbertin, "The Status of MD5 After a Recent Attack," *RSA Laboratories' CryptoBytes*, Vol. 2, 1996, No. 2.

[16] U.S. National Institute of Standards and Technology (NIST), "Data Encryption Standard," FIPS PUB 46, January 1977.

[17] X. Lai, *On the Design and Security of Block Ciphers*, Ph.D. thesis, ETH No. 9752, ETH Zürich, Switzerland, 1992.

[18] J. L. Massey, "SAFER K-64: A Byte-Oriented Block Ciphering Algorithm," *Proceedings of Fast Software Encryption Workshop*, 1994, pp. 1–17.

[19] B. Schneier, "Description of a New Variable-Length Key, 64-Bit Block Cipher (Blowfish)," *Proceedings of Fast Software Encryption Workshop*, 1994, pp. 191–204.

[20] C. Adams, "The CAST-128 Encryption Algorithm," Request for Comments 2144, May 1997.

[21] W. Diffie and M. E. Hellman, "New Directions in Cryptography," *IEEE Transactions on Information Theory*, IT-22(6), 1976, pp. 644–654.

[22] B. Pfitzmann, *Digital Signature Schemes*, Springer-Verlag, Berlin, Germany, 1996.

[23] J. Feghhi, J. Feghhi, and P. Williams, *Digital Certificates: Applied Internet Security*, Addison-Wesley Longman, Reading, MA, 1999.

[24] ITU-T X.509, *The Directory—Authentication Framework*, November 1987.

[25] ISO/IEC 9594-8, *Information Technology—Open Systems Interconnection—The Directory—Part 8: Authentication Framework*, 1990.

[26] R. L. Rivest, A. Shamir, and L. Adleman, "A Method for Obtaining Digital Signatures and Public-Key Cryptosystems," *Communications of the ACM*, 21(2), February 1978, pp. 120–126.

[27] T. ElGamal, *Cryptography and Logarithms over Finite Fields*, Ph.D. thesis, Stanford University, 1984.

[28] T. ElGamal, "A Public Key Cryptosystem and a Signature Scheme Based on Discrete Logarithm," *IEEE Transactions on Information Theory*, IT-31(4), 1985, pp. 469–472.

[29] U.S. National Institute of Standards and Technology (NIST), *Digital Signature Standard (DSS)*, FIPS PUB 186, May 1994.

[30] D. Eastlake, S. Crocker, and J. Schiller, "Randomness Recommendations for Security," Request for Comments 1750, December 1994.

[31] L. J. Hoffman, *Building in Big Brother: The Cryptographic Policy Debate*, Springer-Verlag, New York, 1995.

[32] S. A. Baker and P. R. Hurst, *The Limits of Trust: Cryptography, Governments, and Electronic Commerce*, Kluwer Law International, Cambridge, MA, 1998.

[33] M. Blaze, et al., "Minimal Key Lengths for Symmetric Ciphers to Provide Adequate Commercial Security," Business Software Alliance, January 1996.

Chapter 6

Authentication and Key Distribution

In this chapter, we overview and briefly discuss two basic building blocks for network security in general, and Internet and intranet security in particular: authentication and key distribution. More specifically, we address authentication in Section 6.1 and key distribution in Section 6.2. Note that many authentication schemes, such as one-time passwords and challenge-response mechanisms, are inherently strong but still vulnerable to specific attacks (e.g., session hijacking attacks). One possibility to protect against some of these attacks is to combine authentication and key distribution, and to use the distributed keys to transparently authenticate or encrypt all data that are transmitted after authentication has taken place. An attacker who does not have the correct keys is not able to hijack the session accordingly. Also note that this chapter focuses on the fundamentals, and that specific authentication and key distribution systems (e.g., the Kerberos system) will be explored in Chapter 16.

6.1 AUTHENTICATION

In general, *authentication* refers to the process of verifying the claimed identity of a principal. Authentication results in authenticity, meaning that the verifying

111

principal (i.e., the *verifier*) can be sure the verified principal (i.e., the *claimant*) is the one he or she claims to be.

It is common to divide the techniques that are used for authentication into four categories, depending on whether a technique is based on:

- Something the claimant possesses (proof by possession);

- Something the claimant knows (proof by knowledge);

- Some biometric characteristics of the claimant (proof by property);

- Somewhere the claimant is located (proof by location).

As of this writing, it is commonly agreed that the first three categories are categories of their own, whereas it is not commonly agreed that the fourth category is also a category of its own. Because of its increased importance in contemporary security architectures, however, it is considered to be a category of its own in this book. Some exemplary authentication techniques are overviewed next. Note that the techniques are not mutually exclusive, and that several techniques can be combined in a proper design.

6.1.1 Proof by Possession

In a proof by possession, the claimant proves his or her identity by proving possession of some physical token. On the verifier side, the proof can be verified manually or automatically. In the second case, a corresponding detector (hardware or software) is required. Examples of physical tokens are:

- Physical keys;

- Identification cards;

- Magnetic stripe cards;

- Smart cards;

- USB tokens.

Physical keys have been in widespread use for at least a couple of centuries, whereas all other examples itemized above are relatively new. For example, the use of smart cards and USB tokens to store cryptographic keys has evolved only in the last couple of years and is still considered to be in its infancy.

The major advantage of a proof by possession is that it is very simple and straightforward to use by human beings, whereas the major disadvantages are related to the production, distribution, and management of the physical tokens and the corresponding detectors (if the proofs must be verified automatically). The result of these disadvantages are difficulties in large-scale deployment and operational costs that are often prohibitive. Consequently, proofs by possession are seldom used in networked and distributed systems.

6.1.2 Proof by Knowledge

In a proof by knowledge, the claimant proves his or her identity by proving knowledge of some secret information (e.g., a password or a cryptographic key). This information, in turn, may either be static or dynamically changing in time. Roughly speaking, static information can be used to implement weak authentication mechanisms, whereas dynamically changing information can be used to implement strong authentication mechanisms. Note that in either case, the secret information may be too large or include too much entropy to be kept in memory by human users. Consequently, the use of some auxiliary technologies to store and make available the secret information is common today. Examples include magnetic-stripe cards, smart cards, and USB tokens. Also, the use of personal digital assistants (PDA) to store secret information (possibly in encrypted form) is widespread. Note, however, that contrary to the use of these technologies in a proof by possession, these technologies are only used to extend the capacities of human users in a proof by knowledge. The existence of the physical device is not verified. Obviously, it is possible and makes a lot of sense to combine a proof by possession with a proof by knowledge. For example, if we want to withdraw money from an automatic teller machine (ATM) we usually insert an ATM card into the machine and enter a personal identification number (PIN) into the terminal associated with the machine. In this example, the insertion of the ATM card represents a proof by possession, whereas the fact that the user enters a PIN represents a proof by knowledge.

Static Information

Examples of static information that may be used in a proof by knowledge include PINs, passwords, and passphrases. As of this writing, passwords are by far the most widely deployed authentication mechanisms used in computer networks and distributed systems. This is because they are simple to implement and use. Unfortunately, however, passwords and the way they are used today have two major security problems:

1. Users tend to select passwords that are easy to remember. Consequently, such passwords are not randomly distributed and are easy to guess [1, 2]. Password guessing is the process of correctly guessing the password of a legitimate user. Dan Klein analyzed the feasibility of password-guessing attacks for approximately 15,000 user accounts in 1990. As a result, he found that he could guess 2.7% of the passwords in the first 15 minutes and 21% within the first week [3]. It is assumed that these numbers have not changed much since their original publication in 1990. To make things worse, there are many tools available on the Internet that can be used for password-guessing attacks (e.g., L0phtcrack).

2. The transmission of passwords (which may be well chosen or not) is exposed to passive eavesdropping and subsequent replay attacks. This is because the passwords are often transmitted in the clear. Also, if passwords are not transmitted in the clear but "encrypted" using a well-known one-way function, it is still possible to launch a password guessing attack by simply "encrypting" password candidates with the one-way function and checking whether the result matches the string that has been transmitted at first place.

Obviously, these security problems do not only apply to passwords and are equally true for any other static information that may be employed in a proof by knowledge (e.g., PINs or passphrases). Consequently, the use of static information in a proof by knowledge is not suitable anymore in contemporary computer networks and distributed systems. In fact, the information is too easy to intercept and reuse. While this vulnerability had been known for a very long time, it was not until 1994 that it was demonstrated on a large scale with the discovery of planted password collecting routines at some critical points within the Internet.[1] We have mentioned this vulnerability and the feasibility of corresponding eavesdropping attacks in the preface and Chapter 3. To improve the level of security of a proof by knowledge, we must use information that is dynamically changing in time.

Dynamically Changing Information

The basic idea of using dynamically changing information in a proof by knowledge is that each authentication process uses a unique piece of authentication information,

---

[1] Compare CERT Advisory CA-94:01, "Ongoing Network Monitoring Attacks," 1994.

and that this piece of authentication information cannot be (mis)used at some later point in time. Consequently, if an attacker is able to eavesdrop on an authentication protocol execution and grab the relevant authentication information, he or she will will not be able to (mis)use this information in a replay attack. The information will not be valid a second time.

The use of dynamically changing information is not a new idea. In fact, we have been using transaction authentication numbers (TANs) for a long time. In short, a TAN is a piece of authentication information that can be used for one single authentication process or transaction. It is randomly chosen by the verifier and provided to the claimant using some secure channel (i.e., a trusted courier). The use of TANs is simple and straightforward, and as such there are many applications for them. For example, banks have been using TANs (together with passwords) to authenticate users and account owners. Similarly, many e-government applications can provide client authentication using TANs that are provided to the citizens using certified mail.

If the number of authentication processes or transactions increases beyond a certain threshold, the generation, distribution, and management of TANs becomes very difficult (i.e., the use of TANs does not scale). In this situation, it is generally a good idea to use cryptographic techniques to come up with authentication schemes that make use of dynamically changing information [4]. Some examples are overviewed and briefly discussed next.

One-Time Password Schemes. As its name suggests, a one-time password is a password that can only be used once, meaning that it can only be used for one single authentication process. As such, a one-time password is conceptually similar to a TAN. The major difference is that TANs are generated randomly by the verifier and distributed to the claimant using some secure channel, whereas one-time passwords are typically generated dynamically and deterministically by the claimant and verifier.

Against this background, a one-time password scheme is an authentication scheme that uses one-time passwords. There are many one-time password schemes and corresponding systems available today:

- SecurID tokens[2] as marketed by RSA Security, Inc., are the most important and most widely deployed one-time password system in use today. Roughly speaking, each SecurID token contains a cryptographic processor that implements the

---

[2]http://www.rsasecurity.com/products/securid/index.html

DES, a secret DES key, a clock that is synchronized with the verifier (i.e., an ACE/server), and a small display. The one-time passwords are generated by having the token read out the time from its clock and encrypt the corresponding value with the secret DES key. At each time interval (e.g., each minute), the SecurID token generates a new one-time password and shows it on its display. If the holder of the SecurID token (i.e., the user) wants to authenticate himself or herself, he or she reads from the token's display the currently valid one-time password and types it in at the login prompt (together with a constant password).

- An alternative one-time password scheme that does not require the implementation of a cryptosystem was originally proposed by Leslie Lamport in the early 1980s [5]. In this scheme, the claimant (i.e., the user) begins with a secret password pw. A one-way function h is then used to generate a sequence of t one-time passwords: pw, $h(pw)$, $h(h(pwd))$, ..., $h^t(pw)$. This sequence is used by the claimant in the reverse order, meaning that the one-time password for the ith authentication process, $1 \leq i \leq t$, is defined to be $h^{t-i}(pw)$. This password is used by the claimant to authenticate himself or herself to the verifier. Lamport's one-time password scheme was implemented at Bell Communications Research (Bellcore) in a one-time password system called S/Key [6].[3] S/Key uses MD4 as a one-time function. More recently, the use of MD4 was replaced with MD5 in a similar system called One-Time Passwords in Everything (OPIE) developed at the U.S. Naval Research Laboratory (NRL). S/Key and OPIE both conform to the one-time password system specified in [7].

In addition to SecurID tokens, S/Key, and OPIE, there are many other one-time password systems commercially or freely available on the Internet.

Challenge-Response Mechanisms. One-time password schemes and corresponding systems are simple and straightforward. The major advantage is that they do not require an interaction between the claimant and the verifier. The claimant simply provides a piece of authentication information to the verifier, and the verifier can verify the validity of it (without interacting with the claimant). The major disadvantage, however, is that the claimant and verifier must be synchronized in one way or another (e.g., they must have synchronized clocks).

Like one-time password schemes, challenge-response mechanisms are authentication schemes that make use of dynamically changing information. Unlike one-time password schemes, however, challenge-response mechanisms require the claimant

---

[3]`ftp://thumper.bellcore.com/pub/nmh/skey`

and verifier to interact but generally do not require them to be synchronized. In a challenge-response mechanism, the verifier provides the claimant with a challenge (i.e., a randomly chosen number), and the claimant must compute and provide a valid response for this challenge. Again, there is some sort of cryptographic secret (e.g., key) that must be known on either side to compute and verify the claimant's response.

For example, a digital signature scheme can be used to implement a simple challenge-response mechanism. If the claimant holds a private key and the verifier holds a corresponding public key (or public key certificate), the verifier can challenge the claimant with a randomly chosen number and the claimant can respond with the digital signature for that number. Because the verifier holds the public key (certificate), he or she can easily verify the validity of the claimant's response. Note, however, that this exemplary challenge-response mechanism is far too simple to be used for real applications. It would be too dangerous for a claimant to digitally sign arbitrary values that claim to be legitimate challenges. What would happen, for example, if the claimant were challenged with a one-way hash value computed from the message string "I owe you $1,000"? In this case, the claimant would respond with the digital signature for a message he or she would not have signed in the first place. Consequently, the design and analysis of challenge-response mechanisms are very tricky and must be considered with care.

There is a special class of challenge-response mechanisms and corresponding protocols that have a property called zero-knowledge. Using such a protocol, a claimant can proof knowledge of a secret (e.g., a cryptographic key) while revealing no information whatsover about the secret [8]. It is possible and very likely that zero-knowledge protocols will become important and widely used in the future.

6.1.3 Proof by Property

In a proof by property, the claimant proves his or her identity by proving some biometric characteristics. The biometric characteristics, in turn, are measured and compared with a reference pattern by the verifier. Historically, the first biometric characteristics that were used for authentication were fingerprints. Today, it is possible to use other characteristics, such as facial images, retinal images, and voice patterns. In fact, the recent past has shown an increased interest in biometric technologies and applications.

In practice, the use of biometric characteristics to authenticate users in computer networks and distributed systems is difficult because:

1. Foremost, all terminals and end systems must be equipped with devices that are

able to read biometric characteristics from users. This is difficult and expensive to deploy.

2. All communication lines between the readers and the verifier must be made secure (i.e., physically or cryptographically protected).

3. The use of biometric characteristics also requires some form of live testing.

4. There are still some privacy concerns related to the widespread use of biometric technologies and applications.

Because of these difficulties in practical deployment, the use of biometric characteristics is still not widespread today.

6.1.4   Proof by Location

In a proof by location, the claimant proves his or her identity by proving his or her current location. There are several incarnations of this idea:

- For example, a dial-back system implements a proof by location, because the claimant is called back by the verifier using some defined number (i.e., a number that is bound to a specific network access point).

- Similarly, an address-based authentication scheme as employed, for example, by the BSD UNIX r-tools (rlogin, rsh, and rcp) also implements a proof by location. Address-based authentication does not rely on sending passwords across the network, but rather assumes that the identity of the source can be inferred based on the network address from which packets arrive. The basic idea is that each host stores information that specifies accounts on other hosts that should have access to its resources. Each host may have a file named /etc/hosts.equiv containing a list of trusted hostnames. Users with the same username on both the local and the trusted host may use the r-tools without having to supply a password. Individual users may set up a similar private equivalence list with the .rhosts file in their home directories. Each line in this file may contain a hostname and a username separated by a space. An entry in a user's remote .rhosts file permits the user who is logged into the system specified by hostname to log into the remote system without having to supply a password. Instead of logging into the host, the user can also remotely execute commands or copy files. Note that the idea of trusted hosts is no general solution to the authentication problem in computer networks and distributed systems, and trusted hosts may even pose more serious security threats. The point is that host authentication mechanisms can always be defeated, and if an attacker is able to break into an account in a host that is trusted by other hosts, the users' accounts on these other hosts are usually compromised as well. The use of .rhosts files poses an additional security threat because the system administrator is, in general, unable to exclusively control access to the system via the r-tools. Users are likely to tailor their .rhosts files more for convenience than for security. Depending on the environment, address-based authentication may be more or less secure than sending passwords in the clear. In either case, it is more convenient, and it is therefore the authentication mechanism of choice in many networked environments.

- In a more sophisticated location-based authentication scheme, the verifier may check the geodetic location of a claimant. The corresponding information may be provided, for example, by the Global Positioning System (GPS). The use of GPS signals for location-based authentication has been pioneered by a company called CyberLocator.[4] At the time of this writing, it is still too early to tell whether the GPS-based authentication scheme will withstand a more serious analysis or attack.

In any case, it is possible and very likely that information about the current location of a user will play an increasingly important role in future user authentication schemes.

6.2   KEY DISTRIBUTION

Most of the security services that are enumerated in the OSI security architecture are based on cryptographic mechanisms, and the use of these mechanisms generally requires a corresponding key management infrastructure. According to RFC 2828, the term *key management* refers to the "process of handling and controlling cryptographic keys and related material (such as initialization values) during their life cycle in a cryptographic system, including ordering, generating, distributing, storing, loading, escrowing, archiving, auditing, and destroying the material" [9]. As such, key distribution is certainly an important part of key management, and key distribution has often turned out to be the Achilles heel of any network security architecture. Key distribution is carried out with protocols, and many of the important properties of key distribution protocols do not depend on the underlying cryptographic algorithms, but rather on the structure of the messages exchanged.

---

[4]http://www.cyberlocator.com

Therefore, security leaks and vulnerabilities do not come from weak cryptographic algorithms, but rather from mistakes in higher levels of the protocol design.

The Institute of Electrical and Electronic Engineers (IEEE) WG 802.10 was formed in May 1988 to address the security needs of local and metropolitan area networks and to specify standards for interoperable LAN/MAN security (SILS).[5] The WG was cosponsored by the IEEE Technical Committee on Computer Communications and by the IEEE Technical Committee on Security and Privacy. Within IEEE 802.10, work on cryptographic key management began in May 1989 and was formally approved in 1998 [10]. As such, the IEEE 802.10 WG is in "hibernation" but can still be contacted for assistance.

The key management model and protocols specified in IEEE 802.10 support three classes of key distribution techniques: manual key distribution, center-based key distribution, and certificate-based key distribution. This classification is useful and also used in this book.

6.2.1   Manual Key Distribution

Manual key distribution techniques are the simplest techniques one can use to distribute cryptographic keys. Using manual key distribution, off-line delivery methods are used to establish pairwise or multicast cryptographic keys among the communicating peers.

Manual key distribution techniques are simple and straightforward. They are appropriate for small numbers of communicating peers. If the number of communicating peers increases beyond a certain threshold, however, the scalability problems become obvious and the use of manual key distribution techniques is too cumbersome. Also, manual key distribution techniques do not provide any authentication other than that provided by the corresponding off-line delivery method. Therefore, the strength of the procedures used for off-line delivery of the cryptographic keys is extremely important. In many cases, manual delivery of cryptographic keys is required at least once per user, and distribution of additional keying material can be performed using the manually distributed key as a key encryption key (KEK). The encrypted keying material can then be distributed using any convenient method.

6.2.2   Center-Based Key Distribution

Center-based key distribution techniques may be used to establish pairwise or multicast cryptographic keys among communicating peers by way of trusted third parties

---

[5]http://grouper.ieee.org/groups/802/10/

(TTPs). A TTP, in turn, may act as:

- A *key distribution center* (KDC);

- A *key translation center* (KTC).

In either case, the TTP shares a secret with each principal in its domain. This secret is used to establish a secure channel between the TTP and the principal. In the case of a KDC, the TTP generates the cryptographic keys and distributes them to either principal using a secure channel. In the case of a KTC, the TTP receives the cryptographic keys from one secure channel and forwards them to another. In this case, the TTP simply acts as a relay that possibly decrypts and reencrypts the cryptographic keys.

Most existing center-based key distribution methods have been tailored to specific scenarios and applications. For example, any scheme relying on time stamps favors the local environment, where all users have access to a commonly trusted time server. While requiring tightly synchronized clocks in the wide area is conceivable, it is certainly harder. More important, existing schemes make specific assumptions about network configuration and connectivity models. For instance, they may dictate a specific communication paradigm for contacting a trusted server or KDC. When a principal A needs a key to communicate with another principal B, Kerberos, for example, requires that A obtain the desired key from the KDC before communicating with B. This paradigm is sometimes referred to as the *pull model*. By contrast, in the same situation, the U.S. standard for financial institution key management (ANSI X9.17) specifies that A must contact B first, and let B get the necessary key from the KDC. This paradigm is sometimes referred to as the *push model*. In short, A pushes B to contact the KDC and request a session key accordingly. It is important to note that neither the push model nor the pull model is better than the other, and that both models are justified in their respective environments. In a local area environment, for which Kerberos was originally designed, requiring clients to obtain the keys makes a lot of sense because it distributes the burden over many clients, thus alleviating the task of the few shared servers. In a wide area environment for which X9.17 was designed, however, the opposite approach is justified because there are typically many more clients than servers, and KDCs are typically located closer to servers than clients. Under such circumstances, the amount of system definition in terms of configuration, and the costs of the connections between clients and the KDCs required by the Kerberos approach may become prohibitive in a wide area environment. It is even possible to combine the two approaches and to come up with a mixed model for center-based key distribution.

6.2.3   Certificate-Based Key Distribution

Certificate-based key distribution techniques may be used to establish pairwise cryptographic keys. In this case, the use of public keys and public key certificates is mandatory. There are two classes of certificate-based key distribution techniques to be distinguished:

- A public key cryptosystem is used to encrypt a locally generated cryptographic key and to protect it while it is being transferred to a remote key management entity. This is called a *key transfer*.

- A cryptographic key is cooperatively generated at both the local and remote key management entity. This is called a *key exchange* or *key agreement*. The best example for a key agreement protocol is the Diffie-Hellman key exchange as discussed earlier in this chapter.

We postpone the discussion of public keys and public key certificates to Chapter 19, when we elaborate on public key infrastructures (PKIs).

In general, certificate-based key distribution techniques may not be directly used to establish multicast keys. However, once pairwise cryptographic keys are established, they can be used to further protect the distribution of multicast keys.

REFERENCES

[1] R. Morris and K. Thompson, "Password Security: A Case History," *Communications of the ACM*, Vol. 22, 1979, pp. 594–597.

[2] D. C. Feldmeier and P. R. Karn, "UNIX Password Security—Ten Years Later," *Proceedings of CRYPTO '89*, 1990, pp. 44–63.

[3] D. V. Klein, "Foiling the Cracker: A Survey of, and Improvements to, Password Security," *Proceedings of USENIX UNIX Security Symposium*, August 1990, pp. 5–14.

[4] N. Haller and R. Atkinson, "On Internet Authentication," Request for Comments 1704, October 1994.

[5] L. Lamport, "Password Authentication with Insecure Communication," *Communications of the ACM*, Vol. 24, 1981, pp. 770–772.

[6] N. Haller, "The S/KEY One-Time Password System," Request for Comments 1760, February 1995.

[7] N. Haller and C. Metz, "A One-Time Password System," Request for Comments 1938, May 1996.

[8] J.J. Quisquater and L. Guillou, "How to Explain Zero-Knowledge Protocols to Your Children," *Proceedings of CRYPTO '89*, 1990, pp. 628 – 631.

[9] R. Shirey, "Internet Security Glossary," Request for Comments 2828, May 2000.

[10] IEEE Standard for Interoperable LAN/MAN Security (SILS), Key Mangement (Clause 3), IEEE 802.10c, 1998.

Part II
ACCESS CONTROL

Chapter 7

Overview

In Part II we focus on firewall technologies that can be used to provide access control services for corporate intranets. We start with an advertising query and answer that Trusted Information Systems, Inc.[1], put on its Web site in 1997 to promote its Gauntlet Internet Firewall System:

What do the CIA, MGM/Universal Studios, and the Nation of Islam have in common?

— Their Web sites were hacked and vandalized in 1996.

Against this background, Trusted Information Systems, Inc., suggested two conclusions that may be drawn:

1. One must protect a Web site.

2. One must use a Gauntlet Internet Firewall System to do so.

---

[1]Trusted Information Systems, Inc., was later acquired by Network Associates, Inc.

While one can agree with the first conclusion, the second one is not very obvious and was mainly drawn by marketing people at Trusted Information Systems, Inc. In fact, the Gauntlet Internet Firewall System as it was marketed by Trusted Information Systems, Inc., in 1997 is no longer available today (the product is now called Gauntlet Firewall and marketed by Network Associates, Inc.). As we explain in Part II, firewall technologies are very mature today, and many sophisticated implementations and products are available that compete with one another for the market share.

The aim of this chapter is to introduce the various firewall technologies that populate the Internet security market. More specifically, we overview and briefly discuss the rationale and the basic principles of firewalls in Section 7.1, elaborate on the basic components of a firewall configuration (i.e., packet filters and application gateways) in Section 7.2, and give some sources for further information in Section 7.3.

7.1   INTRODUCTION

While Internet connectivity offers enormous benefits in terms of increased availability and access to information, Internet connectivity is not always a good thing, especially for sites with low levels of security. As we discussed in Part I, the Internet suffers from glaring security problems that, if ignored, could have disastrous impacts for unprepared sites. Inherent problems with the TCP/IP protocols and services, the complexity of host and site configuration, vulnerabilities introduced in the software development process, and a wide variety of other factors all contribute to making unprepared sites open for intruder activities and other security-related threats. For example, host systems and access controls are usually complex to configure and test for correctness. As a result, they are sometimes accidentally misconfigured, and this may result in intruders gaining unauthorized and illegitimate access to system and information resources. It is a rather astonishing fact that some vendors still ship their systems with access controls configured for maximum (i.e., least secure access), which can result in unauthorized and illegitimate access if left as is.[2] Furthermore, a number of security incidents have occurred that are due in part to vulnerabilities discovered by intruders. Because many UNIX systems have their network code derived from BSD UNIX that is publicly available in source code, intruders have been able to study the code for bugs (e.g., buffer overflows)

---

[2]For example, the attack against the database of the World Economic Forum (WEF) that occured in early 2001 exploited an initial password that was neither modified nor removed.

and error conditions that may be exploited to gain unauthorized and illegitimate access. The bugs exist in part because of the complexity of the software and the inability to test it under all circumstances and in all the environments in which it must operate. Sometimes the bugs can be discovered and corrected; other times, however, little can be done except to rewrite the entire software, which is usually the last-resort option. Because of its open source distribution, the same argument also holds for the Linux operation system.

Host security is generally hard to achieve and does not scale well in the sense that as the number of hosts increases, the ability to ensure that security is at a high level for each host usually decreases. Given the fact that secure management of just one single system can be a demanding task, managing many such systems could easily result in mistakes and omissions. A contributing factor is that the role of system administration is often undervalued and performed in a difficult situation. As a result of this, some systems will be less secure than others, and these systems will probably be the ones that ultimately break the security of either a site or an entire corporate intranet. This book does not address host and site security. There is an informational RFC specifying a site security handbook published in 1997 [1]. You may refer to this reference for a comprehensive overview about issues related to host and site security.

In days of old, brick walls were built between buildings in apartment complexes so that if a fire broke out, it would not spread from one building to another. Quite naturally, these walls were and still are called *firewalls*.

Today, when a private network (i.e., intranet) is connected to a public network (i.e., Internet), its users are usually enabled to communicate with the outside world. At the same time, however, the outside world can also interact with the private network and its computer systems. In this situation, an intermediate system can be plugged between the private network and the public network to establish a controlled link, and to erect a security wall or perimeter. The aim of the intermediate system is to protect the private network from network-based attacks that originate from the outside world, and to provide a single choke point where security and audit can be imposed. Note that all traffic in and out of the private network can be enforced to pass through this single, narrow choke point. Also note that this point provides a good place to collect information about system and network use and misuse. As a single point of access, the intermediate system can record what occurs between the private network and the outside world. Quite intuitively, these intermediate systems are called *firewall systems*, or *firewalls*. In other literature, Internet firewalls are also referred to as *secure Internet gateways* or *security gateways*. We are not going to use these alternative terms in this book.

In essence, a firewall system represents a blockade between a privately owned and protected network, which is assumed to be secure and trusted, and another network, typically a public network or the Internet, which is assumed to be nonsecure and untrusted. The purpose of the firewall is to prevent unwanted and unauthorized communications into or out of the protected network.

In addition to the physical firewall analogy mentioned earlier, there are other analogies that may help to better understand and motivate for the use of firewalls:

- Passports are generally checked at the border of a country.

- Apartments are usually locked at the entrance and not necessarily at each door.

- Similarly, offices do not usually have a door to the outside world.

- And yet, a bank still has a vault to store money and valuable goods.

Other analogies include the toll booth on a bridge, the ticket booth at a movie theater, and the checkout line at a supermarket.

These analogies and the first three analogies itemized above illustrate the fact that it sometimes makes a lot of sense to aggregate security functions at a single point. Nevertheless, the last analogy itemized also illustrates that additional security precautions may be required under some circumstances. Note that a firewall is conceptually similar to locking the doors of a house or employing a doorperson. The objective is to ensure that only properly authenticated and authorized people are able to physically enter the house. Unfortunately, this protection is not foolproof and can be defeated with enough effort. The basic idea is to make the effort too big for a burglar, so that he or she will eventually go away and find another, typically more vulnerable, house. However, just in case the burglar does not go away and somehow manages to enter the house, we usually lock up our valuable goods in a safe. According to this analogy, the use of a firewall may not always be sufficient, especially in high-security environments in which we live these days. This point is emphasized by the last analogy itemized and will (hopefully) become more clear in the rest of Part II.

There are several possibilities to define the term *firewall*. For example, according to [2], a *firewall* refers to "an internetwork gateway that restricts data communication traffic to and from one of the connected networks (the one said to be 'inside' the firewall) and thus protects that network's system resources against threats from the other network (the one that is said to be 'outside' the firewall)." This definition is fairly broad and not too accurate.

In their pioneering book [3] and article [4] on firewalls and Internet security, William Cheswick and Steven Bellovin defined a firewall (system) as a collection of components placed between two networks that collectively have the following three properties:

- All traffic from inside to outside, and vice versa, must pass through the firewall.

- Only authorized traffic, as defined by the local security policy, will be allowed to pass.

- The firewall itself is immune to penetration.

Note that these properties are design goals. A failure in one aspect does not necessarily mean that the collection is not a firewall, simply that it is not a good one. Consequently, there are different grades of security that a firewall can achieve. In either case, there must be a security policy for the firewall to enforce.

This definition is more accurate than the one given in [2]. If, however, one wanted to exclude the fact that a simple packet filter can be called a firewall, one would have to come up with an even more complex definition for the term *firewall*. In this case, a system can be called a firewall if it is able:

- To enforce strong authentication for users who wish to establish inbound or outbound[3] connections;

- To associate data streams that are allowed to pass through the firewall with previously authenticated and authorized users.

---

[3]In this book, the terms *inbound* and *outbound* are used to refer to connections or IP packets from the point of view of the protected network, which is typically the intranet. Consequently, an outbound connection is a connection initiated from a client on an internal machine to a server on an external machine. Note that while the connection as a whole is outbound, it includes both outbound IP packets (those from the internal client to the external server) and inbound IP packets (those from the external server to the internal client). Similarly, an inbound connection is a connection initiated from a client on an external machine to a server on an internal machine. Following this terminology, the inbound interface for an IP packet refers to the physical network interface on a screening router on which the packet actually appeared, while the outbound interface refers to the physical network interface on which the packet will go out if it is not denied by the application of a specific packet-filtering rule.

Again, it is a policy decision if a data stream is allowed to pass through a firewall. Thus, this definition also leads to the necessity of an explicitly specified firewall policy, similar to the definition of Cheswick and Bellovin.

Later in this chapter, we will distinguish between packet filters and application gateways. It is interesting to note at this point that the last definition requires the use of application gateways (i.e., circuit-level gateways or application-level gateways). Because application gateways operate at the higher layers of the OSI-RM, they typically have access to more information than packet-filtering devices (e.g., screening routers) and can therefore be programmed to operate more intelligently and to be more secure as well. Some vendors, perhaps for marketing reasons, blur the distinction between a packet filter and a firewall to the extent that they call any packet filtering device a firewall. For the sake of clarity, however, this book makes a clear distinction between packet filters (operating at the network and transport layers of the OSI-RM) and firewalls (operating at the higher layers of the OSI-RM). This distinction is emphasized by the last definition given above. Note that the definition can be applied not only to TCP/IP-based firewalls, but also to modem pools with serial line interfaces that provide support for strong user authentication.

From a more pragmatic point of view, a firewall refers to a collection of hardware, software, and policy that is placed between a private network, typically a corporate intranet, and an external network, typically the Internet. As such, the firewall implements parts of a network security policy by enforcing that all data traffic is directed or routed to the firewall, where it can be examined and evaluated accordingly. A firewall seeks to prevent unwanted and unauthorized communications into or out of a corporate intranet, and to allow an organization to enforce a policy on traffic flowing between its intranet and the Internet. Typically, a firewall also requires its users to strongly authenticate themselves before any further action is deployed. The last definition given above has made this requirement mandatory for a firewall. In this case, strong authentication mechanisms are used to replace password-based or address-based authentication schemes.

The general reasoning behind firewall usage is that without a firewall, a site is more exposed to inherently insecure host operating systems, TCP/IP protocols and services, and probes and attacks from the Internet. In a firewall-less environment, network security is totally a function of each host, and all hosts must, in a sense, cooperate to achieve a uniformly high level of security. The larger the network, the less manageable it usually is to maintain all hosts at the same level of security. As mistakes and lapses in security become more common, break-ins can occur not only as a result of complex attacks, but also because of simple errors in configuration files and inadequately chosen passwords. Assuming that software is buggy, one can conclude that most host systems have security holes that can eventually be exploited by intruders. Firewalls are designed to run less software, and hence may potentially have fewer bugs, vulnerabilities, and security holes than conventional hosts. In addition, firewalls generally have advanced logging and monitoring facilities and can be professionally administered. With firewall usage, only a few hosts are exposed to attacks from the Internet, which considerably simplifies the task of securing the intranet environment.

Later in this book, we will discuss the advantages and disadvantages of the firewall technology as a whole. Probably one of the main disadvantages is due to the fact that a firewall cannot protect sites and corporate intranets against insider attacks. For that matter, internal firewalls may be used to control access between different administration and security domains, or to protect sensitive parts of a corporate intranet. Internal firewalls are sometimes also called *intranet firewalls*. From a purely technical point of view, there is nothing that distinguishes an intranet firewall from an Internet firewall except for the policy it enforces. Consequently, we are not going to differentiate between intranet and Internet firewalls in this book.

7.2 BASIC COMPONENTS

We already mentioned that a firewall provides basic access control services for sites and corporate intranets. In accordance with a specific security policy, the firewall intercepts data traffic and permits only authorized and legitimate traffic to pass through. The access control services can be provided either at the network and transport layers using packet filters, or at a higher layer using application gateways.

In this section we overview the basic components of which a firewall typically consists: a firewall policy, packet filters, and application gateways. In addition, a contemporary firewall typically provides other functions, such as network address translation or network layer encryption. These issues are addressed later in Part II.

7.2.1 Firewall Policy

There are two levels of policy that directly influence the design, installation, and use of a firewall system:

- The higher level policy, the *service access policy*, defines the TCP/IP protocols and services that should be allowed or denied from the protected network, how these services should be used, and how exceptions to this policy are handled.

- The lower level policy, the *firewall design policy*, describes how the firewall actually restricts access and filtering the TCP/IP protocols and services according to the service access policy.

Before we further address the two levels of policy, we want to note that a firewall policy should always be as flexible as possible. This need for flexibility is mainly due to the fact the Internet itself is in flux, and that an organization's needs may change over time as the Internet offers new services, methods, and possibilities for doing business. New TCP/IP protocols and services are emerging on the Internet, which offer more benefits to organizations using the Internet, but sometimes also result in new security concerns. Consequently, a firewall policy must be able to reflect and adequately address these concerns.

Service Access Policy

A *network security policy* (NSP) is a document that describes an organization's network security concerns and specifies the way network security should be achieved in that organization's environment. Parts of the NSP must include a *service access policy* that defines the TCP/IP protocols and services that should be accessible for internal and external use. As such, the service access policy extends the overall organizational policy regarding the protection of informational resources.

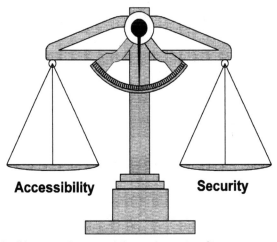

Accessibility   **Security**

Figure 7.1   Tradeoff between the accessibility and security of intranet resources.

A firewall can implement a number of service access policies. In general, a service access policy is focused more on keeping outsiders out than trying to police insiders. For example, a typical policy is to allow no inbound access to a corporate intranet, but to allow full outbound access to the Internet. Another typical policy would be to allow some inbound access from the Internet, but perhaps only to selected systems, such as information servers or e-mail gateways. Also, firewalls sometimes implement service access policies that allow access from the Internet to selected internal systems, but this access would be granted only if necessary and only if it is combined with strong user authentication and data encryption.

For a firewall to be successful, its service access policy must be realistic and reflect the level of security required for the intranet. For example, a site with top secret and classified data does not need a firewall at all. They should not be hooked up to the Internet in the first place, or the systems with the really secret data should be isolated from the rest of the intranet. A realistic service access policy is one that provides a balance between protecting intranet resources from known risks, while still protecting users access to external resources, such as the Internet.

In general, there is a tradeoff between the accessibility and security of intranet resources. This tradeoff can be symbolized with a balance as illustrated in Figure 7.1. It is quite easy to provide either full accessibility or full security. In the first case, one simply connects a corporate intranet to the Internet without caring about security, whereas in the second case, one established two physically separated networks, one with Internet connectivity and one without. The challenge is to find an appropriate balance between the accessibility and security of intranet resources, and this balance must be reflected in the service access policy of the corresponding firewall configuration.

Firewall Design Policy

The service access policy must be refined in a *firewall design policy* that is unique to a specific firewall configuration. The firewall design policy specifies the rules used by the firewall to implement the service access policy.

Formulating a firewall design policy is a difficult task, because one cannot design it in a vacuum isolated from understanding issues such as firewall capabilities and limitations, as well as threats and vulnerabilities associated with TCP/IP protocols and services. A key decision in the firewall design policy is the stance of the firewall design. The stance reflects the attitude of the firewall designers. It is determined by the cost of failure of the firewall and the designers' estimate of that likelihood. Obviously, it is also based on the designers' opinions of their own abilities. In general, a firewall may implement one of the following two stances:

- Permit any service unless it is expressly denied;

- Deny any service unless it is expressly permitted.

A firewall that implements the first stance allows all TCP/IP protocols and services by default, with the exception of those that the service access policy identifies as disallowed. In other words, anything that is not expressly prohibited is permitted by default. From a security point of view, this stance is less desirable, as it offers more avenues for circumventing the firewall. For example, users could access new services currently not denied by the policy or run denied services at nonstandard ports that are not expressly denied by the policy.

A firewall that implements the second stance denies all TCP/IP protocols and services by default, and passes only those that are identified as allowed. Obviously, this stance better fits the traditional access control model that is usually used in information security: Anything that is not expressly permitted is prohibited by default. From a security point of view, this stance is preferable. Note, however, that it is usually also more difficult to implement and may affect users more in that certain TCP/IP protocols and services must be blocked or restricted heavily.

7.2.2   Packet Filters

As further addressed in Chapter 8, a *packet filter* is a multiported internetworking device that applies a set of rules to each incoming IP packet in order to decide whether it will be forwarded or discarded. IP packets are filtered based on information usually found in packet headers, such as:

- Protocol numbers;

- Source and destination IP addresses;

- Source and destination port numbers;

- TCP connection flags;

- Some other options.

Routers that are able to screen and selectively filter IP packets are also called *screening routers*. Note that a screening router is always a packet filter, whereas the opposite is not always the case (note that a packet filter may not be able to route IP packets, and that a packet filter is not necessarily a screening router). However, in the text that follows we are going to use the terms *packet filter* and *screening router* synonymously most of the time.

In general, packet filters are stateless, meaning that each IP packet is examined isolated from what has happened in the past, forcing the filter to make a decision to permit or deny each packet based upon the packet-filtering rules. In Chapter 8, however, we elaborate on *dynamic packet filtering* as a technology to enhance the capabilities and to improve the security of a packet filtering device. Dynamic packet filtering is sometimes also referred to as *stateful multilevel inspection*, or *stateful inspection*. Stateful inspection can be used to increase the expressibility of packet-filtering rules considerably.

A firewall configuration that only consists of a screening router is sometimes also referred to as a *packet-filtering-only firewall*, or *packet-filtering gateway* in short. Perhaps one justification of the term *gateway* is that filtering based on port numbers and TCP connection flags done at the transport layer is not a pure function of a router that typically operates at the network layer of the OSI-RM. The packet-filtering-only firewall is perhaps the most common and easiest to employ for small, uncomplicated sites. Basically, one installs a screening router as a gateway to the Internet and configures the packet-filtering rules in accordance with a service access and firewall design policy. More often than not, such a service access policy allows internal systems to fully access the Internet, while all or most access from the Internet is blocked. The packet-filtering gateway suffers from a number of disadvantages and is less secure than the other firewall configurations discussed in the rest of Part II.

7.2.3 Application Gateways

In general, an *application gateway* or *gateway* refers to an internetworking device that interconnects one network to another for a specific application. Therefore, the gateway must understand and implement the corresponding application protocol. In the client-server model, an application gateway refers to an intermediate process running between the client that requests a particular service and the server that provides the service. In this model, the application gateway functions as a server from the client's point of view, and as a client from the server's point of view.

Again referring to the Internet model, an application gateway can either work at the application layer or at the transport layer [3, 4]:

- If the gateway works at the application layer, it is usually called an *application-level gateway*, or *proxy server*.

- If the gateway works at the transport layer, it is usually called a *circuit-level gateway*.

Most application gateways used in firewall configurations work at the application layer and represent application-level gateways or proxy servers accordingly. In either case, the application gateway runs on a firewall host and performs a specific function as a proxy on the user's behalf. If the application gateway is an application-level gateway, then the function is application-specific. Otherwise, the function is not application-specific and the application gateway is actually a circuit-level gateway. Circuit-level gateways and application-level gateways are further addressed in Chapters 9 and 10.

The Internet community often uses the term *bastion host* to refer to an exposed firewall system that hosts an application gateway. The term *bastion* comes from the heavily fortified projections on the exteriors of castles in medieval times. A bastion host should be configured to be particularly secure because it is exposed to direct attacks from the Internet. Typically, a bastion host is located in a secure environment by residing on a secure operating system. In this case, the secure operating system must protect the firewall code and files from outside attacks. More often than not, the firewall code is the only application that is permitted to execute on the bastion host. Absence of other applications reduces the possibility of unauthorized attempts to penetrate the firewall. Despite the fact that most bastion hosts run a modified and downstripped (or "hardened") version of the UNIX or Linux operating system, there is increasing demand for Windows NT-based firewalls. Also, there are some firewalls that come along with a special and highly secure operating system. One example of this kind is the Sidewinder firewall developed and marketed by the Secure Computing Corporation.[4]

Depending on its basic components and their configuration, several grades of firewall security can be obtained. For example, there is no security by allowing unrestricted access between a corporate intranet and the Internet. Next, packet filters or screening routers can be added to obtain a basic level of traffic interception. Also, the firewall can include both packet filters and application gateways. A variety of circuit-level or application-level gateways can be added along with different strengths of the corresponding authentication schemes. We can also improve the overall security for the intranet by adding e-mail gateway and name services

---

[4]http://www.securecomputing.com

to the firewall. The firewall can also reside on a secure operating system, thereby improving the underlying security for the firewall code and files. A firewall can also provide support for Internet layer security protocols (e.g., IPsec). This facility can be used to build secure tunnels between firewall-protected sites and to build virtual private networks (VPNs) accordingly. Finally, a company can also deny any access to and from the Internet, thereby ensuring isolation and complete security from the outside world. Although this is seemingly a theoretical option in the euphoric time for Internet access we live in these days, for certain highly secure environments it is still the only prudent approach to follow.

7.3   SOURCES FOR FURTHER INFORMATION

There are many books available that entirely cover the firewall technologies that are available today. As a matter of fact, most books that have addressed Internet and intranet security in the past are actually books on firewalls [3, 5, 6], or put the main emphasis on firewalls [7]. There are also many research papers and reports that address specific topics related to firewalls. You may refer to the proceedings of any conference or workshop related to network security. As part of the Computer Operations, Audit, and Security Technology (COAST) project at Purdue University, Eugene H. Spafford has also collected many resources related to Internet firewalls.[5]

In addition, there is the Firewalls Mailing List that is archived at several sites (e.g., `http://lists.gnac.net/firewalls/`). Communications in the mailing list is summarized in a FAQ document addressing various aspects of Internet firewalls. The document was maintained by Marcus J. Ranum until 1998 and is now being maintained by Matt Curtin. It is available in either HTML, PostScript, and PDF formats from the URL mentioned above as well as several other sites.

If you are interested in building a Linux-based firewall, you may refer to Mark Grennan's *Firewall and Proxy Server HOWTO* document.[6]

Finally, a more or less comprehensive list of firewall products is available at `http://www.thegild.com/firewall/`. You may also refer to the Web sites of the various firewall vendors to get a more comprehensive and accurate picture about the current trends in firewall technologies.

---

[5]`http://www.cerias.purdue.edu/coast/firewalls/`
[6]`http://www.grennan.com/Firewall-HOWTO.html`

REFERENCES

[1] B. Fraser, "Site Security Handbook," Request for Comments 2196, September 1997.

[2] R. Shirey, "Internet Security Glossary," Request for Comments 2828, May 2000.

[3] W. R. Cheswick and S. M. Bellovin, *Firewalls and Internet Security: Repelling the Wily Hacker*, Addison-Wesley, Reading, MA, 1994.

[4] W. R. Cheswick and S. M. Bellovin, "Network Firewalls," *IEEE Communications Magazine*, September 1994, pp. 50–57.

[5] K. Siyan and C. Hare, *Internet Firewalls and Network Security*, New Riders Publishing, Indianapolis, IN, 1995.

[6] E. D. Zwicky, et al., *Building Internet Firewalls*, 2nd Edition, O'Reilly & Associates, Sebastopol, CA, 2000.

[7] S. Garfinkel and G. Spafford, *Practical UNIX and Internet Security*, 2nd Edition, O'Reilly & Associates, Sebastopol, CA, 1996.

Chapter 8

Packet Filtering

In this chapter, we elaborate on packet filtering as one of the core technologies employed by many firewall configurations. More specifically, we introduce the technology in Section 8.1, discuss packet filter rules in Section 8.2, overview some packet filtering products in Section 8.3, address stateful inspection (also known as dynamic packet filtering) in Section 8.4, and draw some conclusions in Section 8.5. In this chapter it should become clear that packet filtering is useful but not sufficient to provide appropriate access control services for corporate intranets.

8.1 INTRODUCTION

A router is an internetworking device that usually runs a specialized operating system (e.g., Cisco IOS) to transfer packets between two or more physically separated network segments.[1] It operates at the network layer in the OSI-RM, or the Internet layer in the Internet model, respectively. As such, it routes IP packets by consulting tables that indicate the best path the IP packet should take to reach its

---

[1] Despite the fact that most routers in use today are able to route multiple protocols, we mainly focus on IP routing in this book. This is because IP is by far the most dominant network layer protocol used in the Internet.

final destination. More accurately, a router receives an IP packet on one network interface and forwards it on another network interface, possibly in the direction of the destination IP address that is included in the IP header. If the router knows on which interface to forward the packet, it does so. Otherwise, it is not able to route the packet. In this case, the router usually returns the packet using an ICMP destination unreachable message to the source IP address.

Because every IP packet contains a source and a destination IP address, packets originating from or destined to a particular host or network segment can be selectively filtered by a packet-filtering device. Also, transport layer protocols such as TCP or UDP add a source and destination port number to each segment or datagram as part of the header information. These port numbers indicate which processes on each host finally will receive the data encapsulated within the IP packet. This information can also be used to selectively filter IP packets. In the late 1980s and early 1990s, several scientific papers and articles were published that describe how to use packet filters to provide basic access control services for corporate intranets [1–5]. Some of these papers describe the use of packet filtering in early firewall configurations at AT&T [2] and Digital Equipment Corporation (DEC) [3].[2]

Today, most commercial router products also provide the capability to screen IP packets and filter them in accordance with a set of packet filter rules that implement a specific service access policy. For example, routers from Cisco Systems use a fairly simple syntax to define packet-filtering rules [6–8]. Each network interface on a Cisco router can be assigned an access group, which is basically an integer number that references the interface. Packet-filtering commands for that interface are then expressed in access lists[3] that are associated with access groups. The router, in turn, matches each IP packet routed to a particular network interface against the access lists associated with the access group of that particular interface.

We said in Chapter 7 that routers that provide packet-filtering capabilities are sometimes also called *screening routers*. In general, screening routers can provide an efficient mechanism to control the type of network traffic that can exist (i.e., enter and/or leave) on a particular network segment. By controlling the type of network traffic that can exist on a network segment, they can also control the types of services that may exist. Services that eventually compromise the security of the

---

[2]The DEC firewall was designed and implemented by Marcus J. Ranum. The same firewall was also used to secure the Web site of the White House at http://www.whitehouse.gov.

[3]More accurately, Cisco routers provide support for two types of access lists: standard access lists and extended access lists. We refer to [6–8] and the relevant product documentations for more information on this topic.

network segment can be effectively and efficiently restricted.

Remember that a packet filter or a screening router is a multiported internet-working device that applies a set of rules to each incoming IP packet to decide whether it will be forwarded or discarded. As such, the packet filter or screening router has several ports or network interfaces. Each port may connect the packet filter to a network segment, and the network segments are classified as either internal or external: *Internal* network segments belong to the intranet, whereas *external* network segments typically belong to the Internet. Consequently, it is up to the packet filter to intercept and control data traffic between internal and external network segments.

Upon receiving an IP packet, the packet filter parses the header of the packet and applies the corresponding packet filter rules to determine whether the packet should be forwarded toward its destination IP address or dropped and discarded.[4] We mentioned in Chapter 7 that IP packets are filtered based on information that is usually found in packet headers:

- Protocol numbers;

- Source and destination IP addresses;

- Source and destination port numbers;

- TCP connection flags;

- Some other options.

Note that routers do not normally look at (TCP or UDP) port numbers when making routing decisions, but do for filtering purposes, knowing the source and destination port number allows selective filtering based on the service being used. For example, a Telnet server usually listens at port 23, and an SMTP server usually listens at port 25. Selective filtering by port numbers also takes advantage of how ports are assigned. Although a Telnet server uses port 23 most of the time, a

---

[4]Some packet-filtering implementations with only rudimentary capabilities do not actually parse the headers of IP packets, but instead require the administrator to specify byte ranges within the header to examine and the patterns for which to look in those ranges [4]. This is almost useless, as it requires the administrator to have a very detailed understanding of the structure of an IP packet. Also, it is totally unworkable for packets using IP option fields, which cause the location of the beginning of the transport layer protocol headers, such as TCP or UDP headers, to vary. This variation, in turn, makes it very difficult to find and examine the TCP or UDP port number fields.

Telnet client port number is not fixed, but assigned dynamically. In a UNIX or Linux environment, for example, the client port is assigned a number greater than 1,023. Also note that screening routers can filter on any of the TCP connection flags summarized in Table 2.5, but that the SYN and ACK flags are the most frequently used flags for packet filtering (this is because these two flags collectively determine whether a TCP connection is established inbound or outbound). For example, all TCP segments except the first one (i.e., the TCP connection request message) carry an ACK flag.

Unfortunately, not all screening routers are able to filter IP packets based on all header fields mentioned earlier. For example, some screening routers are not able to consider the source port of an IP packet. This can make packet-filtering rules more complex and can even open up holes in the entire packet filtering scheme. There is, for example, such a problem if a site wishes to allow both inbound and outbound SMTP traffic for e-mail. Remember that in the case of a client establishing an SMTP connection to a server, the client's source port number would be randomly chosen at or above 1,024, and the destination port number would be 25, the port at which an SMTP server conventionally resides. Consequently, the SMTP server would return IP packets with a source port number of 25 and a destination port number equal to the port number randomly chosen by the client. In this scenario, a packet filter must be configured to allow destination and source port numbers greater than 1,023 to pass through in either direction. If the router is able to filter on the source port, it can block incoming SMTP traffic with a destination port greater than 1,023 and a source port other than 25. Without this ability, however, the router cannot consider the source port and must therefore permit incoming SMTP traffic with a destination port greater than 1,023 and an arbitrary source port number. Consequently, legitimate but malicious users could conceivably make use of this situation and run servers at ports greater than 1,023 to circumvent the service access policy enforced by the packet filter. For example, a Telnet server that normally listens at port 23 could be told to listen at port 7,777 instead. Users on the Internet could then use a normal Telnet client to connect to this internal server even if the packet filter blocks destination port 23.

In addition to the header information itemized, some packet-filtering devices also allow the administrator to specify packet-filtering rules based on which network interface an IP packet actually entered and on which interface the packet is destined to leave. Being able to specify filters on both inbound and outbound interfaces allows an administrator significant control over where the packet filter appears in the overall scheme and is very convenient for useful filtering on screening routers with more than two network interfaces. As described later, this ability has turned out to be very useful, and essential to protect against sequence number guessing and IP spoofing attacks. Unfortunately, not all screening routers can actually filter on both inbound and outbound interfaces, and many routers implement packet filtering only on the outbound interface for efficiency reasons. Note that for outgoing IP packets, the filter rules can be applied when the router consults its routing tables to determine the interface to send the packet out on. At this point, however, the router no longer knows on which interface the packet entered; it has lost some important information.

Screening routers filter IP packets according to specific packet filter rules. More accurately, when an IP packet arrives at a network interface of a filtering device, the packet headers are parsed. As described earlier, most packet filters examine the fields in only the IP and the TCP or UDP headers. Each packet-filtering rule is applied to the packet in the order in which the packet-filtering rules are stored. If a rule blocks the transmission or reception of a packet, the packet is not allowed. If a rule allows the transmission or reception of a packet, the packet is allowed to proceed. If a packet does not satisfy any rule, it is either allowed or blocked depending on the stance of the firewall. In general, it is good practice to block the IP packet in this case.

We mentioned previously that packet filters are stateless, meaning that each IP packet must be examined isolated from what has happened in the past, forcing the filter to make a decision to permit or deny each packet individually based upon the packet-filtering rules. Routers are generally optimized to shuffle IP packets quickly. The packet filters of a screening router take time and can defeat the overall optimization efforts. In fact, packet filtering is a slow operation that may considerably reduce routing throughput. Logging of IP packets also occurs without regard to past history, and enabling logging results in another hit on performance. More often than not, packet filtering and logging are not enabled in routers primarily to achieve better throughput and performance. If enabled and used, packet filtering and logging are typically installed at the edge of an administrative domain.

8.2 PACKET-FILTERING RULES

We saw in Chapter 7 that the service access policy defines the TCP/IP protocols and services that are allowed or denied to pass through a firewall, and that the firewall design policy describes how the firewall actually restricts access and filters TCP/IP protocols and services. Consequently, packet-filtering rules must adequately reflect and implement the service access and firewall design policies. Note that packet-filtering rules often are defined at firewall installation time, although they may be later modified, added, or deleted as well.

In essence, a *packet-filtering rule* consists of two parts: selection criteria and an action field.

- The *selection criteria* of a packet-filtering rule use information typically found in headers to decide whether a particular IP packet should be selected or not, and whether the appropriate action specified in the action field of the packet-filtering rule should be taken.

- The *action field* of a packet filter rule specifies the action to be taken if an IP packet meets the selection criteria and is selected by that rule. Two types of action are usually permitted:

  - BLOCK (or DENY) implies that the selected IP packet should be rejected and discarded.

  - PERMIT (or ALLOW) implies that the selected IP packet should be accepted and forwarded toward its destination IP address.

With regard to source and destination IP address, a selection criterion can work either with full IP addresses or address masks. Therefore, an address selection usually is accomplished by specifying two dotted-decimal IP addresses. In this case, the first IP address is the desired address and the second IP address is an address mask that selects the relevant bits in the address field. If a mask bit is 1, the corresponding bit in the address is ignored and any value is allowed. For example, suppose we want to select any packet with a source IP address that begins with 157.4.5. Therefore, we put 157.4.5.0 as the desired source IP address and 0.0.0.255 as the address mask for selecting the relevant bits. So, for this address mask, the first 3 bytes of the mask would select all of the 24 bits of the first 3 bytes of a packet's source IP address. Next, the selected 24 bits are compared against 157.4.5. If there is a match, the packet is selected. Obviously, an equal mechanism can be used for the destination IP address.

It is worth mentioning that most packet-filtering implementations apply the rules in the sequence specified by the administrator until they find a rule that meets the selection criteria for a particular IP packet. When an IP packet arrives at a packet filter, it is tested against the first packet-filtering rule. If the rule applies to the packet, the specified action for that rule is carried out (i.e., the packet is forwarded or discarded). If the rule does not apply to the packet, the second rule is checked, and so on. Note that for each rule, if the IP packet satisfies the selection criteria, the action specified for that rule is carried out and the filter processing for that packet is completed.

Suppose the IP packet is not selected by any of the rules, up to the last one. The last rule, however, specifies to discard all packets. So, the last rule takes effect, and the packet is discarded. Consequently, the default action for packet filtering in this case would be to discard the packet, unless otherwise specified by a previous packet-filtering rule. This is a strongly recommended policy that may help prevent unauthorized IP packets getting into the protected area of a corporate intranet. Unfortunately, there also are some packet-filtering implementations that enforce a particular order of rule application based on the selection criteria in the rules, such as source and destination IP address, regardless of the order in which the rules are specified. Some implementations, for example, apply packet-filtering rules in the same order as routing table entries; that is, they apply rules referring to more specific addresses before rules with less-specific addresses. In general, routers that apply packet-filtering rules in the order specified by the administrator, without reordering them, are easier to understand, configure, and manage, and are therefore more likely to yield correct and complete rulesets.

Packet filtering can be used in a variety of ways to block IP traffic from or to specific sites and network segments. For example, a site may wish to block connections from certain IP addresses that it considers to be untrustworthy or hostile. Alternatively, a site also might wish to block connections from all IP addresses external to the site (with certain exceptions, such as SMTP connections for handling e-mail traffic).

As an example of a packet-filtering scenario, consider a service access policy that permits only certain connections to a network of address 123.4.*.*. Telnet connections will be allowed to only one host, 123.4.5.6, which may be a Telnet application gateway. Similarly, SMTP connections will be allowed to two hosts, 123.4.5.7 and 123.4.5.8, which may be e-mail application gateways. NNTP traffic is allowed only from the site's feed system, 129.6.48.254, and only to the site's NNTP server, 123.4.5.9, whereas NTP traffic is allowed to all hosts. All other services and corresponding IP traffic must be blocked by default. An exemplary set of packet-filtering rules that implement this policy are summarized in Table 8.1. Note that each type of packet-filtering device usually has its own set of rules and syntax on how to program packet-filtering rules. Therefore, one must read the packet-filtering device documentation and learn the peculiarities of the syntax for that particular device. In our example of packet-filtering rules, we use an abstract syntax that is not usually found in commercial products.

The first rule allows TCP traffic from any source IP address and port number greater than 1,023 on the Internet to the destination address of 123.4.5.6 and port number 23 on the intranet. This port number is associated with the Telnet server, and all Telnet clients should have unprivileged source ports of 1,024 or higher. The second and third rules work in a similar fashion, except that traffic to destination addresses 123.4.5.7 and 123.4.5.8, and port number 25 for SMTP, is permitted. The fourth rule permits IP packets to the site's NNTP server, but only from source IP address 129.6.48.254 to destination IP address 123.4.5.9 and port number 119. Note that 129.6.48.254 is the only NNTP server that news should be received from, thus access for NNTP is restricted to only that IP address. The fifth rule permits NTP traffic, which uses UDP instead of TCP, from any source to any destination address on the intranet. Finally, the sixth rule denies all other traffic and corresponding IP packets. If this rule were not present in the ruleset, the router may or may not deny all subsequent packets.

In Chapter 2, we briefly mentioned the problem of IP fragmentation. Note that IP supports the notion that any router along a packet's delivery path may fragment that packet into smaller packets to accommodate the limitations of underlying transport media, to be reassembled into the original IP packet at the destination. For example, an FDDI frame may be much larger than an Ethernet frame. So, a router between an FDDI ring and an Ethernet network may split an IP packet that fits in a single FDDI frame into multiple fragments that fit into the smaller Ethernet frames. The problem with this, from a packet-filtering point of view, is that only the first of the IP fragments comprises the upper-layer protocol headers (i.e., TCP or UDP headers) from the original packet, which may be necessary to make a useful filtering decision concerning the fragment. Different packet-filtering implementations take a variety of responses to this situation. Some implementations apply packet-filtering

Table 8.1
Exemplary Set of Packet-Filtering Rules

No.	Type	Source Address	Dest. Address	Source Port	Dest. Port	Action
1	TCP	*	123.4.5.6	> 1023	23	Permit
2	TCP	*	123.4.5.7	> 1023	25	Permit
3	TCP	*	123.4.5.8	> 1023	25	Permit
4	TCP	129.6.48.254	123.4.5.9	> 1023	119	Permit
5	UDP	*	123.4.*.*	> 1023	123	Permit
6	*	*	*	*	*	Deny

rules only to the first fragment of an IP packet that actually contains the upper-layer protocol header, and simply route the remaining fragments. The assumption is that if the first fragment of an IP packet is dropped by the packet filter, the rest of the fragments cannot be reassembled into a full IP packet and will therefore cause no harm. Note, however, that it is dangerous to suppress only the first fragment of an outbound IP packet; one may still be leaking data in subsequent fragments that are routed out of the intranet. To defeat this problem, it is possible to keep a cache of recently seen first fragments and the filtering decision that was reached, and to look up subsequent fragments in this cache in order to apply the same decision. This approach is conceptually very closely related to dynamic packet filtering or stateful inspection, as discussed later.

The question on how to filter TCP/IP application protocols and services depends on the chosen service access policy (i.e., which systems should have Internet access and the type of access to permit). Many books have been written that focus entirely on that question. Again, we refer to the books that were referenced in Chapter 7. In particular, we refer to appendix B of [9], where the packet-filtering characteristics for various TCP and UDP ports are summarized.

In short, there are many TCP-based application protocols and services that can be effectively addressed with packet filters and screening routers. Examples include FTP, Telnet, SMTP, DNS, HTTP, and NNTP.

In regard to FTP, it is worth mentioning that two TCP connections are actually used between a client and a server: a control connection (port 21 on the server side) and a data connection (port 20 on the server side). It is up to the client to establish the control connection, whereas it is up to the server to establish backward the data connection. In an intranet environment, the data connection can generally be established. If, however, the FTP client is located on the intranet and the FTP server is located on the Internet, the data connection is inbound and may be rejected by a screening router controlling access to the intranet environment. We come back to this problem when we discuss dynamic packet filtering and stateful inspection later in this chapter. In the meantime, a bypass is available if the client and server both provide support for passive mode FTP [10]. In passive mode FTP, the data connection is also established from the client to the server (similar to the control connection). As such, both connections are outbound and may be easily handled by a screening router.

With regard to DNS it is also worth mentioning that the service can be based on TCP or UDP, and that it is usually provided at port 53 (in either case). The UDP-based service is usually used for queries, while the TCP-based service is used for server-to-server zone transfers. One implementation characteristic of the Berkeley

Internet Name Daemon (BIND) is that server-to-server proxy queries are made by way of UDP, with both ends of a connection using port 53. Packet-filtering rules can take advantage of this characteristic, as DNS is sometimes the only UDP-based protocol that is allowed bidirectionally between internal machines and the outside world.

Not all systems require general access to all services. For example, restricting Telnet or FTP access from the Internet to only those systems that actually require it can improve the overall security at almost no cost to user convenience. Other protocols and services such as NNTP may seem to pose little threat, but restricting them to only those systems that actually require them may help to create a cleaner intranet environment and reduce the likelihood of exploitation from yet-to-be-discovered vulnerabilities and corresponding threats. Finally, TCP/IP protocols and services that are inherently vulnerable to abuse should generally be blocked by a screening router being part of a firewall configuration. Typical examples include the Trivial FTP (TFTP) and protocols used by the X11 window system.

Unfortunately, there are also some TCP/IP protocols and services that cannot be addressed effectively with packet filters and screening routers:

- Protocols and services that are layered on top of UDP are generally hard to handle with packet filters. This is because UDP is a connectionless transport layer protocol that does not establish and make use of connections. Each UDP is sent individually and there is no possibility to decide whether the application it actually belongs to is used inbound or outbound. This makes it very difficult to intelligently filter IP packets. Unfortunately, UDP is used by an increasingly large number of applications and application protocols, mainly for real-time and multicast communications.

- Similarly, protocols and services that use dynamically assigned port numbers are hard to handle with packet filters. For example, the actual port number of an RPC-based protocol and service is dynamically assigned by the portmapper service (typically running at the well-known port number 111). The portmapper service maps an RPC service number to the particular UDP or TCP port number that the service is currently using on the machine being queried. Because RPC-based protocols and services might be on any port, the filtering implementation has no sure way of recognizing what is and what is not RPC.

Obviously, protocols and services that combine the use of UDP and dynamically assigned port numbers are particularly hard to handle using packet-filtering techniques only.

We have mentioned the sequence number guessing and related IP spoofing attacks several times throughout the previous chapters of this book. We now have a brief look at the way a firewall and its packet-filtering component can be configured to protect against them. Remember that these attacks usually exploit the weakness that the source address of an IP packet header must not be authentic (since it is not authenticated). In fact, a host can very easily change the source IP address of a packet to appear as if it is coming from another host, such as a trusted host. In this case, the packet may include a system command that would be executed without prior authentication of the corresponding user.

To protect against this kind of attack, the packet-filtering rules must be designed to discard any packet arriving at an inbound network interface that contains an internal source IP address. The reason is that a packet originating from the outside with the source IP address of an internal machine implies that the packet is somehow fraudulent. Consequently, the packet-filtering rules must specify to discard the packet. Suppose the network or firewall administrator has detected that a certain host on the Internet is sending fraudulent packets by spoofing the source IP address. The administrator can then add a new rule to discard packets arriving from any host with that particular source IP address. Similarly, if a given host is under attack, the new filter rule can discard IP packets destined for that particular host. The new rule should be added at the beginning of the existing ruleset, thereby avoiding any impact to other network traffic.

8.3   PACKET-FILTERING PRODUCTS

As mentioned in Section 8.2, a steadily increasing number of commercial router products (e.g., Cisco Systems, Nortel Networks, and 3Com) provide support for packet filtering, and these routers are commonly referred to as screening routers. In either case, it is always a good idea to disable IP source routing on a screening router. Whether IP source routing can be disabled at all, whether it is enabled or disabled by default, and how to disable it vary from product to product. For example, for a Cisco router, one can usually disable source routing by using the command `no ip source-route`. Other vendors use a similar command syntax.

In addition to screening routers, there are several tools and utilities available on the Internet that can be used for IP packet filtering:

- For example, the `screend` software package was originally designed and developed by Jeff Mogul [1] and is now being maintained by Paul Vixie. The `screend` package provides a daemon and kernel modifications to allow all packets to be

filtered based on source IP address, destination IP address, or any other byte
or set of bytes in the packet. The software works on most systems that use
Berkeley-style networking in the kernel, but requires some kernel modifications.

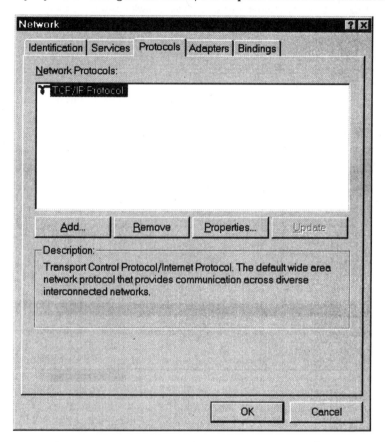

Figure 8.1   The Network Protocols panel of Microsoft NT. © 2000 Microsoft Corporation.

- Similarly, there are several PC-based packet-filtering products available that are
  not able to route IP packets and therefore act as a bridge between the network
  segments they interconnect. Probably the two most widely used and deployed
  examples are Drawbridge and KarlBridge.

— Drawbridge comes along with the copyrighted but publicly and freely available Texas A&M University (TAMU) security tools [11].[5]

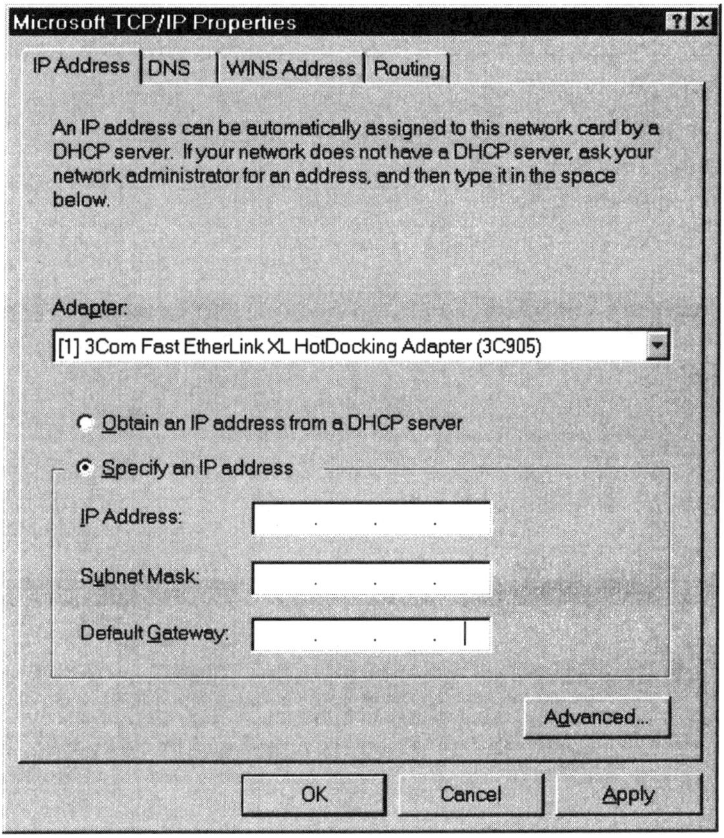

Figure 8.2   The IP Address panel of Microsoft NT. © 2000 Microsoft Corporation.

— The KarlBridge has evolved from a simple PC program that was originally written by Doug Karl at Ohio State University. Karl later cofounded Karl-

---

[5]You may refer either to `ftp://net.tamu.edu/pub/security/TAMU/` (using FTP) or to `http://www.net.tamu.edu/ftp/security/TAMU/` (using HTTP).

Net, Inc.[6] to commercialize the program and to develop and market similar products.

Installation and configuration of Drawbridge and the KarlBridge are described in [12] and are not further addressed in this book.

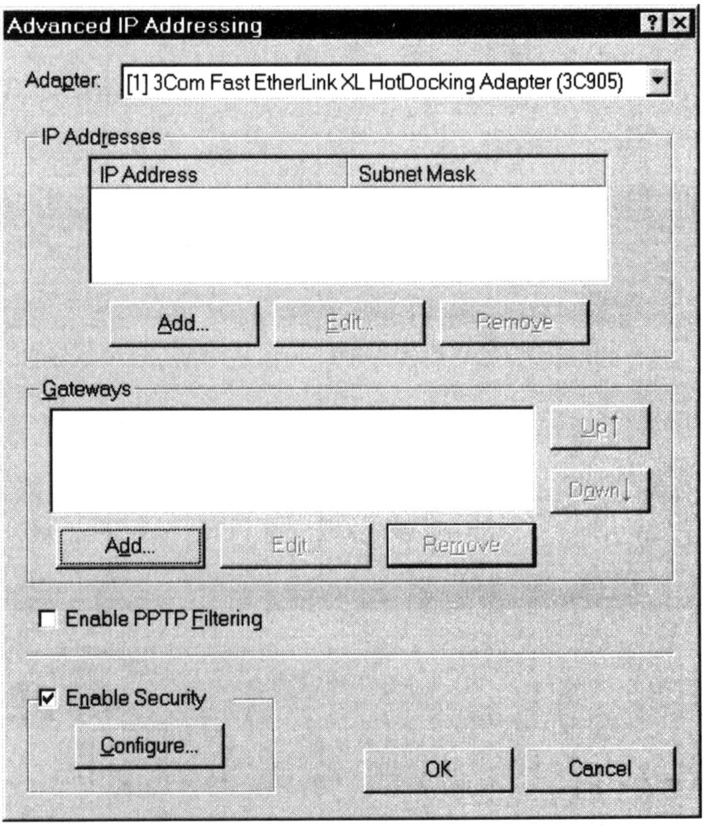

Figure 8.3   The Advanced IP Addressing panel of Microsoft NT. © 2000 Microsoft Corporation.

---

[6]http://www.karlnet.com

- Finally, there is an increasingly large number of software packages that include packet-filtering capabilities as an additional feature. For example, the latest version of PGP (i.e., PGP Desktop Security 7.0) incorporates a personal firewall that can also be configured to implement an IP packet filter.

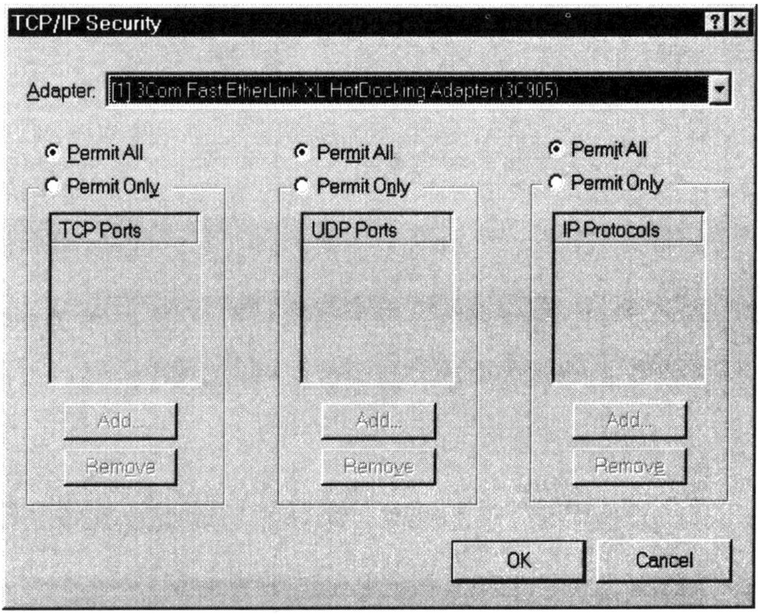

Figure 8.4   The TCP/IP Security panel of Microsoft NT. © 2000 Microsoft Corporation.

Today, it is more and more common to have packet-filtering capabilities built into (network) operating systems. Systems running Windows NT or Windows 2000 can be configured to implement quite sophisticated packet-filtering rules. For example, in the case of Windows NT, you start with the Control Panel and press the Network icon. On the Network Protocols panel illustrated in Figure 8.1, you press the Properties button and come to the IP Address panel as illustrated in Figure 8.2. On the bottom right of this panel, there is an "Advanced..." button. If you press this button, you come to the Advanced IP Addressing panel illustrated in Figure 8.3. Finally, if you click the "Configure..." button on the bottom left, you are able to configure Windows NT's packet-filtering rules in a window similar to the one illustrated in Figure 8.4. In this TCP/IP Security panel, it is possible to collectively or selectively permit TCP and UDP ports, as well as IP protocols. The use of this panel is intuitive and need not be further explained in this book.

8.4   STATEFUL INSPECTION

Earlier in this chapter we mentioned FTP and its use of two TCP connections to actually transfer a file (i.e., an FTP control connection and an FTP data connection). We also said that because of the nature of the FTP data connection, it is quite difficult to set up appropriate packet-filtering rules. The problem is related to the fact that the data connection is typically established inbound (i.e., from the FTP server to the FTP client) and that inbound connections are very likely to be rejected by a properly configured packet filter or screening router.

For example, imagine a situation in which an intranet client wishes to establish an outbound FTP session to a server located somewhere on the Internet. According to the normal FTP specification, the client would first establish an outbound TCP connection from a randomly chosen port X to the FTP control port (i.e., port 21) of the server. Among other things, this connection would be used by the client to inform the server on which port Y it is going to listen for the incoming FTP data connection (using the PORT command of the FTP protocol). The server, in turn, would establish an inbound TCP connection from its FTP data port (i.e., port 20) to port Y on the client side. A file requested by the client would then be transferred on this TCP connection to the client.

Now imagine what happens if Internet connectivity is mediated through a screening router and the corresponding packet-filtering rules are configured in a restrictive way (meaning that inbound TCP connections are not allowed and rejected). In this situation, the second TCP connection (i.e., the FTP data connection) would be denied and the corresponding file transfer would not be able to take place. The underlying problem is that due to the stateless nature of (static) packet filtering, it is not possible to recognize that the second TCP connection (i.e., the FTP data connection) logically belongs to the first TCP connection (i.e., the FTP control connection), and that the two connections collectively represent an FTP session. Consequently, the screening router simply sees an Internet server trying to establish an inbound TCP connection from server port 20 to client port Y. According to its policy and configuration, it is very likely that the screening router is going to refuse this TCP connection establishment request.

We have also already mentioned that passive mode FTP as specified in [10] provides a simple solution for this particular problem. Note, however, that the problem is more fundamental and that an increasingly large number of network applications use multiple connections and randomly chosen port numbers. For these applications, it is getting increasingly difficult to specify appropriate packet-filtering rules.

Remember that packet filters are stateless, meaning that each IP packet is examined isolated from what has happened in the past, forcing the packet filter to make a decision to permit or deny each packet based upon the packet-filtering rules. Contrary to that, the notion and technology of *stateful inspection* or *dynamic packet filtering* was created by the developers of the FireWall-1 at CheckPoint Software Technologies, Ltd.[7] In short, stateful inspection refers to a technology in which a packet filter maintains state information about past IP packets to make more intelligent decisions about the legitimacy of present and future IP packets. For example, a dynamic packet filter compares the first packet in a connection to the packet-filtering rules, and if the packet is permitted, state information is added to an internal database. One might think of this state information as representing an internal virtual circuit in the stateful inspection device on top of the transport layer association. This information permits subsequent packets in that association to pass quickly through the stateful inspection device. If the rules for a specific type of service require examining application data, then part of each packet must still be examined. As an example, FireWall-1 can react to seeing an FTP PORT command by creating a dynamic rule permitting a connection back from the FTP server to that particular port number on the client's side.

In summary, stateful inspection provides much better possibilities to define packet-filtering rules and to filter IP packets accordingly (as compared to static packet filtering). Whenever possible (and available in products), stateful inspection should therefore be used to improve the capabilities of packet-filtering devices.

8.5   CONCLUSIONS

As of this writing, static and dynamic packet filtering are used and widely deployed on the Internet. There are at least three reasons for its success:

1. Packet filtering is a low-cost technology. We have seen that packet-filtering capabilities are already integrated into many commercial off-the-shelf (COTS) products (and will continue to be integrated in future COTS products).

---

[7]The technology is covered by U.S. patent US 5,606,668 that specifies a "system for securing inbound and outbound data packet flow in a computer network." The patent was granted to Checkpoint Software Technologies, Ltd., on February 25, 1997.

2. The use of packet filtering is transparent to both application programs and users. There is no need to make an application program aware of (static or dynamic) packet filtering. This level of transparency is also available but more complicated to achieve for other firewall technologies.

3. Vendors have promoted the technology, since it is not based on cryptography and has not been export-controlled accordingly. This feature has allowed a worldwide distribution and promotion of products that make use of packet filtering.

Because of these advantages, it is possible and very likely that we will see a further proliferation and sophistication of packet-filtering techniques and corresponding implementations in the future. Stateful inspection and its integration in many networking products are one example of this trend.

But packet filtering is not a panacea for network security, particularly in the form in which it is currently implemented by many vendors. As a matter of fact, packet filters and screening routers suffer from a number of weaknesses and disadvantages [4]. The primary weakness relates to the complexity of correctly configuring and managing packet filter rules. There are two points here:

1. Correctly specifying packet-filtering rules is still a difficult and error-prone process.

2. Reordering packet-filtering rules makes correctly specifying rules even more difficult by turning a ruleset that works if evaluated in the order given into a ruleset that does not work. The difficulty is somehow related to the complexity of correctly setting up rules in knowledge-based expert systems.

In general, the way in which packet-filtering rules must be specified and the order in which they are applied are key determinants of how useful and powerful certain packet-filtering capabilities really are. Most implementations require the administrator to specify filters in ways that make the filters easy to parse and apply, but make them rather difficult for the administrator to fully understand and properly manage. Also, the configuration process requires intricate knowledge of TCP/IP networking and addressing. Note that most users still consider networking activities in terms of "connections," while packet filtering, by definition, is concerned only with IP packets (that eventually make up a connection or virtual circuit on a higher layer). For example, an inbound connection must usually be translated into at least two packet-filtering rules, namely, one for the inbound IP packets and one for the outbound packets. To make things worse, the concept of a connection is applied even when considering a connectionless protocol, such as ICMP, UDP, or UDP-based application protocols. This mismatch among the abstractions commonly used and the mechanisms provided by many packet-filtering implementations contributes to the difficulties of correctly and completely specifying packet-filtering rules.

As a result, network and firewall administrators may very well commit mistakes in setting up packet filter rules. Often, exceptions to rules must be made to allow certain types of access that normally would be blocked. Unfortunately, such exceptions make a packet-filtering ruleset so complex as to be unmanageable. For example, it is relatively simple and straightforward to specify a rule to block all inbound connections to a Telnet server that is running on port 23. If exceptions are made (i.e., if certain systems need to accept direct Telnet connections from the outside), then a rule for each system must be added to the ruleset. Sometimes the addition of certain rules may complicate the entire packet-filtering scheme. This is due to the fact that the simple syntax used in most packet-filtering implementations makes it easy for the screening router but difficult for the administrator.

Brent Chapman compares the task of specifying packet-filtering rules with the task of programming in assembly language [4]. Instead of being able to use some high-level language abstractions, the administrator is forced to produce a tabular representation of the packet-filtering rules. However, the desired behavior may or may not map on to a tabular representation. Fortunately, the industry direction is to make it more simple to specify packet-filtering rules. In addition, utilities and tools are being developed to test and validate packet-filtering rules, perhaps including test suites and automatic test case generators. There are also tools available that can be used to derive packet-filtering rules directly from a given router network specification.

In summary, the advantages of packet filters and screening routers are simplicity and low cost, whereas the disadvantages are related to the difficulties in setting up packet-filtering rules correctly, as well as the lack of user authentication. It is very important to note that any packet filter has to decide whether to forward or discard packets based on information that may not be authentic. Because the authenticity of an IP source address is not protected, a given host can spoof another host by simply changing the source IP address of the packets it sends out. The sequence number guessing attack described in Chapter 3 exploits this vulnerability. A countermeasure to reduce or even eliminate this vulnerability is cryptographic authentication, as implemented, for example, by the IP security authentication header (AH) mechanism (the IPsec AH mechanism is described in Chapter 14). Using such a mechanism, a screening router could be configured to drop and silently discard any IP packet that is not properly authenticated using a valid AH.

REFERENCES

[1] J. C. Mogul, "Simple and Flexible Datagram Access Controls for UNIX-Based Gateways," *Proceedings of the USENIX Summer Conference*, 1989, pp. 203–221.

[2] B. Cheswick, "The Design of a Secure Internet Gateway," *Proceedings of the USENIX Summer Conference*, 1990, pp. 233–237.

[3] M. J. Ranum, "A Network Firewall," *Proceedings of World Conference on System Administration and Security*, July 1992, pp. 153–163.

[4] D. B. Chapman, "Network (In)Security Through IP Packet Filtering," *Proceedings of USENIX UNIX Security Symposium III*, September 1992, pp. 63–76.

[5] F. Avolio and M. J. Ranum, "A Network Perimeter with Secure Internet Access," *Proceedings of the Internet Society Symposium on Network and Distributed System Security*, February 1994, pp. 109–119.

[6] Cisco Systems, *Cisco IOS 12.0 Configuration Fundamentals*, Cisco Press, 1999.

[7] Cisco Systems, *Cisco IOS 12.0 Network Security*, Cisco Press, 1999.

[8] M. Wenstrom (Ed.), *Managing Cisco Network Security*, Cisco Press, 2001.

[9] W. R. Cheswick and S. M. Bellovin, *Firewalls and Internet Security: Repelling the Wily Hacker*, Addison-Wesley, Reading, MA, 1994.

[10] S. M. Bellovin, "Firewall-Friendly FTP," Request for Comments 1579, February 1994.

[11] D. R. Safford, D. K. Hess, and D. L. Schales, "The TAMU Security Package: An Ongoing Response to Internet Intruders in an Academic Environment," *Proceedings of USENIX UNIX Security Symposium*, October 1993, pp. 91–118.

[12] K. Siyan and C. Hare, *Internet Firewalls and Network Security*, New Riders Publishing, Indianapolis, IN, 1995.

Chapter 9

Circuit-Level Gateways

In this chapter, we elaborate on circuit-level gateways in general, and one major implementation of a circuit-level gateway (i.e., SOCKS) in particular. More specifically, we briefly introduce the technology in Section 9.1, elaborate on SOCKS in Section 9.2, and draw some conclusions in Section 9.3. In summary, circuit-level gateways provide an interesting technology to build applications that provide support for authenticated firewall traversal. They are particularly interesting for applications for which application-level gateways (i.e., proxy servers) are not readily available.

9.1 INTRODUCTION

As already mentioned in Chapter 7, the idea of an application gateway is fundamentally different from a packet filter (i.e., a static or dynamic packet filter). This is equally true for a circuit-level gateway. In essence, a circuit-level gateway is a proxy server for TCP.[1] As illustrated in Figure 9.1, a circuit-level gateway is typically located and running on the firewall of a corporate intranet to relay TCP connections.

---

[1]This statement is not completely true, as contemporary circuit-level gateways also are able to handle UDP-based application protocols. This will be explained later in this chapter.

More specifically, the circuit-level gateway does the following three things when a client wants to establish a TCP connection to a destination server:

1. It receives the TCP connection establishment request that is sent out by the client (because the client is configured that way).

2. It authenticates and possibly authorizes the client (or the user behind the client).

3. It establishes a second TCP connection to the destination server on the client's behalf.

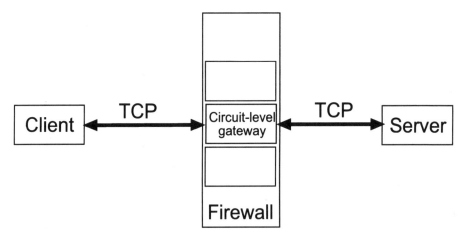

Figure 9.1   The placement and use of a circuit-level gateway.

After having successfully established the second TCP connection, the circuit-level gateway simply relays data forth and back between the two TCP connections. As such, it does not interfere with the data stream. This differentiates a circuit-level gateway from an application-level gateway or proxy server that is able to actually understand the application protocol employed by the two endpoints of the connection. What this basically means is that the circuit-level gateway must not understand the application protocol in use. This simplifies the implementation and deployment of circuit-level gateways considerably.

Note that the only difference between a circuit-level gateway and a simple port forwarding mechanism is that with a circuit-level gateway, the client is aware of the intermediate system, whereas in the case of a simple port-forwarding mechanism, the client must not be aware and may be completely oblivious of the existence of the intermediary. Also, a circuit-level gateway is generic, and any TCP connection can be handled by the same gateway (if enabled in its configuration). Contrary to that, a port-forwarding mechanism is usually specific to a given service, meaning that all qualifying TCP segments are forwarded to a specific port of the destination server.

The most important circuit-level gateway in use today is SOCKS.[2] SOCKS and the SOCKS protocols are currently being marketed by NEC USA, Inc. (e.g., as part of NEC's e-Border product line).

9.2   SOCKS

SOCKS is a circuit-level gateway that follows a customized client approach, meaning that it requires customizations and modifications to the client software (i.e., no change is usually required to user procedures). More precisely, SOCKS requires modifications either to the client software or the TCP/IP stack to accommodate the interception at the firewall between the client and the server:

- A client that has been modified to handle SOCKS interactions is commonly referred to as a *socksified client*. Following this terminology, Netscape Navigator and Microsoft Internet Explorer are both socksified clients, as they accommodate interactions with a SOCKS server. A socksified client issues SOCKS calls that are transparent to the users.

- Socksified TCP/IP stacks are also available, which may obviate the need for client software modifications.

In either case, the SOCKS server resides at the firewall and interacts with the socksified clients or TCP/IP stacks. There are no further changes required for the servers that may reside either on the Internet or intranet.

SOCKS and the original SOCKS protocol for communications between a socksified client and a SOCKS server were originally developed by David and Michelle Koblas and proposed in a paper at the 1992 USENIX Security Symposium [1]. The original implementation consisted of two components: a SOCKS server or daemon (i.e., sockd) and a SOCKS library that can be used to replace regular Sockets calls in the client software. More specifically, the application developer has to recompile

---

[2]http://www.socks.nec.com

Table 9.1
Sockets Calls and SOCKS Counterparts

SOCKS Call	Socket Call
Rconnect	connect
Rbind	bind
Rlisten	listen
Rselect	select
Rgetsockname	getsockname
Raccept	accept

and link the client software with a few preprocessor directives to intercept and replace the regular TCP/IP networking Sockets calls with their SOCKS counterparts, as summarized in Table 9.1. This is sufficiently easy to be used on a large scale.

The design goal of SOCKS was to provide a general framework for TCP/IP applications to securely use (and traverse) a firewall. Complying with these design goals, SOCKS is independent of any supported TCP/IP application protocol. When a socksified intranet client requires access to an destination server on the Internet, it must first open a TCP connection to the appropriate port on the SOCKS server residing on the firewall system (the SOCKS server conventionally listens at TCP port 1080). If this first TCP connection is established, the client uses the SOCKS protocol to have a second TCP connection to the destination server be established by the SOCKS server.

The SOCKS protocol used between the socksified client (i.e., the client using the SOCKS library routines) and the SOCKS server basically consists of the following two commands:

1. The CONNECT command takes as arguments the IP address and port number of the destination server, as well as a username. It basically requests that the SOCKS server establishes a TCP connection to the given IP address and port number.

2. The BIND command takes as arguments the client IP address and a username. It is used only in protocols that require the client to accept connections back from the destination server. As we have seen in Chapter 8, FTP is an example of such a protocol (since it requires the client to accept a data connection from the server).

In either case, the username is a string passed from the requesting client to the SOCKS server for the purposes of authentication, authorization, and accounting.

After having received a request (i.e., a CONNECT and/or BIND command), the SOCKS server evaluates the information provided by the client. The evaluation is performed against a `sockd` configuration file that may include a ruleset. Each rule in the set either permits or denies communications with one or several systems (the syntax of the rules is specified in [1]). In either case, the SOCKS server sends a reply back to the client. Among other things, the reply includes information indicating whether the request was successful. Once the requested second connection is established, the SOCKS server simply relays data back and forth between the client and the destination server (without looking into or interpreting the data stream).

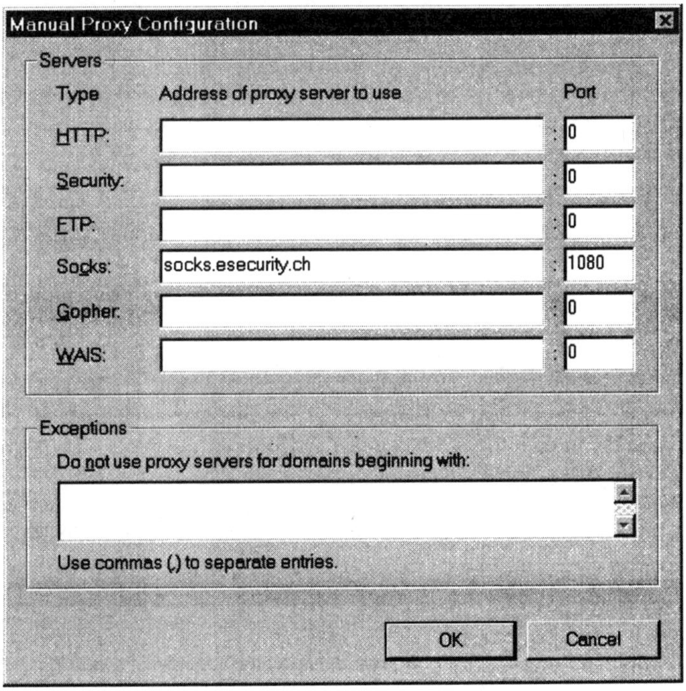

Figure 9.2   Manual Proxy Configuration menu of Netscape Navigator. © 2001 Netscape Communications Corporation.

The original SOCKS implementation of [1] was further refined into a SOCKS package and a protocol that is widely deployed and commonly referred to as SOCKS protocol version 4, or SOCKS V4. Many client software packages have been socksified in the past. For example, most Web browsers we use today (e.g., Netscape Navigator and Microsoft Internet Explorer) have been socksified. Figures 9.2 and 9.3 illustrate the corresponding manual proxy configuration and proxy settings menus of Netscape Navigator and Microsoft Internet Explorer. In either case, the browser is configured to make use of a SOCKS server that runs on port 1080 of a system with the host name `socks.esecurity.ch`.

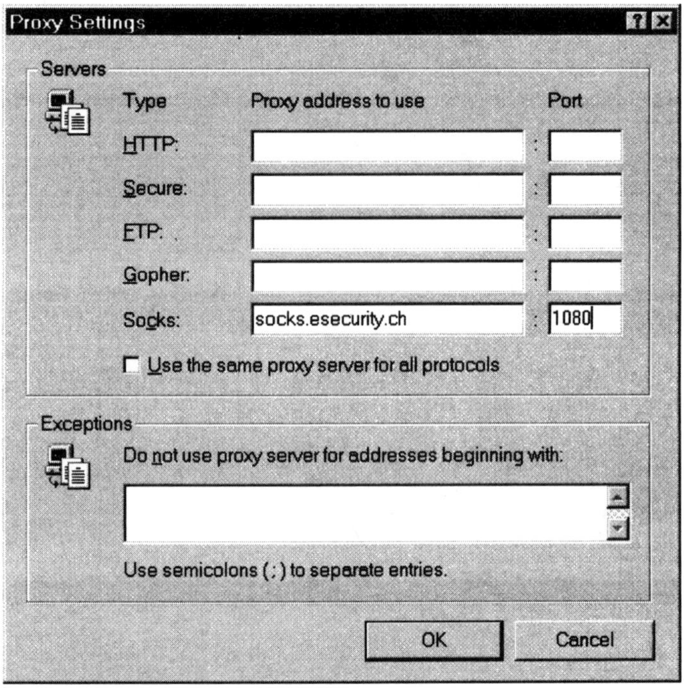

Figure 9.3   Proxy Settings menu of Microsoft Internet Explorer. © 2001 Microsoft Corporation.

After the successful deployment of SOCKS V4, the IETF chartered an Authenticated Firewall Traversal (AFT) WG to "start with the SOCKS system described" in [1], and to "specify a protocol to address the issue of application-layer support for firewall traversal" in 1994.[3] The major result of the IETF AFT WG was the specification of the SOCKS protocol version 5 (SOCKS V5) in March 1996 [2].[4] As such, SOCKS V5 has been submitted to the Internet standards track as a Proposed Standard. It is possible and very likely that the protocol will become an Internet Standard in the future.

As compared with SOCKS V4, SOCKS V5 provides some additional features. These features are related to user authentication, communication security, UDP support, and extended addressing schemes:

- In SOCKS V4, user authentication is relatively simple and straightforward. It basically consists of a username that is sent from the socksified client to the SOCKS server as part of the CONNECT or BIND method. In addition to this simple authentication scheme, SOCKS V5 supports a handshake between the client and the SOCKS server for authentication method negotiation. The first message is sent by the client to the SOCKS server. It declares the authentication methods the client is currently able to support. The second message is sent from the SOCKS server back to the client. It selects a particular authentication method according to the SOCKS server's security policy. If none of the methods declared by the client meets the security requirements of the SOCKS server, communications are dropped. After the authentication method has been negotiated, the client and SOCKS server start the authentication process using the chosen method. Two authentication methods are specified in corresponding RFC documents: password-based authentication in [3] and Kerberos V5 GSS-API authentication in [4].[5] The approach for use of GSS-API in SOCKS V5 is to authenticate the client and server by successfully establishing a security context. This context can then be used to protect messages that are subsequently exchanged. Prior to use of GSS-API primitives, the client and server should be locally authenticated and have established default GSS-API credentials.

- Depending on the underlying authentication methods implemented via GSS-API, a client can negotiate with the SOCKS server about the security of subsequent messages. In the case of Kerberos V5, either integrity and/or confidentiality services are provided for the rest of messages, including the client's requests, the SOCKS server's replies, and all application data. Note that this feature is

---

[3]http://www.ietf.org/html.charters/aft-charter.html

[4]At the time of this writing, an updated version of the SOCKS protocol version 5 specification is published as an Internet-Draft.

[5]The term *GSS-API* will be explained when we discuss the Kerberos authentication system and its application programming interface (API) in Section 16.2.

particularly well suited for use by reverse proxy servers, because it supports data encryption between clients (on the Internet) and the SOCKS server.

- As mentioned, SOCKS V4 is only able to handle TCP applications. Unfortunately, an increasingly large number of TCP/IP applications are making use of UDP (e.g., applications that make use of real-time and/or multicast communications). Against this background, the SOCKS protocol has been extended to additionally provide support for UDP. More specifically, a new method, called UDP ASSOCIATE, has been added to the SOCKS V5 protocol specification [2]. The UDP ASSOCIATE request sent from the client to the SOCKS server is used to establish an association within the UDP relay process to handle UDP datagrams. According to this association, the SOCKS server relays UDP datagrams to the requesting client. Obviously, this approach is conceptually similar to stateful inspection or dynamic packet filtering as discussed in Chapter 8. The UDP association terminates when the TCP connection that the UDP ASSOCIATE request arrived on terminates. As a result, the SOCKS V5 library can now be used to socksify both TCP- and UDP-based applications.

- Finally, SOCKS V5 supports DNS names and IP version 6 addresses in addition to normal IP version 4 addresses.

Because of their fundamental differences, the SOCKS V5 protocol specification does not require any provision for supporting the SOCKS V4 protocol. However, it is a simple matter of implementation to enable SOCKS V5 servers to communicate with V5 and V4 clients. In fact, most SOCKS V5 servers that are available today provide this backward compatibility.

9.3   CONCLUSIONS

In summary, a circuit-level gateway (e.g., a SOCKS server) provides an interesting technology and possibility to have applications and application protocols securely traverse a firewall. A clear advantage of circuit-level gateways is their generality, meaning that a circuit-level gateway can act as a proxy server for any TCP-based application and application protocol (not just one of them). This generality, however, also has negative impacts on security. For example, a SOCKS server is not able to scan application data for specific commands or executable content (e.g., Java applets or ActiveX controls).

Circuit-level gateways are particularly useful for applications and application protocols for which application-level gateways (i.e., proxy servers) do not exist or are conceptually hard to design and implement. For example, many application programs (e.g., Web browsers) are distributed in socksified form. Other application programs can be socksified if the client software is available in source code (since it must be recompiled and linked with the SOCKS library). Note that this requirement is quite strong and does not generally apply for proprietary and commercially distributed software packages. It does, however, apply for an increasingly large number of software packages that are distributed under an open source licensing agreement. These packages can easily be modified and extended to make use of SOCKS.

One application protocol that is particularly hard to deal with (using packet-filtering technologies and application-level gateways) is the Internet Inter-ORB Protocol that is widely used in environments and applications that conform to the Common Object Request Broker Architecture (CORBA). The difficulty stems from the fact that the IIOP makes heavy use of UDP and dynamically assigned port numbers. Against this background, a group of vendors have jointly specified the use of SOCKS V5 to have IIOP communications securely traverse a firewall.[6] This is likely to be something we are going to see deployed in the future.

REFERENCES

[1] D. Koblas and M. R. Koblas, "SOCKS," *Proceedings of USENIX UNIX Security III Symposium*, September 1992, pp. 77–82.

[2] M. Leech, et al., "SOCKS Protocol Version 5," Request for Comments 1928, March 1996.

[3] M. Leech, "Username/Password Authentication for SOCKS V5," Request for Comments 1929, March 1996.

[4] P. McMahon, "GSS-API Authentication Method for SOCKS Version 5," Request for Comments 1961, June 1996.

---

[6]http://www.socks.nec.com/corba-firewall.pdf

Chapter 10

Application-Level Gateways

In this chapter, we elaborate on application-level gateways and proxy servers. More specifically, we introduce the technology in Section 10.1, elaborate on user authentication and authorization in Section 10.2, overview some proxy servers in Section 10.3, and draw some conclusions in Section 10.4.

10.1 INTRODUCTION

Remember from our previous discussions that an application gateway can either work at the transport or application layer, and that one distinguishes between circuit-level gateways and application-level gateways accordingly. Circuit-level gateways have been overviewed and discussed in Chapter 9, whereas application-level gateways are addressed in this chapter.

To clarify the difference between a circuit-level gateway and an application-level gateway, imagine the situation in which the packet filter of a firewall configuration blocks all inbound Telnet and FTP sessions, unless the sessions are terminated by a bastion host (that is also part of the firewall configuration). The bastion host, in turn, hosts an application gateway that operates at the transport or application layer. The situation is slightly different in either case:

171

- If the application gateway operates at the transport layer, a circuit-level gateway (e.g., a SOCKS server) must be running on the bastion host.

- If the application gateway operates at the application layer, there are basically two application-level gateways or proxy servers that must be running on the bastion host (i.e., a proxy server for Telnet and another proxy server for FTP).

In either case, a user who wishes to connect inbound to an intranet server must have his or her Telnet or FTP client connect to the application gateway running on the bastion host. The application gateway, in turn, would then authenticate and authorize the user. In the positive case, it would set up a secondary TCP connection to the intranet server and relay application data between the two TCP connections back and forth. If the application gateway is a circuit-level gateway, it would not look into the application data it relays. If, however, the application gateway is an application-level gateway, it would be able to look into and fully control the application data stream. In an attempt to make it hard to retrieve internal files from systems located on the Internet, an application-level gateway could, for example, be configured in a way that permits the use of the FTP PUT command but denies the use of the FTP GET command. Similarly, an application-level gateway for HTTP could be configured to screen data traffic and filter out Java applets and ActiveX controls to protect internal hosts from executable content and software-driven attacks. This kind of filtering is simply not possible in the case of a circuit-level gateway.

From the client's point of view, interaction with an application gateway requires some additional steps. This is equally true for circuit-level gateways and application-level gateways. In the case of a SOCKS server we saw in Chapter 9 that the additional steps are hidden from the user and that the corresponding client software must be modified to be aware of the SOCKS server (i.e., it must be "socksified").

In general, the use of an application gateway requires some customization and modification of either user procedures or client software:

- The customization and modification of user procedures is an obvious approach to implement application gateway support. Following this approach, the user first establishes a connection to the application gateway and then requests the establishment of a second connection to the destination server. An important benefit is that the customization of user procedures, in general, requires no impact to client software. Given the extensive presence of client software, this approach is attractive for implementing Internet access (in fact, the first Internet firewalls worked that way). The main disadvantage of this approach is that the user has to be trained for an extra step to logon to the proxy server. For organizations that have been using TCP/IP applications for a long time, the corresponding user training may be a time-consuming and expensive process.

- The other approach to implement application gateway support is to customize and modify the client software (similar to the process of "socksifying" a client). The main advantage of this approach is that it may provide transparency to users in accessing the Internet and traversing firewall systems. The main disadvantage, however, is that it obviously requires modifications to client software. This is not always possible, and is very seldom easy to accomplish.

Note that both approaches to implement application gateway support have severe disadvantages, as they require customization and modification of either user procedures or client software. Consequently, it would be nice to have a firewall that maintains all software modifications required for application gateway support in the firewall. In this case, neither the user procedures nor the client software would have to be customized or modified accordingly. This idea has led to the development of transparent firewalls. In fact, many vendors have come up with transparent firewall products in the past.

In short, a *transparent firewall* is configured to listen on the network segment of the firewall for outgoing TCP connections and to autonomously relay these connections on the client's behalf. Note, however, that transparency is not necessarily provided in both directions. As a matter of fact, inbound transparency is seldom required or used, as users must usually authenticate themselves at a firewall system. Also note that a transparent firewall still requires that all messages to and from the Internet be transmitted through the firewall. However, the existence of the firewall system can be hidden entirely from both the users and the clients. We will return to the idea of transparent firewalls when we talk about network address translation (NAT) in Chapter 11.

We will have a closer look at an example in which a Telnet client tries to connect to a Telnet server making use of a proxy server, as illustrated in Figure 10.1. Note that the black rectangle that is part of the firewall represents the Telnet proxy server. Also note the similarity of Figure 10.1 to Figure 9.1. The only differences are that the SOCKS server in Figure 9.1 is replaced with a Telnet proxy server in Figure 10.1, and that the two TCP connections in Figure 9.1 are replaced with Telnet sessions in Figure 10.1. The procedure to establish a Telnet session can be summarized as follows:

1. The Telnet client acting on behalf of the user requests a TCP connection to the Telnet proxy server running on the firewall (at an arbitrary but fixed port number). If a screening router is put in front of the firewall, the connection must be authorized according to the packet-filtering rules.

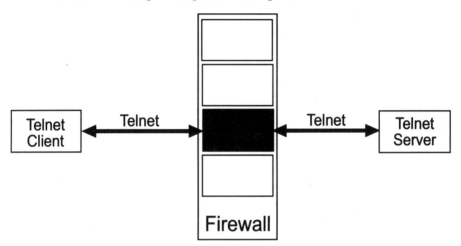

Figure 10.1   The placement and use of a Telnet proxy server.

2. The Telnet proxy server, in turn, checks the source IP address of the client machine. The connection request is accepted or rejected according to some preconfigured access control information.

3. In addition to the source IP address check of the client machine, the user may also need to authenticate himself or herself (e.g., using a username and password).

4. If the user is properly authenticated, the client must provide the address or name of the destination Telnet server (again, this step can be and will be made transparent to the user).

5. The Telnet proxy server then establishes a second TCP connection to the Telnet destination server. Again, this connection request may have to pass through a screening router. In this case, the packet-filtering rules of the screening router must be configured so that they let packets through that are originated by a firewall system.

6. After having established the second TCP connection to the Telnet destination server, the Telnet proxy server relays Telnet data between the two connections. In addition, the Telnet proxy server also may scan the data traffic for specific Telnet commands and filter them out. Also, the Telnet proxy server may log all command executions to build an audit trail.

To properly authenticate the user, the Telnet proxy server must have access to some identification and authentication information. This is generally true for any application-level gateway or proxy server that provides support for user-level authentication (not only for a Telnet proxy server). User authentication and authorization are addressed next.

10.2 USER AUTHENTICATION AND AUTHORIZATION

As mentioned in Section 10.1, one of the key functionalities of an application-level gateway or proxy server is user authentication and authorization. In Section 6.1, we overviewed and briefly discussed several user authentication schemes that can be used by an application-level gateway or proxy server. For example, HTTP version 1.1 specifies a Basic authentication mechanism in which the client sends the username and password in the clear (i.e., in Base-64 encoded form) to the HTTP proxy server [1]. Contrary to that, a more sophisticated and more secure Digest authentication mechanism is specified in [2]. Following this specification, a one-way hash is computed from the username, the password, a challenge provided by the proxy server, and some additional information. The resulting authentication mechanism is more secure because user passwords are never transmitted in the clear.

In general, there are several user authentication and authorization schemes that an application-level gateway or proxy server could implement and use:

- The simplest scheme is notably to have a proxy server hold a pair of lists of client IP addresses that are allowed to connect inbound (first list) or outbound (second list). Obviously, this scheme is not very secure, since IP spoofing is possible and can be used to spoof authorized IP addresses to get intranet or Internet access.

- Another scheme is to have a client (or user) and a proxy server share a secret, such as a password. When the client connects to the proxy server, the server requests the secret, and the client has to provide it. If the secret is transmitted in the clear, the resulting authentication scheme is weak (i.e., a passive attacker gets authentication information he or she can reuse to spoof a legitimate user). The HTTP Basic authentication mechanism is an example of a weak authentication scheme. In such a scheme, authorization is done implicitly, meaning that someone equipped with a shared secret is also authorized to gain intranet or Internet access.

- A more secure scheme is to use strong authentication mechanisms to have users authenticate to a proxy server, and to handle authorization accordingly. In this case, it is no longer possible for a user to simply spoof the IP address of another user's authorized client machine to get Internet access. Examples of strong authentication mechanisms include HTTP Digest authentication as mentioned earlier, as well as one-time password and challenge-response mechanisms.

In practice, the firewall policy must define the authentication and authorization schemes that must be used in either direction and for each service. Many policies use the simplest scheme mentioned above for outbound connections and a strong authentication scheme for inbound connections.

In either case, the application-level gateway or proxy server must have access to some reference information it can use to verify whether the authentication information provided by a client (or user) is valid and legitimate (e.g., a one-way hash value of a user password or the public key certificate of a user). The reference information can be stored either locally or remotely. For obvious reasons, the second approach is preferable since it makes it possible to aggregate security information and functions for several firewall systems and network access servers (NAS) at a single point. Typically, a standardized protocol is used to retrieve the reference information from a centralized security server. There are currently two competing protocol proposals:

- Livingston Enterprises, Inc., has developed and implemented a protocol called Remote Authentication Dial-In User Service (RADIUS) [3].[1] In short, the RADIUS protocol can be used to carry authentication, authorization, and configuration information between an NAS that desires to authenticate its users and a shared authentication or security server. Livingston Enterprises, Inc., also has made publicly and freely available corresponding RADIUS security server software. A companion protocol that can be used to carry accounting information between an NAS and a shared authentication or security server server is specified in [4].

- The terminal access controller access control system (TACACS) was originally developed by BBN under ARPA funding in the early 1980s. It was used to authenticate users to terminal access computers on the ARPANET. Later, Cisco

---

[1]As of this writing, the RADIUS protocol has reached the status of a Draft Standard.

Systems developed, implemented, and deployed a family of protocols that are based on TACACS [5]. While the TACACS and extended TACACS (XTACACS) protocols are no longer in use, TACACS+ is a protocol in current use. Refer to the Cisco manuals for the corresponding TACACS, XTACACS, and TACACS+ commands.

Both protocols (RADIUS and the protocol family for the TACACS derivates) are widely supported by commercial firewall systems and network access servers. They are not further addressed in this book.

There also are some alternative proposals to handle user authentication reference information. For example, some time ago, Ravi Ganesan implemented an application gateway that uses the Kerberos[2] system to authenticate connection requests [6]. Once the application gateway has satisfied itself about the identity of the requesting user, it establishes a corresponding connection to the destination server.

After having successfully authenticated and authorized the client (or user), the proxy server sets up a secondary TCP connection to the requested application server. From the user's point of view, a secondary authentication may now be required and actually take place, since the application server may want to authenticate and authorize the client (or user) as well. This secondary authentication step is beyond the scope of the firewall. If the user is successfully authenticated and authorized, the application server usually starts serving the request.

10.3 PROXY SERVERS

Because proxy servers run at the application layer, separate servers are usually required for each application. Commercial firewalls typically come along with proxy server support for Telnet, FTP, SMTP, HTTP, and many other TCP-based applications and application protocols. Refer to Figures 9.2 and 9.3 for illustrations of the panels that can be used to configure the various proxy servers for Netscape Navigator and Microsoft Internet Explorer. Other software packages use similar panels to configure relevant proxies.

In addition to commercial firewalls that come along with many application-level gateways and proxy servers, there are also software packages that can be used to build and customize firewall systems. For example, in the early 1990s, Trusted

---

[2]We address the Kerberos system in Section 16.2, when we talk about authentication and key distribution systems.

Information Systems, Inc.,[3] developed an Internet Firewall Toolkit (FWTK) that is widely used and deployed on the Internet [7]. Because the TIS FWTK is written in the C programming language it should, with some effort at portability, run on most versions of the UNIX operating system. It is important to note that the TIS FWTK does not constitute a turnkey firewall solution, but rather provides the components from which an application-level gateway can be assembled and built. Components of the FWTK, while designed to work together, also can be used in isolation or can be combined with other firewall software components. The TIS FWTK provides proxy servers for most TCP-based applications in use today, such as Telnet, Rlogin, FTP, HTTP, Gopher, SMTP, NNTP, and X11. Also, the toolkit provides an authentication server that all proxy servers can use. The authentication server, in turn, supports many authentication mechanisms, ranging from simple passwords to one-time passwords and challenge-response mechanisms (e.g., S/Key, SecureNet Key, and SecurID). Also, the toolkit supports several firewall configurations, including dual-homed firewalls, screened host firewalls, and screened subnet firewalls.

The TIS FWTK software was officially released in October 1993. It is publicly and freely available but is copyrighted and must be licensed for commercial use.[4] Much of the functionality of the commercial Gauntlet Firewall from Network Associates, Inc., is built on top of the FWTK.

10.4   CONCLUSIONS

Application-level gateways and proxy servers provide a sophisticated and advanced technology to secure TCP-based applications and application protocols for the Internet. There are advantages and disadvantages that should be kept in mind when discussing the suitability of application-level gateways and proxy servers:

- The advantages are related to user authentication and authorization, application protocol control, logging, and accounting. We have discussed user authentication and authorization, as well as application protocol control in Section 10.2. In regard to the other points, it is important to note that an application gateway always acts as an intermediate that can handle logging and accounting in a simple and straightforward way.

---

[3]As mentioned in Chapter 7, Trusted Information Systems, Inc., was acquired by Network Associates, Inc.

[4]Refer to the README file found at `ftp://ftp.tis.com/pub/firewalls/toolkit/`.

- The major disadvantages are related to the following points:

  - A proxy server must be built specifically for each application protocol. In other words, if a firewall hosts proxy servers for Telnet and FTP, then only Telnet and FTP traffic is allowed into and out of the protected area of the intranet, and all other services must be blocked. In many cases, this degree of security is important, as it guarantees that only those services that are considered trustworthy are actually allowed through the firewall. It also prevents other untrusted services from being implemented behind the backs of the firewall administrator. This fact may severely limit the usefulness and deployment of new applications.

  - Application gateways (i.e., circuit-level and application-level gateways) are notoriously bad at handling UDP-based application protocols.

  - Finally, note that to code and set up a proxy server, one must at least know the application protocol. This is not always the case, because proprietary application protocols are in widespread use today (e.g., Lotus Notes, SQLnet, and SAP). If an application protocol specification is not available it is generally not possible to implement a proxy server.[5] Consequently, proprietary application protocols are inherently difficult to be handled with application-level gateways and proxy servers.

Against this background (i.e., the second disadvantage), an interesting field of study refers to the secure handling of multicast traffic. Note that multicast traffic, as deployed on the Multicast Backbone (MBone), is based on UDP as a transport layer protocol. MBone holds great potential for many organizations because it supports low-cost audio- and video-conferencing and carries live broadcasts of an increasing number of public interest events. MBone conferences are transmitted by way of unauthenticated multicast traffic, which unfortunately conveys significant security vulnerabilities to any system that receives them. For this reason, most application gateways block MBone traffic sent from the Internet and prevent it from reaching internal hosts. It is not until recently that firewall vendors have begun to address the UDP and multicast challenge. For example, in 1999, Trusted Information Systems, Inc., extended its set of proxy servers for the FWTK version 2.0 with a set of facilities that can be used to participate in MBone conferencing [8]. The basic idea is to have proxy servers running on the

---

[5]It would still be possible, if the application protocol were reverse-engineered.

firewall that forward inbound multicast traffic using unicast addressing on the corporate intranet. Obviously, this approach is appropriate for individual users participating in MBone conferencing. However, this approach is not very efficient and may run into scalability problems if too many users on the corporate intranet want to participate in multicast sessions. In this case, the efficiency advantages of multicast routing are entirely lost.

Now that the basic components of a firewall configuration (i.e., packet filters and application gateways) have been introduced and examined, we can combine them to provide some higher levels of security and flexibility than if either were used alone. In Chapter 11 we provide some examples of firewall configurations to give a more concrete and comprehensive understanding of the firewall technology as a whole.

REFERENCES

[1] R. Fielding, et al., "Hypertext Transfer Protocol—HTTP/1.1," Request for Comments 2068, January 1997.

[2] J. Franks, et al., "An Extension to HTTP: Digest Access Authentication," Request for Comments 2069, January 1997.

[3] C. Rigney, et al., "Remote Authentication Dial-In User Service (RADIUS)," Request for Comments 2138, April 1997.

[4] C. Rigney, "RADIUS Accounting," Request for Comments 2139, April 1997.

[5] C. Finseth, "An Access Control Protocol, Sometimes Called TACACS," Request for Comments 1492, July 1993.

[6] R. Ganesan, "BAfirewall: A Modern Design," *Proceedings of Internet Society Symposium on Network and Distributed System Security*, February 1994.

[7] F. Avolio and M. J. Ranum, "A Network Perimeter with Secure External Access," *Proceedings of Internet Society Symposium on Network and Distributed System Security*, February 1994.

[8] K. Djahandri and D. F. Sterne, "An MBone Proxy for a Firewall Toolkit," *Proceedings of IEEE Symposium on Security and Privacy*, Oakland, CA, May 1997.

Chapter 11

Firewall Configurations

A firewall configuration typically consists of packet filters and application gateways (i.e., circuit-level and application-level gateways). In theory, there are many possibilities to combine these components. In practice, however, there are only three firewall configurations that are used and widely deployed on the Internet [1, 2]. In Sections 11.1 to 11.3, we overview and briefly discuss dual-homed firewall, screened host firewall, and screened subnet firewall configurations. Furthermore, we address network address translation (NAT) in Section 11.4, possibilities to protect a firewall against denial of service attacks in Section 11.5, and firewall certification in Section 11.6.

11.1 DUAL-HOMED FIREWALL CONFIGURATIONS

In TCP/IP parlance, the term *multihomed host* refers to a host with multiple network interfaces. Usually, each network interface is connected to a separate network segment and the multihomed host can typically forward or route IP packets between those network segments. If, however, IP forwarding and IP routing are disabled on the multihomed host, it provides isolation between the network segments and may be used in a firewall configuration accordingly. To disable IP routing is usually a relatively simple and straightforward task. It basically means to turn off any program that might be advertising the host as a router. To disable IP forwarding is considerably more difficult and may require modifying the operating system kernel. Fortunately, a number of operating system vendors provide a simple possibility to make this kernel modification and to turn off IP forwarding accordingly.

A dual-homed host is a special case of a multihomed host, namely one that has exactly two network interfaces. Again, IP routing and IP forwarding can be disabled to provide isolation between the two network segments the dual-homed host interconnects.

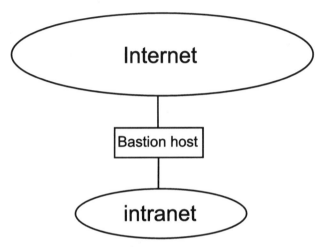

Figure 11.1   A simple dual-homed firewall configuration.

As illustrated in Figure 11.1, a simple *dual-homed firewall* configuration may consist of a dual-homed host (i.e., a host with two network interfaces) that serves as a bastion host. IP routing and IP forwarding are disabled so that IP packets can no longer be routed or forwarded between the two network interfaces. Consequently, any data received from one network interface and sent to the other network interface must be processed by an application-level process (i.e., the application gateway) running on the bastion host. Note that Figure 11.1 is simplified in the sense that the routers are not illustrated (they are assumed to be part of the intranet and Internet environments).

Contrary to Figure 11.1, Figure 11.2 illustrates a more realistic configuration of a dual-homed firewall. In this configuration, the bastion host's external network interface is connected to an outer network segment and the bastion host's internal network interface is connected to an inner network segment:

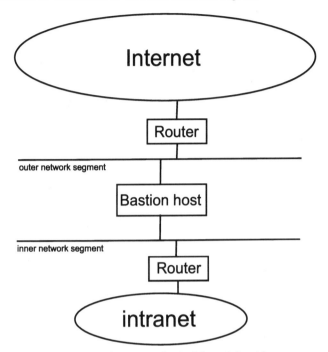

Figure 11.2 A more realistic configuration of a dual-homed firewall.

- The outer network segment hosts a screening router that is interconnected (and serves as an access router) to the Internet. The aim of the screening router is to ensure that any outbound IP packet carries the IP address of the bastion host as its source IP address, and that any inbound IP packet carries the IP address of the bastion host as its destination IP address. The packet-filtering rules must be configured accordingly.

- Similarly, the inner network segment hosts a screening router that is interconnected to the intranet. The aim of this screening router is to make sure that any outbound IP packet carries the IP address of the bastion host as its destination IP address, and that any inbound IP packet carries the IP address of the bastion host as its source IP address. Again, the packet-filtering rules must be configured accordingly.

In the firewall configuration illustrated in Figure 11.2, the outer network segment can also be used to host specific (noncritical) server systems, such as public Web servers, DNS servers with public information, or access servers for other networks (e.g., modem pools for the PSTN or ISDN). This is common practice to make server systems and corresponding services publicly available and accessible from the Internet. In some literature, the outer network segment is labeled "red" and the inner network segment is labeled "blue" to refer to their different sensitivity and security status.

It is fairly obvious that the bastion host (and the application gateways running on it) can be replicated an arbitrary number of times in a dual-homed firewall configuration (e.g., to improve throughput). The resulting configuration is sometimes also called a *parallel dual-homed firewall*. It may consist of several bastion hosts that are all connected to the same inner and outer network segments.

The dual-homed firewall is a simple and highly secure firewall configuration. The security originates from the fact that all data must pass an application gateway to get from one network interface of the bastion host to the other. There is no possibility of bypassing the bastion host or its application gateways. There are, however, also several disadvantages that are important in practice, and that should be considered with care accordingly:

1. Performance is a problem because the bastion host may become a bottleneck (note that all data must pass the bastion host).

2. The bastion host represents a single point of failure. If it crashes, Internet connectivity is also lost.

3. There are some practical problems related to TCP/IP application protocols with no proxy support (e.g., proprietary protocols). In this case, the dual-homed firewall configuration turns out to be rather inflexible, and this inflexibility could turn out to be disadvantageous.

In summary, the dual-homed firewall configuration is used and widely deployed on the Internet. It is highly secure but rather inflexible. Contrary to this, the screened host and screened subnet firewall configurations discussed next are more flexible but also less secure. Consequently, where throughput and flexibility are important or required, these configurations may in fact be the preferable choices.

11.2   SCREENED HOST FIREWALL CONFIGURATIONS

As illustrated in Figure 11.3, a *screened host firewall* configuration basically consists of a screening router that interconnects the intranet to the Internet, and a bastion host that is logically situated on the intranet. Contrary to the bastion host of a dual-homed firewall, the bastion host of a screened host firewall is single-homed, meaning that it has only one network interface that interconnects it with an internal network segment (i.e., a network segment that is part of the intranet).

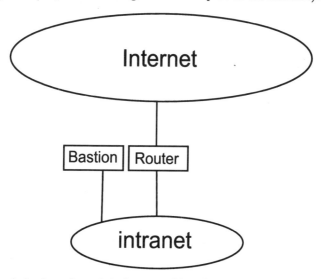

Figure 11.3   A simple configuration of a screened host firewall.

In a screened host firewall configuration, the screening router has to make sure that IP packets destined for intranet systems are first sent to an appropriate application gateway on the bastion host. If a specific TCP/IP application protocol is assumed to be "secure," the screening router also can be configured to bypass the bastion host and to send the corresponding IP packets directly to the destination system. For very obvious reasons, this possibly increases flexibility but also decreases security.

Similar to the dual-homed firewall configuration, the bastion host and its application gateways can also be replicated an arbitrary number of times in the screened host firewall configuration. In fact, this is likely to be the preferred configuration, as different application gateways are typically running on different hosts (all of them representing bastion hosts for the applications they serve as a gateway).

In summary, the screened host firewall configuration is very simple and straight-forward. As compared with the dual-homed firewall configuration, it is more flexible but also potentially less secure. This is because the bastion host can be bypassed (by configuring the screening router that interconnects the intranet and the Internet accordingly). Due to the dual-homed nature of the bastion host, this is not possible in the dual-homed firewall configuration.

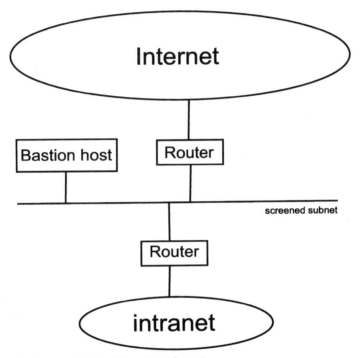

Figure 11.4   A screened subnet firewall configuration.

11.3   SCREENED SUBNET FIREWALL CONFIGURATIONS

As illustrated in Figure 11.4, a *screened subnet firewall* configuration basically con-sists of a subnet that is screened by a single-homed bastion host. The outer screening router has to make sure that all (or at least most) data pass an application gateway running on a bastion host. Consequently, the bastion host screens the subnet located between the outer and the inner screening router, and this screened subnet is sometimes also referred to as a *demilitarized zone* (DMZ).[1]

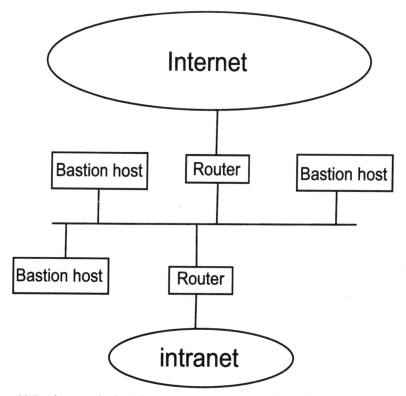

Figure 11.5   A screened subnet firewall configuration with multiple bastion hosts.

Similar to the other configurations discussed thus far, the bastion host also can be replicated an arbitrary number of times in a screened subnet firewall configuration. A corresponding screened subnet firewall configuration with multiple bastion hosts is illustrated in Figure 11.5. The big advantage of this configuration is that dedicated hosts can be used to provide specific services. The resulting separation

---

[1]The DMZ is named after the strip of no-man's-land between North and South Korea.

of servers and services is an interesting feature from a security point of view.

Note that the two screening routers provide redundancy in that an attacker would have to subvert both routers in order to access intranet systems. Also note that the bastion host and the additional servers on the DMZ could be set up to be the only systems seen from the Internet; no other system name would be known or used in a DNS database that is made accessible to the outside world.

A screened subnet firewall configuration can be made more flexible by permitting certain services to pass around the bastion host and the corresponding application gateways. As an alternative to passing services directly between the intranet and Internet, you may also locate the systems that need these services directly on the screened subnet. In fact, this would be the preferred configuration but is not always possible.

In summary, the screened subnet firewall configuration is flexible and provides a reasonable level of security. As such, it has been a preferred firewall configuration in the past.

11.4   NETWORK ADDRESS TRANSLATION

Many contemporary firewall systems provide support for what is known as *network address translation* (NAT). NAT basically means that an organization can use private IP addresses on its own network (i.e., the intranet) to increase its address space. If IP packets are sent to the Internet, the private IP addresses are dynamically converted to IP addresses that have been officially assigned to the organization and that are routable on the Internet. Similarly, if IP packets are received from the Internet, the officially assigned IP addresses are converted back to the appropriate private IP addresses. Based on the private IP addresses, the IP packets are then routed on the intranet to their appropriate destination.

In RFC 1918 and BCP 5 [3], three blocks of the IP address space are reserved for private use. The blocks are summarized in Table 11.1.

Table 11.1
Private IP Address Blocks (According to [3])

10.0.0.0	- 10.255.255.255	24-bit block
172.16.0.0	- 172.31.255.255	20-bit block
192.168.0.0	- 192.168.255.255	16-bit block

A firewall that supports NAT works similarly to a transparent firewall. IP packets with unknown destination IP addresses are routed to the network segment that hosts the firewall configuration. The firewall, in turn, grabs the the IP packets that request a TCP connection establishment and establishes the connection on behalf of the client. In addition, a firewall that supports NAT also substitutes the private IP addresses (used on the intranet) with officially assigned IP addresses (used on the Internet). Obviously, this substitution is reversed in the opposite direction.

For example, we assume a company that is officially assigned an IP class C address. For its internal use, the company uses IP addresses from the 20-bit block itemized in Table 11.1 (i.e., 172.16.0.0 to 172.31.255.255). As illustrated in Figure 11.6, an FTP client (on the left) with a private IP address C wants to retrieve a file from a destination FTP server with IP address S located somewhere on the Internet (on the right). Therefore, the client makes use of a transparent firewall with IP address F (in the middle). The transparent firewall, in turn, actively supports NAT.

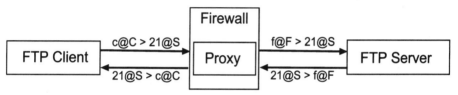

Figure 11.6   A firewall supporting NAT.

In this situation, the following steps are performed to establish a connection between the FTP client and the FTP server:

1. The FTP client sends out a TCP connection establishment request message to port 21 of the destination FTP server (the notation c@C > 21@S indicates that a message is sent out from source IP address C and port number c to destination IP address S and port number 21). Because the FTP server is not directly reachable by the client, the message is forwarded to the network segment that hosts the firewall and its proxy servers.

2. The FTP proxy server of the firewall grabs the initial TCP connection establishment request message, authenticates and authorizes the user, and eventually forwards the message to the destination FTP server. In this case, however, the message source is initialized with an IP address F and a randomly chosen and

dynamically assigned port number (the port number is specific for this particular FTP session).

3. The destination FTP server receives the TCP connection establishment request message and eventually establishes a TCP connection to the FTP proxy server. Any FTP command that is sent out by the FTP client is then automatically forwarded by the FTP proxy server to the destination FTP server.

In the opposite direction, FTP application data are sent from the destination FTP server to the proxy server of the firewall, and from the proxy server to the FTP client. Note that in this direction, the source IP address is usually not substituted by the proxy server, and that officially assigned IP addresses may appear on the intranet accordingly (in the source IP address fields).

Transparent application gateways provide the most recent and most sophisticated firewall technology available today. Whenever possible, this technology should be the preferred one to use, as it does not require user procedures or client software to be modified. Unfortunately, most firewalls that implement this technology also must use NAT. The IETF has debated NAT for some time and there is considerable feeling that it is an unfortunate technical approach that is justified only when an organization is unable to acquire adequate IP address space. Because of its increased address space, the use and wide deployment of IPv6 will make NAT obsolete in the future.

11.5   PROTECTION AGAINST DENIAL OF SERVICE

In Chapter 3, we introduced and briefly discussed the TCP SYN flooding attack. In this attack, a number of TCP SYN messages are sent to a server to flood its backlog queue. Unfortunately, this attack is always possible and protection against it requires some major modifications in TCP and the way TCP connections are established (e.g., the use of SYN cookies). These modifications will take some time to be specified, standardized, implemented, and deployed. When they become available, it is strongly recommended to install them on all systems as soon as possible.

In the meantime, there are ad hoc solutions offered by some firewall vendors. For example, CheckPoint Software Technologies, Ltd., offers a tool called SYNDefender for its FireWall-1 customers. In fact, the SYNDefender provides two different solutions for the problem of protecting internal systems against TCP SYN flooding attacks: SYNDefender Relay and SYNDefender Gateway.

The *SYNDefender Relay* protects an internal system by making sure that a three-way TCP connection establishment handshake with an external host is completed (i.e., the connection is valid) before an initial SYN message is sent to the internal system. More specifically, the SYNDefender Relay that resides on the firewall and receives a SYN message from an external system returns a SYN-ACK message to that system. The external system must then finish the connection establishment with an ACK message, before the SYNDefender Relay establishes a secondary TCP connection to the internal system on the external system's behalf. From then on, the SYNDefender Relay simply relays data between the two TCP connections back and forth. The corresponding message flows are illustrated on the top of Figure 11.7. Note that one of the key capabilities the SYNDefender Relay employs is the ability to translate the sequence numbers, which are now different for either connection.

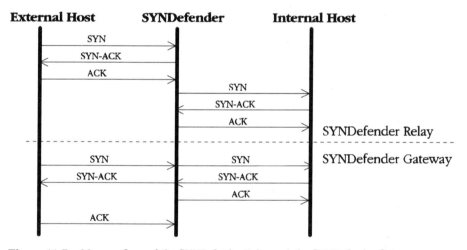

Figure 11.7   Message flows of the SYNDefender Relay and the SYNDefender Gateway.

For the resetting of SYN connection attempts to be effective against the TCP SYN flooding attack, the reset timer must be small enough to keep the internal system's backlog queue from filling up, while at the same time being big enough to allow users coming over slow links to connect. The *SYNDefender Gateway* solution surmounts this problem by making sure that an ACK message is sent in immediate response to the internal system's SYN-ACK message. When the internal system receives the ACK message, the connection is moved out of the backlog queue and becomes an open connection. Again, the SYNDefender Gateway resides on the firewall. Whenever it receives a SYN message from an external system, it simply forwards the message to the internal system. The internal system, in turn, sends back a SYN-ACK message that the SYNDefender Gateway forwards to the external system. In addition, the SYNDefender Gateway returns an ACK message to the internal system to establish the connection. If a proper ACK message from the external system is received within a certain time frame, the destined connection is established and the SYNDefender Gateway simply relays data back and forth. If, however, the SYNDefender Gateway does not receive a proper ACK message from the external system, it closes the connection by sending an RST message to the internal system. The message flows of the SYNDefender Gateway are illustrated at the bottom of Figure 11.7.

The main advantage of the SYNDefender Relay is that the internal system will not receive any invalid connection establishment request. If the host has limited memory or often reaches an overloaded state, then the SYNDefender Relay's filtering of invalid connection establishment requests might be advantageous in the event of an attack. Users making connections to an internal system may, however, experience a slightly longer connection setup time, which is not the case with the SYNDefender Gateway solution.

11.6 FIREWALL CERTIFICATION

The idea of having security properties of IT products and systems evaluated and certified by some trusted party is not new and has led to the development of various criteria catalogs, such as the Trusted Computer System Evaluation Criteria (TC-SEC), also known as Orange Book in the United States, the Information Technology Security Evaluation Criteria (ITSEC) in Europe, and the Common Criteria (CC) for the international market. In theory, the same or slightly modified and enhanced versions of these catalogs could also be used to evaluate and certify firewall systems. In practice, however, there are only a few firewalls that have been evaluated and certified thus far.

Meanwhile, some companies and organizations have independently started to evaluate and certify the security properties of some commercial firewall products. For example, the ICSA Labs,[2] a division of TruSecure Corporation,[3] have become active in the field.[4] In fact, the ICSA Labs host a Firewall Product Developers

---

[2]http://www.icsalabs.com

[3]http://www.trusecure.com

[4]The ICSA Labs evolved from the National Computer Security Association (NCSA) that was later renamed the International Computer Security Association (ICSA).

Consortium (FWPD) Community that has released a set of firewall product certification criteria (currently in version 3.0a). In short, the criteria define functionality and security requirements for firewall products:

- The functionality requirements specify TCP/IP protocols and services that must be provided to internal clients and external users. In particular, the protocols include Telnet, FTP, HTTP (with and without SSL support), SMTP, and DNS. In addition, the functionality requirements also address firewall management.

- Upon demonstration of its functionality, a firewall product is also subjected to a couple of tests to demonstrate protection against a standardized and evolving suite of attacks. These tests are performed with several tools, including a port scanning tool, the ISS Security Scanner, and some proprietary tools developed in-house.

There are too many firewall products that have met the ICSA Labs and FWPD criteria and that are authorized to carry the ICSA Certified logo in their marketing and other literature accordingly. Unfortunately, in a market in which almost all products are authorized to carry a specific logo, the value of this logo to differentiate products is negligible. Unfortunately, this is the current situation with the ICSA Certified logo in the firewall market.

REFERENCES

[1] W. R. Cheswick and S. M. Bellovin, *Firewalls and Internet Security: Repelling the Wily Hacker*, Addison-Wesley, Reading, MA, 1994.

[2] E. D. Zwicky, et al., *Building Internet Firewalls*, 2nd Edition, O'Reilly & Associates, Sebastopol, CA, 2000.

[3] Y. Rekhter, et al., "Address Allocation for Private Internets," Request for Comments 1918 (BCP 5), February 1996.

Chapter 12

Conclusions and Outlook

If properly designed, implemented, deployed, and administered, a firewall can provide effective access control services for corporate intranets. Consequently, more and more network administrators are setting up firewalls as their first line of defense against outside attacks. After having introduced and discussed the fundamentals and the underlying principles of the firewall technology, its components (i.e., packet filters, circuit-level gateways, and application-level gateways), and some possible configurations, we use this chapter to conclude Part II, to give a brief overview about the current state-of-the-art and future directions in firewall research and development, and to elaborate on the role of firewalls in future IT landscapes.

First of all, it is important to note that firewalls are a fact of life on the Internet and that it is not likely that they will disappear in the future. In fact, the firewall technology is the most widely deployed security technology on the Internet. Many companies and organizations regularly perform market surveys and publish corresponding results. In a world of multiple vendors, interoperability is becoming a critical requirement. Against this background, CheckPoint Software Technologies, Inc., founded the open platform for security (OPSEC[1]) in 1997. Initiatives like OPSEC are very important for the evolution of the firewall technology in the future.

---

[1] http://www.checkpoint.com/opsec/

In spite of their commercial success, however, the firewall technology has remained an emotional topic within the Internet community. We briefly summarize the major arguments:

- Firewall advocates consider firewalls as important security measures and additional safeguards because they aggregate security functions in a single point, simplifying installation, configuration, and administration. Many companies and organizations use firewalls as corporate ambassadors to the Internet and use them to store public information about products and services, files to download, software patches, and so forth. From a U.S. manufacturer and vendor's point of view, the firewall technology is interesting mainly because it does not use cryptographic techniques and is therefore exportable. In addition to that, the technology's use is restricted neither to the TCP/IP protocols nor to the Internet, and very similar techniques can be used in any packet-switched data network, such as X.25 data networks.

- Firewall detractors are usually concerned about the difficulty of properly setting up, administering, and using firewalls, as well as their interference with the usability and vitality of the Internet as a whole. They claim that firewalls foster a false sense of security, leading to lax security within the firewall perimeter.

At the least, firewall advocates and detractors both agree that firewalls are a powerful tool for network security, but that they are not by any means a panacea or a magic bullet for all network and Internet-related security problems. Consequently, they should not be regarded as a substitute for careful security management within a corporate environment. Also, a firewall is useful only if it is configured to handle all data traffic to and from the Internet. This is not always the case, as many sites permit dial-in access to modems that are located at various points throughout the intranet. This is a potential backdoor and could negate all the protection provided by the firewall. A much better method for handling modems is to concentrate them into a modem pool. In essence, a modem pool consists of several modems connected to a terminal server. A dial-in user connects to the terminal server and then connects from there to other internal systems. Some terminal servers provide security features that can restrict connections to specific systems, or require users to strongly authenticate themselves. Obviously, RADIUS or TACACS+ can be used to secure communications between the terminal server and a centralized security server. Sometimes, authorized users also wish to have a dial-out capability. These users, however, need to recognize the vulnerabilities they may be creating if they are careless with the use of modems. A dial-out capability may easily become a dial-in capability if proper precautions are not taken. In general, dial-in and dial-out capabilities should be considered in the design of a firewall and incorporated into it. Forcing outside users to go through the strong authentication of the firewall should be reflected in the firewall policy.

In addition to unauthorized modems, there are at least two types of security problems that firewalls cannot address:

- Firewalls cannot protect against insider attacks. This is because the insider—as the name suggests—operates from the inside and must not pass the firewall at all. Consequently, the firewall is not aware of anything that happens inside the perimeter it protects. Protection against insider attacks can only be achieved by designing, implementing, and deploying appropriate authentication, authorization, and access control mechanisms inside the firewall. Furthermore, intranet firewalls can be used to limit the scope of an inside attack.

- Similarly, firewalls generally cannot protect against data-driven attacks, such as those employed by users downloading virus-infected software from archives or transferring corresponding program files in MIME-type attachments of e-mail messages. Because these program files may be encoded, compressed, and encrypted in any number of ways, a firewall is not always able to scan them to search for known virus signatures with any degree of accuracy. The same is true for macro viruses that may be included in innocent-looking data files (e.g., Word documents or PowerPoint presentations). It is possible and very likely that this problem will become more severe in the future, simply because more data traffic is encrypted on an end-to-end basis. Using end-to-end encryption, however, it is generally no longer possible for an intermediate system (e.g., a firewall or proxy server) to decrypt the data traffic and to make intelligent decisions about the nonexistence of malicious code. Protection against data-driven attacks can only be achieved by having users be restrictive in terms of software they accept, install, and execute, as well as having them use recent releases of antivirus software products.

With regard to computer viruses and data-driven attacks, it is important to note that the use and wide proliferation of executable content and mobile code, as provided, for example, by Java applets and ActiveX controls, has dramatically intensified the security problems [1–3].[2] If, for example, a user downloads a Java

---

[2]In some literature, Java has also been attributed to be an "automatic malicious software distribution system" [4].

applet or ActiveX control to a client machine that is configured to accept it by default, the Java applet or ActiveX control is automatically executed without asking the user for further permission. As such, the Java applet or ActiveX control may potentially compromise the security of the system.[3] The situation is dangerous, simply because the user imports a program that is executed locally without knowing exactly what the program is all about or what functions it actually implements. Think of this situation as something conceptually similar to a reverse remote procedure call (RPC).

As further addressed in Chapters 9 and 11 of [3], there are only a few technologies that can be used to address the security problems related to executable content and mobile code. For example, the Java security architecture employs the concept of a sandbox that can be configured to heavily restrict the runtime environment and the permissions of a Java applet. Similarly, the authenticity of an ActiveX control can be verified using digital signatures. With its lack of a concept similar to the Java sandbox, ActiveX is going to pose even more severe security problems than Java. For example, some time ago the German Chaos Computer Club demonstrated the danger of using ActiveX when they wrote and put on the Web an ActiveX control that was actually a Trojan horse. In the background, the ActiveX control prepared a money transfer order for the Microsoft Quicken software and put it in the corresponding payment queue. So, when the user had Quicken transfer its money orders the next time, the faked money transfer order generated by the Trojan horse would also be transferred. If the amount of transferred money is not too large, chances are that the user does not realize the manipulation.

It is also worthwhile mentioning that firewalls offer strong protection, but that tunnels can always be used to circumvent and bypass them. In essence, tunneling refers to the technique of encapsulating a data unit from one protocol in another, and using the facilities of the second protocol to traverse parts of the network. At the destination point, the encapsulation is stripped off, and the original data unit is reinjected into the local network. There are many uses for tunneling, and in some cases, a protocol may also be encapsulated within itself. For example, IP tunneling is used in both the evolving Multicast Backbone (MBone) and the IPv6 Backbone (6Bone).

- With regard to the MBone, IP multicast packets are tunneled using IP unicast packets. More precisely, IP packets with multicast destination addresses are encapsulated in IP packets with unicast destination addresses and tunneled through

---

[3]Access the WWW home page of DigiCrime, Inc., at URL http://www.digicrime.com to learn how executable content could, in fact, damage your system.

the existing Internet accordingly. Only destinations that are able to handle multicast traffic decapsulate the packets and eventually reinject them into their local networks.

- Similarly, IPv6 migration suggests the use of IP tunneling for transmitting IPv6 packets in the existing IPv4-based Internet. In this case, IPv6 packets are tunneled using IPv4 packets. More precisely, IPv6 packets are encapsulated in IPv4 packets and tunneled through the existing Internet. Only destinations that are able to handle IPv6 packets decapsulate the IPv6 packets and eventually reinject them into their local networks. Later, when IPv6 has become more widely deployed, it is possible and very likely that IPv4 traffic will be tunneled through an IPv6-based Internet.

Unfortunately, IP tunneling can also be misused to circumvent and bypass firewalls. We assume that a firewall permits at least one type of traffic to pass through bidirectionally. In this case, an insider and an outsider who dislike the firewall and wish to bypass it can build a tunnel between an internal system and an external system. What they basically do is encapsulate arbitrary IP packets in legitimate IP packets or some higher layer messages that are authorized to pass through the firewall. As such, the legitimate IP packets or some higher layer messages are transmitted to the destination system, where they are decapsulated to retrieve the original IP packets. Consequently, the two accomplices have established a tunnel that allows the free flow of IP packets through the firewall. From a security point of view, an unauthorized tunnel is far worse than a simple outbound connection, since inbound connections are usually permitted through the tunnel as well. Unauthorized tunnels are, in the final analysis, a management problem, not a technical one. If insiders do not generally accept the need for information security, firewall systems and other access control mechanisms will always be futile. The establishment of unauthorized tunnels is actually an insider problem, as it requires the cooperation of a legitimate inside user.

One should also notice that tunnels through firewalls also have their good sides. When properly configured and employed, they can be used to bypass the limitations of a particular firewall configuration. For example, a tunnel could be used to interconnect two physically separated sites. Firewalls at each location would provide protection from the outside, while a tunnel provides connectivity. If the tunnel is entirely encrypted, then the risks of such a configuration are low and the benefits are high.

To some people, the notion of a firewall is questionable. They argue that in most situations, the network is not the resource at risk; rather, the endpoints of the network are threatened. Given that the target of the attackers is the hosts on the network, should they not be suitably configured and armored to resist all possible attacks? The answer is that they should be, but probably cannot be. There will be bugs, either in the network programs or in the administration of the systems. Consequently, firewalls have been constructed and are used for pragmatic reasons by organizations interested in a higher level of security than may be possible without them. According to Steven Bellovin, firewalls are not a solution to network security problems, but rather a network response to a host security problem [4]. More precisely, they are a response to the dismal state of software engineering. Taken as a whole, the industry has missed the opportunity to produce software that is correct, secure, and easy to administer.

Firewall systems provide basic access control services for corporate intranets. But firewalls are not going to solve all security problems. A pair of historical analogies can help us better understand the role of firewall technology for the current and future Internet [5]:

- Our Stone Age predecessors lived in caves, each inhabited by a family whose members knew one another quite well. They could use this knowledge to identify and authenticate one another. Someone wanting to enter the cave would have to be introduced by a family member trusted by the others. Human history has shown that this security model is too simple to work on a large scale. As families grew in size and started to interact with one another, it was no longer possible for all family members to know all other members of the community, or even to reliably remember all persons who had ever been introduced to them.

- In the Middle Ages, our predecessors lived in castles and villages surrounded by town walls. The inhabitants were acquainted with one another, but this web of knowledge was not trusted. Instead, identification, authentication, authorization, and access control were centralized at a front gate. Anyone who wanted to enter the castle or village had to pass the front gate and was thoroughly checked there. Those who managed to pass the gate were implicitly trusted by all inhabitants. But human history has shown that this security model does not work either. For one thing, town walls do not protect against malicious insider attacks; for another, town walls and front gates do not scale easily. Many remnants of medieval town walls bear witness to this lack of scalability.

Using these analogies, the Internet has just entered the Middle Ages. The simple security model of the Stone Age still works for single hosts and local area networks (LANs). But it no longer works for wide area networks (WANs) in general and the Internet in particular. As a first (and let's hope intermediate) step, firewalls have been erected at the intranet gateways. Because they are capable of selectively dropping IP datagrams, firewalls restrict the connectivity of the Internet as a whole. The Internet's firewalls are thus comparable to the town walls and front gates of the Middle Ages. Screening routers correspond to general-purpose gates, whereas application gateways correspond to more specialized gates.

We do not see town walls anymore. Instead, countries issue passports to their citizens to use worldwide for identification and authentication. The Internet may need a similar means of security. TTPs and CAs could issue locally or globally accepted certificates or tickets for Internet principals, and these certificates or tickets could then be used to provide security services such as authentication, data confidentiality and integrity, access control, and non-repudiation services. In the remainder of this book, we are going to elaborate on these approaches (i.e., how to use cryptographic techniques to provide security services for an intranet or the Internet).

REFERENCES

[1] G. McGraw and E. W. Felton, *Java Security: Hostile Applets, Holes and Antidotes*, John Wiley & Sons, New York, 1996.

[2] A. D. Rubin, D. Geer, and M. J. Ranum, *Web Security Sourcebook*, John Wiley & Sons, New York, 1997.

[3] R. Oppliger, *Security Technologies for the World Wide Web*, Artech House, Norwood, MA, 2000.

[4] R. R. Schell, "The Internet Rules but the Emperor Has No Clothes," *Proceedings of 12th Computer Security Applications Conference*, San Diego, CA, December 1996, pp. xiii–xix.

[5] S. M. Bellovin, "An Introduction to Firewalls," Presentation held at the *IEEE Computer Society Symposium on Internet Security*, San Francisco, CA, November 12, 1994.

Part III

COMMUNICATION SECURITY

Chapter 13

Network Access Layer Security Protocols

In this chapter, we focus on some security protocols that have been proposed, specified, implemented, and deployed for the network access layer of the Internet model. More specifically, we introduce the topic in Section 13.1, elaborate on three conceptually similar network access layer security protocols in Sections 13.2 to 13.4, and draw some conclusions in Section 13.5.

13.1 INTRODUCTION

As mentioned in Chapter 2, the network access layer handles issues related to local area networking and dial-up connectivity in the Internet model and the corresponding TCP/IP communications protocol stack. Protocols that operate at this layer[1] include Ethernet (IEEE 802.3), token bus (IEEE 802.4), token ring (IEEE 802.5), FDDI, and protocols for serial line dial-up networking, such as the Serial Line IP (SLIP) protocol [1] and the Point-to-Point Protocol (PPP) [2]. SLIP and PPP both define encapsulation mechanisms for transporting multiprotocol data across layer two point-to-point links (e.g., serial lines). For all practical purposes, Ethernet is

---

[1]Remember that the protocols that operate at this layer are generally referred to as media access layer protocols or network access layer protocols.

205

the most widely used and deployed technology for local area networking, and PPP is the most widely deployed protocol for dial-up networking.

In the late 1980s, the IEEE started to address issues related to LAN and metropolitan area network (MAN) security. In particular, the IEEE 802.10 working group (WG) was formed in May 1988 to address LAN and MAN security. Meanwhile, the IEEE 802.10 WG specified several *standards for interoperable LAN/MAN security* (SILS) that are compatible with existing IEEE 802 and OSI specifications [3, 4]. Unfortunately, SILS has not been commercially successful, and there are hardly any products that implement the SILS specifications. Consequently, we do not address the work of the IEEE 802.10 WG in this book. Instead, we elaborate on recent work that was done to secure dial-up connections using PPP with some security enhancements.

Figure 13.1   Graphical illustration of the problem facing a conference attendee who is traveling in the United States and wants to connect his or her laptop computer to his or her corporate intranet in Europe.

First of all, we consider the problem that a European conference attendee traveling in the United States faces if he or she wants to connect his or her laptop computer to his or her corporate intranet in Europe (e.g., to read e-mail messages or download a PowerPoint presentation). The situation is illustrated in Figure 13.1. There are at least two solutions for this problem:

1. A very obvious solution for the problem is to use the public-switched telephone network (PSTN) or the integrated switched digital network (ISDN) to connect to a remote access server (RAS) located on the corporate intranet (e.g., a modem pool), to set up a PPP connection, and to use this connection to log into the destination server located on the corporate intranet. The major advantages of

this solution are availability and simplicity, whereas the major disadvantages are related to security and costs:

- The problem related to security is that the data traffic between the laptop computer and the intranet server goes unencrypted and unprotected.

- The problem related to costs is that the user is charged a long-distance call (or the company is charged the fees in the case of a modem pool with free charging or dial-back facilities).

2. A more sophisticated solution for the problem is to use a virtual private network (VPN) channel or tunnel. As we discuss later, there are many technologies that refer to and make use of the term VPN. Some of these technologies use cryptography to encapsulate data traffic and to establish and maintain cryptographically protected tunnels between the communicating peers. There are basically two approaches to create a VPN tunnel:

- One possibility is to encapsulate a given network layer protocol, such as IP, IPX, or AppleTalk, inside PPP, to cryptographically protect the PPP frames and to encapsulate the data inside a tunneling protocol, which is typically IP (but could also be ATM or Frame Relay). This approach is commonly referred to as "layer 2 tunneling" because the passenger of the tunneling scheme is actually a layer 2 protocol (i.e., PPP).

- Another possibility is to encapsulate a given network layer protocol, such as IP, IPX, or AppleTalk, directly into a tunneling protocol, such as 3Com's Virtual Tunneling Protocol (VTP), and to encapsulate the data inside a tunneling protocol (e.g., IP). This approach is commonly referred to as "layer 3 tunneling" because the passenger of the tunneling scheme is actually a layer 3 protocol (i.e., VTP).

Figure 13.2 illustrates and puts into perspective the layer 2 tunneling and layer 3 tunneling encapsulation schemes (for IPX encapsulated inside IP). The major advantages of VPN tunnels are related to the fact that data traffic is encapsulated in IP packets that can be routed over the Internet and that cryptographic techniques can then be used to protect the IP packets.

The first solution is simple and straightforward; it does not deserve further explanation. In the following sections we elaborate on the second solution. In particular, we briefly overview and partly discuss the layer 2 forwarding/tunneling protocols that have been proposed and deployed in the past (layer 3 tunneling protocols are addressed in Chapter 14). Today, there is a strong consensus that the Layer 2 Tunneling Protocol (L2TP) is the preferred choice for applications that want to use layer 2 tunneling. Therefore, the layer 2 tunneling protocol used in Figure 13.2 is the L2TP.

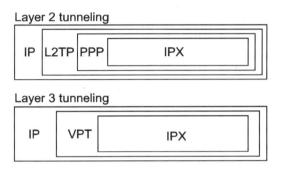

Figure 13.2   The layer 2 and layer 3 tunneling encapsulation schemes.

Figure 13.3 illustrates the layer 2 forwarding/tunneling solution to the conference attendee problem previously mentioned. In this solution, the connection is tunneled from the Internet service provider's point of presence (POP) to the RAS or network access server (NAS) that is typically located at the firewall of the corporate intranet.

Figure 13.3   Graphical illustration of the layer 2 forwarding/tunneling solution for the conference attendee problem.

Following the terminolgy introduced by the L2TP specifications, the following terms and acronyms are used in Figure 13.3 and the remainder of this chapter (instead of POP and RAS[2]):

- A *remote system* or *dial-up client* is a computer system or router that is either the initiator or recipient of a layer 2 tunnel. In Figure 13.3, the white bullet on the left represents the remote system or dial-up client.

- An *L2TP access concentrator* (LAC) is a node that acts as one side of a layer 2 tunnel endpoint and is a peer to the layer 2 tunneling protocol server (e.g., the L2TP network server discussed next). As such, the LAC sits between the remote system or dial-up client and the server and forwards packets to and from each. The connection from the LAC to the remote system is either local or a PPP link. In Figure 13.3, the second case is illustrated, meaning that the remote system uses PPP to connect to the LAC. Contrary to that, IP packets exchanged between the LAC and the server require tunneling with a layer 2 forwarding/tunneling protocol.

- Finally, an *L2TP network server* (LNS) is a node that acts as one side of a layer 2 tunnel endpoint and is a peer to the LAC. As such, the LNS is the logical termination point of a PPP session that is being tunneled from the remote system by the LAC.

Note that the LAC and the LNS require a common understanding of the encapsulation protocol so that layer 2 frames (e.g., PPP frames) can be successfully transmitted and received across the Internet. Also note that in this terminology, an NAS is a device providing local network access to users across a remote access network, such as the PSTN or ISDN. As such, an NAS may serve as either a LAC, LNS, or both.

In the following sections, we briefly overview and discuss three layer 2 forwarding/tunneling protocols that have been developed, proposed, implemented, and deployed in the past.

13.2   LAYER 2 FORWARDING PROTOCOL

Historically, the first layer 2 forwarding/tunneling protocol was the *Layer 2 Forwarding* (L2F) protocol originally developed and proposed by Cisco Systems. It addressed two areas of standardization:

---

[2]Because the term RAS is heavily used in the PPTP implementation of Microsoft, we use it when we discuss MS-PPTP later in this chapter.

- The encapsulation of layer 2 frames (i.e., PPP frames) within the L2F protocol. Each L2F frame, including an L2F header and a payload, is then encapsulated and sent within an IP packet or a UDP datagram, respectively. Contrary to more recent layer 2 forwarding/tunneling protocol proposals, the L2F protocol does not take into account the use of cryptography to protect the confidentiality of the encapsulated layer 2 frames.

- The connection management for the layer 2 tunnel (i.e., how the tunnel is initiated and terminated).

Both areas are specified in RFC 2341 [5]. According to this specification, the L2F protocol uses the well-known UDP port 1701 (for both source and destination ports).

Because the L2F protocol is only of historical value,[3] we do not delve into the technical details of the L2F protocol specification in this book. You may refer to the referenced RFC document if you are interested in history (or if you are an administrator in charge of installing and configuring an implementation of the L2F protocol).

13.3   POINT-TO-POINT TUNNELING PROTOCOL

Similar to the L2F protocol, the *Point-to-Point Tunneling Protocol* (PPTP) was originally developed and designed to solve the problem of creating and maintaining VPN tunnels over public TCP/IP-based networks using the PPP [6, 7].[4] The PPTP is the result of joint efforts of Microsoft and a set of product vendors, including, for example, Ascend Communications, 3Com/Primary Access, ECI Telematics, and U.S. Robotics. These companies originally constituted the PPTP Forum, whose resulting PPTP specification was made publicly available and submitted to the IETF Point-to-Point Protocol Extensions (PPPEXT[5]) WG for possible consideration as an Internet Standard in 1996.[6] PPTP is documented in a series of Internet-Drafts[7] that have all since expired.

As illustrated in Figures 13.1 and 13.3, a typical deployment of the PPTP would start with a remote system or dial-up client, such as a laptop computer, that must

---

[3]Note that the category of the referenced RFC document is "historic."

[4]http://www.microsoft.com/technet/winnt/winntas/technote/pptpudst.asp

[5]http://www.ietf.org/html.charters/pppext-charter.html

[6]Note that the IETF PPPEXT WG is situated in the IETF's Internet area (not in the security area).

[7]draft-ietf-pppext-pptp-*.txt

be interconnected to an LNS located on a corporate intranet using an LAC. As such, the PPTP can be used to encapsulate PPP frames in IP packets for transmission over the Internet or any other publicly accessible TCP/IP-based network. More specifically, the remote system can connect to the LNS in two ways:

- Directly using the PPTP (if the remote system supports PPTP);

- Using an Internet service provider's LAC that supports inbound PPP connections (if the remote system does not directly support the PPTP).

In the first case, the situation is comparably simple. The remote system first establishes a PPP connection to the Internet service provider's LAC and then uses PPTP to send encapsulated PPP frames to the LNS. The IP packets that encapsulate the PPP frames are simply forwarded by the LAC.

In the second case, however, the situation is more complicated. In this case, the LAC must use the PPTP to encapsulate the PPP frames in IP packets on behalf of the remote system. Consequently, the LAC must play the role of an intermediate or proxy server in one way or another. In fact, there are two connections. The first connection uses the PPP to interconnect the remote system and the LAC, whereas the second connection uses the PPTP to interconnect the LAC and the LNS. PPP frames received by the LAC are encapsulated in IP packets using the PPTP.

Figure 13.4   The PPTP encapsulation scheme.

In either case, the PPTP uses a sophisticated encapsulation scheme to tunnel PPP frames through the Internet (or any other TCP/IP-based network that interconnects the LAC and the LNS). As illustrated in Figure 13.4, network or Internet layer protocol data units (e.g., IP packets, IPX packets, or NetBEUI messages) are first framed using PPP. The resulting PPP frames are then encapsulated using a generic routing encapsulation (GRE) header [8] as well as an IP header that is used to route the frame through the Internet. Finally, the resulting IP packets are framed with still another media-specific header before they can be forwarded to the interface connected to the Internet (the media-specific header is not even illustrated in Figure 13.4).

In addition to the data channel that uses IP encapsulation to transmit data, the PPTP uses a TCP connection for signaling. The corresponding messages that are sent or received over this connection are used to query status and to convey signaling information between the LAC (i.e., the PPTP client) and the LNS (i.e., the PPTP server). The control channel is always initiated by the PPTP client to the PPTP server using TCP port number 1723. In most cases, it is a bidirectional channel where the client can send messages to the server and vice versa. Note that the notion of an outband signaling channel is something very specific for PPTP. Most other security protocols (e.g., the IPsec protocols) use inband signaling, meaning that signaling information is transported together with the protected data units.

The PPTP specification does not mandate the use of specific algorithms for authentication and encryption. Instead, it provides a framework for the negotiation of particular algorithms. This negotiation is not specific to PPTP, and relies on existing PPP option negotiations contained within the PPP compression protocol (CCP) [9], the challenge handshake authentication protocol (CHAP) [10], and some other PPP extensions and enhancements. Also outside the world of the PPTP, PPP sessions have been able to negotiate compression algorithms as well as authentication and encryption algorithms [11, 12].

In spite of the fact that the PPTP specification was submitted to the IETF PPPEXT WG for consideration as an Internet Standard, its standardization effort has been abandoned. It is currently available only for networks served by Windows NT 4.0 or the Linux operating systems. This is not likely to change in the future, as most vendors move to the L2TP as a replacement for the PPTP. Against this background, Microsoft's implementation of the PPTP (i.e., MS-PPTP) is still the most widely deployed protocol for virtual private networking and providing VPN connectivity. It is part of the Windows NT server software distribution and is also used extensively in other VPN products. The Microsoft PPTP server only runs under Windows NT, whereas the client software is also available for Windows 95 and Windows 98 (and probably all future releases of the Windows operating systems). Configuration issues are fully addressed in Chapter 6 of [6]. They are not covered in this book. In the rest of this section, we focus on the security properties of MS-PPTP. Keep in mind, however, that the PPTP is somehow outdated and that the industry is steadily replacing both the L2F protocol and PPTP with L2TP.

13.3.1   MS-PPTP Authentication

MS-PPTP currently supports three authentication methods:

- *Clear password.* The client authenticates to the server by sending it a password in the clear.

- *Hashed password.* The client authenticates to the server by sending it a one-way hash value of the password.

- *Challenge-response.* The client and the server authenticate each other using MS-CHAP [13], which is Microsoft's version of the commonly used CHAP [10].

For obvious reasons, the clear password authentication option (i.e., clear password) is susceptible to password sniffing and cannot be considered to be secure. In regard to the hashed password authentication option (i.e., hashed password), Microsoft's implementation of PPTP for Windows NT actually uses two one-way hash functions: the LAN Manager hash function[8] and the Windows NT hash function[9]:

- The LAN Manager hash function is based on the DES encryption algorithm. It basically works as follows:

  1. The password is turned into a 14-character string, either by truncating longer passwords or padding shorter passwords with zeros.

  2. All lowercase characters are converted to uppercase (numbers and non-alphanumeric characters remain unaffected).

  3. The 14-byte string is split into two 7-byte strings, and a fixed constant is DES-encrypted using each 7-byte string as a key. Consequently, this step yields two 8-byte encrypted strings.

  4. The two resulting 8-byte encrypted strings are concatenated to create a single 16-byte hash value.

- Contrary to that, the Windows NT hash function is based on the MD4 one-way hash function. It basically works in two steps:

  1. The password (up to 14 characters long and case-sensitive) is converted to Unicode.

  2. The password is hashed using the MD4 one-way hash function, yielding a 16-byte hash value.

---

[8]The LAN Manager hash function was originally developed by Microsoft for IBM's OS/2 operating system, and was later integrated into Windows for Workgroups and optionally in Windows 3.1.

[9]The Windows NT hash function was developed by Microsoft specifically for Windows NT.

For obvious reasons, dictionary attacks are possible and quite easy to be launched to break the security of the LAN Manager hash function.[10]   The Windows NT hash function is an improvement over the LAN Manager hash function, because case sensitivity provides more entropy for the passwords, passwords can be longer than 14 characters, and hashing the entire password together instead of in small sections is better.   However, neither of the two hash functions provides support for a salt mechanism, such as is employed, for example, by the UNIX and Linux operating systems.[11]   Consequently, two people with the same password will always have the same LAN Manager and Windows NT hash values, so comparing a file of hashed passwords with a precomputed dictionary of hashed password candidates is still a fruitful attack. Also note that both hash values are always sent together. Therefore, it is possible to brute-force the password using the weaker hash function (i.e., the LAN Manager hash function), and then test various lowercase alternatives to actually find the other hash value (i.e., the Windows NT hash value). In fact, Peter Mudge developed a software called L0phtcrack to automate the process of recovering passwords from their corresponding hash values. Today, the tool is widely deployed on the Internet and it is being marketed by Security Software Technologies, Inc.[12]

When using MS-CHAP [13], the challenge-response option of MS-PPTP au-thentication, the client first requests a login challenge, and the server sends back an 8-byte random challenge. The client then calculates the LAN Manager hash value, adds five zero-bytes to create a 21-byte string, and partitions the string into three 7-byte keys. Each key is then used to encrypt the challenge with the DES

---

[10]Note that all characters are converted to uppercase, making the number of possible passwords smaller. Also, there is no salt mechanism (as addressed in the following footnote), causing two users with the same password to always have the same hashed password. Finally, the two 7-byte halves of the password are hashed independently, enabling the two halves to be attacked with brute force independently.

[11]In many operating systems, user passwords are stored in the one-way encrypted form. The one-way function that is used for this transformation is publicly known, so anybody could generate a codebook with password candidates transformed with this one-way function. In order to make it more difficult to generate such a codebook, the UNIX operating system uses a salt mechanism. The basic idea is to use a random number (which is also called "salt" or "salt value") as a parameter for the one-way function, and to store the salt as cleartext in the password file (together with the one-way encrypted password). When the operating system wants to check the user-supplied password, it has to feed the one-way function with the appropriate salt value (the one it reads from the password file). As a consequence, an attacker can only launch a dictionary attack against a specific salt value, and a dictionary attack against the entire set of users is no longer possible (or at least more difficult).

[12]http://www.securitysoftwaretech.com/l0phtcrack/

encryption algorithm, resulting in a 24-byte encrypted string. This string is sent to the server as a response. In addition, the client does the same with the Windows NT hash functions, resulting in another 24-byte encrypted string. The server, in turn, looks up one of the two hash values in its local database, reconstructs the three DES keys, encrypts the challenge with these keys, and compares the results with the encrypted hash values it has received from the client. If all three values match, the authentication process is successful. Note that, in principle, the server could make the comparison on the LAN Manager or Windows NT hash value. In either case, the result should be the same. Which hash value the server should use depends on a flag set in the client's response message. If the flag is set, the server tests against the Windows NT hash value; if the flag is not set, the server tests against the LAN Manager hash value.

In either case, MS-CHAP must be used for subsequent PPTP data traffic to be encrypted. With either of the other two authentication options (clear or hashed password), no encryption is available in MS-PPTP.

13.3.2   MS-PPTP Encryption

In addition to the various PPTP authentication options, the *Microsoft Point-to-Point Encryption* (MPPE) protocol makes it possible to encrypt PPTP data traffic [14]. In short, the MPPE protocol assumes the existence of a secret key that is shared between a client and a server and then uses the RC4 stream cipher to transparently encrypt the data traffic between them. In the past, there was a U.S. domestic version and an international version of MS-PPTP encryption (the U.S. domestic version used 128-bit keys, whereas the international version was restricted to 40-bit keys). Again, this distinction no longer applies and it is now possible to also use strong cryptography (i.e., long keys) outside the United States and Canada.

One question that arises immediately is how the client and the server come into possession of a shared secret key. One possibility would be to use the outband signaling channel to perform a Diffie-Hellman key exchange and to subsequently authenticate this key exchange using digital signatures. As discussed in Chapter 14, this approach is similar to the key exchange mechanism used for the IPsec protocols. The developers of the MPPE, however, traded security against efficiency and came up with a much simpler scheme (as discussed later, the scheme is actually too simple to provide a sufficient level of security).

- A 40-bit RC4 key was generated by first generating a deterministic 64-bit key from the LAN Manager hash value of the user's password using SHA-1, and then setting the high-order 24 bits of the key to 0xD1269E.[13]

- Similarly, a 128-bit RC4 key was generated by first concatenating the Windows NT hash value of the user's password and a 64-bit random nonce created by the server during the execution of MS-CHAP, and then generating a deterministic 128-bit key again using SHA-1.

In either case, the resulting key was used to initialize the RC4 stream cipher in the usual manner, and then to encrypt the data stream. After every 256 packets, a new RC4 key—64 bits long for 40-bit encryption and 128 bits long for 128-bit encryption—was generated by hashing the previous key and the original key with SHA-1. Again, if the required key was 40 bits, the high-order 24 bits of the key were set to the hexadecimal value mentioned above.

13.3.3   Security Analysis

In 1998, Bruce Schneier and Peter Mudge cryptanalyzed the first version of MS-PPTP [15]. In summary, they found this version of MS-CHAP to be weak and easily susceptible to dictionary attacks. For example, one problem stems from the fact that the LAN Manager and the Windows NT hash values are both transmitted (even in a Windows NT-only environment), and that it is therefore possible to attack the weaker hash function (i.e., the LAN Manager hash function). Another problem with MS-CHAP is that only the client is authenticated. Consequently, an attacker who hijacks a connection can easily masquerade as the server. If encryption is enabled, the attacker will not be able to send and receive messages (unless he or she also breaks the encryption), but by reusing an old challenge value, he or she can obtain two sessions encrypted with the same key. This can be further explored by the attacker to break the encryption.

With regard to the MPPE protocol, the situation is even worse. It is important to note that the RC4 key is deterministically derived from the hash value of the user password. Consequently, the security of the key is no greater than the security of the password. In other words, the entropy of the key is bounded by the entropy of the password.[14] To make things worse, the 40-bit RC4 encryption suffers from

---

[13]The MPPE protocol specification includes a flag for calculating the 40-bit RC4 key based on the Windows NT hash instead of the LAN Manager hash, but this feature was not implemented in the first version of MPPE.

[14]In information theory, the entropy of a random variable X measures the amount of information provided by an observation of X. Equivalently, it is also the uncertainty about the outcome before an observation of X. Entropy is particularly useful for approximating the average number of bits

even more serious weaknesses. Because there is no salt mechanism,[15] an attacker can precompute a dictionary of ciphertext headers and then quickly look up a given ciphertext in this dictionary. Moreover, the same 40-bit RC4 key is generated every time a user initializes PPTP. Because RC4 is an output feedback (OFB) mode stream cipher, it is possible to break the encryption from the ciphertext from two sessions. Unfortunately, the same key is used in both the forward and backward direction, guaranteeing that the same keystream is used to encrypt two different plaintexts. The 128-bit RC4 encryption uses a 64-bit nonce in the key generation process, making precomputed dictionary attacks impractical. Nevertheless, brute-force attacks against the password are still much more efficient than brute-force attacks against the keyspace. The use of the nonce also means that two sessions using the same password will have two different 128-bit RC4 keys, although the same key will be used to encrypt the plaintext in both directions. Remember that RC4 is an OFB mode stream cipher, and that MPPE does not provide authentication and integrity of the ciphertext stream. Consequently, an attacker can undetectably flip arbitrary bits in the ciphertext stream and compromise the integrity of the data stream accordingly. This attack does not require the attacker to know the secret key or the client's password (of course, higher-level protocols might detect or prevent these sorts of attacks).

In addition to the attacks against MS-CHAP and the MPPE protocol, Schneier and Mudge also showed how an attacker can either spoof resynchronization requests or forge MPPE packets with incorrect coherency counts. If this is done continuously just before the 256th packet exchange, in which the session key would normally be updated, an attacker can succeed in forcing the encrypted communications channel to never rekey. In addition, they described a number of other attacks against MS-PPTP, including, for example, passive monitoring of PPTP servers, spoofing PPP negotiation parameters, and several denial-of-service attacks against the server.

In June 1998, Microsoft posted a preliminary answer to the security problems. In fact, they argued that for reasons of legacy compatibility, Microsoft had continued to support both the LAN Manager and the Windows NT hash function in its PPTP implementation, and that future releases of PPTP software would provide administrators with the ability to configure a PPTP server so that it would only accept the cryptographically stronger Windows NT hash function. With regard to the problem of having the session keys derived from the password's hash, Microsoft

---

required to encode the elements of X. For example, the English language has about 1.3 bits of entropy per character, and case variations, numbers, and nonalphanumeric characters increase this value significantly.

[15]The rationale behind the salt mechanism is explained in footnote 8.

recommended the use of 128-bit encryption and that administrators enforce the use of strong passwords.

More recently, Microsoft released an upgrade for its MS-PPTP implementation. Commonly referred to as MS-PPTP version 2, or as MS-PPTP V2, several improvements were made. For example, MS-CHAP was upgraded to something similar to, but incompatible with, MS-CHAP version 1 [16]. Also, MS-PPTP V2 uses a unique key in either direction to make certain cryptanalytical attacks more difficult (the keys for each direction are still derived from the same value, the user's password Windows NT hash value, but differently depending on the direction). Furthermore, the LAN Manager hash value of the user's password is no longer sent along with the stronger Windows NT hash value. Unfortunately (and because of the lack of a salt mechanism for password hashing), MS-PPTP V2 is still vulnerable to offline password-guessing attacks, such as employed by L0phtcrack. Furthermore, version rollback attacks are possible to invoke the cryptanalytically weaker MS-CHAP V1 and to attack the user's LAN Manager hash value accordingly. Refer to [17] for a more comprehensive security analysis of MS-PPTP V2. The paper is electronically available on-line.[16]

13.4   LAYER 2 TUNNELING PROTOCOL

In June 1996, Microsoft and Cisco Systems proposed and submitted a combination of MS-PPTP and the L2F protocol to the IETF PPPEXT WG. The proposal was named *Layer 2 Tunneling Protocol* (L2TP) [18]. This collaborative protocol specification was particularly good news, as it meant that there would be just one industrywide IETF specification for a layer 2 tunneling and VPN dial-up protocol.

Similar to the L2F protocol and PPTP, the L2TP facilitates the tunneling of encapsulated PPP frames across an intervening network in a way that is as transparent as possible to both end users and applications. Contrary to the other protocols, however, L2TP uses and even requires the use of IPsec security associations (SAs) to cryptographically protect data that are transmitted between LACs and LNSs. IPsec and IPsec SAs are further addressed in Chapter 14.

After this initial release, the L2TP specification was further refined. In August 1999, a preliminary release was published in RFC 2661 [19] and submitted to the Internet standards track. As such, the L2TP is likely to replace both the L2F protocol and PPTP in the future (this is equally true for Microsoft and Cisco products).

---

[16]http://www.counterpane.com/pptpv2-paper.html

13.5 CONCLUSIONS

In this chapter we elaborated on a few network access layer security or layer 2 forwarding/tunneling protocols, including, for example, the L2F protocol, PPTP, and L2TP. The protocols provide some means for virtual private networking. It is, however, important to note that if a protocol or protocol implementation's cryptography is weak or inherently flawed (e.g., MS-PPTP), the resulting security is no better than the security of a protocol that does not use cryptography at all. In fact, the resulting security may even be worse (because the claimed use of crytography may seduce people into transmitting sensitive data they would not transmit under normal circumstances). Note, however, that the fact that weak or inherently flawed cryptography can make the overall security worse is true for any protocol, not just the layer 2 forwarding/tunneling protocols addressed so far. This argument should always be kept in mind and considered with care when cryptography is used.

Because of the weak cryptography that is typically built into layer 2 tunneling protocols, the use of L2TP and IPsec SAs between the LACs and the LNSs provides an interesting possibility to establish VPN channels or tunnels. In Chapter 14, we focus entirely on layer 3 tunneling in general and the IPsec protocols in particular.

A final word is due to the term VPN. We have said that layer 2 tunneling and layer 3 tunneling protocols can be used for virtual private networking. According to RFC 2828, a VPN is "a restricted-use, logical computer network that is constructed from the system resources of a relatively public, physical network (such as the Internet), often by using encryption, and often by tunneling links of the virtual network across the real network" [20]. According to this definition, the use of encryption is not mandatory for VPNs. Consequently, there are some alternative technologies and notions of virtual private networking in use today. These technologies use controlled route leaking (i.e., route filtering) or label switching instead of cryptography to provide VPNs. For example, *multi-protocol label switching* (MPLS) is a heavily promoted and widely deployed technology to provide a feature similar to a closed user group in a TCP/IP-based network [21, 22]. MPLS implements label switching to make sure that IP packets can only reach legitimate members of a particular host group. There is no cryptographic protection in use. Consequently, any subscriber of an MPLS network has to trust the provider not to eavesdrop on its communications and not to manipulate the IP traffic. Sometimes this level of trust is justified. Sometimes, however, this level of trust is not justified and the subscriber is then well advised to look into and consider the use of VPN technologies that employ cryptography in one way or another.

REFERENCES

[1] J. Romkey, "A Nonstandard for Transmission of IP Datagrams over Serial Lines: SLIP," Request for Comments 1055, STD 47, June 1988.

[2] W. Simpson, "The Point-to-Point Protocol (PPP)," Request for Comments 1661, STD 51, July 1994.

[3] IEEE 802.10, "IEEE Standards for Local and Metropolitan Area Networks: Interoperable LAN/MAN Security (SILS)," 1998.

[4] IEEE 802.10c, "Supplements to IEEE Std 802.10, Interoperable LAN/MAN Security (SILS): Key Management (Clause 3)," 1992.

[5] A. Valencia, M. Littlewood, and T. Kolar, "Cisco Layer Two Forwarding (Protocol) L2F," Request for Comments 2341, May 1998.

[6] C. Scott, P. Wolfe, and M. Erwin, *Virtual Private Networks*, 2nd Edition, O'Reilly & Associates, Sebastopol, CA, 1998.

[7] S. Brown, *Implementing Virtual Private Networks*, McGraw-Hill, New York, 1999.

[8] S. Hanks, et al., "Generic Routing Encapsulation (GRE)," Request for Comments 1701, October 1994.

[9] D. Rand, "The PPP Compression Control Protocol (CCP)," Request for Comments 1962, June 1996.

[10] W. Simpson, "PPP Challenge Handshake Authentication Protocol (CHAP)," Request for Comments 1994, August 1996.

[11] G. Meyer, "The PPP Encryption Control Protocol (ECP)," Request for Comments 1968, June 1996.

[12] L. Blunk and J. Vollbrecht, "PPP Extensible Authentication Protocol (EAP)," Request for Comments 2284, March 1998.

[13] G. Zorn and S. Cobb, "Microsoft PPP CHAP Extensions," Request for Comments 2433, October 1998.

[14] G. S. Pall and G. Zorn, "Microsoft Point-to-Point Encryption (MPPE) Protocol," Request for Comments 2118, April 1998.

[15] B. Schneier and P. Mudge, "Cryptanalysis of Microsoft's Point-to-Point Tunneling Protocol," *Proceedings of ACM Conference on Communcations and Computer Security*, November 1998.

[16] G. Zorn, "Microsoft PPP CHAP Extensions, Version 2," Request for Comments 2759, January 2000.

[17] B. Schneier and P. Mudge, "Cryptanalysis of Microsoft's PPTP Authentication Extensions (MS-CHAPv2)," June 1999.

[18] R. Shea, *L2TP: Implementation and Operation*, Addison-Wesley, Reading, MA, 1999.

[19] W. Townsley, et al., "Layer Two Tunneling Protocol 'L2TP'," Request for Comments 2661, August 1999.

[20] R. Shirey, "Internet Security Glossary," Request for Comments 2828, May 2000.

[21] B. S. Davie and Y. Rekhter, *MPLS: Technology and Applications*, Morgan Kaufmann Publishers, San Francisco, CA, 2000.

[22] U. Black, *MPLS and Label Switching Networks*, Prentice-Hall, Englewood Cliffs, NJ, 2001.

Chapter 14

Internet Layer Security Protocols

In this chapter, we focus on the security protocols that have been developed, proposed, and specified by the IETF IP Security (IPSEC) WG for the Internet layer of the TCP/IP protocol stack. More specifically, we briefly address some previous work in Section 14.1, overview the standardization efforts of the relevant IETF working groups in Section 14.2, elaborate on the IP security architecture in Section 14.3, further describe the IPsec[1] protocols in Section 14.4, and focus on some relevant key management protocols in Section 14.5. Furthermore, we address implementation issues in Section 14.6 and conclude with some final remarks in Section 14.7. Note that the topic addressed in this chapter (i.e., the IPsec protocols) is very complex, and that the explanations are rather short and not at all comprehensive. Further information can be found in any book on IPsec and virtual private networking [1–3]. Among these books, I particularly recommend [3].[2]

---

[1]The acronym "IPsec" is used inconsistently. Sometimes "IPSec" is used instead of "IPsec" or "IPSEC." In this book, we use "IPSEC" to refer to the IETF WG of the same name, and "IPsec" to refer to the corresponding security architecture and suite of security protocols.

[2]This book is also published in Artech House's Computer Security Series.

14.1 PREVIOUS WORK

In most network architectures and corresponding communications protocol stacks, network layer protocol data units are transmitted in the clear, meaning that they are not cryptographically protected during their transmission. Consequently, it is relatively simple to do malicious things, such as inspecting the contents of the data units, forging the source or destination addresses, modifying the contents, or even replaying old data units. There is no guarantee that data units received are in fact from the claimed originators (i.e., the claimed source addresses), that they are delivered to the proper recipients, that they contain the original contents, and that the contents have not been inspected by an eavesdropper while the data units were transmitted from the originators to the recipients. The lack of built-in security is particularly true for IP packets.[3]

Against this background, the idea of having a standardized network or Internet layer security protocol (to protect network or Internet layer protocol data units) is not new, and several protocols had been proposed before the IETF IPSEC WG started to meet:

- The *Security Protocol 3* (SP3) was a network layer security protocol jointly developed and proposed by the U.S. National Security Agency (NSA) and the National Institute of Science and Technology (NIST) as part of the secure data network system (SDNS) suite of security protocols [4]. Outside the U.S. military, the SDNS and its security protocols have not seen widespread use. This is particularly true for SP3.

- The *Network Layer Security Protocol* (NLSP) was developed by the ISO to secure the Connectionless Network Protocol (CLNP) [5]. Similar to IP in the Internet model, CLNP provides a connectionless and unreliable network layer service to the higher layers in the OSI-RM. As such, the aim of the NLSP is to secure the network layer service and to provide some basic security services to the higher layers. The NLSP is an incompatible descendent of SP3.

- The *Integrated NLSP* (I-NLSP) was originally developed and proposed by Robert K. Glenn at the NIST to provide security services for both IP (i.e., IPv4) and CLNP.[4] Again, the security function of I-NLSP is roughly similar to that of

---

[3]Note that IP packets are the protocol data units for the network layer protocol of the Internet architecture, namely, the Internet Protocol (IP).

[4]I-NLSP was specified in an Internet-Draft that expired long ago.

SP3, although some details differ. For example, I-NLSP provides some additional functionality, such as security label processing.

- A protocol named *swIPe* was yet another experimental Internet layer security protocol that was developed and prototyped by John Ioannidis and Matt Blaze [6]. The prototype implementation is publicly and freely available on the Internet.[5] It was often used in UNIX environments and it is still in use today.

The network and Internet layer security protocols listed are more alike than they are different. In fact, they all use encapsulation as their basic enabling technique. What this basically means is that authenticated or encrypted network layer protocol data units are contained within other data units. In the case of IP encapsulation, for example, outgoing plaintext IP packets are authenticated or encrypted and encapsulated in new IP packets by adding new IP headers that are used to route the packets through the internetwork. At the peer systems, the incoming IP packets are decapsulated, meaning that the outer IP headers are stripped off and the inner IP packets are authenticated or decrypted and then forwarded to the intended recipients.

Figure 14.1   Encapsulated IP packet.

An encapsulated IP packet is illustrated in Figure 14.1. Note that the original IP header and IP payload are collectively treated as the payload for the new IP packet, and that a new IP header must be prepended to this new payload. Consequently, the new IP header must not be encrypted, since it must be used to route (or "tunnel") the new IP packet through the (inter)network. Such an encapsulation or tunneling scheme is convenient, since it means that no changes are required to the existing Internet routing infrastructure: authenticated or encrypted IP packets have an unencrypted, normal-looking outer IP header, and this IP header can be used to route and process the packet as usual. This transparency is convenient for the large-scale deployment of encapsulation and tunneling schemes in general, and IP encapsulation or tunneling in particular. In fact, similar IP encapsulation or

---

[5]`ftp://ftp.csua.berkeley.edu/pub/cypherpunks/swIPe/swipe.tar.Z`

tunneling schemes can be used to transfer multicast or IPv6 traffic through unicast or IPv4 network segments.

14.2   IETF STANDARDIZATION

When the IETF started to develop the next version of IP (i.e., IPv6), it was commonly agreed that this version had to incorporate strong security features (at least for users who desire security). The security features had to be algorithm-independent so that the cryptographic algorithms could be altered without affecting the other parts of an implementation. Furthermore, the security features should be useful in enforcing a wide variety of security policies, and yet they should be designed in a way that avoids adverse impacts on Internet users who do not need security services for the protection of their IP traffic at all.

Against this background, the IETF chartered an IPSEC WG in 1992. The aim was to define a security architecture (mainly for IPv6), and to standardize both an IP Security Protocol (IPSP) and a related Internet Key Management Protocol (IKMP). Soon it was realized that the same security architecture that was being developed for IPv6 could also be used for IPv4. Consequently, the charter of the IETF IPSEC WG was revised to target both IPv6 and IPv4, and the resulting security architecture had to be the same. The main difference is that the security mechanisms specified in the IP security architecture have to be retrofitted into IPv4 implementations, whereas they must be present in all IPv6 implementations at the beginning.

In August 1995, the IETF IPSEC WG published a series of RFC documents that collectively specified a first version of the IP security architecture and the IPSP [7–11]. This version was incomplete and rushed to publication mainly to satisfy a perceived industry need. Nevertheless, the IESG approved the IPSP specification to enter the Internet standards track as a Proposed Standard, and the participants of the IETF IPSEC WG continued their work to refine the IP security architecture and the IPSP specification, as well as to standardize the IKMP [12, 13]. As explained later in this chapter, the discussion on the standardization of the IKMP was very controversial. In the end, two protocol proposals, namely, the Internet Security Association and Key Management Protocol (ISAKMP) and the OAKLEY Key Determination Protocol, were merged to become the IKMP. Furthermore, the acronym IPSP was replaced with the term *IPsec protocols* (as it consists of two subprotocols), and the acronym IKMP was replaced with the term *Internet Key Exchange* (IKE). Consequently, the IP security architecture as we understand it today comprises both a series of IPsec protocols and an IKE protocol.

In November 1998, the IETF IPSEC WG published a series of RFC documents that collectively specify a revised version of the IP security architecture [14], including revised versions of the IPsec [15–20] and IKE [21–23] protocols.[6] In addition, an informational RFC was published that provides a road map for the various documents that are released under the auspices of the IETF IPSEC WG [24]. Further information about the current status of the various protocol specifications can be found on the home page of the IETF IPSEC WG.[7]

Soon after the release of the revised series of RFC documents, it was realized that two topics deserved further study:

- The use of policies in IPsec environments;

- The use of IPsec technologies to secure remote access services.

In early 2000, the IETF chartered an IP Security Policy (IPSP)[8] WG to address the first topic and an IP Security Remote Access (IPSRA)[9] WG to address the second topic. As of this writing, the two WGs are still in the process of defining their aims and scope, as well as their goals and milestones. Consequently, their work is not further addressed in this book. You may refer to the home pages of the two WGs to get an overview about the current status of their work.

14.3   IP SECURITY ARCHITECTURE

As mentioned in Section 14.2, the IP security architecture comprises an entire suite of security protocols, including, for example, the IPsec protocols (formerly known as IPSP) and the IKE protocol (formerly known as IKMP). Furthermore, the IPsec protocols comprise two subprotocols, namely the Authentication Header (AH) and the Encapsulating Security Payload (ESP). Similarly, the IKE protocol has evolved from two major key management protocol proposals (i.e., ISAKMP and OAKLEY). All of these protocols and subprotocols are introduced and put into perspective later in this chapter.

A high-level overview of the IP security architecture is given in Figure 14.2. In short, an IPsec module is a (hardware or software) module that implements the IPsec architecture and its protocols. The primary goal of an IPsec module is

---

[6]As of this writing, the protocol specifications refer to Proposed Standards.

[7]http://www.ietf.org/html.charters/ipsec-charter.html

[8]http://www.ietf.org/html.charters/ipsp-charter.html

[9]http://www.ietf.org/html.charters/ipsra-charter.html

to secure IP traffic that is sent to or received from another IPsec module. What this basically means in terms of security services and mechanisms is specified in a corresponding *security association* (SA). The aim of the IKE protocol is to establish SAs and the aim of the IPsec protocols is to make use of these SAs. On either side of an SA, the security parameters of that SA (e.g., encryption algorithm and session key) are stored in a *security association database* (SAD). Each SA and corresponding entry in the SAD is indexed with three values:

- A *security parameters index* (SPI);

- An IP destination address;

- A security protocol identifier (i.e., AH or ESP).

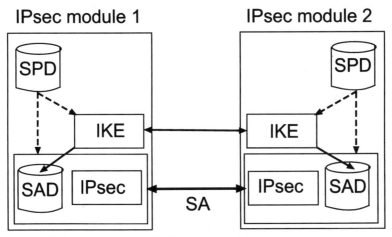

Figure 14.2   High-level overview of the IP security architecture.

As will be explained later, each IPsec-protected packet carries an SPI value that can be used by the recipient to retrieve the correct SA parameters from its SAD. In addition to the SAD, there is a security policy database (SPD) in each IPsec module. The SPD provides detailed specifications of the security services accorded to each packet.

In accordance to this high-level overview, the concept of an SA is at the core of the IP security architecture. An SA specifies the security services and mechanisms that must be implemented and used between two endpoints or IPsec modules. The endpoints, in turn, may be hosts or network security gateways, such as IPsec-enabled routers or application gateways. For example, an SA may require the provision of data confidentiality services through the use of the IPsec ESP protocol (this protocol will be explained later in this chapter). Furthermore, the SA may specifiy the parameters for this protocol, such as the encryption algorithm (e.g., the DES algorithm), the mode of operation (e.g., the CBC mode), and its initialization vector (IV). The SA is a simplex "connection" or "relationship." Security services are afforded to an SA by the use of AH, or ESP, but not both. If both AH and ESP protection is applied to a data stream, then two SAs must be established and maintained. Similarly, to secure bidirectional communications between two hosts or security gateways, two SAs (one in each direction) are required. The term *SA bundle* refers to a set of SAs through which traffic must be processed to satisfy a specific security policy.

The IPsec architecture allows the user or system administrator to control the granularity at which security services are offered. In the first series of RFCs [7–11], three approaches of how to feed SAs with security parameters and cryptographic keys were distinguished:

- *Host-oriented keying* has all users on one host share the same session key for use on traffic destined for all users on another host.

- *User-oriented keying* lets each user on one host have one or more unique session keys for the traffic destined for another host (such session keys are not shared with other users).

- *Session-unique keying* has a single session key being assigned to a given IP address, upper-layer protocol, and port number triple (in this case, a user's FTP session may use a different key than the same user's Telnet session).

From a security point of view, user-oriented and session-unique keying are superior and therefore preferred. This is due to the fact that in many cases, a single computer system will have at least two suspicious users that do not mutually trust each other. When host-oriented keying is used and mutually suspicious users exist on a system, it is sometimes possible for a user to determine the host-oriented key by cryptanalytical attacks. Once this user has improperly obtained the key in use, he or she can either read another user's encrypted traffic or forge traffic from this particular user. Some possible attacks that follow and take advantage of this line of argumentation can be found in [25, 26]. When user-oriented or session-unique keying is used, certain kinds of attack from one user onto another user's data traffic are simply not possible. Unfortunately, the distinction between the three keying approaches is no longer used in the current protocol specifications of the IETF IPSEC WG. In reality, all we see today is host-oriented keying.

The SPD of an IPsec implementation defines at a high level of abstraction the security requirements for the IP packets that are forwarded or routed. As such, the SPD is established and maintained by a user or system administrator (or by an application operating within constraints established by either of them). Each entry in the SPD defines the traffic to be protected, how to protect it, and with whom the protection is shared. For each IP packet entering or leaving the IPsec implementation, the SPD must be consulted for the possible application of the IPsec security services. More specifically, an SPD entry may define one of the three actions to take upon a traffic match:

- *Discard:* A packet is not left in or out.

- *Bypass:* A packet is left in and out without applying IPsec security services.

- *Apply:* A packet is only left in or out after having applied IPsec security services.

As such, the SPD provides access control enforcement equivalent to a (static) packet filter.

In general, the IPsec protocols (i.e., AH and ESP) are largely independent of the associated SA and key management techniques and protocols, although the techniques and protocols involved do affect some of the security services offered by the protocols. The IPsec protocols and the corresponding key management protocols (including the IKE protocol) are overviewed next.

14.4   IPSEC PROTOCOLS

According to the terminology introduced in the OSI security architecture, the IPsec protocols provide the following security services:

- A data origin authentication service;

- A connectionless data integrity service (including protection against replay attacks);

- A data confidentiality service;

- An access control service;

- A limited traffic flow confidentiality service.

The security services are provided at the Internet layer, offering protection for IP and upper-layer protocols. As mentioned previously, the security services are provided by two subprotocols, namely, the AH and the ESP. Each protocol can be used to protect either only the upper-layer payload of an IP packet or the entire IP packet. This distinction is handled by considering two different modes of operation:

- *Transport mode* is used to protect the upper-layer payload of an IP packet.

- *Tunnel mode* is used to protect an entire IP packet (in this case, IP encapsulation is used as an enabling technique).

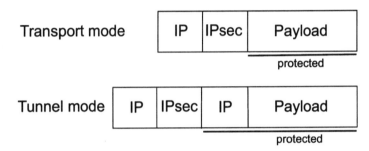

Figure 14.3   IPsec transport and tunnel modes.

Figure 14.3 illustrates the IPsec transport and tunnel modes. In transport mode, an IPsec header (i.e., an AH or ESP header) is inserted between the original IP header and payload (i.e., the TCP segment or UDP datagram). This is true for both IPv4 and IPv6:

- In IPv4, the transport mode IPsec header appears immediately after the IP header (with or without options), but before the upper-layer protocol data (e.g., TCP or UDP).

- In IPv6, the IPsec header appears after the base IP and some extension headers, but before destination options and the upper-layer protocol data.

In tunnel mode, the original IP packet is encapsulated into another IP packet. What this means is that there are two IP headers:

- An inner IP header that carries the original IP header (specifying the original source and destination IP addresses);

- An outer IP header that carries the new IP header (specifying new source and destination IP addresses).

The tunnel mode IPsec header appears between the outer IP header and the inner IP header.

Both IPsec protocols—AH and ESP—can operate in either transport or tunnel mode. Transport mode is typically used to secure IP traffic between two endpoints (i.e., computer systems), whereas tunnel mode is typically used to secure IP traffic between two points that are not necessarily the endpoints of the communications. For example, one of the points may be a security gateway for a corporate intranet. In this case, the IP traffic is encapsulated (i.e., using IPsec in tunnel mode) between the remote system and the security gateway (making sure that the systems located on the corporate intranet must not be able to handle IPsec). Note that whenever either endpoint is a security gateway, IPsec must be used in tunnel mode (in the case where traffic is destined for a security gateway, e.g., SNMP commands, the security gateway is acting as a host and transport mode is also allowed).

14.4.1   Authentication Header

The IPsec AH protocol provides data origin authentication and connectionless data integrity for IP packets (collectively referred to as "authentication" in this section). The precision of the authentication is a function of the granularity of the SA with which AH is employed. Depending on which cryptographic algorithm is used and how keying is performed, the AH may also provide non-repudiation of origin services. Finally, the AH may offer an antireplay service at the discretion of the receiver, to help counter specific denial-of-service attacks.

The IANA has assigned the protocol number 51 for the AH protocol, so the header immediately preceding the AH must include 51 in its protocol or next header field. As specified in RFC 2402 [15] and illustrated in Figure 14.4, the AH header consists of the following fields:

- An 8-bit Next Header field;

- An 8-bit Payload Length field;

- A 16-bit field that is reserved for future use;

- A 32-bit SPI field;

- A 32-bit Sequence Number field;

- A variable-length $n*32$-bit Authentication Data field.

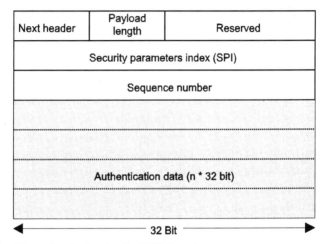

Next header	Payload length	Reserved
Security parameters index (SPI)		
Sequence number		
Authentication data (n * 32 bit)		

◀————————— 32 Bit —————————▶

Figure 14.4 The authentication header (AH) format.

The authentication data is computed by using an authentication algorithm and a cryptographic key specified in the corresponding SA. The sender computes the data before sending the IP packet, and the receiver verifies it upon reception. Several algorithms for authentication data computation and verification have been proposed in the past. In particular, RFC 2403 [16] suggests the use of the HMAC construction with MD5 and RFC 2404 [17] suggests the use of the same construction with SHA-1 (instead of MD5). The HMAC construction is fully explained in [27]. In short, the HMAC construction takes as input the message M and the authentication key K, and produces as output the following expression:

$$HMAC_K(M) = h(K \oplus opad, h(K \oplus ipad, M))$$

This expression looks more complicated than it really is. To compute $HMAC_K(M)$, the key K and an inner pad value *ipad* (*ipad* refers to the byte

0x36 repeated several times) are first added modulo 2. The result is then concatenated with the message M and hashed with the one-way hash function h (which can be either MD5 or SHA-1). Similarly, the result is then concatenated with the sum of K and an outer pad value *opad* (*opad* refers to the byte 0x5C repeated several times) modulo 2. Finally, this result is hashed with the appropriate one-way hash function h (MD5 or SHA-1), and the resulting authentication data is truncated to 96 bits.[10] Depending on the one-way hash function in use, the resulting HMAC constructions are called HMAC-MD5-96 (in the case of MD5) and HMAC-SHA-1-96 (in the case of SHA-1).

As the AH protocol does not provide data confidentiality services, implementations thereof may be widely deployed, even in countries where controls on encryption would preclude deployment of technology that potentially offered data confidentiality services. Consequently, AH is an appropriate protocol to employ when confidentiality is not required.

14.4.2   Encapsulating Security Payload

As its name suggests, the IPsec ESP protocol uses IP encapsulation to provide data confidentiality and partial traffic flow confidentiality (in tunnel mode and with the invocation of padding data to hide the size of an IP packet). Similar to the AH, the ESP protocol may also provide authentication (referring to data origin authentication and connectionless data integrity services). Note, however, that the scope of the authentication offered by the ESP is narrower than that for the AH (i.e., the IP headers below the ESP header are not protected). If only the upper-layer protocols need to be authenticated, then ESP authentication is an appropriate choice and is more space efficient than use of an AH encapsulating an ESP.

The IANA has assigned the protocol number 50 for the ESP protocol, so the header immediately preceding the ESP must include 50 in its protocol or next header field. The ESP format is specified in RFC 2406 [19] and illustrated in Figure 14.5. It consists of the following fields:

- A 32-bit SPI field (not encrypted);

- A 32-bit Sequence Number field (not encrypted);

- A variable-length Payload Data field;

---

[10]The truncation was introduced because of a desire to achieve a specific packet alignment goal, to avoid devoting all 128 or 160 bits to the authentication function, and to have a uniform size MAC whether MD5 or SHA-1 is employed.

- A variable-length Padding field;

- An 8-bit Pad Length field;

- An 8-bit Next Header field;

- In addition, the ESP may also include a variable-length $n*32$-bit Authentication Data field.

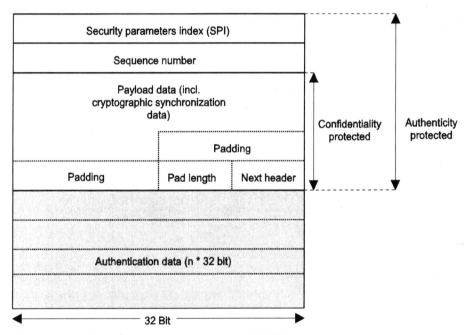

Figure 14.5 The encapsulating security payload (ESP) format.

In RFC 2405 [18], the DES in cipher block chaining (CBC) mode with an explicit initialization vector (IV) is introduced as the default algorithm to encrypt the ESP Payload Data field. But this default algorithm may be replaced by any other algorithm at will. For example, RFC 1851 specifies the experimental use of 3DES. In the future, it is possible and very likely that we will see more AES implementations instead of DES or 3DES implementations. Unfortunately, export, import, and use of specific encryption algorithms may be regulated in some countries. The algorithms for computing the authentication data are the same as the ones suggested for the AH.

Note that both AH and ESP are also vehicles for access control, based on the distribution of cryptographic keys and the management of traffic flows relative to these security protocols. Also note that full protection from traffic analysis is not provided by any of the two IPsec subprotocols. At the most, tunnel mode ESP can provide a partial traffic flow confidentiality service. In fact, the ESP protocol can be used to create a secure tunnel between two security gateways. In this case, anyone eavesdropping on the communications between the security gateways is not able to see what hosts are actually sending and receiving IP packets from behind the security gateways. Nevertheless, it is fair to mention that only a few Internet users worry about traffic analysis at all.

A final word should be said about the interdependence between data compression and encryption. Note that when encryption is employed at the Internet layer, it prevents effective data compression by lower protocol layers. Unfortunately, the suite of IPsec protocols in its current form does not provide support for a data compression service. Such a service may be provided by higher layer protocols, or, in the future, by IP itself.

14.5 KEY MANAGEMENT PROTOCOLS

The IP security architecture mandates support for both manual and automated SA and key management (using a key management protocol, such as IKE). For several years, the IETF IPSEC WG had been struggling with competing proposals for an automated SA and key management protocol:

- IBM proposed a Modular Key Management Protocol (MKMP) for its IP Secure Tunnel Protocol (IPST) [28].

- Sun Microsystems proposed and is using its Simple Key-Management for Internet Protocols (SKIP) [29].

- Phil Karn from Qualcomm originally proposed and prototyped a Photuris Key Management Protocol[11] [30, 31] that is conceptually similar to the Station-to-Station (STS) protocol originally proposed in [32]. The Photuris protocol combines an ephemeral Diffie-Hellman key exchange with a subsequent authentication

---

[11]Phil Karn was later joined by Bill Simpson to write the experimental Photuris protocol specifications.

step to protect against man-in-the-middle attacks. To protect the participanting peers against resource clogging attacks, the Photuris protocol introduced a cookie exchange [33].

- Hugo Krawczyk from IBM proposed a variation and generalization of the Photuris protocol, called Photuris Plus or SKEME [34].

- Because of the fact that Bill Simpson (one of the coauthors of the latest Photuris Key Management Protocol specification) refused to make changes to protocol specification in accordance to suggestions provided by the IETF IPSEC WG chairs, the Photuris Key Management Protocol was dropped from consideration and Hilaire Orman from the University of Arizona drafted a version of the Photuris and SKEME protocols that was called OAKLEY Key Determination Protocol [35]. In this protocol, several parameters are negotiable, including, for example, the mathematical structure in which the Diffie-Hellman key exchange is supposed to take place and the authentication method that is being used.

- A group of researchers from the NSA Office of INFOSEC Computer Science proposed a general Internet Security Association and Key Management Protocol (ISAKMP).

The protocol proposals and their tradeoffs are overviewed and fully discussed in the first edition of this book. In the first half of the 1990s, the developers of the various key management protocols competed with one another within the IETF IPSEC WG. There were basically two groups: SKIP and the group of Photuris-like protocols, including, for example, the OAKLEY Key Determination Protocol. Also, because of the fact that SKIP does not make use of SAs at all, the ISAKMP is useful only for the second group of protocols. Consequently, the two major contenders were SKIP and ISAKMP/OAKLEY.

In September 1996, the IETF Security Area Director[12] posted a document to the Internet to end the controversy. In this document, the two contenders (i.e., SKIP and ISAKMP/OAKLEY) were reviewed, and it was concluded that ISAKMP/OAKLEY should be the way to go and become the mandatory standard. The following three major arguments were used to explain this decision:

---

[12]The IETF Security Area Director was (and still is) Jeffrey Schiller from MIT.

1. ISAKMP/OAKLEY provides perfect forward secrecy (PFS),[13] whereas SKIP—at least in its native form—is not able to provide PFS.

2. Given an arbitrarily chosen pair of hosts, it is likelier that ISAKMP/OAKLEY results in a working SA than in SKIP.

3. The ISAKMP/OAKLEY approach seems to more closely follow the goals defined in the charter of the key management part of the IETF IPSEC WG.

This line of arguments is not very convincing. As explained later, SKIP can easily be modified to provide PFS. Also, SKIP is not good in establishing SAs because it does not use SAs at all. Finally, the third argument looks a bit arbitrary and is not well justified.

There are, however, good reasons to use ISAKMP/OAKLEY instead of SKIP. For example, SKIP does not rely on SAs, and as such, it incurs greater per-packet overhead. This is potentially advantageous for purely connectionless applications (because it avoids the need to create a session for a short-lived communication), but it is a serious disadvantage for connection-oriented applications. The vast majority of Internet applications are still connection-oriented, which favors the ISAKMP/OAKLEY-style approach. Also, over time we have added a number of parameters to the SA establishment procedure, which would also not have been possible using SKIP.

In either case, moving ISAKMP/OAKLEY forward on the Internet standards track was an important step (because it finished the struggle between the promoters of SKIP and the promoters of ISAKMP/OAKLEY). Finally, it was agreed that ISAKMP/OAKLEY would become the mandatory key management standard for the Internet (named IKE), and that SKIP could still become an elective standard for the Internet. As such, Sun Microsystems has continued to promote and market the SKIP technology. SKIP and IKE are overviewed and briefly discussed next.

14.5.1 SKIP

Most key distribution and management schemes and protocols are session-oriented, meaning that they establish and maintain an SA that lasts at least a certain amount of time. In contrast, many network and Internet layer protocols, such as IP and

---

[13]In short, PFS refers to the property of a key establishment protocol that the compromise of a long-term secret does not necessarily reveal all session keys that have been or will be established in the past (future). For all practical purposes, PFS requires a key agreement protocol, such as a Diffie-Hellman key exchange.

CLNP, are connectionless in nature and provide a connectionless datagram delivery service. To use a session-oriented key distribution scheme with IP, one has to create and implement a pseudosession layer underneath IP for the establishment and updating of IP traffic authentication and encryption keys. In fact, this layer is represented by the SA. While this is possible, it may be far less cumbersome to use a scheme that does not entail the overhead of such a pseudosession layer.

Against this background, Ashar Aziz from Sun Microsystems developed, proposed, and patented[14] a key distribution and management scheme and protocol that is not session-oriented, meaning that it does not make use of SAs, in the early 1990s. As mentioned, the resulting key distribution and management scheme and protocol was named SKIP and is being marketed by Sun Microsystems. You may refer to the SKIP home page[15] to learn about the availability of SKIP products and their interoperability with other VPN products.

Contrary to most other key distribution and management schemes and protocols that have been submitted to the IETF IPSEC WG, SKIP is not session-oriented. Instead of having the communicating peers establish and maintain an SA, SKIP uses packet-specific encryption keys that are communicated inband with the IP packets (in cryptographically protected form). More specifically, SKIP uses predistributed and authenticated Diffie-Hellman public keys to have two entities share an implicit master key from which a key encryption key (KEK) may be derived. The KEK, in turn, is used to encrypt a randomly chosen packet key and the packet key is used to encrypt the IP packet. Finally, the encrypted packet key is prepended to the encrypted IP packet.

Let us assume that all SKIP entities share a large prime p and a generator g of Z_p^*. We further assume that principal A has a private Diffie-Hellman key x_A and a corresponding public key $y_A = g^{x_A} (\text{mod } p)$, and that principal B has another private key x_B and a corresponding public key $y_B = g^{x_B} (\text{mod } p)$. Both public keys are distributed in the form of public key certificates and retrieved using a protocol, such as the Certificate Discovery Protocol (CDP), specified for SKIP. According to the Diffie-Hellman key exchange, A and B then share the secret key $K'_{AB} = g^{x_A x_B} (\text{mod } p)$. This key is implicit and does not need to be communicated explicitly to either entity (i.e., each entity can compute the shared secret based on knowledge of the other entity's identity and public key certificate). This mutually authenticated long-term secret key K'_{AB} can be used to derive a master key or

---

[14]The relevant patents for SKIP are U.S. Patent 5,588,060, "Method and Apparatus for a Key-Management Scheme for Internet Protocols" and U.S. Patent 5,548,646, "System for Signatureless Transmission and Reception of Data Packets Between Computer Networks."

[15]http://skip.incog.com

KEK K_{AB} to provide IP-packet-based authentication and encryption. K_{AB} can be derived, for example, by taking the low-order key size bits of K'_{AB}. However, there are at least two reasons for updating the KEK periodically:

1. It minimizes the exposure of any given KEK, making cryptanalysis more difficult.

2. Updating the KEK prevents the reuse of compromised packet keys.

The KEK is updated by sending in the packet a counter n that only increments and is never decremented. K_{AB} then becomes a function of this counter n as follows: $K_{ABn} = h(K'_{AB}, n)$. Again, h refers to a one-way hash function, such as MD5, SHA-1, or RIPEM. A simple and stateless way of implementing n is to let n be equal to the number of time units since the more recent of A's or B's certificates. In the absence of a clock, n can be constructed simply by using a counter.

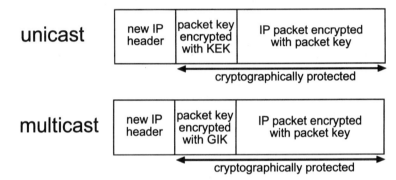

Figure 14.6   The use of SKIP to encrypt unicast and multicast IP packets.

To encrypt an individual IP packet, A randomly generates a packet key K_p and digitally envelopes the packet with this key and the KEK that he or she implicitly shares with the recipient B. More accurately, A encrypts both the packet with K_p and K_p with K_{AB}, and encapsulates both ciphertexts in a new IP packet. Note that because K_{AB} can be cached for efficiency, it allows packet keys to be modified very rapidly without incurring the computational overhead of public key operations. The packet keys can be changed as frequently as desired in line with a key management policy. If necessary, packet keys can be changed on a per-packet basis. When B receives the encrypted packet, he or she looks up A's certificate (using, for example, the SKIP CDP). Using the corresponding long-term public key and his or her own long-term private key, B can compute K'_{AB} and hence K_{AB}. Using K_{AB}, B can finally decrypt both K_p and the entire IP packet.

Figure 14.6 illustrates the use of SKIP to encrypt unicast and multicast IP packets. The use of SKIP to encrypt unicast packets has been described. The traditional approach for key distribution in a multicast environment is to set up and run a KDC that distributes the traffic keys to the legitimate and authorized members of a group. This one shared key is then used by the group members to encrypt and decrypt data. There are at least two problems related to this approach:

1. Key change cannot be done efficiently and does not scale well to large groups. Key change policies need to be a function of the amount of data encrypted with a given key, and not merely a function of time alone. This means that for high-speed data transmission links the keys must be updated far more frequently than for slower links, for the same key change policy. For a large number of members in a multicast group, however, it may become increasingly difficult or prohibitive for a multicast KDC to be rapidly supplying updated keys to all group members.

2. Use of the same key by all members of a multicast group precludes the use of certain stream ciphers. This is because using the same key will result in the same key stream being used to encrypt different plaintexts. Because key stream reuse is catastrophic to the security of some stream ciphers, it should be avoided generally. Nevertheless, it is important to allow stream ciphers to be used in conjunction with IP multicast. A common use of IP multicast is videoconferencing. Because video is a demanding application in terms of speed and throughput, it is important to allow the use of ciphers that can be efficiently implemented in software. Some of the most widely used and efficient ciphers are stream ciphers such as RC4. Because of key stream reuse issues, it is not possible to use a stream cipher like RC4 for IP multicast if all members of the multicast group use the same traffic key.

A simple modification of the basic SKIP protocol solves both problems. Instead of distributing a traffic key to the group members, a group owner may distribute a group interchange key (GIK) to them. As illustrated in Figure 14.6, the GIK can then be used to encrypt multicast IP packets (the GIK plays the role of the KEK for unicast traffic). To send encrypted data to a multicast group, a member first has to request the GIK from the group owner. The group owner's identity has to be known to the requesting principal. The request is made using the unicast SKIP protocol. Once the group owner determines that the requesting principal is on the group's access control list (ACL), it will provide the GIK to him or her. The requesting principal then encrypts the multicast traffic using one (or more) randomly generated packet keys. The packet keys are in turn encrypted using the

GIK, and sent in-line with the corresponding IP packets. Note that changing the multicast traffic encryption key is simple. Each source can do this by randomly generating a new traffic key and communicating it in-line with the multicast IP packets (encrypted using the GIK). Multicast traffic encryption keys can be updated rapidly, even every packet if so desired, with no further communications overhead. Also note that because each source of encrypted traffic generates random traffic keys, all sources of encrypted traffic naturally use different keys. This allows any kind of stream cipher to be used for multicast traffic encryption as well.

Contrary to most other key distribution and management schemes and protocols that have been submitted to the IETF IPSEC WG, the original form of SKIP did not provide PFS. There is, however, a simple solution for this problem. In fact, it is possible to use a simple handshake that implements an additional ephemeral Diffie-Hellman key exchange to provide PFS. The ephemeral Diffie-Hellman key exchange, in turn, is authenticated using the KEK K_{AB}. Note, however, that any ephemeral Diffie-Hellman key exchange introduces greater bilateral state and overhead than is present in the base SKIP protocol. Consequently, when using SKIP PFS, certain features of the base SKIP protocol that rely on its statelessness become unavailable. In general, there is an interesting tradeoff between the statelessness of a key management protocol and its ability to provide PFS [36]. This tradeoff has not been investigated sufficiently and is not well understood today.

14.5.2   IKE

Contrary to SKIP and similar to most other key distribution and management schemes and protocols that have been submitted to the IETF IPSEC WG, the IKE protocol is session-oriented, meaning that it is used to establish and maintain SAs. If no SA is available for an inbound or outbound IP packet, the IKE protocol is first used to establish one. In fact, the whole purpose of the IKE protocol is to establish shared security parameters and authenticated keys—in other words, SAs—among communicating IPsec modules.

IKE refers to a combination of ISAKMP and OAKLEY. In short, ISAKMP defines how two peers communicate, how the messages they use to communicate are constructed, and through which state transitions they go to secure their communications. It provides the means to authenticate a peer, to exchange information for a key exchange, and to negotiate security services. It does not, however, define how a particular authenticated key exchange is done, nor does it define the attributes necessary for the establishment of SAs. These issues are left to a specific key exchange protocol, such as OAKLEY. As such, ISAKMP is a general-purpose security exchange protocol that may be used for policy negotiation and establishment of keying material for a variety of needs. The specification of what IKE is being used for is done in a *domain of interpretation* (DOI). The IP security DOI for ISAKMP is specified in RFC 2407 [21]. More specifically, RFC 2407 defines how ISAKMP can be used to negotiate IKE and IPsec SAs. If and when IKE is used by other protocols, they will each have to define their own DOI.[16] In other words, ISAKMP defines the language to establish authenticated session keys, whereas OAKLEY defines the steps two peers must actually take to establish the keys.

The IKE protocol is a request-response type of protocol with an initiator and a responder. The IKE initiator is the party that is instructed by its IPsec module to establish an SA or an SA bundle as a result of an outbound packet matching an SPD entry. The SPD of IPsec is used to instruct IKE what to establish but does not instruct IKE how to do so. In fact, how IKE establishes the IPsec SAs is based on its own policy settings. IKE defines policy in terms of protection suites. Each protection suite must define at least the encryption algorithm, the hash algorithm, the Diffie-Hellman group, and the method of authentication used. IKE's policy database then is the list of all protection suites weighted in order of preference.

The establishment of an IPsec SA (or an SA bundle) using IKE is a two-phase process:

- In phase one, an IKE SA is established. The IKE SA defines the way in which the two peers communicate, for example, which algorithm to use to encrypt IKE traffic, how to authenticate the remote peer, and so on.

- In phase two, the IKE SA is used to establish any given number of IPsec SAs between the communicating peers. The IPsec SAs established by IKE may optionally have PFS of the keys and, if desired, also of the peer identity.

Phase One: Establishing an IKE SA

The establishment of an IKE SA basically consists of three steps and corresponding exchanges:

- A cookie exchange;

---

[16]At the time of this writing, no other DOI is available.

- A value exchange;

- An authentication exchange.

In short, the cookie exchange protects the responder from simple resource clogging attacks. Once initiator and responder cookies have been established, a value exchange and a subsequent authentication exchange are used to implement an authenticated Diffie-Hellman key exchange, and to provide the initiator and responder with an authenticated shared secret accordingly.

Cookie Exchange: To protect the responder from simple resource clogging attacks, the initiator must provide a valid cookie whenever he or she wants to enter a value exchange and initiate a computationally expensive Diffie-Hellman key exchange accordingly. A valid cookie, in turn, is a value that can be computed and verified only by the responder. For example, it can be a keyed one-way hash value of the initiator's and responder's IP addresses and port numbers. In this case, the key must be known only to the responder. The cookie exchange and the rationale behind it are beyond the scope of this book. Refer to [33] for a more detailed explanation and analysis.

Value Exchange: A value exchange establishes a shared secret key between the communicating peers. In general, there is more than one way to establish a key, but IKE always uses a Diffie-Hellman key exchange. Consequently, the act of doing a Diffie-Hellman key exchange is not negotiable, but the parameters to use are. In fact, IKE borrows five groups from the OAKLEY specification; three are traditional exchanges doing exponentiation modulo a large prime, and two are elliptic curve groups. Upon completion of the value exchange, the two peers share a key and this key still needs to be authenticated.

Authentication Exchange: In a final step, the Diffie-Hellman key and, therefore, the IKE SA must be authenticated. There are five methods of authentication defined in IKE: preshared keys, digital signature using DSS, digital signature using RSA, and two methods that use an encrypted nonce exchange with RSA.

There are basically two modes and corresponding exchanges that can be used in phase one: a main mode exchange and an aggressive mode exchange.

- In a *main mode exchange*, the request and response messages for each of the three exchanges are sent and received one after the other, totaling six messages.

- Contrary to that, some of the messages are sent together in an *aggressive mode exchange*, totaling three messages. Most important, an aggressive mode exchange cannot use cookies to protect against resource clogging attacks.

In short, aggressive mode is faster but main mode is more flexible. Once phase one is completed, phase two may commence and the required IPsec SAs may be created.

Phase Two: Establishing IPsec SAs

Contrary to phase one, there is a single phase two exchange, and this exchange has been named *quick mode exchange*. This exchange negotiates IPsec SAs under the protection of the IKE SA, which was created in phase one. The keys used for the IPsec SAs are, by default, derived from the IKE secret state. Pseudorandom nonces are exchanged in quick mode and hashed with the secret state to generate keys and guarantee that all SAs have unique keys. All such keys do not have the property of PFS as they are all derived from the same root key (i.e., the IKE shared secret). To provide PFS, Diffie-Hellman public values, and the group from which they are derived, are exchanged along the nonces and IPsec SA negotiation parameters. The resulting secret is used to generate the IPsecSA keys to guarantee PFS.

14.6   IMPLEMENTATIONS

In general, there are three possibilities to implement the IPsec architecture (with or without key management) and to place the implementation in a host or security gateway:

- The most simple and straightforward possibility is to integrate the IPsec protocols into a native IP implementation. This is applicable to hosts and security gateways, but requires access to the corresponding source code.

- Another possibility is provided by so-called "bump-in-the-stack" (BITS) implementations. In these implementations, IPsec is implemented underneath an existing IP stack, between the native IP implementation and the local network drivers. Source code access for the IP stack is not required in this case, making it appropriate for use with legacy systems. This approach, when it is adopted, is usually employed with hosts.

- A somewhat related possibility is provided by so-called "bump-in-the-wire" (BITW) implementations. Similar to BITS implementations, source code access for the IP stack is not required for BITW implementations. But in addition to BITS implementations, additional hardware in the form of outboard cryptographic processors are typically used. This is a common design feature of network security systems used by the military, and of some commercial systems as well. BITW implementations may be designed to serve both hosts and security gateways.

As of this writing, most IPsec implementations are either BITS or BITW. For example, PGPnet is a BITS implementation, whereas most firewall products that support IPsec for virtual private networking are BITW implementations. The dominance of BITS or BITW implementations is expected to change in the future, because more vendors of networking software have integrated or are about to integrate the IPsec protocols into their products. For example, Windows 2000 comes along with IPsec support and the Cisco IOS also provides support for the IPsec protocols in the more recent releases.

14.7   CONCLUSIONS

The IP security architecture as discussed in this chapter is not an overall security architecture for the Internet. It addresses security only at the Internet layer, provided through the use of a suite of security protocols (i.e., the IPsec protocols and the IKE protocol) and a corresponding API (i.e., the PF_KEY key management API version 2 as specified in [37]). Related topics, such as securing the routing infrastructure, the DNS, and network management, are further addressed in [12]. Also, the current status of the IP security architecture does not even address all aspects of Internet layer security. Topics for further study include the use of Internet layer security protocols in conjunction with NAT, a more complete support for IP multicast, issues related to interoperability and benchmark testing. Note that the evolving nature of the IP architecture and the corresponding suite of security protocols make true interoperability hard to achieve.

There are advantages and disadvantages related to security protocols that operate at the Internet layer in general, and the IPsec protocols in particular:

- The main advantage is that applications must not be changed to use the IPsec protocols. Another advantage is that providing security at the Internet layer works for both TCP- and UDP-based applications. This is advantageous because a steadily increasing number of applications are based on UDP that is hard to secure at the transport layer (we will further address this point in Chapter 15).

- The main disadvantage is that IP stacks must either be changed or extended. Because of the inherent complexity of the IKE protocol, the changes or extensions are not at all trivial. In the long term, high-speed networking may also provide a performance problem. As of this writing, it is not clear whether encryption rates and key agility properties of IPsec implementations will meet the performance requirements of future high-speed networks.

Because of the disadvantages of providing security at the Internet layer, some alternative approaches have appeared in the past (as discussed in the other sections of this chapter). The current trend in industry suggests that the IPsec protocols will primarily be used for virtual private networking and connecting mobile users to corporate intranets. As mentioned in Chapter 13, the combination of L2TP and IPsec is a particularly interesting technology for virtual private networking today.

REFERENCES

[1] N. Doraswamy and D. Harkins, *IPSec: The News Security Standard for the Internet, Intranets, and Virtual Private Networks*, Prentice Hall PTR, Upper Saddle River, NJ, 1999.

[2] E. Kaufman and A. Neuman, *Implementing IPSec: Making Security Work on VPNs, Intranets, and Extranets*, John Wiley & Sons, New York, 1999.

[3] S. Frankel, *Demystifying the IPsec Puzzle*, Artech House, Norwood, MA, 2001.

[4] R. Nelson, "SDNS Services and Architecture," *Proceedings of National Computer Security Conference*, 1987, pp. 153–157.

[5] ISO/IEC 11577, Information Technology—Telecommunications and Information Exchange Between Systems—Network Layer Security Protocol, Geneva, Switzerland, 1993.

[6] J. Ioannidis and M. Blaze, "The Architecture and Implementation of Network-Layer Security Under Unix," *Proceedings of the USENIX UNIX Security Symposium IV*, October 1993, pp. 29–39.

[7] R. J. Atkinson, "Security Architecture for the Internet Protocol," Request for Comments 1825, August 1995.

[8] R. J. Atkinson, "IP Authentication Header," Request for Comments 1826, August 1995.

[9] R. J. Atkinson, "IP Encapsulating Security Payload," Request for Comments 1827, August 1995.

[10] P. Metzger and W. Simpson, "IP Authentication Using Keyed MD5," Request for Comments 1828, August 1995.

[11] P. Karn, P. Metzger, and W. Simpson, "The ESP DES-CBC Transform," Request for Comments 1829, August 1995.

[12] R. J. Atkinson, "Towards a More Secure Internet," *IEEE Computer*, Vol. 30, January 1997, pp. 57–61.

[13] R. Oppliger, "Security at the Internet Layer," *IEEE Computer*, Vol. 31, No. 9, September 1998, pp. 43–47.

[14] S. Kent and R. Atkinson, "Security Architecture for the Internet Protocol," Request for Comments 2401, November 1998.

[15] S. Kent and R. Atkinson, "IP Authentication Header," Request for Comments 2402, November 1998.

[16] C. Madson and R. Glenn, "The Use of HMAC-MD5-96 Within ESP and AH," Request for Comments 2403, November 1998.

[17] C. Madson and R. Glenn, "The Use of HMAC-SHA-1-96 Within ESP and AH," Request for Comments 2404, November 1998.

[18] C. Madson and N. Doraswamy, "The ESP DES-CBC Cipher Algorithm with Explicit IV," Request for Comments 2405, November 1998.

[19] S. Kent and R. Atkinson, "IP Encapsulating Security Payload (ESP)," Request for Comments 2406, November 1998.

[20] R. Glenn and S. Kent, "The NULL Encryption Algorithm and Its Use with IPsec," Request for Comments 2410, November 1998.

[21] D. Piper, "The Internet IP Security Domain of Interpretation for ISAKMP," Request for Comments 2407, November 1998.

[22] D. Maughan, et al., "Internet Security Association and Key Management Protocol (ISAKMP)," Request for Comments 2408, November 1998.

[23] D. Harkins and D. Carrel, "The Internet Key Exchange (IKE)," Request for Comments 2409, November 1998.

[24] R. Thayer and N. Doraswamy, "IP Security Document Roadmap," Request for Comments 2411, November 1998.

[25] S. M. Bellovin, "Problem Areas for the IP Security Protocols," *Proceedings of the 6th USENIX Security Symposium*, 1996, pp. 1–16.

[26] S. M. Bellovin, "Probable Plaintext Cryptanalysis of the IP Security Protocols," *Proceedings of the Symposium on Network and Distributed System Security*, 1997, pp. 155–160.

[27] M. Oehler and R. Glenn, "HMAC-MD5 IP Authentication with Replay Prevention," Request for Comments 2085, February 1997.

[28] P. C. Cheng, et al., "A Security Architecture for the Internet Protocol," *IBM Systems Journal*, Vol. 37, No. 1, 1998, pp. 42–60.

[29] G. Caronni, et al., "SKIP—Securing the Internet," *Proceedings of WET ICE '96*, Workshops on Enabling Technologies: Infrastructure for Collaborative Enterprises, June 1996, pp. 62–67.

[30] P. Karn and W. Simpson, "Photuris: Session-Key Management Protocol," Request for Comments 2522, March 1999.

[31] P. Karn and W. Simpson, "Photuris: Extended Schemes and Attributes," Request for Comments 2523, March 1999.

[32] W. Diffie, P. C. van Oorshot, and M. J. Wiener, "Authentication and Authenticated Key Exchanges," *Designs, Codes and Cryptography*, Kluwer Academic Publishers, Norwell, MA, 1992, pp. 107–125.

[33] R. Oppliger, "Protecting Key Exchange and Management Protocols Against Resource Clogging Attacks," *Proceedings of the IFIP TC6 and TC11 Joint Working Conference on Communications and Multimedia Security*, September 1999, Kluwer Academic Publishers, Norwell, MA, pp. 163–175.

[34] H. Krawczyk, "SKEME: A Versatile Secure Key Exchange Mechanism for Internet," *Proceedings of Internet Society Symposium on Network and Distributed System Security*, February 1996.

[35] H. Orman, "The OAKLEY Key Determination Protocol," Request for Comments 2412, November 1998.

[36] R. Oppliger, "Internet Security: Firewalls and Beyond," *Communications of the ACM*, Vol. 40, No. 5, May 1997, pp. 92–102.

[37] D. McDonald, C. Metz, and B. Phan, "PF_KEY Key Management API, Version 2," Request for Comments 2367, July 1998.

Chapter 15

Transport Layer Security Protocols

In this chapter, we focus on some security protocols that have been proposed, specified, implemented, and deployed for the transport layer of the Internet model. More
specifically, we have a look at previous work in Section 15.1, overview and discuss
the Secure Sockets Layer (SSL) and Transport Layer Security (TLS) protocols in
Section 15.2 and 15.3, address firewall traversal in Section 15.4, and draw some
conclusions in Section 15.5. Note that some parts of this chapter are taken from
Chapter 6 of [1]. Also note that all transport layer security protocols we look at
in this chapter (i.e., the SSL and TLS protocols) are layered on top of TCP and
its connection-oriented transport layer service. Consequently, these protocols could
also be named *session layer security protocols*. This term, however, would not match
the Internet model and its four layers. Consequently, we do not use the term in this
book.

15.1 PREVIOUS WORK

The promoters of transport layer security protocols generally have an application
developer in mind. For such a developer it would be nice to have a possibility
to establish secure network connections (instead of insecure network connections).

Consequently, the application developer needs a development environment and a library that allows him or her to establish secure network connections. Having this idea in mind, several transport layer security protocols have been proposed in the past (in addition to the SSL and TLS protocols):

- Similar to the SP3, the *Security Protocol 4* (SP4) is a transport layer security protocol that was jointly developed by the NSA and NIST as part of the SDNS suite of security protocols [2].

- The *Transport Layer Security Protocol* (TLSP) was developed and standardized by the ISO [3].

- Steven Bellovin and Matt Blaze from AT&T Bell Laboratories developed and prototyped a transport layer security protocol in a software package called *Encrypted Session Manager* (ESM) [4].

The SP4 and the TLSP are full-fledged transport layer security protocols, whereas the ESM—similar to the SSL and TLS protocols—only runs on top of a connection-oriented and reliable transport layer service, such as provided by TCP. Consequently, these protocols could also be named "session layer security protocols." As previously mentioned, however, this term does not match the four layers of the Internet model and is therefore not used in this book.

As of this writing, the SSL and TLS protocols are still the major examples of transport layer security protocols. They are overviewed and briefly discussed next.

15.2   SSL PROTOCOL

In general, there are several possibilities to cryptographically protect HTTP data traffic. For example, in the early 1990s the CommerceNet consortium proposed Secure HTTP (S-HTTP). As will be briefly mentioned in Chapter 16, S-HTTP was basically a security-specific enhancement of HTTP. An implementation of S-HTTP was made publicly available in a modified version of the NCSA Mosaic browser that users had to purchase (contrary to the "normal" NCSA Mosaic browser that was publicly and freely available on the Internet). At the same time, however, Netscape Communications introduced SSL and a protocol of the same name with the first version of Netscape Navigator.[1] Contrary to the CommerceNet consortium,

---

[1]On August 12, 1997, Netscape Communications was granted U.S. patent 5,657,390, "Secure Socket Layer Application Program Apparatus and Method" for the technology employed by the SSL protocol.

Netscape Communications did not charge its customers for the implementation of its security protocol. Consequently, SSL became the predominant protocol to provide security services for HTTP data traffic after 1994, and S-HTTP silently sank into oblivion.

So far, we have seen three versions of SSL:

- SSL version 1.0 was used internally only by Netscape Communications. It contained some serious flaws and was never released in public.

- SSL version 2.0 was incorporated into Netscape Navigator versions 1.0 through 2.x. It had some weaknesses related to specific incarnations of the man-in-the-middle attack. In an attempt to leverage public uncertainty about SSL's security, Microsoft also introduced the competing Private Communication Technology (PCT) protocol in its first release of its Internet Explorer in 1996.

- Netscape Communications responded to Microsoft's PCT challenge by introducing SSL version 3.0 that addressed the problems in SSL 2.0 and added some new features. At this point, Microsoft backed down and agreed to support SSL in all versions of its TCP/IP-based software (although its own software still supports PCT for backward compatibility).

The latest specification of SSL 3.0 was officially released in March 1996. It is implemented in both Netscape Navigator 3.0 (and higher) and Microsoft Internet Explorer 3.0 (and higher). As discussed later in this chapter, SSL 3.0 has also been adapted by the IETF Transport Layer Security (TLS) WG. In fact, the TLS 1.0 protocol specification is a derivative of SSL 3.0.

The architecture of SSL and the corresponding SSL protocol are illustrated in Figure 15.1. According to this figure, SSL refers to an intermediate (security) layer between the transport layer and the application layer. SSL is layered on top of a connection-oriented and reliable transport service, such as provided by TCP. It is conceptually able to provide security services for arbitrary TCP-based application protocols, not just HTTP. As a matter of fact, one major advantage of transport layer security protocols in general, and the SSL protocol in particular, is that they are application-independent, in the sense that they can be used to transparently secure any application protocol layered on top of TCP. Figure 15.1 illustrates several exemplary application protocols, including NSIIOP, HTTP, FTP, Telnet, IMAP, IRC, and POP3. They can all be secured by layering them on top of SSL (the appended letter "S" in the corresponding protocol acronyms indicates the use of SSL). Note, however, that SSL has a strong client-server orientation and does not really meet the requirements of peer application protocols.

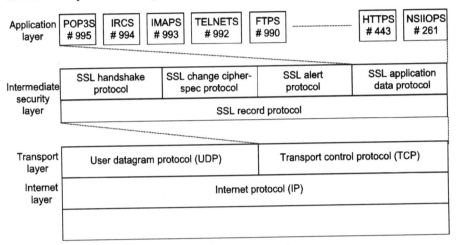

Figure 15.1   The architecture of SSL and the SSL protocol.

In short, the SSL protocol provides communication security that has three basic properties:

1. The communicating parties (i.e., the client and the server) can authenticate each other using public key cryptography.

2. The confidentiality of the data traffic is protected, as the connection is transparently encrypted after an initial handshake and session key negotiation has taken place.

3. The authenticity and integrity of the data traffic is also protected, as messages are transparently authenticated and integrity-checked using MACs.

Nevertheless, it is important to note that SSL does not protect against traffic analysis attacks. For example, by examining the unencrypted source and destination IP addresses and TCP port numbers, or examining the volume of transmitted data, a traffic analyst can still determine what parties are interacting, what types of services are being used, and sometimes even recover information about business or personal relationships. We have already mentioned in this book that users generally consider the threat of traffic analysis to be relatively low, and so the developers of SSL have not attempted to address it, either. Furthermore, SSL does not protect against attacks directed against the TCP implementation, such as TCP SYN flooding or session hijacking attacks.

To use SSL protection, both the client and server must know that the other side is using SSL. In general, there are three possibilities to address this issue:

1. Use dedicated port numbers reserved by the IANA. In this case, a separate port number must be assigned for every application protocol that uses SSL.

2. Use the normal port number for every application protocol, and to negotiate security options as part of the (now slightly modified) application protocol.

3. Use a TCP option to negotiate the use of a security protocol, such as SSL, during the normal TCP connection establishment phase.

Table 15.1
Port Numbers Assigned for Application Protocols That Run on Top of SSL/TLS

Keyword	*Port*	*Description*
nsiiops	261	IIOP name service over TLS/SSL
https	443	HTTP over TLS/SSL
smtps	465	SMTP over TLS/SSL (former **ssmtp**)
nntps	563	NNTP over TLS/SSL (former **snntp**)
ldaps	636	LDAP over TLS/SSL (former **sldap**)
ftps-data	989	FTP (data) over TLS/SSL
ftps	990	FTP (control) over TLS/SSL
telnets	992	TELNET over TLS/SSL
imaps	993	IMAP4 over TLS/SSL
ircs	994	IRC over TLS/SSL
pop3s	995	POP3 over TLS/SSL (former **spop3**)

The application-specific negotiation of security options (i.e., the second possibility) has the disadvantage of requiring each application protocol to be modified to understand the negotiation process. Also, defining a TCP option (i.e., the third possibility) would be a fine solution, but has not been seriously discussed so far. In practice, separate port numbers have been reserved and assigned by the IANA for every application protocol that may run on top of SSL or TLS (i.e., the first possibility).[2] Note, however, that the use of separate port numbers also has the

---

[2]http://www.isi.edu/in-notes/iana/assignments/port-numbers

disadvantage of requiring two TCP connections if the client does not know what the server supports. First the client must connect to the secure port, and then to the unsecure port, or vice versa. It is very possible that future protocols will abandon this approach and go for the second possibility. For example, the Simple Authentication and Security Layer (SALS) defines a method for adding authentication support to connection-based application protocols [5]. According to the SALS specification, the use of authentication mechanisms is negotiable between the client and server of a given application protocol. As of this writing, SALS is primarily used to secure communications between IMAP4 clients and servers. It is not clear at the moment whether SALS or similar mechanisms will also be used to secure other application protocols.

The port numbers assigned by the IANA for application protocols that run on top of SSL/TLS are summarized in Table 15.1 and partly illustrated in Figure 15.1. Note that some acronyms for application protocols that run on top of SSL/TLS have changed since the publication of the first edition of this book. Today, the "S" indicating the use of SSL is consistently appended (postfixed) to the acronyms of the corresponding application protocols (in some earlier terminologies, the "S" was inconsistently used and prepended (prefixed) to some acronyms).

Table 15.2
SSL Session State Information Elements

Element	Description
Session ID	Identifier chosen by the server to identify an active or resumable session state.
Peer certificate	X.509 version 3 certificate of the peer entity.
Compression method	Algorithm used to compress data prior to encryption.
Cipher spec	Specification of the data encryption and MAC algorithms.
Master secret	48-byte secret shared between the client and server.
Is resumable	Flag that indicates whether the session can be used to initiate new connections.

In general, an SSL session is stateful and the SSL protocol must initialize and maintain the state information on either side of the session. The corresponding session state information elements, including a session ID, a peer certificate, a compression method, a cipher spec, a master secret, and a flag that indicates whether the session is resumable, are summarized in Table 15.2. An SSL session can be used for several connections, and the corresponding connection state information elements are summarized in Table 15.3. They include cryptographic parameters, such as server and client random byte sequences, server and client write MAC secrets, server and client write keys, an initialization vector, and a sequence number. In either case, it is important to note that communicating parties may use multiple simultaneous SSL sessions and sessions with multiple simultaneous connections.

Table 15.3
SSL Connection State Information Elements

Element	Description
Server and client random	Byte sequences that are chosen by the server and client for each connection.
Server write MAC secret	Secret used for MAC operations on data written by the server.
Client write MAC secret	Secret used for MAC operations on data written by the client.
Server write key	Key used for data encryption by the server and decryption by the client.
Client write key	Key used for data encryption by the client and decryption by the server.
Initialization vector	Initialization state for a block cipher in CBC mode. This field is first initialized by the SSL Handshake Protocol. Thereafter, the final ciphertext block from each record is preserved for use with the following record.
Sequence number	Each party maintains separate sequence numbers for transmitted and received messages for each connection.

As illustrated in Figure 15.1, the SSL protocol consists of two main parts, the SSL Record Protocol and several SSL subprotocols layered on top of it:

- The *SSL Record Protocol* is layered on top of a connection-oriented and reliable transport layer service, such as provided by TCP, and provides message origin authentication, data confidentiality, and data integrity services (including such things as replay protection).

- The SSL subprotocols are layered on top of the SSL Record Protocol to provide support for SSL session and connection establishment management.

The most important SSL subprotocol is the SSL Handshake Protocol. This protocol, in turn, is an authentication and key exchange protocol that can be used to negotiate, initialize, and synchronize security parameters and corresponding state information located at either endpoint of an SSL session or connection.

After the SSL Handshake Protocol has completed, application data can be sent and received using the SSL Record Protocol and the negotiated security parameters and state information elements. The SSL Record and Handshake Protocols are overviewed next.

15.2.1   SSL Record Protocol

The SSL Record Protocol receives data from higher layer SSL subprotocols and addresses data fragmentation, compression,[3] authentication, and encryption. More precisely, the protocol takes as input a data block of arbitrary size, and produces as output a series of SSL data fragments (further referred to as SSL records) of less than or equal to $2^{14} - 1 = 16,383$ bytes each.

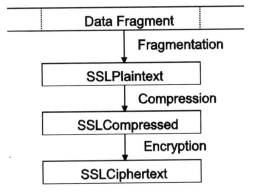

Figure 15.2   The SSL Record Protocol steps.

The various steps of the SSL Record Protocol that lead from a raw data fragment to an SSLPlaintext (fragmentation step), SSLCompressed (compression step), and SSLCiphertext (encryption step) record are illustrated in Figure 15.2. Finally, each SSL record contains the following information fields:

- Content type;

- Protocol version number;

---

[3]Data compression as addressed by the SSL Record Protocol is not supported by the major SSL implementations in use today.

- Length;

- Data payload (optionally compressed and encrypted);

- MAC.

The content type defines the higher layer protocol that must be used to subsequently process the SSL record data payload (after proper decompression and decryption). The protocol version number determines the SSL version in use (typically 3.0). Each SSL record data payload is compressed and encrypted according to the current compression method and cipher spec defined for the SSL session. At the start of each SSL session, the compression method and cipher spec are usually defined as null. They are both set during the initial execution of the SSL Handshake Protocol. Finally, a MAC is appended to each SSL record. It provides message origin authentication and data integrity services. Similar to the encryption algorithm, the algorithm that is used to compute and verify the MAC is defined in the cipher spec of the current session state. By default, the SSL Record Protocol uses a MAC construction that is similar but still different from the newer HMAC construction specified in RFC 2104 [6]. There are three major differences between the SSL MAC construction and the HMAC construction:

1. The SSL MAC construction includes a sequence number in the message before hashing to protect against specific forms of replay attacks.

2. The SSL MAC construction includes the record length.

3. The SSL MAC construction uses concatenation operators, whereas the HMAC construction uses the addition modulo 2.

All these differences exist mainly because the SSL MAC construction predates the adoption of the HMAC construction in almost all Internet security protocol specifications. The HMAC construction was also adopted for the more recent TLS protocol specification.

As illustrated in Figure 15.1, several SSL subprotocols are layered on top of the SSL Record Protocol. Each subprotocol may refer to specific types of messages that are sent using the SSL Record Protocol. The SSL 3.0 specification defines the following three SSL protocols:

- Alert Protocol;

- Handshake Protocol;

- ChangeCipherSpec Protocol.

In short, the SSL Alert Protocol is used to transmit alerts (i.e., alert messages) via the SSL Record Protocol. Each alert message consists of two parts, an alert level and an alert description.

The SSL Handshake Protocol is the major SSL subprotocol. It is used to mutually authenticate the client and the server and to exchange a session key. As such, the SSL Handshake Protocol is overviewed and briefly discussed in the following section.

Finally, the SSL ChangeCipherSpec Protocol is used to change between one cipher spec and another. Although the cipher spec is normally changed at the end of an SSL handshake, it can also be changed at any later point in time.

In addition to these SSL subprotocols, an SSL Application Data Protocol is used to directly pass application data to the SSL Record Protocol.

15.2.2   SSL Handshake Protocol

The SSL Handshake Protocol is the main SSL subprotocol that is layered on top of the SSL Record Protocol. Consequently, SSL handshake messages are supplied to the SSL record layer, where they are encapsulated within one or more SSL records, which are processed and transmitted as specified by the compression method and cipher spec of the current SSL session, and the cryptographic keys of the corresponding SSL connection. The aim of the SSL Handshake Protocol is to have a client and server establish and maintain state information that is used to secure communications. More specifically, the protocol is to have the client and server agree on a common SSL protocol version, select the compression method and cipher spec, optionally authenticate each other, and create a master secret from which the various session keys for message authentication and encryption may be derived.

In short, an execution of the SSL Handshake Protocol between a client C and a server S can be summarized as follows (the messages that are put in square brackets are optional):

$$
\begin{array}{lll}
1 : C & \longrightarrow & S : \text{ClientHello} \\
2 : S & \longrightarrow & C : \text{ServerHello} \\
: & & : [\text{Certificate}] \\
: & & : [\text{ServerKeyExchange}] \\
: & & : [\text{CertificateRequest}] \\
: & & : \text{ServerHelloDone} \\
3 : C & \longrightarrow & S : [\text{Certificate}] \\
: & & : \text{ClientKeyExchange} \\
: & & : [\text{CertificateVerify}] \\
: & & : \text{ChangeCipherSpec} \\
: & & : \text{Finished} \\
4 : S & \longrightarrow & C : \text{ChangeCipherSpec} \\
: & & : \text{Finished}
\end{array}
$$

When the client C wants to connect to the server S, it establishes a TCP connection to the HTTPS port (not included in the protocol description) and sends a ClientHello message to the server in step 1 of the SSL Handshake Protocol execution. The client can also send a ClientHello message in response to a HelloRequest message or on its own initiative to renegotiate the security parameters of an existing connection. The ClientHello message includes the following fields:

- The number of the highest SSL version understood by the client (typically 3.0);

- A client-generated random structure that consists of a 32-bit timestamp in standard UNIX format, and a 28-byte value generated by a pseudorandom number generator;

- A session identity the client wishes to use for this connection;

- A list of cipher suites that the client supports;

- A list of compression methods that the client supports.

Note that the session identity field should be empty if no SSL session currently exists or if the client wishes to generate new security parameters. In either case, a nonempty session identity field is to specify an existing SSL session between the client and the server (i.e., a session whose security parameters the client wishes to reuse). The session identity may be from an earlier connection, this connection, or another currently active connection. Also note that the list of supported cipher suites, passed from the client to the server in the ClientHello message, contains the combinations of cryptographic algorithms supported by the client in order of preference. Each cipher suite defines both a key exchange algorithm and a cipher spec. The server will select a cipher suite or, if no acceptable choices are presented, return an error message and close the connection accordingly. After having sent the CLIENTHELLO message, the client waits for a SERVERHELLO message. Any other message returned by the server except for a HELLOREQUEST message is treated as an error at this point in time.

In step 2, the server processes the CLIENTHELLO message and responds with either an error or SERVERHELLO message. Similar to the CLIENTHELLO message, the SERVERHELLO message includes the following fields:

- A server version number that contains the lower version of that suggested by the client in the CLIENTHELLO message and the highest supported by the server;

- A server-generated random structure that also consists of a 32-bit timestamp in standard UNIX format, and a 28-byte value generated by a pseudorandom number generator;

- A session identity corresponding to this connection;

- A cipher suite selected by the server from the list of cipher suites supported by the client;

- A compression method selected by the server from the list of compression algorithms supported by the client.

If the session identity in the CLIENTHELLO message was nonempty, the server looks in its session cache for a match. If a match is found and the server is willing to establish the new connection using the corresponding session state, the server responds with the same value as supplied by the client. This indicates a resumed session and dictates that both parties must proceed directly to the CHANGE-CIPHERSPEC and FINISHED messages as addressed further below. Otherwise, this field contains a different value identifying a new session. The server may also return an empty session identity field to indicate that the session will not be cached and therefore cannot be resumed later. Also note that in the SERVERHELLO message, the server selects a cipher suite and a compression method from the lists provided by the client in the CLIENTHELLO message. The key exchange, authentication, encryption, and message authentication algorithms are determined by the cipher suite selected by the server and revealed in the SERVERHELLO message. The cipher suites that have been defined for the SSL protocol are essentially the same as the ones that are specified for the TLS protocol (as summarized in Tables 15.4 to 15.7).

In addition to the SERVERHELLO message, the server may also send other messages to the client. For example, if the server is using certificate-based authentication (which is currently almost always the case), the server sends its site certificate to the client in a corresponding CERTIFICATE message. The certificate type must be appropriate for the selected cipher suite's key exchange algorithm, and is generally an X.509v3 certificate. The same message type will be used later for the client's response to the server's CERTIFICATEREQUEST message. In the case of X.509v3 certificates, a certificate may actually refer to an entire chain of certificates, ordered with the sender's certificate first followed by any CA certificates proceeding sequentially upward to a root CA (that will be accepted by the client).

Next, the server may send a SERVERKEYEXCHANGE message to the client if it has no certificate, a certificate that can be used only for verifying digital signatures, or uses the FORTEZZA token-based key exchange algorithm (KEA).[4] Obviously, this message is not required if the site certificate includes an RSA public key that can be used for encryption. Also, an unanonymous server can optionally request a personal certificate to authenticate the client. It therefore sends a CERTIFICATEREQUEST message to the client. The message includes a list of the types of certificates requested, sorted in order of the server's preference, as well as a list of distinguished names for acceptable CAs. At the end of step 2, the server sends a SERVERHELLODONE message to the client to indicate the end of the SERVERHELLO and associated messages.

Upon receipt of the SERVERHELLO and associated messages, the client verifies that the server provided a valid site certificate,[5] if required, and checks that the security parameters provided in the SERVERHELLO message are indeed acceptable. If the server has requested client authentication, it sends a CERTIFICATE message that includes a personal certificate for the user's public key to the server in step 3. Next, the client sends a CLIENTKEYEXCHANGE message, whose format depends on the key exchange algorithm selected by the server:

- If RSA is used for server authentication and key exchange, the client generates a 48-byte premaster secret,[6] encrypts it with the public key found in the site

---

[4]Netscape Communications was paid a large amount of money by the NSA to include support for the FORTEZZA KEA in the SSL protocol specification.

[5]A site certificate is considered to be valid if its server's common name field entry matches the host part of the URL the client wants to access.

[6]The premaster secret is 48 bytes long and consists of 2 bytes specifying the protocol version and 46 bytes of randomly generated data.

certificate or the temporary RSA key from the SERVERKEYEXCHANGE message, and sends the result back to the server in the CLIENTKEYEXCHANGE message. The server, in turn, uses the corresponding private key to decrypt the premaster secret. We will return to this key exchange algorithm later in this section when we talk about a specific attack.

- If FORTEZZA tokens are used for key exchange, the client derives a token encryption key (TEK) using the KEA. The client's KEA calculation uses the public key from the server certificate along with some private parameters in the client's token. The client sends public parameters needed for the server to also generate the TEK, using its private parameters. It generates a premaster secret, wraps it using the TEK, and sends the result together with some initialization vectors to the server as part of the CLIENTKEYEXCHANGE message. The server, in turn, can decrypt the premaster secret accordingly. This key exchange algorithm is not widely used in practice.

- If a Diffie-Hellman key exchange is performed, the server and client exchange their public parameters as part of the SERVERKEYEXCHANGE and CLIENT-KEYEXCHANGE messages. Obviously, this is only required if the Diffie-Hellman public parameters are not included in the site and personal certificates. The negotiated Diffie-Hellman key can then be used as premaster secret. Because a Diffie-Hellman key exchange involves both parties in a key exchange, the resulting key exchange is less vulnerable to weak pseudorandom number generators in client software packages. Consequently, it is possible and very likely that we will see more widespread use of the Diffie-Hellman key exchange in the future.

For RSA, FORTEZZA, and Diffie-Hellman key exchange, the same algorithms are used to convert the premaster secret into a 48-byte master secret (stored in the corresponding SSL session state), and to derive session keys for encryption and message authentication from this master secret. Nevertheless, some key exchange algorithms, such as FORTEZZA token-based key exchange, may also use their own procedures for generating encryption keys. In this case, the master secret is only used to derive keys for message authentication. The procedures to derive master and session keys, as well as initialization vectors, are fully described in the SSL protocol specification and are not further addressed in this book.

If client authentication is required, the client also sends a CERTIFICATEVERIFY message to the server. This message is used to provide explicit verification of the user's identity based on the personal certificate. It is only sent following a client certificate that has signing capability (all certificates except those containing fixed Diffie-Hellman parameters). Finally, the client finishes step 3 by sending a CHANGE-CIPHERSPEC message and a corresponding FINISHED message to the server. The FINISHED message is always sent immediately after the CHANGECIPHERSPEC message to verify that the key exchange and authentication processes were successful. As a matter of fact, the FINISHED message is the first message that is protected with the newly negotiated algorithms and session keys. It can only be generated and verified if these keys are properly installed on both sides. No acknowledgment of the FINISHED message is required; parties may begin sending encrypted data immediately after having sent the FINISHED message. The SSL Handshake Protocol execution finishes up by also having the server send a CHANGECIPHERSPEC message and a corresponding FINISHED message to the client in step 4.

After the SSL handshake is complete, a secure connection is established between the client and the server. This connection can now be used to send application data that is encapsulated by the SSL Record Protocol. More accurately, application data may be fragmented, compressed, encrypted, and authenticated according to the SSL Record Protocol, as well as the session and connection state information that is now established (according to the execution of the SSL Handshake Protocol).

The SSL Handshake Protocol can be shortened if the client and server decide to resume a previously established (and still cached) SSL session or duplicate an existing SSL session. In this case, only three message flows and a total of six messages are required. The corresponding message flows can be summarized as follows:

$$
\begin{array}{llll}
1: & C \longrightarrow & S & : \text{CLIENTHELLO} \\
2: & S \longrightarrow & C & : \text{SERVERHELLO} \\
 & : & & : \text{CHANGECIPHERSPEC} \\
 & : & & : \text{FINISHED} \\
3: & S \longrightarrow & C & : \text{CHANGECIPHERSPEC} \\
 & : & & : \text{FINISHED}
\end{array}
$$

In step 1, the client sends a CLIENTHELLO message to the server that includes a session identity to be resumed. The server, in turn, checks its session cache for a match. If a match is found, and the server is willing to resume the connection under the specified session state, it returns a SERVERHELLO message with the same session identity in step 2. At this point, both the client and the server must send CHANGECIPHERSPEC and FINISHED messages to each other in steps 2 and 3. Once the session reestablishment is complete, the client and server can begin exchanging application data.

In summary, the SSL protocol can be used to establish secure TCP connections between clients and servers. In particular, it can be used to authenticate the server, to optionally authenticate the client, to perform a key exchange, and to provide message authentication, as well as data confidentiality and integrity services for arbitrary application protocols layered on top of TCP. Although it may seem that not providing client authentication goes against the principles that should be espoused by a secure system, an argument can be made that the decision to optionally support it helped SSL gain widespread use in the first place. Support for client authentication requires public keys and personal certificates for each client, and because SSL support for HTTP must be embedded in the corresponding browser software, requiring client authentication would involve distributing public keys and personal certificates to every user on the Internet. In the short term, it was believed to be more crucial that consumers be aware of with whom they are conducting business than to give the merchants the same level of assurance. Furthermore, because the number of Internet servers is much smaller than the number of clients, it is easier and more practical to first outfit servers with the necessary public keys and site certificates. As of this writing, however, support for client-side public keys and personal certificates is growing as people generally push the use of PKI technologies.

A comprehensive security analysis of SSL 3.0 was performed by Bruce Schneier and David Wagner in [7]. Except for some minor flaws and worrisome features that could be easily corrected without overhauling the basic structure of the SSL protocol, they found no serious vulnerability or security problem in their analysis. Consequently, they concluded that the SSL protocol provides excellent security against eavesdropping and other passive attacks, and that people implementing the protocol should be aware of some sophisticated active attacks.

In 1998, Daniel Bleichenbacher from Bell Laboratories found an adaptive chosen ciphertext attack against protocols based on the public key cryptography standard (PKCS) #1 [8]. In short, an RSA private key operation (a decryption or digital signature operation) can be performed if the attacker has access to an oracle that, for any chosen ciphertext, returns only 1 bit telling whether the ciphertext corresponds to some unknown block of data encrypted using PKCS #1 [9]. Because this attack is quite sophisticated and requires some basic understanding of cryptanalysis, you may skip the following paragraphs and continue to read Section 15.3, which addresses currently available SSL implementations.

To understand the Bleichenbacher attack, it is necessary to have a look at PKCS #1. In fact, there are three block formats specified in PKCS #1: block types 0 and 1 are used for RSA digital signatures, and block type 2 is used for RSA encryption. Recall from our previous discussion that if the RSA algorithm is used for server authentication and key exchange, the client randomly generates a 46-byte premaster secret, prepends the two bytes 03 (the SSL protocol version number) and 00 to the premaster secret, encrypts the result using the public key of the server, and sends it in a CLIENTKEYEXCHANGE message to the server. As such, the CLIENTKEYEXCHANGE message carrying the encrypted premaster secret must conform to the format specified in PKCS #1 block type 2. The format is illustrated in Figure 15.3.

Figure 15.3   PKCS #1 block format for encryption.

Now, assume there is an attacker who can send an arbitrary number of randomly looking messages to an SSL server, and the server responds for each of these messages with a bit indicating whether a particular message is correctly encrypted and encoded according to PKCS #1 (the server thus acts as an oracle). Under this assumption, Bleichenbacher developed an attack to illegitimately perform an RSA operation with the private key of the server (either a decryption or a digital signature operation). When applied to decrypt a premaster secret of a previously sent CLIENTKEYEXCHANGE message, the attacker can rebuild the premaster secret and the session keys that are derived from it accordingly. Consequently, the attacker can then decrypt the entire session (if he or she has monitored and stored the data stream of that session).

The attack is primarily of theoretical interest. Note that experimental results have shown that typically between 300,000 and 2 million chosen ciphertexts are required to actually perform the (decryption or digital signature) operation. To make things worse, the attack can only be launched against an SSL server that is available on-line (since it must act as an oracle). From the attacker's point of view, it may be difficult to send this huge number of chosen ciphertexts to the SSL server without causing the server administrator to become suspicious.

There are several possibilities to protect against the Bleichenbacher attack. First of all, it is not necessary for the server to respond with an error message after having received a CLIENTKEYEXCHANGE message that does not conform to PKCS #1. Another possibility is to change the PKCS #1 block format for encryption and to remove the leading 00 and 02 bytes, as well as the 00, 03, and 00 bytes in the middle of the message (as illustrated in Figure 15.3). Finally, another possibility is to use plaintext-aware encryption schemes, such as the one proposed by Mihir Bellare and Phillip Rogaway [10], or any other public key cryptosystem that is provably secure against adaptive chosen ciphertext attacks [11].[7] For example, in the aftermath of the publication of Bleichenbacher's results, IBM launched a marketing initiative to promote such a cryptosystem jointly developed by Ronald Cramer and Victor Shoup [12].

Before Bleichbacher published his attack, he had been collaborating with RSA Laboratories to update PKCS #1 and to specify a version 2 that is secure against adaptive chosen ciphertext attacks [13]. Meanwhile, all major vendors of SSL servers have incorporated and implemented PKCS #1 version 2 into their products. As a result, this attack does not work anymore due to recent releases of SSL server software.

Finally, it may be interesting to know that most banks that offer their services over the Internet have their corresponding home banking client software based on SSL. This decision also conforms to the strategic view of the European Committee for Banking Standards (ECBS) [14]. As of this writing, the SSL protocol is by far the most pervasive security protocol for the Internet in general, and the WWW in particular. In fact, many Web servers and browsers have been modified to use SSL. For example, the Apache Web server has been modified to incorporate the SSLeay mentioned below [15]. Typically, Web servers that use SSL (or TLS) are called "secure" or "commerce servers." Note, however, that these servers are not necessarily more secure than any other Web server; they just support SSL to secure the data traffic that is transmitted between the client and the server. On the client side, most browsers support SSL. In particular, Netscape Navigator and Microsoft Internet Explorer both provide support for SSL. Most of these products support the RC4 algorithm for encryption and the MD2 and MD5 one-way functions for hashing. In addition, there are many implementations of SSL. Examples include *SSLref*, a reference implementation of SSL from Netscape Communications; *SSLeay*, an internationally distributed implementation written by Eric Young in Australia; and

---

[7]Note that plaintext awareness always implies security against chosen ciphertext attacks.

OpenSSL, an open source implementation of SSL.[8] Finally, there is an interesting software called *Stunnel* that can be used to add SSL protection to existing TCP-based application servers in a UNIX environment without requiring changes to the corresponding code. The software can be invoked from the Internet daemon (i.e., `inetd`) as a wrapper for any number of services or run standalone, accepting network connections itself for a particular service. Refer to the Stunnel home page[9] for further information about the software package.

For obvious reasons, the use of SSL slows the speed of a browser interacting with an HTTPS server. This performance degradation is in fact noticeable by the user. It is primarily due to the public key encryption and decryption operations that are required to initialize the SSL session and connection state information elements. In practice, users experience an additional pause of a few seconds between opening a connection to the HTTPS server and retrieving the first HTML page from it. Because SSL is designed to cache the master secret between subsequent sessions, this delay affects only the first SSL connection between the browser and the server. Compared with the session establishment, the additional overhead of encrypting and decrypting the data traffic using one of the supported encryption algorithms, such as DES, RC2, or RC4, is practically insignificant (and not necessarily noticeable by the user). Consequently, for users that have a fast computer and a relatively slow network connection to an HTTPS server, the overhead of SSL is insignificant, especially if a large amount of data is sent afterward over the SSL session or over multiple SSL sessions that use a shared master secret. However, administrators of very busy SSL servers should consider getting either extremely fast computers or hardware assistance for the public key operations.

15.3 TLS PROTOCOL

Early in 1996, the IETF chartered a TLS WG within the security and transport areas. The objective of the IETF TLS WG was to write Internet standards track RFCs for a TLS protocol using the currently available specifications of SSL (2.0 and 3.0), PCT (1.0), and the secure shell (SSH) version 2 as a basis.[10] Shortly before the IETF meeting in December 1996, a first TLS 1.0 document was released as an Internet-Draft. The document was essentially the same as the SSL 3.0 specification.

---

[8]http://www.openssl.org

[9]http://www.stunnel.org

[10]Note that at this point in time the SSH protocol had been investigated by the IETF TLS WG, and that the IETF later chartered a SECSH WG to update and standardize the SSH protocol independently of the TLS protocol. The SSH protocol is overviewed and discussed in Chapter 16.

In fact, it was the explicit strategy of the IETF TLS WG to have the TLS 1.0 specification be based on SSL 3.0, as opposed to SSL 2.0, PCT 1.0, SSH version 2, or any other transport layer security protocol proposal. At least three major modifications were suggested for SSL 3.0 to be incorporated into TLS 1.0:

1. The HMAC construction developed in the IETF IPsec WG should be adopted and consistently used in TLS 1.0.

2. The FORTEZZA token-based KEA should be removed from TLS 1.0, since it refers to a proprietary and unpublished technology. Instead, a DSS-based key exchange mechanism should be included in TLS 1.0.

3. The TLS Record Protocol and the TLS Handshake Protocol should be separated out and specified more clearly in related documents.

After having adopted these modifications, the resulting TLS protocol was specified in a series of Internet-Drafts. In January 1999, the TLS protocol version 1.0 was specified in RFC 2246 [16] and submitted to the Internet standards track (as a Proposed Standard). The differences between TLS 1.0 and SSL 3.0 are not huge, but they are significant enough that TLS 1.0 and SSL 3.0 do not easily interoperate. Nevertheless, TLS 1.0 does incorporate a mechanism by which a TLS implementation can back down to SSL 3.0.

Similar to the SSL protocol, the TLS protocol is a layered protocol that consists of a TLS Record Protocol and several TLS subprotocols layered on top of it:

- On the lower layer, the *TLS Record Protocol* takes messages to be transmitted, fragments them into manageable data blocks (so-called "TLS records"), optionally compresses them, computes and appends a MAC to each record, encrypts the result, and transmits it. Again, similar to SSL, the resulting records are called TLSPlaintext, TLSCompressed, and TLSCiphertext. A received TLSCiphertext record, in turn, is decrypted, verified, decompressed, and reassembled before it is delivered to the appropriate application protocol. A TLS connection state is the operating environment of the TLS Record Protocol. It specifies compression, encryption, and message authentication algorithms, and determines parameters for these algorithms, such as encryption and MAC keys and IVs for a connection in both the read and write directions. There are always four connection states outstanding: the current read and write states and the pending read and write states. All records are processed under the current read and write states. The security parameters for the pending states are set by the TLS Handshake Protocol, and the handshake protocol selectively makes either of the pending states current, in which case the appropriate current state is disposed of and replaced with the pending state; the pending state is then reinitialized to an empty state.

Table 15.4
TLS 1.0 Cipher Suites as Specified in [16]

Cipher Suite	Exportable
TLS_NULL_WITH_NULL_NULL	yes
TLS_RSA_WITH_NULL_MD5	yes
TLS_RSA_WITH_NULL_SHA	yes
TLS_RSA_EXPORT_WITH_RC4_40_MD5	yes
TLS_RSA_WITH_RC4_128_MD5	no
TLS_RSA_WITH_RC4_128_SHA	no
TLS_RSA_EXPORT_WITH_RC2_CBC_40_MD5	yes
TLS_RSA_WITH_IDEA_CBC_SHA	no
TLS_RSA_EXPORT_WITH_DES40_CBC_SHA	yes
TLS_RSA_WITH_DES_CBC_SHA	no
TLS_RSA_WITH_3DES_EDE_CBC_SHA	no
TLS_DH_DSS_EXPORT_WITH_DES40_CBC_SHA	yes
TLS_DH_DSS_WITH_DES_CBC_SHA	no
TLS_DH_DSS_WITH_3DES_EDE_CBC_SHA	no
TLS_DH_RSA_EXPORT_WITH_DES40_CBC_SHA	yes
TLS_DH_RSA_WITH_DES_CBC_SHA	no
TLS_DH_RSA_WITH_3DES_EDE_CBC_SHA	no
TLS_DHE_DSS_EXPORT_WITH_DES40_CBC_SHA	yes
TLS_DHE_DSS_WITH_DES_CBC_SHA	no
TLS_DHE_DSS_WITH_3DES_EDE_CBC_SHA	no
TLS_DHE_RSA_EXPORT_WITH_DES40_CBC_SHA	yes
TLS_DHE_RSA_WITH_DES_CBC_SHA	no
TLS_DHE_RSA_WITH_3DES_EDE_CBC_SHA	no
TLS_DH_anon_EXPORT_WITH_RC4_40_MD5	yes
TLS_DH_anon_WITH_RC4_128_MD5	no
TLS_DH_anon_EXPORT_WITH_DES40_CBC_SHA	no
TLS_DH_anon_WITH_DES_CBC_SHA	no
TLS_DH_anon_WITH_3DES_EDE_CBC_SHA	no

- On the higher layer, there are several TLS subprotocols layered on top of the TLS Record Protocol. For example, the *TLS Handshake Protocol* is used to negotiate session and connection information elements that comprise a session identifier, a peer certificate, a compression method, a cipher spec, a master key, and a flag whether the session is resumable and can be used to initiate new connections. These items are used to create security parameters for use by the TLS Record Protocol when protecting application data. In addition, there are a *TLS Change Cipher Spec Protocol* and a *TLS Alert Protocol*. Both are similar to the corresponding SSL protocols (and are not further addressed in this book).

Table 15.5
TLS 1.0 Key Exchange Algorithms as Specified in [16]

Key Exchange Algorithm	Description	Key Size Limit
DHE_DSS	Ephemeral DH with DSS signatures	None
DHE_DSS_EXPORT	Ephemeral DH with DSS signatures	DH = 512 bits
DHE_RSA	Ephemeral DH with RSA signatures	None
DHE_RSA_EXPORT	Ephemeral DH with RSA signatures	DH = 512 bits
DH_anon	Anonymous DH, no signatures	None
DH_anon_EXPORT	Anonymous DH, no signatures	DH = 512 bits
DH_DSS	DH with DSS-based certificates	None
DH_DSS_EXPORT	DH with DSS-based certificates	DH = 512 bits
DH_RSA	DH with RSA-based certificates	None
DH_RSA_EXPORT	DH with RSA-based certificates	DH = 512 bits
NULL	No key exchange	N/A
RSA	RSA key exchange	None
RSA_EXPORT	RSA key exchange	RSA = 512 bits

After a TLS handshake has been performed, the client and server can exchange application data messages. These messages are carried by the TLS Record Protocol and fragmented, compressed, authenticated, and encrypted accordingly. The messages are treated as transparent data to the TLS record layer.

The cipher suites that are specified for TLS 1.0 are summarized in Table 15.4. The key exchange and encryption mechanisms, as well as the one-way hash function that are used in a particular cipher suite, are all encoded in its name. For example, the cipher suite TLS_RSA_WITH_RC4_128_MD5 uses RSA public key encryption for key exchange, RC4 with 128 bit session keys for encryption, and MD5 for computing one-way hash function results. Similarly, the cipher suite TLS_DH_DSS_WITH_3DES_EDE_CBC_SHA uses the Diffie-Hellman key exchange algorithm (DH) for key exchange, the digital signature standard (DSS) to compute and verify digital signatures, Tripe-DES in CBC mode for encryption, and SHA-1 for computing one-way hash function results. Consequently, a TLS cipher suite is always named TLS_X_WITH_Y_Z, where X refers to the key exchange algorithm, Y to the encryption algorithm, and Z to the one-way hash function that is being used. The key exchange and encryption algorithms, as well as the one-way hash functions that are specified in TLS 1.0, are itemized and further explained in Tables 15.5 to 15.7. Note that Tables 15.4 and 15.6 also indicate whether a particular implementation of a cipher suite or encryption algorithm is exportable from the United States. In Table 15.6, the type of a cipher indicates whether it is a stream cipher or a block cipher running in CBC mode. Similarly, the key length indicates the number of bytes that are used for generating the encryption keys, whereas the expanded key length indicates the number of bytes actually fed into the encryption algorithm. Finally, the effective key bits measure how much entropy is in the key material being fed into the encryption routine, and the IV size measures how much data needs to be generated for the IV.

Table 15.6

TLS 1.0 Encryption Algorithms as Specified in [16]

Cipher	Exportable	Type	Key Length	Expanded Key Length	Effective Key Bits	IV Size	Block Size
NULL	Yes	Stream	0	0	0	0	N/A
IDEA_CBC	No	Block	16	16	128	8	8
RC2_CBC_40	Yes	Block	5	16	40	8	8
RC4_40	Yes	Stream	5	16	40	0	N/A
RC4_128	No	Stream	16	16	128	0	N/A
DES40_CBC	Yes	Block	5	8	40	8	8
DES_CBC	No	Block	8	8	56	8	8
3DES_EDE_CBC	No	Block	24	24	168	8	8

TLS 1.0 as specified in RFC 2246 [16] was submitted to the IESG for consideration as a Proposed Standard for the Internet in January 1999. Meanwhile, two other standards track RFC documents and have been officially released by the IETF TLS WG:

- RFC 2712 specifies the addition of Kerberos Cipher Suites to TLS [17].

- RFC 2817 specifies how to upgrade to TLS Within HTTP/1.1 [18].

In addition, an informational RFC document specifies the use of HTTP over TLS (i.e., HTTPS) [19]. Finally, there are various Internet-Drafts specifying specific issues related to TLS or the use of TLS to secure TCP-based application protocols. Refer to the home page of the IETF TLS WG for an overview about the most recent developments and achievements.

Table 15.7
TLS 1.0 One-Way Hash Functions as Specified in [16]

Hash Function	Hash Size	Padding Size
NULL	0	0
MD5	16	48
SHA	20	40

15.4 FIREWALL TUNNELING

As of this writing, SSL and TLS in general, and HTTPS in particular, are widely used and deployed on the Internet and the WWW. Unfortunately, the protocols do not easily interoperate with application gateways (i.e., circuit-level gateways and application-level gateways). Note that an SSL or TLS connection is always established on an end-to-end basis, and that any application gateway or proxy server running at the firewall (between the client and the origin server) must be considered to be a "man-in-the-middle." Also note that different protocols generally have different requirements for proxy servers.

In general, an application protocol can either be proxied or tunneled through a proxy server [20]:

- When we say that an application protocol is being proxied, we actually mean that the corresponding proxy server is aware of the specifics of the protocol and can understand what is happening on the protocol level. This allows such things as protocol-level filtering, access control, accounting, and logging. Examples of protocols that are usually proxied include Telnet, FTP, and HTTP.

- Contrary to that, we say that an application protocol is being tunneled when we actually mean that the corresponding proxy server (which is basically acting as a circuit-level gateway) is not aware of the specifics of the protocol and cannot understand what is happening on the protocol level accordingly. It is simply relaying, or "tunneling," the data between the client and the server, and does not necessarily understand the protocol being used. Consequently, it cannot perform such things as protocol-level filtering, access control, and logging to the same extent as is possible for a full-fledged proxy server. Examples of protocols that are usually tunneled by proxy servers or circuit-level gateways include SSL-enhanced protocols, such as HTTPS, as well as the IIOP used in CORBA environments.

In an early attempt to address the problem of having SSL/TLS or HTTPS traffic going through a proxy-based firewall, Ari Luotonen from Netscape Communications proposed an *SSL Tunneling Protocol* that basically allows an HTTP proxy server to act as a tunnel for SSL-enhanced protocols. The protocol allows an SSL (or HTTPS) client to open a secure tunnel through an HTTP proxy server that resides on the firewall. When tunneling SSL, the proxy server must not have access to the data being transferred in either direction (for the sake of confidentiality). The proxy server must merely know the source and destination addresses (IP addresses and port numbers), and possibly, if the proxy server supports user authentication, the name of the requesting user. Consequently, there is a handshake between the client and the proxy server to establish the connection between the client and the remote server through the intermediate proxy server. To make the SSL tunneling extension be backward compatible, the handshake must be in the same format as normal HTTP/1.0 requests, so that proxy servers without support for this feature can still determine the request as impossible for them to service, and provide proper error notifications. As such, SSL tunneling is not really SSL specific. It is rather a general way to have a third party establish a connection between two endpoints, after which bytes are simply copied back and forth by this intermediary.

Using the SSL Tunneling Protocol, the client connects to the proxy server and uses the CONNECT method to specify the hostname and the port number to connect to (the hostname and port number are separated by a colon). The `host:port` part is then followed by a space and a string specifying the HTTP version number (e.g., HTTP/1.0 or HTTP/1.1), and the line terminator. After that, there is a series of zeros or more of HTTP request header lines, followed by an empty line. After this empty line, if the handshake to establish the connection was successful, SSL can actually transfer data. Consequently, an SSL tunneling sequence may look as follows:

```
CONNECT www.esecurity.ch:443 HTTP/1.0
User-agent: Mozilla/4.05 [en] (WinNT; U)

... SSL data ...
```

The SSL tunneling handshake is freely extensible using arbitrary HTTP/1.0 headers. For example, to enforce client authentication, the proxy may use the 407 status code and the Proxy-authenticate response header to ask the client to provide some authentication information to the proxy. Consequently, the SSL tunneling sequence looks as follows:

```
HTTP/1.0 407 Proxy authentication required
Proxy-authenticate: ...

... SSL data ...
```

In this case, the client would send the required authentication information in a message that looks as follows:

```
CONNECT www.esecurity.ch:443 HTTP/1.0
User-agent: Mozilla/4.05 [en] (WinNT; U)
Proxy-authorization: ...

... SSL data ...
```

Note that the CONNECT method provides a lower level function than the other HTTP methods. Think of it as some kind of an "escape mechanism" for saying that the proxy server should not interfere with the transaction, but merely serve as a circuit-level gateway and forward the data stream. In fact, the proxy server should not need to know the entire URL that is being requested—only the information that is actually needed to serve the request, such as the hostname and port number of the origin Web server. Consequently, the proxy server cannot verify that the protocol being spoken is really SSL, and the proxy server configuration should therefore explicitly limit allowed (tunneled) connections to well-known SSL ports, such as 443 for HTTPS or 563 for NNTPS (the port numbers are assigned by the IANA). As of this writing, SSL tunneling is supported by most HTTP proxy servers and browsers that are commercially available, including, for example, Netscape Navigator and Microsoft Internet Explorer.

The primary use of SSL tunneling is to let internal users within a corporate intranet access external HTTPS servers on the Internet (in this case, it is seldom necessary to check the destination port number, because outbound HTTP connections are allowed in most security policies). Nevertheless, SSL tunneling can also be used in the opposite direction, namely, to make internal HTTPS servers visible and accessible to the outside world (to the users located on the Internet). In this case, however, the proxy server acts as an inbound proxy[11] for the SSL data traffic. What this basically means is that HTTPS connections originating from the outside world are simply relayed by the inbound proxy to the internal HTTPS servers, where the requesting users should be strongly authenticated. Therefore, the internal Web servers must implement the SSL or TLS protocol. Unfortunately, this is not always the case and most internal Web servers are still not SSL or TLS-enabled (and do not represent HTTPS servers accordingly). In this case, the inbound proxy must authenticate the requesting clients and connect them to the appropriate internal Web servers. To make this possible (and to make these servers visible to the outside world), several SSL gateways or SSL proxy servers have been developed and are being marketed today. For example, a group of researchers from the DEC Systems Research Center proposed the use of a combination of SSL client authentication (at the inbound proxy) and URL rewriting techniques in a technology called "secure Web tunneling" [21]. Since then, several products have been developed that implement similar ideas. One example is the Trusted Entry Security Server (TESS) jointly developed by two Swiss companies.[12]

A final word is due to the fact that the use of SSL, TLS, or any other transport layer security protocol to secure (i.e., encrypt) HTTP data traffic also negatively influences the usefulness of proxy servers for caching. If a resource is encrypted end-to-end, it is encrypted in a way that is useful only for the server and one particular client (i.e., the client that has requested the resource and holds the corresponding session key). Consequently, there is no use in caching the encrypted resource for other clients.

15.5 CONCLUSIONS

In this chapter, we focused on some security protocols that have been proposed for the transport layer. In particular, we overviewed and discussed the SSL and TLS protocols. In addition, we mentioned the PCT protocol as being a simple derivative from SSL version 2. With the official release of the TLS protocol specification and its submission to the Internet standards track, Microsoft has abandoned the PCT protocol. In addition to SSL, PCT, and TLS, the first edition of this book also discussed the SSH protocol in the chapter referring to transport layer security

---

[11]In the literature, inbound proxies are called *reverse proxies* most of the time. In this book, however, we use the term "inbound proxy," as there is no reverse functionality involved. In fact, a reverse proxy is doing nothing differently than a normal proxy server. The only difference is that it primarily serves inbound connections (instead of outbound connections).

[12]http://www.tess.ch

protocols. This is arguably correct because SSH provides similar functionalities to SSL and TLS (i.e., it provides a mutually authenticated and encrypted session between two endpoints). Contrary to SSL and TLS, however, SSH is most often used as a replacement for more traditional terminal access protocols, such as Telnet or Rlogin. Consequently, we overview and discuss SSH when we talk about security-enhanced terminal access protocols in the following chapter.

Given the current situation on the Internet security market, it is possible and very likely that the TLS protocol will be one of the most important security protocols for the Internet. This is particularly true for the HTTP and the WWW. It is, however, also true for other applications (protocols) layered on top of TCP. For example, one can reasonably expect that future releases of software packages for Telnet, FTP, SMTP, POP3, and IMAP4 will implement and support the TLS protocol as well.

The big advantage of SSL/TLS is simplicity and wide deployment. There are, however, also two disadvantages that should be considered with care:

1. Both the SSL and the TLS protocols are layered on top of TCP. They neither address nor meet the security requirements of applications and application protocols that are layered on UDP. Unfortunately, there is an increasingly large number of applications and application protocols layered on UDP (e.g., protocols for real-time or multicast communications). For all these applications and application protocols, the SSL and the TLS protocols do not provide a viable solution. There are at least two conclusions one can draw from this situation:

   • There is room for further research to address the question of how to secure UDP-based applications on the transport layer (e.g., a preliminary study is done in [22]).

   • There is room for security protocols that operate either below or above the transport layer. This is the reason why Part III includes other chapters on Internet and application layer security.

   The second conclusion is particularly important as it counters the argument that all other security protocols have become obsolete with the wide deployment of SSL/TLS.

2. The SSL and TLS protocols work poorly with application gateways in general, and application-level gateways (i.e., proxy servers) in particular. Note that both

protocols have been specifically designed to provide end-to-end security between a client and a server, and to protect against man-in-the-middle attacks accordingly. Consequently, these protocols cannot be proxied in the traditional sense (because the protocols consider a proxy server to be a man-in-the-middle). Sometimes, it is possible to use an SSL gateway. In other situations, however, the secure connection must be end-to-end and cannot be broken by an intermediary. In these situations, there are several strategies to solve (or circumvent) the problem:

- The simple solution is to use a packet filter instead of an application-level gateway. The packet filter can be configured to allow all traffic to and from a specific port (e.g., port number 443 for HTTPS).

- A more complicated solution is to use a circuit-level gateway (e.g., SOCKS server) to relay the data traffic that is secured using the transport layer security protocol. In this case, the client is authenticated by the circuit-level gateway on the server's behalf.

- Finally, still another solution is to use a special tunneling protocol, such as the one we have discussed in the contect of HTTP tunneling. In this case, the client is authenticated directly by the server (contrary to the use of a circuit-level gateway).

Obviously, the use of a packet filter instead of application-level gateways is dangerous, as the trusted port numbers can always be used for applications that are not secured using SSL or TLS. If all that is needed are TCP and UDP restrictions based on client and server IP addresses, SOCKS works fine. However, most proxy servers work at the application level and have the ability to understand header information related to the application protocol as well. Under these circumstances, the use of a special tunneling protocol seems to be advantageous.

In [1] and the first edition of this book, the problem of using SSL- and TLS-enabled software with limited cryptographic strength is also addressed. Due to the liberalized U.S. export controls, this problem has become obsolete in most parts of the world. Consequently, we are not going to repeat the discussion in this edition of the book.

REFERENCES

[1] R. Oppliger, *Security Technologies for the World Wide Web*, Artech House, Norwood, MA, 2000.

[2] R. Nelson, "SDNS Services and Architecture," *Proceedings of National Computer Security Conference*, 1987, pp. 153–157.

[3] ISO/IEC 10736, *Information Technology—Telecommunications and Information Exchange Between Systems—Transport Layer Security Protocol*, Geneva, Switzerland, 1993.

[4] M. Blaze and S. M. Bellovin, "Session-Layer Encryption," *Proceedings of USENIX UNIX Security Symposium*, June 1995.

[5] J. Myers, "Simple Authentication and Security Layer," Request for Comments 2222, October 1997.

[6] H. Krawczyk, M. Bellare, and R. Canetti, "HMAC: Keyed-Hashing for Message Authentication," Request for Comments 2104, February 1997.

[7] D. Wagner and B. Schneier, "Analysis of the SSL 3.0 Protocol," *Proceedings of 2nd USENIX Workshop on Electronic Commerce*, November 1996, pp. 29–40.

[8] D. Bleichenbacher, "Chosen Ciphertext Attacks Against Protocols Based on the RSA Encryption Standard PKCS #1," *Proceedings of CRYPTO '98*, August 1998, pp. 1–12.

[9] RSA Data Security, Inc., *PKCS #1: RSA Encryption Standard*, Redwood City, CA, November 1993.

[10] M. Bellare and P. Rogaway, "Optimal Asymmetric Encryption," *Proceedings of EURO-CRYPT '94*, 1994, pp. 92–111.

[11] M. Bellare, et al., "Relations Among Notions of Security for Public-Key Encryption Schemes," *Proceedings of CRYPTO '98*, August 1998.

[12] R. Cramer and V. Shoup, "A Practical Public Key Cryptosystem Provably Secure Against Adaptive Chosen Ciphertext Attack," *Proceedings of CRYPTO '98*, August 1998, pp. 13–25.

[13] B. Kaliski and J. Staddon "PKCS #1: RSA Cryptography Specifications Version 2.0," Request for Comments 2437, October 1998.

[14] European Committee for Banking Standards (ECBS), *Secure Banking over the Internet*, March 1997.

[15] B. Laurie and P. Lauried, *Apache: The Definitive Guide*, O'Reilly & Associates, Sebastopol, CA, 1997.

[16] T. Dierks and C. Allen, "The TLS Protocol Version 1.0," Request for Comments 2246, January 1999.

[17] A. Medvinsky and M. Hur, "Addition of Kerberos Cipher Suites to Transport Layer Security (TLS)," Request for Comments 2712, October 1999.

[18] R. Khare and S. Lawrence, "Upgrading to TLS Within HTTP/1.1," Request for Comments 2817, May 2000.

[19] E. Rescorla, "HTTP over TLS," Request for Comments 2818, May 2000.

[20] A. Luotonen, *Web Proxy Servers*, Prentice Hall PTR, Upper Saddle River, NJ, 1998.

[21] M. Abadi, et al., "Secure Web Tunneling," *Proceedings of 7th International World Wide Web Conference*, April 1998, pp. 531–539.

[22] S. Mittra and T. Y. C. Woo, "A Flow-Based Approach to Datagram Security," *Proceedings of ACM SIGCOMM*, September 1997.

Chapter 16

Application Layer Security Protocols

In this chapter, we focus on security protocols that have been proposed, specified, implemented, and deployed for the application layer of the Internet model. Providing security at the application layer has in fact often turned out to be the most intrusive option. It is also the most flexible, because the scope and strength of the protection can be tailored to meet the security requirements of specific applications. Roughly speaking, there are two possibilities to provide security services at the application layer:

1. Take a given application protocol as it is and enhance it with security features. The result is a secure version of the given application protocol.

2. Follow a more generic approach to provide a security system that can be used by many application protocols to incorporate security features.

The first possibility leads to security-enhanced application protocols, whereas the second possibility leads to the development and use of authentication and key distribution systems that provide a standardized API. We overview and discuss security-enhanced application protocols in Section 16.1 and authentication and key distribution systems in Section 16.2. Finally, we draw some conclusions in Section 16.3.

283

16.1 SECURITY-ENHANCED APPLICATION PROTOCOLS

There are several application protocols that have been enhanced to provide integrated security services. In the following subsections, we address security enhancements for terminal access, file transfer, electronic mail, WWW transactions, DNS, and distributed file systems. Take them as examples; there are many other application protocols that can be enhanced with security features but are not addressed in this book (e.g., SNMP).

16.1.1 Terminal Access

Telnet [1] and Rlogin [2] are the protocols of choice to provide terminal access services for systems running the TCP/IP communications protocol stack. From a security point of view, Telnet is the preferred protocol, as it employs a password-based authentication scheme (contrary to Rlogin, which employs an address-based authentication scheme that depends on and makes use of trusted hosts).

Referring to the introductory remarks, it is possible to use an authentication and key distribution system to provide security services for a particular application protocol, such as Telnet or Rlogin. More accurately, an authentication and key distribution system provides an API that applications can use to incorporate and provide the security services they require. While something like Kerberos-mediated Telnet encryption [3] might be an ultimate goal, it takes a big effort to deploy. The same is true for any other authentication and key distribution system one may think of (e.g., SPX [4]).

Instead of waiting until authentication and key distribution systems are used and widely deployed on the Internet, several security-enhanced Telnet software packages have been developed in the past. In Chapter 15, for example, we learned about the SSL and TLS protocols being able to secure any application protocol layered on top of TCP. Consequently, these protocols can also be used to secure Telnet. Exemplary implementations include SSLtelnet and SSLTel. In fact, the port number 992 has been assigned by the IANA to run Telnet on top of SSL/TLS.

In addition to these possibilities, there are a number of technological approaches and corresponding products that can be used to secure applications that provide terminal access. For example, we also mentioned in Chapter 15 that Steven Bellovin and Matt Blaze developed the ESM that may serve as a secure Telnet replacement for 4.4BSD UNIX [5]. The ESM implements a Diffie-Hellman key exchange and the Interlock protocol originally invented and proposed by Ron Rivest and Adi Shamir [6] to protect against the man-in-the-middle attack. Because the software is not widely deployed on the Internet, some other software packages are described next. In either case, it is important to use such a software package as a replacement for Telnet or Rlogin in an intranet environment. It is even more important to use such a replacement software package if users regularly connect to intranet hosts from the Internet.

Secure RPC Authentication

The *Secure RPC Authentication* (SRA) software package was originally developed and distributed by a group of researchers at the Texas A&M University (TAMU) [7]. SRA is based on Sun Microsystems' Secure RPC implementation to protect Telnet and FTP connection establishment handshakes against password sniffing attacks.

When an SRA-enhanced client connects to an SRA-enhanced Telnet (or FTP) server, a Diffie-Hellman key exchange is performed to negotiate a session key. This session key is then used to encrypt the user's authentication information, which typically consists of a username and password. Unfortunately, the remainder of the Telnet (or FTP) traffic is left unencrypted. There are two major problems related to the use of SRA:

1. The length of the modulus used with Sun Microsystems' implementation of the Secure RPC Diffie-Hellman key exchange is only 192 bits and thus far too small to protect against more serious cryptanalytical attacks [8].

2. The Secure RPC and hence also SRA are vulnerable to the man-in-the-middle attack. An attacker can decrypt and reencrypt user identification and authentication information such as a password or an encrypted time stamp.

In addition to that, the SRA software package also contains a DES library that was not exportable from the United States and Canada. Nevertheless, there had been software packages available overseas that combined the SRA basic software with publicly available DES libraries.

Secure Telnet

Secure Telnet (STEL) is another Telnet replacement that was developed at the University of Milan in cooperation with the Italian CERT [9].

Again, the purpose of STEL is to provide its users remote terminal access, very similar to Telnet and Rlogin. The main differences, however, are that the authentication mechanisms employed by STEL are much stronger than their traditional counterparts and that all data traffic between the client and the server is transparently encrypted. The client software is intended to be directly run by users, whereas the server software can be run as a standalone daemon by the superuser or automatically be invoked by inetd.

Similar to SRA, STEL uses a Diffie-Hellman key exchange with a shared prime number p (either 512 or 1,024 bits) and a shared generator $g = 3$ to have a client and a server agree on a common session key. The actual session key is derived from the Diffie-Hellman value by hashing it with MD5. To protect against the man-in-the-middle attack, STEL also implements the Interlock protocol. In addition, a variety of methods are currently supported by STEL to provide client authentication (e.g., UNIX passwords, S/Key, and SecurID). With regard to UNIX passwords, it should be noted that the communication channel between the client and server is transparently encrypted and that this encrytion provides a reasonable level of security for the transmission of the password.

After the Diffie-Hellman key exchange and client authentication, all data traffic is transparently encrypted using the specified encryption algorithm keyed with the session key. The default encryption algorithm is DES, because it is fast, but Triple-DES and IDEA are also available. Because the STEL software has been developed entirely outside the United States and Canada, there is no problem in distributing the software package internationally.

Secure Shell

Probably the most important and most widely used and deployed replacement for Telnet and Rlogin on the Internet is the Secure Shell (SSH).[1] SSH is a relatively simple program that can be used to securely log into a remote system, execute commands on that system, and move files from one system to another. SSH provides strong authentication and secure communications over insecure network connections. As such, it was originally designed to replace the Berkeley r-tools (e.g., rlogin, rsh, rcp, and rdist), but can also be used to replace Telnet in many cases. Furthermore, any application protocol layered on top of TCP (including, for example, the X protocol) can be secured using the integrated port forwarding mechanism of SSH. There are currently two versions of the SSH protocol:

---

[1]Refer to footnote 6 for an explanation of why SSH is addressed in this chapter.

- SSH version 1, or SSH V1, refers to the protocol that was originally developed by Tatu Ylönen at the Helsinki University of Technology in Finland [10]. The corresponding implementation, including source code, documentation, and configuration scripts, was made publicly and freely available on the Internet. It was ported to many platforms and is in widespread use today. For example, most Linux software distribution packages come along with SSH V1 support. In addition, there are many commercial implementations of SSH V1 that are being sold by various companies, including, for example, the SSH Communications Security Corporation,[2] a company founded by Ylönen after the public release of the first SSH software package. Refer to [11] for an overview about SSH V1 implementations.

- SSH version 2, or SSH V2, refers to the protocol that is specified by the participants of the IETF Secure Shell (SECSH) WG.[3] The first Internet-Draft specifying SSH V2 was submitted to IETF in 1997 and has been further refined in a series of Internet-Drafts since then. Again, there are many commercial and noncommercial implementations of SSH V2 [11]. For example, the commercial version that is being marketed by the SSH Communications Security Corporation is called the SSH Secure Shell (currently in version 2.4). Also, another Finnish company, called F-Secure, distributes a commercial version of SSH that is widely used and deployed on the Internet today.

In either case, there are open source implementations of SSH commonly referred to as OpenSSH.[4] OpenSSH is being developed under the auspices of the OpenBSD project[5] and is freely usable under a BSD license.

SSH V1 and V2 both utilize a generic transport layer security protocol.[6] When used over TCP/IP, the server normally listens for TCP connection establishment requests on port 22. This port number has been registered with the IANA and is officially assigned for SSH. In short, the SSH protocol provides support for both host authentication and user authentication, together with data compression and data confidentiality and integrity protection.

---

[2]http://www.ssh.com

[3]http://www.ietf.org/html.charters/secsh-charter.html

[4]http://www.openssh.com

[5]http://www.openbsd.org

[6]Because of the existence of this generic transport layer security protocol, SSH was discussed in the chapter entitled "Transport Layer Security Protocols" in the first edition of this book. In fact, SSH provides similar functionality like SSL and TLS, and should therefore be covered in the same chapter. Mainly because SSH is primarily used as a replacement for Telnet and Rlogin, however, it is being discussed in this chapter.

The SSH V1 protocol is simple and straightforward. It requires the server be equipped with two public key pairs:

- A long-term *host public key pair* with a relatively long key size (typically 1,024-bit RSA);

- A short-term *server public key pair* with a shorter key size (typically 768-bit RSA).

Contrary to the host public key pair, the server public key pair changes periodically (i.e., every hour by default). The aim of having two public key pairs and having one of them (i.e., the server public key pair) change periodically is to provide something like PFS (refer to Chapter 14 for a discussion of PFS and key management protocols that provide PFS). Note that the purpose of the host public key is to bind the connection to the desired server host, whereas the purpose of the periodically changing server public key is to make decrypting recorded traffic impossible even in the case of a private host key being compromised. To achieve PFS, however, it must be ensured that the server private key never be saved to disk.

When a user wants to use SSH V1 to get terminal access to an SSH server, the SSH client sends an authentication request to the server. The server, in turn, sends back both of its public keys. The client now compares the received host key against its own database of manually distributed and preconfigured host keys. The client normally accepts the key of an unknown host and stores it in its database for future use. This makes the use of SSH practical in most environments. However, in more secure environments it is also possible to configure the SSH client to refuse access to any host whose public key has not been properly registered in the client database. If the client accepts the host key, it generates a 256-bit random number that serves as a session key. Furthermore, the client chooses an encryption algorithm from those supported by the server, typically Blowfish, DES, or 3DES in CBC mode. The client pads the session key with random bytes, double encrypts it with the public host and server RSA keys, and sends the result to the server. The server, in turn, decrypts the RSA double encryption and recovers the session key accordingly. Both parties can now start using the session key to transparently encrypt and decrypt data transmitted over the connection. The server sends an encrypted confirmation to the client. Receipt of this confirmation tells the client that the server has been able to successfully decrypt the session key, and must therefore hold its private keys. From that moment on, the client assumes the server to be authentic and transport layer encryption and integrity protection to be in proper use.

In certain cases, user authentication may also be required. The corresponding message exchange is initiated by the client who sends an authentication request to the server. The request declares the user name to log in. Depending on the authentication method in use, the dialogue that takes place between the client and the server may look different. There are two authentication methods supported in SSH V1:

- In the case of *password authentication*, the user password is transmitted over the communication channel in transparently encrypted form.

- In the case of *RSA authentication*, the server challenges the client with a random number that is encrypted with the public key of the user. In this case, the server must also have access to a database of manually distributed and preconfigured public keys for registered users. The client can only decrypt the challenge if it knows the private key of the user. It therefore requests a passphrase that is needed to temporarily unlock the user's private key. To authenticate to the server, the client must respond with a correct MD5 hash value of the decrypted challenge and some additional data that binds the result to the current session.

In either case, the server must respond with an authentication success or failure. If client authentication is not required, or if the client has been able to successfully authenticate to the server, it can now request a service. In particular, it can securely log in to a remote system (using the `slogin` command), remotely execute commands (using the `ssh` command), transfer files (using the `scp` command), and so on. Session keys can also be reexchanged dynamically.

SSH V2 is being standardized by the participants of the IETF SECSH WG. In a first step, the protocol used in SSH version 1 was divided into three subprotocols:

- The SSH transport layer protocol (i.e., SSH-TRANS);

- The SSH authentication protocol (i.e., SSH-USERAUTH);

- The SSH connection protocol (i.e., SSH-CONN).

All of these subprotocols are being specified in separate Internet-Drafts. A fourth document specified in an Internet-Draft describes the overall SSH protocol architecture (i.e., SSH-ARCH).

SSH V1 and SSH V2 differ considerably. For example, in SSH V2 all algorithms can be negotiated between the client and the server. Also, SSH V2 uses a Diffie-Hellman key exchange to provide PFS (instead of encrypting the session key with an additonal server key). Furthermore, SSH V2 is designed to provide support for public key certificates. Most importantly, SSH V1's weak CRC-32 integrity check has been replaced in SSH V2 with a stronger MAC construction.[7]

In summary, SSH provides a well established and widely used and deployed alternative for Telnet and the Berkeley r-tools (e.g., `rlogin`, `rcp`, `rsh`, ...). As such, its use is highly recommended and server systems should be remotely administered only using SSH. The major disadvantage of SSH in the past was the lack of certificate-based key management, meaning that public keys had to be manually configured on both the client and server side. This disadvantage has been resolved and the latest releases of SSH are also able to handle public key certificates (either X.509 or PGP certificates).

16.1.2   File Transfer

The *File Transfer Protocol* (FTP) [12] is the protocol of choice for transferring files in TCP/IP-based networks. We briefly touched upon FTP when we discussed the uncompleteness of static packet filtering techniques in Part II (in fact, we used the FTP to motivate to use dynamic packet filtering techniques).

Many things that have been said for secure terminal access also apply for secure file transfer:

1. It is possible to use an authentication and key distribution system, such as Kerberos or SPX, to secure the transfer of files. In this case, however, the corresponding software on either side (i.e., the client and server software) must be modified to make use of the authentication and key distribution system and the corresponding API.

2. It is possible to layer FTP on top of SSL/TLS. The corresponding protocol has been acronymed FTPS and the IANA has assigned the two port numbers 989 (for the FTPS data connection) and 990 (for the FTPS control connection) to it (instead of 20 and 21 as in the case of the FTP data and control connections). For example, SSLftp implements FTPS.

---

[7]The weak CRC-32 integrity check was exploited in an SSH insertion attack in 1998. You may refer to `http://www.core-sdi.com/advisories/ssh-advisory.htm` for an overview about the attack.

3. SRA and SSH can be used to securely transfer files in TCP/IP-based networks. For example, the SSH utility `scp` can be used to securely transfer (i.e., copy) files from one system to another, and SSH V2 provides an `sftp` utility that implements FTP on top of the SSH V2 transport layer security protocol.

It would be very important to use any of these possibilities to securely transfer files in TCP/IP-based networks. Unfortunately, this is seldom done and file transfers often occur without proper protection put in place.

16.1.3   Electronic Mail

There are two RFC documents that collectively define the mode of operation of an Internet-based electronic mail (e-mail) system:

- RFC 822 (STD 11) specifies the formats and syntactical rules for text-based e-mail messages [13].

- RFC 821 (part of STD 10) specifies the SMTP used to send and receive e-mail messages by user agents and message transfer agents [14].

In addition, there are several protocols that either enhance the capabilities of SMTP or provide a possibility to access a user's message store (e.g., POP3 and IMAP4). All of these protocols are fully described in [15, 16] and summarized in Chapter 3 of [17].

Again, there are many possibilities to secure communications in an e-mail system. For example, it is possible to layer the various protocols on top of SSL/TLS. SMTP on top of SSL/TLS combine to form the acronym SMTPS and has a port number of 465. Similarly, POP3 (IMAP4) on top of SSL/TLS has the acronym POP3S (IMAPS) and has a port number of 995 (993). Also, it is possible to use the Kerberos authentication system to have users access their message stores in an authenticated way. For example, the Eudora user agent software provides support for Kerberos-based authentication.

All the possibilities mentioned above target the e-mail system. In addition, there is always the possibility to transform and secure the messages that are sent or received in an e-mail system in a way that is transparent to both the e-mail system and the users of the system. This possibility requires the use of a message security scheme, and we further elaborate on such schemes in Chapter 17.

16.1.4   WWW Transactions

The continuing growth and popularity of the Internet is mainly driven by the HTTP and the WWW. As further explored in [18], there are many technologies that can be used to secure the WWW and corresponding Web transactions. For example, the Digest authentication method has been added to the HTTP to provide a mechanism for strong user authentication [19]. Also, the SSL and TLS protocols are extensively used on the WWW to provide transaction security. As we saw in Chapter 15, HTTP layered on top of SSL/TLS has the acronym HTTPS and has a port number of 443 from the IANA.

In addition to the SSL and TLS protocols and the work that is being done within the IETF TLS WG, the IETF Web Transaction Security (WTS) WG[8] was chartered in 1995. The goal of the WTS WG was (and still is) to "develop requirements and a specification for the provision of security services to Web transaction." The starting point was the specification of the Secure Hypertext Transfer Protocol (S-HTTP) that was developed and originally proposed by Eric Rescorla and Allan Schiffman on behalf of the CommerceNet consortium in the early 1990s.[9] S-HTTP version 1.0 was publicly released in June 1994 and distributed by the CommerceNet consortium. Since 1995, the S-HTTP specification has been further refined under the auspices of the IETF WTS WG. In August 1999, the S-HTTP was specified and released in an experimental RFC document [20]. In addition, the IETF WTS WG released an informational RFC document specifying considerations for Web transaction security in January 1997 [21]. Because S-HTTP is not used and deployed on the Internet, we are not going to delve into the technical details of the corresponding protocol specification. You may refer to the first edition of this book or the RFC document mentioned above to obtain the details.

Finally, there are some complementary proposals to secure WWW transactions. For example, the use of a general-purpose common client interface (CCI) to enhance the security of WWW transactions with PGP messaging was proposed in [22]. The CCI was an early attempt at extending the functionality of WWW browsers. Now largely abandoned, CCI was an experimental protocol that allowed some versions of the NCSA Mosaic WWW browser to be controlled by an HTTP server. Today, many of the more useful functions of CCI are also present in programming and

---

[8]http://www.ietf.org/html.charters/wts-charter.html

[9]Launched in 1994 as a nonprofit organization, CommerceNet is dedicated to advancing electronic commerce on the Internet. Its almost 600 member companies and organizations seek solutions to technology issues, sponsor industry pilots, and foster market and business development. The CommerceNet consortium is available on-line at http://www.commerce.net.

scripting languages, such as Java and JavaScript. The PGP-CCI application was basically a link between a WWW browser and the functionality provided by the PGP software.

16.1.5   Domain Name System

As mentioned in Chapter 4, the DNS has specific vulnerabilities that may be exploited in DNS spoofing attacks. Against this background, the IETF has worked out a couple of security extensions for the DNS, and these security extensions are commonly referred to as DNS Security, or DNSSEC. The extensions are specified in standards track RFC 2535 [23] and are currently being implemented and deployed.

In short, DNSSEC uses public key cryptography and digital signatures to provide data integrity and authentication for the information contained within the DNS and transferred with the DNS protocol. To achieve this goal, DNSSEC incorporates some new RR types:

- The KEY RR for public keys;

- The CERT RR for public key certificates;

- The SIG RR for digital signatures;

- The NXT RR for the nonexistence of specific data.

As such, digital signatures can be used to secure DNS zone data, dynamic updates, and transactions, as well as to prove the nonexistence of DNS data. Furthermore, DNSSEC provides an option to use secret key cryptography rather than public key cryptography to secure DNS transactions. The digital signatures and the public keys used for signature verification are retrieved through queries and responses, just like any other piece of information within the DNS.

What DNSSEC does not provide is access control and privacy. This is important to distinguish from actual implementations, which may or may not choose to include additional mechanisms for access control and privacy. The reason why access control and privacy have been omitted is that the information contained with the original DNS protocol is designed to be public data. With the advent of firewalls, concerns about information leakage of system names and locations, and DoS attacks, there is an increasing desire to have both access control and privacy. This demand is being reflected in the implementation of DNS. For example, the BIND implementation provided access control to prevent unauthorized systems from performing zone transfers. This has also been extended to prevent certain systems from querying servers. To date, privacy has been partially achieved by using firewalls and having what is known as a split DNS configuration, in which the internal DNS information is difficult to access from the Internet.

DNSSEC has many security advantages. Any organization that relies on the Internet should consider DNSSEC a critical component of its security infrastructure because the DNS protocol is vulnerable and can be misused in spoofing attacks. Only DNSSEC, through its cryptographic techniques, can provide data integrity and authentication to all aspects of the DNS. Consequently, it is possible and very likely that DNSSEC will become more important in the future. DNSSEC, however, also has its disadvantages. For example, signing and verifying DNS data create some additional overhead that will negatively affect network and service performance. Furthermore, some operational aspects of DNSSEC are still being worked out, such as exactly how and who will sign public keys and how public key certificates can be revoked. An obvious solution is to establish a hierarchical PKI that matches the structure of the DNS tree. In this case, the PKI has a globally unique root CA.

16.1.6   Distributed File Systems

Another application that is often enhanced with security features is a distributed file system. Note that security professionals may feel well protected with strong encryption mechanisms, such as those provided by IPsec or SSL/TLS. But what good is transferring encrypted data over a network connection if the data are stored unencrypted on local machines that may get compromised? Thus, instead of having each application handle encryption and decryption, it is also possible to enhance a file system so that files are automatically encrypted after they leave applications but before they are sent to the file system. This approach has several advantages with regard to transparency and efficiency. There are at least two file systems that follow this approach:

- Matt Blaze from AT&T Bell Laboratories developed a *Cryptographic File System* (CFS) that is heavily used on UNIX systems [24, 25].

- Another example is the *Andrew File System* (AFS) that was originally designed and developed at Carnegie Mellon University and later marketed by the Transarc Corporation[10] [26, 27]. More recently, Transarc Corporation was acquired by IBM and has become the IBM Transarc Lab. In principle, the AFS refers to a Kerberized file system; it uses Kerberos for authentication and optional encryption, and is designed to work across WANs. Consequently, AFS provides a

---

[10]http://www.transarc.com

considerably higher level of security than does the Network File System (NFS) more commonly used today. NFS is shipped as part of the operating system with most versions of UNIX, while AFS is a commercial third-party product. Because Kerberos and AFS require significant technical expertise to set up and maintain, AFS is not widely used outside of a relatively small number of sites. If WAN file systems must be secured, it may be worth investigating AFS. There have been security problems with some earlier versions of AFS, but those have since been fixed [28].

Given the fact that the CFS is restricted to UNIX systems and the AFS requires the use of the Kerberos authentication system (which is used mainly in UNIX environments), there is not much choice for Windows users to transparently encrypt and decrypt their file systems. In Windows 2000, however, there is at least a possibility to transparently encrypt and decrypt NTFS files. This possibility has been named Encrypting File System (EFS). If a user activates encryption for a file, the EFS selects a random file encryption key and encrypts the file with this key. Furthermore, the file encryption key is encrypted with the public key of the user and the encrypted file encryption key is stored together with the encrypted file on disk. Consequently, file decryption always requires the decryption of the file encryption key, and the decryption of the file encryption key always requires the user's private key. For key recovery purposes it is possible to encrypt the file encryption key with an additional public key.

16.2 AUTHENTICATION AND KEY DISTRIBUTION SYSTEMS

In the late 1980s and early 1990s, a considerable amount of research and development was dedicated to authentication and key distribution systems that could be used to secure arbitrary network applications. Examples include:

- Kerberos, developed at MIT;

- Network Security Program (NetSP), developed by IBM;

- SPX, developed by Digital Equipment Corporation (DEC);[11]

---

[11]DEC has been acquired by Compaq.

- The Exponential Security System (TESS), developed at the University of Karlsruhe.

In addition, several extensions to the Kerberos authentication system have been developed, such as Yaksha, a Secure European System for Applications in a Multi-vendor Environment (SESAME), and the Distributed Computing Environment (DCE) developed by the Open Group.[12] In this section we are not going to describe and discuss all of these systems. Instead, we refer to [29] for a comparative overview.

Among the authentication and key distribution systems mentioned here, only Kerberos and SESAME are still in use. In addition, a Kerberos implementation is used in Windows 2000 to provide a single sign-on service. Kerberos, SESAME, and Windows 2000 are overviewed next.

16.2.1 Kerberos

The authentication and key distribution system Kerberos[13] [30–32] was originally developed at MIT to protect the emerging network services provided by the Athena project [33, 34]. The aim of the Kerberos system was to extend the notion of authentication to the computing and networking environment at MIT. According to Project Athena's technical plan [35], this environment consisted of public and private workstations, centrally operated server systems, and a campus network that interconnects the various components. In this environment, the primary security threats resulted from the potential of a user to forge the identity of another user in order to gain unauthorized access to system resources. These and similar threats are still relevant in many contemporary computing and networking environments.

The first three versions of the Kerberos system were used only at MIT. The first version that was made publicly available was Kerberos version 4 (Kerberos V4), and this version has achieved widespread use beyond MIT.[14] Officially released in December 1992, MIT Kerberos V4 is in its final state. In fact, MIT does not anticipate ever making a new Kerberos V4 software release in the future.

---

[12]The Open Group was formed in early 1996 by the consolidation of two open systems consortia, namely the Open Software Foundation (OSF) and the X/Open Company, Ltd. The Open Group includes a large number of computer vendors, including IBM and Microsoft.

[13]In Greek mythology, Kerberos is the name of the three-headed watchdog of Hades, whose duty it was to guard the entrance of the underworld.

[14]Outside the United States and Canada, the eBones distribution of Kerberos V4 is heavily used and widely deployed. The eBones distribution is available at http://www.pdc.kth.se/kth-krb/.

Some sites require functionality that Kerberos V4 does not provide, while others have a computing and networking environment or administrative procedures that differ from those at MIT. In addition, Steven Bellovin and Michael Merrit published a paper describing some shortcomings and limitations of Kerberos V4 in 1990 [36]. Against this background, work on Kerberos version 5 (V5) commenced in 1989, also fueled by discussions with Kerberos V4 users and administrators about their experience with the Kerberos model in general, and the MIT reference implementation in particular. In September 1993, Kerberos V5 was officially specified in RFC 1510 [37], and as such it was submitted to the Internet standards track.[15] Again, MIT provided a publicly and freely available Kerberos V5 reference implementation.

It should be noted that Kerberos V4 and V5, although conceptually similar, are substantially different from one another, and are even competing for dominance in the marketplace. In short, Kerberos V4 has a greater installed base, is simpler, and has better performance than V5, but works only with IP addresses; whereas Kerberos V5 has a smaller installed base, is less simple and thus less efficient, but provides more functionality than V4. For the purpose of this book, we simplify the Kerberos system and protocol considerably. This simplified form of Kerberos is equally valid for Kerberos V4 and V5. Further and more detailed information can be obtained from Chapter 2 of [29] or [38]. Also, the Kerberos home pages at MIT[16] and the Information Sciences Institute (ISI)[17] of the University of Southern California provide good sources of information. In particular, there is a document originally written by Bill Bryant in 1988. Entitled "Designing an Authentication System: A Dialogue in Four Scenes," the document introduces and discusses the considerations and decisions that led to Kerberos V4 design. The document is highly recommended reading and can be downloaded from the MIT Kerberos home page[18] and many other sites related to network security.

Kerberos is based on authentication and key distribution protocols that were originally proposed in [39, 40] and later modified to use time stamps [41]. In the Kerberos model and terminology, an administration domain is called a *realm*. It is assumed that every company or organization that runs the Kerberos system establishes a realm that is uniquely identified by a realm name. Also, Kerberos is based on the client-server model. Users, clients, and servers implementing and providing specific network services are considered as *principals*, and each principal is uniquely identified by a principal identifier.

---

[15] As of this writing, the protocol is still in the status of a Proposed Standard.
[16] http://web.mit.edu/kerberos/www/
[17] http://nii.isi.edu/info/kerberos/
[18] http://web.mit.edu/kerberos/www/dialogue.html

The aim of Kerberos is to allow a client acting on behalf of a user to authenticate (i.e., prove its identity) to a service (i.e., an application server) without having to send authentication information in the clear across the network. Also, user authentication should be empowered by passwords, but the use of the passwords should be minimized (i.e., they should be used only once during the single sign-on processes). To achieve these goals, the Kerberos system requires the existence of a TTP that acts as KDC. The KDC, in turn, consists of two logically separated components:

- An *authentication server* (AS);

- A set of *ticket-granting servers* (TGSs).

Note that the AS and the TGSs are only logically separated components and that they may be processes running on the same machine. Also note that the machines that provide these services must be carefully protected and located in physically secure environments. If an intruder is able to subvert either the AS or any of the TGSs, he or she may compromise the entire system at will.

The KDC maintains a database that includes an entry for every principal registered in the Kerberos realm. The information a Kerberos KDC stores for each principal P includes (but is not restricted to) the following two items:

- The principal identifier of P;

- The key K_p that is shared between P and the KDC (e.g., a password if P is a user);

For obvious reasons, the confidentiality of the keys (i.e., K_p for each principal P) must be protected. The Kerberos system therefore encrypts all keys with a KDC master key. This encryption allows a system manager to remove copies of the KDC database from the master server, and send copies thereof to slave servers without going to extraordinary lengths to protect the privacy of the copies. Slave servers are required in large realms to provide a highly available Kerberos authentication service. Note that Kerberos does not store the KDC master key in the same database, but manages that key separately.

In prinicple, Kerberos implements a ticketing system. What this basically means is that a central authority (i.e., the KDC) issues tickets that clients and servers can use to mutually authenticate themselves and to agree on a shared secret. The shared secret, in turn, can then be used for subsequent data authentication and encryption. In either case, a Kerberos ticket is a data record that is issued by the Kerberos KDC. Among other things, the ticket contains:

- The session key that will be used for authentication between the client and the server;

- The name of the principal to whom the session key was issued;

- An expiration time after which the session key is no longer valid.

The ticket is not sent directly to the server, but instead sent to the client who forwards it to the server as part of an authentication exchange. A Kerberos ticket is always encrypted with the server key, known only to the AS and the intended server. Because of this encryption, it is not possible for the client to modify the ticket without detection. There are two types of tickets:

- *Ticket-granting tickets* (TGTs) are issued by the Kerberos AS and can be used to request service tickets from a TGS;

- *Service tickets*, or *tickets*, in turn, are issued by a TGS and can be used to authenticate to specific server systems.

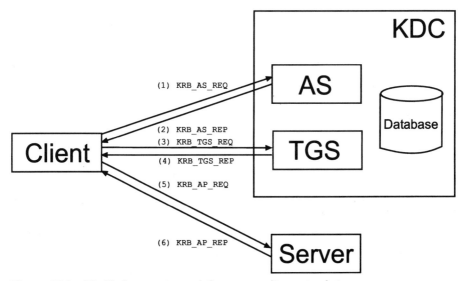

Figure 16.1   The Kerberos system and the corresponding protocol steps.

During the duration of a typical session, a TGT is usually obtained first. The TGT is then locally stored on the client (instead of the user's password) and used to request service tickets for each and every server system the client must authenticate to.

Figure 16.1 illustrates the Kerberos system and the corresponding protocol steps. The six steps can be be formalized as follows:

$$
\begin{array}{llll}
1 : C & \longrightarrow & AS & : \text{KRB\_AS\_REQ}(U, TGS, L_1, N_1) \\
2 : AS & \longrightarrow & C & : \text{KRB\_AS\_REP}(U, T_{c,tgs}, \{TGS, K, T_{start}, T_{expire}, N_1\}K_U) \\
3 : C & \longrightarrow & TGS & : \text{KRB\_TGS\_REQ}(S, L_2, N_2, T_{c,tgs}, A_{c,tgs}) \\
4 : TGS & \longrightarrow & C & : \text{KRB\_TGS\_REP}(U, T_{c,s}, \{S, K', T'_{start}, T'_{expire}, N_2\}K) \\
5 : C & \longrightarrow & S & : \text{KRB\_AP\_REQ}(T_{c,s}, A_{c,s}) \\
6 : S & \longrightarrow & C & : \text{KRB\_AP\_REP}(\{T'\}K')
\end{array}
$$

Furthermore, the six steps can be grouped in three exchanges:

- The *AS exchange* between the client and the AS (steps 1 and 2);

- The *TGS exchange* between the client and the TGS (steps 3 and 4);

- The *AP exchange* between the client and the application server (steps 5 and 6).

Obviously, the AS exchange must be performed only once during the login process, whereas the TGS exchange and the AP exchange must be performed for each server the client wants to access (if the server requires authentication).

When a user U wants to sign on a Kerberos realm, he or she has a client C send a KRB_AS_REQ (Kerberos authentication server request) message to the AS of the Kerberos KDC in step 1. The message basically includes the principal identifier for U, the identifier for a TGS, a desired lifetime L_1 for the TGT, and a randomly chosen nonce N_1.

After having received the KRB_AS_REQ message, the AS looks up and extracts the secret keys for both U and the TGS. If required, the AS preauthenticates the request, and if preauthentication fails, a corresponding error message is returned to C. Otherwise, the AS randomly selects a new session key K, and returns a KRB_AS_REP message to C in step 2. The message includes U, a TGT $T_{c,tgs} = \{U, C, TGS, K, T_{start}, T_{expire}\}K_{tgs}$, and $\{TGS, K, T_{start}, T_{expire}, N_1\}K_U$. The TGT's start and expiration times T_{start} and T_{expire} are set in accordance with the realm's security policy in a way that fits the specified lifespan L_1 of the KRB_AS_REQ message.

After having received the KRB_AS_REP message in step 2, C applies a well-known one-way hash function h to the user-provided password pwd_U to compute the user's master key $K_U = h(pwd_U)$.[19] Equipped with this key, C can decrypt $\{TGS, K, T_{start}, T_{expire}\}K_U$, and extract TGS, K, T_{start}, and T_{expire} accordingly. C is now in the possession of a TGT that is valid from T_{start} to T_{expire}. It can use this TGT to request service tickets from the TGS for any server S in the realm. Note that in a TGT, a lifetime is used like a password expiration time. Limiting the lifetime of a TGT thus limits the amount of damage that can be caused by a compromise of the TGT. In Kerberos, there is generally no possibility to revoke a TGT once it has been issued. Thus, limiting the TGT lifetime implicitly sets a deadline after which the TGT becomes obsolete.

Before initiating a TGS exchange, C must determine in which realm the application server he or she will request a ticket for what has been registered. If C does not already possess a TGT for that realm, C must obtain one. This is first attempted by requesting a TGT for the destination realm from the local Kerberos server (using the KRB_TGS_REQ message recursively). The Kerberos server may return a TGT for the desired realm, in which case C can proceed. Alternatively, the Kerberos server may also return a TGT for a realm which is closer to the desired realm, in which case this step must be repeated with a Kerberos server in the realm specified in the returned TGT. If neither is returned, the request must be retried with a Kerberos server for a realm higher in the hierarchy. This request will itself require a TGT for the higher realm, which must be obtained by recursively applying these directions. Once the client obtains a TGT for the appropriate realm, it determines which Kerberos servers serve that realm, and contacts one. The list might be obtained through a configuration file or a corresponding network service.

In step 3, C sends a KRB_TGS_REQ (Kerberos ticket-granting server request) message to the TGS. The message includes the principal identifier S for the server, a requested lifetime L_2 for the service ticket, a nonce N_2, the TGT $T_{c,tgs}$, and an authenticator $A_{c,tgs}$ to prove legitimate ownership of the TGT. $A_{c,tgs}$ can be regarded as the principal identifier of C and a time stamp, both of them encrypted with the

---

[19]Kerberos V4 did not prompt the user to enter the password until after C has received the KRB_AS_REP message. This is because Kerberos V4 was serious in following the generally good security rule of having C know the user's password only for the minimum time possible. But waiting the few seconds to retrieve the KRB_AS_REP message before asking the user for the password really does not enhance security significantly, and in fact Kerberos V5 has the user enter the password before C sends the KRB_AS_REQ message. The reason for the designers of Kerberos V5 to change the order was that V5 requires C to prove that it knows the user's password before the AS sends the KRB_AS_REP message, which makes it less easy to obtain a quantity with which to launch an offline password guessing attack.

session key K: $A_{c,tgs} = \{C,T\}K$. Note that $T_{c,tgs}$ can have a comparably long lifetime, and could be eavesdropped and replayed. The purpose of the authenticator is thus to show that C holds the secret key, and to thwart this kind of attack. Also note that the use of authenticators generally requires that principals on the network keep reasonably synchronized time. The times can be off by some amount. The allowable time skew is independently set at each server, and therefore some servers may be configured to be fussier than others about times being close. The allowed time skew is usually set to be accurate within 5 minutes without undue administrative burden. In practice, that assumption has turned out to be more problematic than expected. Distributed time services, once deployed, make much tighter synchronization possible.

The KRB_TGS_REQ message is processed in a manner similar to that of the KRB_AS_REQ message, but there are some additional checks to be performed. In step 4, the TGS returns a KRB_TGS_REP message (Kerberos ticket-granting server reply) that shares its format with the KRB_AS_REP message. It includes the principal identifier for the user, a ticket $T_{c,s}$ for the requested server S, and an expression (i.e., $\{S, K', T'_{start}, T'_{expire}, N_2\}$) encrypted with K. Again, the client can use K to decrypt the expression and to extract the identifier for the server, the new session key K' (which the client uses to talk to the server), a lifetime for the ticket, and the nonce N_2.

When the KRB_TGS_REP is received by C, it is processed in the same manner as the KRB_AS_REP processing described above. The primary difference is that the ciphertext part of the response must be decrypted with the session key that is shared with the TGS rather than with the user's master key.

It turns out that there is neither functionality nor security gained by having Kerberos require an authenticator as part of the KRB_TGS_REQ message. If someone who did not know the session key K transmitted $T_{c,tgs}$ to the TGS, the TGS would return a message encrypted with K, which would be of no use to someone who did not know the session key. The reason the designers of Kerberos did it this way is to make the protocol for talking to the TGS be the same as for talking to the other servers. When talking to other servers, the authenticator does indeed provide security, because it authenticates the knowledge of the corresponding session key.

The AP exchange of the Kerberos V4 protocol is used by network applications either to authenticate a client to a server, or to mutually authenticate a client and a server to each other. The client must have already acquired credentials for the server using the AS or TGS exchange.

In step 5, C sends a KRB_AP_REQ (Kerberos application request) message to the server S. The message includes $T_{c,s}$, $A_{c,s} = \{C, T'\}K'$, and some additional bookkeeping information. Authentication is based on the server's current time of day, the ticket $T_{c,s}$, and the authenticator $A_{c,s}$.

To make sure that the KRB_AP_REQ message is not a replay of a request recent enough to look current given the time skew, S should keep all time stamps received within the maximum allowable time skew and check that each received time stamp is different from any of the stored values. Any authenticator older than the maximum allowable time skew would be rejected anyway, so there is no need to remember values older than the threshold value. Kerberos V4, however, does not bother saving time stamps. Saving time stamps does not help if S is a replicated service in which all the instances of the service use the same master key. The threat of an eavesdropper replaying the authenticator C sent to one instance of S to a different instance of S could have been avoided if Kerberos had done something like put the network layer of the instance of S in the authenticator, too.

If no error occurs, and if mutual authentication is required, S has to return a KRB_AP_REP (Kerberos application reply) message to C in step 6. Again, this message is encrypted with the session key K' that is shared between C and S. Since this key was in the ticket encrypted with the server's secret key, possession of this key is proof that S is the intended principal. More accurately, S has to increment the time stamp included in the KRB_AP_REQ message authenticator and reencrypt it with K'.

As described thus far, Kerberos provides mutual authentication services for the client and server. However, a by-product of the Kerberos authentication protocol is the exchange of a session key K' that is shared between the client and the server. This key can then be used by the application to protect the confidentiality and integrity of communications. Typically, communications between the client and server is transparently encrypted and decrypted using the DES and the session key K'.

There are at least two problems that should be considered with care when it comes to the large-scale deployment of the Kerberos system:

1. The fact that one part of the KRB_AS_REP message is encrypted with K_U can be used to launch a verifiable password guessing attack against the user's password. More accurately, it is possible to guess a password candidate, derive a candidate K_U from this value, and decrypt the relevant part of the KRB_AS_REP message with this key. It is then verifiable whether the password candidate was properly guessed. There are several strategies to protect against this type of attack, but

unfortunately, all require the use of public key cryptography or similar constructs.

2. The fact that the Kerberos KDC shares a secret key with each prinicpal in the realm allows the administrator of the KDC to spoof any principal. This is a consequence of the fact that the Kerberos system only uses secret key cryptography.

Furthermore, every network application must be modified to make use of the Kerberos system. The process of modifying a network application to make use of the Kerberos system is commonly referred to as "Kerberizing" it. In general, Kerberizing network applications is usually the most difficult part of installing Kerberos. Fortunately, the MIT reference implementations of the Kerberos system include Kerberized versions of some popular network applications, such as Telnet and the Berkeley r-tools. Other applications have been Kerberized by vendors and are included in their supported products. The availability of Kerberized applications has improved with time, and is expected to further improve in the future. However, a site would still have to arrange itself to add Kerberos support to any application developed in house.

One of the main design principles for an authentication and key distribution system is its use of a standardized API, such as the *Generic Security Services API* (GSS-API) specified by the IETF Common Authentication Technology (CAT) WG. Unfortunately, the use of the GSS-API for Kerberos V5 has not been specified until recently [42]. Also, more work is needed to standardize and eventually simplify the GSS-API, such as demonstrated by GSS-API version 2 or the Simple Public-Key GSS-API Mechanism [43, 44].

Finally, note that the Kerberos system provides authentication, data confidentiality, and data integrity services. By itself, it provides no information as to whether or not the client is authorized to access the server and to use the corresponding services. In general, there are three possibilities to address authorization within the basic Kerberos model:

1. The Kerberos KDC could maintain authorization information for each service and issue tickets to authorized users only.

2. A dedicated service could maintain authorization information by keeping access lists for each service and allowing the client to obtain sealed certification of list membership. The client would then present the sealed certification in addition to a Kerberos ticket to the requested service.

3. Each service could maintain its own authorization information, with the optional help of a service that stores access lists and provides certification of list membership.

The Kerberos model is based on the assumption that each service knows best who its users should be and what form of authorization is appropriate for them. Consequently, the third approach is employed in the Kerberos system. Next we will see that the main difference between Kerberos and SESAME and Windows 2000 is that SESAME and Windows 2000 both employ the second approach to address authorization.

16.2.2   SESAME

SESAME was a European research and development project aimed at developing an authentication and authorization infrastructure (AAI) and system for distributed computing and networking environments [45–47]. It achieved this by including and combining an extended Kerberos V5 authentication service and a privilege attribute service that can be used to provide authorization and corresponding access control services.

Recall that in the Kerberos system a client requests a TGT from the AS, and that the client can use this TGT to request service tickets from the TGS. In the SESAME system, a similar approach is used for authorization and access control. If a client wants to use a service, he or she must not only be authenticated by the AS, but also have his or her other privilege attributes certified by an additional component, a so-called *privilege attribute server* (PAS). In SESAME, the term *privilege attribute certificate* (PAC) is used to refer to a certified set of privilege attributes. In principle, a PAC consists of both the user's privileges and corresponding control information. The user's privileges are data such as the user's identity, role, organizational group, and security clearance, whereas the control information says where and when the PAC can be used and whether it can be delegated or not. Note that a PAC is conceptually similar to an attribute certificate. In short, the client and the PAS must exchange KRB_PAS_REQ and KRB_PAS_REP messages between the AS exchange (using the KRB_AS_REQ and KRB_AS_REP messages) and the TGS exchange (using the KRB_TGS_REQ and KRB_TGS_REP messages). In these messages, the client is provided with a PAC that is relevant for the user on whose behalf it is acting.

Refer to Chapter 6 of [29] or [47] to get a more comprehensive overview and discussion of the SESAME system. Also, the SESAME home page[20] provides a good source of information for further study. With the deployment of similar mechanisms in Windows 2000, interest in SESAME and SESAME-enabled applications has become negligible in the recent past.

16.2.3   Windows 2000

More recently, Microsoft has implemented the Kerberos V5 authentication service with extensions for public key authentication[21] for the Windows 2000 operating system. The Kerberos KDC is integrated with other Windows 2000 security services running on the domain controller and uses the domain's active directory as its security account database.[22]

In addition to the functionality specified in [37], Windows 2000 implements an authorization mechanism in the Kerberos system in a specific and unique way. When the Kerberos protocol is used for authentication, a list of security identifiers (SID) identifying a principal and the principal's group memberships is transported to the client in the authorization data field of a ticket. Authorization data, in turn, are gathered in two steps:

- The first step takes place when the KDC in a Windows 2000 domain prepares a TGT.

- The second step is accomplished when the KDC prepares a service ticket for the server in the domain.

When a user requests a TGT, the KDC in the user's account domain queries the domain's active directory. The user's account record includes the user's SID as well as SIDs for any security group to which the user belongs. The list of SIDs returned by the KDC is placed in the authorization data field of the TGT.[23] In a multiple-domain environment, the KDC also queries the Global Catalog for any universal groups that include the user or one of the user's domain security groups. If any are found, their SIDs are also added to the list in the TGT's authorization data field.

---

[20]http://www.esat.kuleuven.ac.be/cosic/sesame/

[21]These extensions are specified by the IETF CAT WG under the acronym PKINT.

[22]For consistency, the Microsoft documentation uses the term "domain" instead of "realm." Furthermore, the distinction between an AS and a TGS is not made. Both components are collectively referred to as a KDC.

[23]Note that this use of the authorization data field to actually carry authorization information is consistent with revisions to the Kerberos V5 protocol specification [37] submitted to the IETF.

When a user requests a service ticket, the KDC in the server's domain copies the contents of the TGT's authorization data field to the ticket's authorization data field. Furthermore, if the server's domain is different from the user's account domain, the KDC queries the active directory to find out whether any security groups in the local domain include the user or one of the user's security groups. If any are found, their SIDs are also added to the list in the service ticket's authorization data field.

16.3 CONCLUSIONS

In this chapter, we overviewed and briefly discussed various application layer security protocols (either security-enhanced application protocols or authentication and key distribution systems). In Chapter 18, we talk about the end-to-end argument [48] that basically says that the application layer is the appropriate layer to provide services, such as security services.

From a theoretical point of view, the use of authentication and key distribution systems that provide a standardized API is advantageous, as it minimizes the parts that are application-specific and must be implemented for each application individually. But implementation and deployment of authentication and key distribution systems have turned out to be difficult and slow in practice. One of the main reasons is that applications and application programs must be modified to use the systems or the corresponding APIs (i.e., "Kerberized" in the case of the Kerberos system).

This modification is neither simple nor always possible. For example, if an organization is running a proprietary application for which it does not possess the source code, it is generally not possible to modify the application. Also, for applications that are available in source, the modification process is not always possible. Consequently, security-enhanced application protocols have become more and more popular during the last decade. For example, SSH is a very popular tool that is widely used as a security-enhanced replacement for Telnet and Rlogin in the intranet environment. Also, security extensions for the DNS (i.e., DNSSEC) are becoming increasingly important from the point of view of infrastructure security. Without a secure version of the DNS, almost all security technologies, mechanisms, and services can be circumvented by corresponding spoofing attacks.

In either case, adding security to an application protocol remains a difficult and error-prone task. To put it into the words of RFC 2316, "Security is not and cannot be a cookie cutter process. There is no magic pixie dust that can be sprinkled over a protocol to make it secure. Each protocol must be analyzed individually to determine what vulnerabilities exist, what risks they may lead to, what palliative measures can be taken, and what the residual risks are" [49].

Because of the difficulty of enhancing the application layer protocols with security features, it has become increasingly popular to leave the protocols as they are and to layer security on top of them. In Chapter 17, we overview and discuss some of the resulting message security protocols.

REFERENCES

[1] J. Postel and J. Reynolds, "Telnet Protocol Specification," Request for Comments 854 (STD 8), May 1983.

[2] B. Kantor, "BSD Rlogin," Request for Comments 1282, December 1991.

[3] D. Borman, "Telnet Authentication: Kerberos Version 4," Request for Comments 1411, January 1993.

[4] K. Alagappan, "Telnet Authentication: SPX," Request for Comments 1412, January 1993.

[5] M. Blaze and S. M. Bellovin, "Session-Layer Encryption," *Proceedings of USENIX UNIX Security Symposium*, June 1995.

[6] R. L. Rivest and A. Shamir, "How to Expose an Eavesdropper," *Communications of the ACM*, Vol. 27, No. 4, 1984, pp. 393–395.

[7] D. R. Safford, D. K. Hess, and D. L. Schales, "Secure RPC Authentication (SRA) for TELNET and FTP," *Proceedings of USENIX UNIX Security Symposium*, October 1993, pp. 63–67.

[8] B. A. LaMacchia and A. M. Odlyzko, "Computation of Discrete Logarithms in Prime Fields," *Designs, Codes, and Cryptography*, Vol. 1, 1991, pp. 46–62.

[9] D. Vincenzetti, S. Taino, and F. Bolognesi, "STEL: Secure Telnet," *Proceedings of USENIX UNIX Security Symposium*, June 1995.

[10] T. Ylönen, "SSH—Secure Login Connections over the Internet," *Proceedings of USENIX UNIX Security Symposium*, July 1996.

[11] D. J. Barrett and R. E. Silverman, *SSH, the Secure Shell: The Definitive Guide*, O'Reilly & Associates, Sebastopol, CA, 2001.

[12] J. Postel and J. Reynolds, "File Transfer Protocol (FTP)," Request for Comments 959 (STD 9), October 1985.

[13] D. H. Crocker, "Standard for ARPA Internet Text Messages," Request for Comments 822 (STD 11), August 1982.

[14] J. Postel, "Simple Mail Transfer Protocol," Request for Comments 821 (part of STD 10), August 1982.

[15] L. Hughes, *Internet E-Mail: Protocols, Standards, and Implementations*, Artech House, Norwood, MA, 1998.

[16] D. Strom and M. T. Rose, *Internet Messaging*, Prentice Hall, Upper Saddle River, NJ, 1998.

[17] R. Oppliger, *Secure Messaging with PGP and S/MIME*, Artech House, Norwood, MA, 2001.

[18] R. Oppliger, *Security Technologies for the World Wide Web*, Artech House, Norwood, MA, 2000.

[19] J. Franks, et al., "An Extension to HTTP: Digest Access Authentication," Request for Comments 2069, January 1997.

[20] E. Rescorla and A. Schiffman, "The Secure HyperText Transfer Protocol," Request for Comments 2660, August 1999.

[21] G. Bossert, S. Cooper, and W. Drummond, "Considerations for Web Transaction Security," Request for Comments 2084, January 1997.

[22] J. D. Weeks, A. Cain, and B. Sanderson, "CCI-Based Web Security—A Design Using PGP," *Proceedings of 4th International World Wide Web Conference*, December 1995, pp. 381–395.

[23] D. Eastlake, "Domain Name System Security Extensions," Request for Comments 2535, March 1999.

[24] M. Blaze, "A Cryptographic File System for UNIX," *Proceedings of ACM Conference on Computer and Communications Security*, November 1993, pp. 9–16.

[25] M. Blaze, "Key Management in an Encrypting File System," *Proceedings of USENIX Summer Conference*, June 1994, pp. 27–35.

[26] J. H. Howard, "An Overview of the Andrew File System," *Proceedings of USENIX Conference*, 1988, pp. 23–26.

[27] M. L. Kazar, "Synchronization and Caching Issues in the Andrew File System," *Proceedings of USENIX Conference*, 1988, pp. 27–36.

[28] P. Honeyman, L. B. Huston, and M. T. Stolarchuk, "Hijacking AFS," *Proceedings of USENIX Conference*, 1992, pp. 175–182.

[29] R. Oppliger, *Authentication Systems for Secure Networks*, Artech House, Norwood, MA, 1996.

[30] J. G. Steiner, B. C. Neuman, and J. I. Schiller, "Kerberos: An Authentication Service for Open Network Systems," *Proceedings of the USENIX UNIX Security Symposium*, August 1988.

[31] J. Kohl and B. C. Neuman, "The Kerberos Network Authentication Service," Massachusetts Institute of Technology (MIT), Cambridge, MA, December 1990.

[32] J. I. Schiller, "Secure Distributed Computing," *Scientific American*, November 1994, pp. 72–76.

[33] G. A. Champine, D. E. Geer, and W. N. Ruh, "Project Athena as a Distributed Computer System," *IEEE Computer*, Vol. 23, September 1990, pp. 40–50.

[34] G. A. Champine, *MIT Project Athena—A Model for Distributed Computing*, Digital Press, 1991.

[35] S. P. Miller, et al., "Kerberos Authentication and Authorization System," Section E.2.1 of the Project Athena Technical Plan, Massachusetts Institute of Technology (MIT), Cambridge, MA, December 1987.

[36] S. M. Bellovin, and M. Merritt, "Limitations of the Kerberos Authentication System," *ACM Computer Communication Review*, Vol. 20, 1990, pp. 119–132.

[37] J. Kohl and B. C. Neuman, "The Kerberos Network Authentication Service (V5)," Request for Comments 1510, September 1993.

[38] B. Tung, *Kerberos: A Network Authentication System*, Addison-Wesley, Reading, MA, 1999.

[39] R. M. Needham and M. D. Schroeder, "Using Encryption for Authentication in Large Networks of Computers," *Communications of the ACM*, Vol. 21, December 1978, pp. 993–999.

[40] R. M. Needham and M. D. Schroeder, "Authentication Revisited," *ACM Operating Systems Review*, Vol. 21, 1987, p. 7.

[41] D. E. Denning and G. Sacco, "Timestamps in Key Distribution Protocols," *Communications of the ACM*, Vol. 24, 1981, pp. 533–536.

[42] J. Linn, "The Kerberos Version 5 GSS-API Mechanism," Request for Comments 1964, June 1996.

[43] J. Linn, "Generic Security Services Application Program Interface, Version 2," Request for Comments 2078, January 1997.

[44] C. Adams, "The Simple Public-Key GSS-API Mechanism," Request for Comments 2025, October 1996.

[45] T. A. Parker, "A Secure European System for Applications in a Multi-Vendor Environment (The SESAME Project)," *Proceedings of the 14th National Computer Security Conference*, 1991.

[46] P. V. McMahon, "SESAME V2 Public Key and Authorisation Extensions to Kerberos," *Proceedings of the Internet Society Symposium on Network and Distributed System Security*, February 1995, pp. 114–131.

[47] P. Ashley and M. Vandenwauver, *Practical Intranet Security—Overview of the State of the Art and Available Technologies*, Kluwer Academic Publishers, Norwell, MA, 1999.

[48] J. H. Saltzer, D. P. Reed, and D. D. Clark, "End-to-End Arguments in System Design," *ACM Transactions on Computer Systems*, Vol. 2, No. 4, November 1984, pp. 277–288.

[49] S. Bellovin, "Report of the IAB Security Architecture Workshop," Request for Comments 2316, April 1998.

Chapter 17

Message Security Protocols

In this chapter, we focus on the security protocols that operate above the application layer, meaning that the messages that are transmitted by application protocols are cryptographically protected before they are submitted for transmission. These protocols are called *message security protocols* in this book. We start this chapter with an introduction in Section 17.1, elaborate on some protocols that have been proposed and that are being used for secure messaging in Section 17.2, and draw some conclusions in Section 17.3.

17.1 INTRODUCTION

Consider the situation in which you have to securely transfer a stream of bits and bytes (e.g., a file or a message) through a computer network or distributed system. There are basically two possibilities to do so:

1. You may use a secure transfer protocol. If no such protocol is available, you may consider enhancing a given transfer protocol (e.g., FTP) with security features and use this security-enhanced transfer protocol to actually transfer the stream of bits and bytes.

2. You may use any given (insecure) transfer protocol and secure the stream of bits and bytes before it is submitted for transfer.

The first possibility leads to a situation in which the security services are provided at the application layer, whereas the second possibility leads to a situation in which the security services are provided above the application layer. To make this distinction more accurate, the security protocols that implement the second possibility are referred to as *message security protocols* in the rest of this book. Note that this is an artificial term, and that there is no such thing as a "message layer" in the Internet model. Also note that the first possibility (i.e., application layer security protocols) was addressed in Chapter 16, whereas the second possibility (i.e., message security protocols) is discussed in this chapter. More specifically, we discuss the problem of securely transfering e-mail messages (using a secure messaging protocol) next.

Another topic that could be addressed in this chapter is related to the security features of the Extensible Markup Language (XML) as specified by the World Wide Web Consortium (W3C). In fact, the use of XML makes it possible to encrypt or digitally sign data segments (e.g., messages) in a standardized way before they are transmitted in computer networks or distributed systems. Because XML security is a very new and still transient topic, it is not further addressed in this book. Note, however, that the IETF XMLDSIG WG[1] has been asked "to develop an XML compliant syntax used for representing the signature of Web resources and portions of protocol messages (anything referencable by a URI) and procedures for computing and verifying such signatures." As of this writing, the IETF XMLDSIG WG has released a standards track RFC document [1] as well as two informational RFC documents [2, 3].[2]

17.2   SECURE MESSAGING PROTOCOLS

One possibility to securely transfer an e-mail message is to cryptographically protect it in a way that is useful only for the intended recipients. For example, the message can be digitally enveloped to protect its confidentiality or digitally signed to protect its authenticity and integrity:

- As explained in Section 5.5, the message is digitally enveloped by encrypting it with a randomly chosen message key, encrypting the message key with the recipient's public key, and sending both—the encrypted message and the encrypted

---

[1] http://www.ietf.org/html.charters/xmldsig-charter.html
[2] Furthermore, an Internet-Draft has been released that is going to replace [1].

message key—to the recipient. The recipient, in turn, can decrypt the message key with his or her private key and decrypt the message with the resulting message key. If there are multiple recipients, the message key is encrypted with the public key of each recipient.

- As explained in Section 5.4, the message is digitally signed by computing a one-way hash from the message and encrypting the hash value with the sender's private key.

All secure messaging schemes and protocols that are relevant today follow this approach and provide support for both digital envelopes and digital signatures [4]:

- Privacy enhanced mail (PEM) and MIME object security services (MOSS);

- Pretty Good Privacy (PGP) [5–7];

- Secure MIME (S/MIME).

In short, PEM was an early standardization effort initiated by the IRTF Privacy and Security Research Group and later by the IETF PEM WG [8].[3] In fact, PEM was the first serious effort to provide security services for Internet messaging. The work led to the publication of a four-part PEM specification in February 1993 [9–12]. The specification was submitted to the Internet standards track as a Proposed Standard. Unfortunately, PEM was never a recognized success in terms of commercial deployment. One of the main reasons for its lack of success was because it was limited to 7-bit encoded ASCII messages, and was incompatible with the MIME format which was developed around the same time. The other main reason for its lack of commercial success was its strict use of a hierarchy of CAs that serves as a PKI for PEM.

After the publication of the original PEM specifications in 1993, the IETF PEM WG continued to work on the development of PEM-like security services for use in conjunction with MIME messages. This work was completed in 1995 and resulted in two separate specifications which solve two parts of the MIME incompatibility problem:

- RFC 1847, entitled "Security Multiparts for MIME: Multipart/Signed and Multipart/Encrypted," specifies two additional MIME content types for encrypted and digitally signed messages (i.e., `multipart/encrypted` and `multipart/signed`) [13].

---

[3]Both groups no longer exist.

- RFC 1848, entitled "MIME Object Security Services" (MOSS), defines a set of procedures and formats for digitally signing and encrypting MIME body parts for use in conjunction with the content types introduced in RFC 1847 [14]. When a digital signature is applied to a MIME object, the `multipart/signed` content type is used. When encryption is applied, the `multipart/encrypted` content type is used. Contrary to PEM, digital signature and encryption mechanisms can also be used independently (whereas PEM required that encrypted objects are always digitally signed).

Following the terminology introduced in RFC 1848, the entire architecture was named MOSS. It is further described in [15]. In summary, MOSS was an attempt to overcome the limitations and shortcomings of PEM (namely the incompatibility with MIME messages and the far-too-strict PKI requirements). But MOSS also had so many implementation options that it was possible and very likely for two independent software developers to come up with MOSS implementations that would not interoperate. MOSS can be thought of as a framework rather than a specification, and considerable work in implementation profiling remains to be done.[4]

While PEM and MOSS failed to become commercially successful and have sunk into oblivion, the secure messaging schemes that are in widespread use (i.e., PGP and S/MIME) copied the good features of their predecessors while attempting to avoid the bad ones. For example, PEM introduced the use of digital envelopes and the base-64 encoding scheme, and all secure messaging schemes that were proposed afterward have retained these features.

Today, PGP and S/MIME are the way to go for secure messaging on the Internet. S/MIME is a specification, whereas PGP can be thought of as both a specification and a software package. PGP and S/MIME are very similar in nature. For example, they both use public key cryptography and digital enveloping techniques to digitally sign and cryptographically protect e-mail messages. They are overviewed and briefly discussed next. Again, more background information about secure messaging in general and PGP and S/MIME in particular is available in [4].

17.2.1 PGP

PGP is a software package that was originally developed by Philip R. Zimmermann in the early 1990s [5–7]. At that time, Zimmermann selected some of the best available cryptographic algorithms (i.e., MD5, IDEA, and RSA) as building blocks, integrated them into a platform-independent software package that was based on

---

[4]This has not changed so far.

a small set of easy-to-use commands, and made the resulting software and its documentation, including the source code written in the C programming language, publicly and freely available on the Internet (at least for citizens from the United States and Canada). In addition, Zimmermann entered into a legal agreement with a company called Viacrypt to provide a fully compatible commercial version of PGP that was reasonably priced.[5] The commercial version of PGP was primarily intended to satisfy the requirements of users who wanted to have a product with full professional vendor support. There were at least two legal problems related to the first versions of PGP:

1. The PGP software used the RSA algorithm for authentication and key distribution. As mentioned in Chapter 5, the RSA algorithm was protected by a U.S. patent (that expired on September 20, 2000);

2. More important, the U.S. government held that export controls for cryptographic software were violated when the PGP software spread around the world following its publication as freeware.

The first problem was settled with the patent holders of the RSA algorithm by having the PGP software include and make use of a cryptographic subroutine library that was distributed by RSA Security, Inc.[6] More specifically, beginning with version 2.5, the PGP software included and made use of the RSAREF cryptographic subroutine library to perform RSA public key computations. The RSAREF library, in turn, was distributed under a license that allowed noncommercial use within the United States. The commercial use of RSAREF, however, required the payment of a license fee to RSA Security, Inc. Because the commercial version of PGP was sold by Viacrypt, the use of RSAREF in this version was properly licensed.

The second problem was more severe. In fact, it led to a three-year criminal investigation by the U.S. government. Zimmermann was accused of a federal crime because the software had flowed across national borders. The investigation was carefully followed by both the trade press and the general public as further described in [7].

After the government dropped the case in early 1996, Zimmermann founded a company called Pretty Good Privacy, Inc.,[7] which was acquired by McAfee Associates in December 1997. At the same time, Network Associates, Inc. (NAI) was

---

[5]The company no longer exists and the URL www.viacrypt.com leads to the home page of Network Associates, Inc. (NAI).

[6]At that time, RSA Security, Inc., was named RSA Data Security, Inc.

[7]http://www.pgp.com

formed by a merger of McAfee Associates and Network General. Today, NAI is one of the world's largest network security and management software companies with four business units and more than 2,700 employees. Zimmermann was employed by NAI until early in 2001, when he left the company to join Hush Communications.[8]

In the United States and Canada, the PGP software is publicly and freely available for noncommercial use, but must be licensed for commercial use from NAI:

- The noncommercial version of PGP is distributed by MIT.[9]

- The commercial version of PGP is distributed by NAI and its local resellers.

Outside the United States and Canada, the legal situation is less clear. Some years ago, the international PGPi scanning project was initiated and launched.[10] The idea of the project was to export the source code of the PGP software in optical character recognition (OCR) format, and to recompile and rebuild the software entirely outside the United States and Canada. Note that the U.S. Export Administration Regulations (EAR) explicitly state:

"A printed book or other printed material setting forth encryption source code is not itself subject to the EAR (...)"

Consequently, source code is not subject to the EAR and can be exported from the United States. If the source code is recompiled and rebuilt entirely outside the United States, a fully compatible and interoperable software package is created. The resulting versions of the PGP software (also referred to as PGPi) are publicly and freely available from the International PGP home page at http://www.pgpi.org (the site is physically located in Norway). Note that the amount of source code is huge. For example, PGP 5.0i was recompiled and rebuilt from source code that was printed in 12 books containing more than 6,000 pages, whereas PGP version 6.5.1 already came along with 40 books containing more than 20,000 pages.

In addition to the PGPi scanning project, NAI used Network Associates International B.V. in The Netherlands to market PGP products outside the United States and Canada. The corresponding Web site is available at http://www.pgpinternational.com. More specifically, the PGP products sold by Network Associates International B.V. were recompiled and rebuilt by a Swiss

---

[8]http://www.hush.com

[9]http://web.mit.edu/network/pgp.html

[10]The letter "i" stands for "international version." Further information about the PGPi scanning project is available at http://www.pgpi.org/pgpi/project/scanning/.

company called cnlab Software AG[11] based on the C code that was legally exported from the United States (the same source code that is used for the domestic versions of the PGP software). NAI B.V. licensed the PGP software from cnlab Software AG to market it outside the United States and Canada. To comply with the EAR, NAI had to make sure that no technical assistance or support was provided from the United States to cnlab Software AG or to any international users of PGP products, and that all support for international users came from non-U.S. nationals, either from employees of NAI B.V., employees of cnlab Software AG, or anyone else.

This situation has changed and the liberalized U.S. export controls have made it possible for NAI and its PGP Security business unit to legally distribute PGP products on a worldwide scale. In fact, on January 20, 2000, PGP Security announced[12] that its software had been successfully exported from the United States for the first time under the new export regulations. At an event launching the new PGP Security business unit of NAI, the software was exported by sending it as a binary e-mail attachment to a recipient in the United Kingdom. This simple act would have been designated a federal crime until January 14, 2000, when new export regulations were adopted by the U.S. Department of Commerce (DoC) to allow the use of U.S.-developed cryptographic technology worldwide (refer to Chapter 4 for a brief discussion of the new U.S. export regulations). It will be interesting to see how the new export regulations influence the worldwide distribution of PGP software and products. In either case, NAI still recommends buying the software from its local resellers.

As mentioned, the first versions of PGP were implemented by Zimmermann. Major parts of later versions of PGP, however, were implemented by an international collaborative effort involving a large number of contributors. Here, we use the term *PGP* to refer to software developed by NAI (or its PGP Security business unit respectively) or any other software that implements and conforms to the PGP or OpenPGP specifications. There are many versions of PGP in use today:

- PGP 2.6.x was the first version that was widely used and internationally deployed. This version of PGP is specified in the informational RFC 1991 [7]. It requires the use of MD5, IDEA, and RSA.

---

[11]http://www.cnlab.ch

[12]The announcement was made during the RSA Data Security Conference that was held on January 16–20, 2000, in San José, California.

- PGP 5.x was introduced to define new message formats and correct a number of problems in the PGP 2.6.x design. PGP 5.x is also known as PGP 3.

- After the release of PGP 5.x, an IETF OpenPGP WG was formed in the IETF Security Area. The aim of the WG was to use PGP 5.x as a basis and to come up with a new OpenPGP specification. More recently, OpenPGP was specified in RFC 2440 [8] and submitted to the Internet standards track.[13]

- Based on PGP 5.x and the OpenPGP specifications, NAI came up with PGP 6.x that introduced some new features that go beyond a tool for secure messaging. Two of these features include PGPnet, which is basically a "bump-in-the-stack" implementation of the IP security (IPsec) protocol suite (as explained in Chapter 14), and PGPdisk, which allows a user to transparently encrypt and decrypt partitions on local hard disks. The latest and most widely deployed version of PGP 6.x is PGP 6.5.3.

- In September 2000, NAI publicly released PGP Desktop Security 7.0. In addition to the functionality of PGP 6.5.3, PGP Desktop Security 7.0 provides a personal firewall and a personal intrusion detection system (IDS). The reason for this is that any computer system that uses PGPnet to interconnect to an intranet represents a network access point and must be protected accordingly (e.g., using a personal firewall and/or IDS). Furthermore, PGP Desktop Security 7.0 fully integrates with X.509-based PKIs and provides a single sign-on (SSO) mechanism for the Windows 2000 operating system. Finally, PGP Desktop Security 7.0 comes with an optional passphrase recovery mechanism.[14] Support for smartcards (primarily for the European market) and USB tokens (primarily for the U.S. market) was stated to become available in PGP 7.1.

In addition, there are several PGP versions that are marked with special characters. For example, we mentioned in footnote 10 that a PGP version number with an appended character "i" (e.g., PGP version 6.0.2i) refers to an international version that is made available as part of the PGPi scanning project, meaning that the software has been recompiled and rebuilt entirely outside the United States and Canada.

Contrary to MOSS and S/MIME, PGP must not be integrated into the user agent software. A user can create a message with his or her favorite word-processing

---

[13] As of this writing, the OpenPGP specification is a Proposed Standard.

[14] The mechanism uses five personal questions and answers that are provided by the user during the PGP initialization and configuration process.

program (e.g., a "normal" text editor or Microsoft Word), digitally sign or encrypt the file with PGP, optionally encode it for transport with PGP's radix-64 encoding function or any other encoding utility, and finally use a commercial off-the-shelf (COTS) user agent of his or her choice to send the resulting message to the recipient. The point to make and to remember is that PGP must not be part of the user agent that is finally used to send out the message, and that PGP can reside entirely outside the user agent. However, from a user's point of view it is more convenient to have PGP incorporated into and become part of the user agent software. In the simplest case, the user has two buttons, one for signaling the use of digital signatures (to protect the authenticity and integrity of a message) and one for signaling the use of digital envelopes (to protect the confidentiality of a message).

If a user agent is MIME compliant, it may even be possible to combine PGP's functionality with the functionality of MIME. In fact, the approach to combine PGP and MIME is called *PGP/MIME* and the approach to combine OpenPGP and MIME is called *OpenPGP/MIME*:

- *PGP/MIME* is based on the message formats defined in RFC 1991 [16] and further specified in RFC 2015 [17].

- *OpenPGP/MIME* is based on the message formats defined in RFC 2440 [18] and further specified in a pair of Internet-Drafts[15] that are developed by the participants of the IETF OpenPGP WG. By the time you read this book, these Internet-Drafts will probably have become standard track RFC documents.

Note that RFC 1991 requires the use of patented cryptographic algorithms (RSA and IDEA), and that it cannot be submitted to the Internet standards track accordingly (it has been published as an informational RFC document). Because RFC 2015 relies on RFC 1991, it cannot be submitted to the Internet standards track, either. Consequently, PGP/MIME is not going to become an Internet standard. Contrary to that, it is likely and very possible that OpenPGP/MIME as specified in RFC 2440 will be submitted to the Internet standards track and that PGP/MIME implementations will be replaced by OpenPGP/MIME implementations in the future. In the meantime, not all user agents implement the PGP/MIME and OpenPGP/MIME specifications. For example, Qualcomm Eudora version 4.3 implements only PGP/MIME, whereas Microsoft Outlook Express version 5 implements neither of the two specifications.

---

[15]`draft-ietf-openpgp-mime-*.txt` and `draft-ietf-openpgp-multsig-*.txt`

Finally, note that an interesting alternative to NAI products is being developed in Germany. More specifically, the German Federal Ministry of Economics and Technology issued a DM 250,000 grant to the GNU Privacy Guard (GPG) project on November 19, 1999. The aim of the project is to further develop the GnuPG software, a free and open source implementation of the OpenPGP specification. Because GnuPG does not use IDEA or RSA, it can be used without any legal restriction. The software is currently available only as a command line program (a GUI version is planned for the future). Further information about the GPG project in general, and the GnuPG software in particular, is available at `http://www.gnupg.org`.

It is commonly agreed that the (cryptographic) strength of PGP, OpenPGP, and GPG is comparably good. In fact, there have been published only two vulnerabilities so far:

1. A vulnerability was found in the additional decryption key (ADK) feature of PGP in August 2000. In fact, it was possible to add an ADK to a PGP certificate in order to have a specific message key be additionally encrypted with this ADK. Anybody who knows the ADK is able to decrypt the message key and the message accordingly. The vulnerability is further described in CERT Advisory[16] CA-2000-18 entitled "PGP May Encrypt Data with Unauthorized ADKs."

2. Two Czech cryptologists, Vlastimil Klima and Tomas Rosa, publicly announced the discovery of a flaw in the OpenPGP format in March 2001. The flaw was reported in *The New York Times* and refers to the way in which a user's private key is stored in an OpenPGP key ring. More specifically, the integrity of the key is not entirely protected. This allows an attacker (who has physical access to the private key ring) to modify the key and to invoke the use of this key for the generation of future signatures. Equipped with a legitimate signature and a signature that uses the modified key, the attacker can cryptanalyze the user's private key. The flaw is severe. Nevertheless, keep in mind that exploiting the flaw requires physical access to the private key ring, and that by having this kind of access, it is much simpler for the attacker to simply grab the encrypted key ring and use a keylogger to eavesdrop on the passphrase that is required to decrypt the private key.

Unfortunately, it is not clear whether—and if so what—other vulnerabilities have been found in PGP, OpenPGP, and GPG software packages so far.

---

[16]`http://www.cert.org/advisories/CA-2000-18.html`

17.2.2   S/MIME

Earlier in this chapter, we mentioned that PEM was an early IETF-initiated Internet standardization effort for secure messaging that suffered from two major limitations and shortcomings (namely, the incompatibility with the MIME message formats and the far-too-restrictive PKI requirements), and that MOSS was an attempt to overcome them. In parallel with the development of MOSS in the mid-1990s, however, an industry working group led by RSA Security, Inc., started to develop another specification for conveying digitally signed and/or encrypted and digitally enveloped data in accordance to the MIME message formats and some of the earlier specified public key cryptography standards (PKCSs).[17]

The approach and protocol specifications that were developed by the industry working group were named *Secure Multipurpose Internet Mail Extensions* (S/MIME). Similar to PEM and MOSS, S/MIME refers to a specification rather than a product (such as PGP), and similar to MOSS, S/MIME also was designed to add security to e-mail messages that make use of the MIME message formats. Consequently, S/MIME cannot be used with user agents that do not provide support for MIME (contrary to PGP). Unlike PEM and MOSS, however, S/MIME has been successfully deployed in the marketplace.

While the goals of MOSS and S/MIME were largely the same, the final solutions ended up being quite different. This is primarily because S/MIME is built on top of some PKCS specifications (and as such makes heavy use of ASN.1 specifications), whereas PEM, MOSS, and PGP use character-encoding style of protocols. Note, however, that this is not a fundamental difference, but rather an implementation issue. Also note that using established encoding schemes is certainly good practice, as any security analysis does not have to start from scratch.

As of this writing, there are three versions of S/MIME, of which only versions 2 and 3 are used in practice:

- S/MIME version 1 was specified and officially published in 1995 by RSA Security, Inc. [19].

- S/MIME version 2 was specified in a pair of informational RFC documents—RFC 2311 [20] and RFC 2312 [21]—in March 1998.[18]

---

[17]The PKCS specifications are developed by another industry working group also led by RSA Security, Inc. Consequently, RSA Security, Inc., had a vital interest promoting the PKCS specifications and applying them in the field of secure messaging.

[18]The pair was complemented by three informational RFC documents that specify PKCS #1 (RFC 2313), PKCS #7 (RFC 2314), and PKCS #10 (RFC 2315).

- The work was continued in the IETF S/MIME Mail Security (SMIME) WG and resulted in S/MIME version 3 in June 1999. S/MIME version 3, in turn, was specified in a set of five related RFC documents (RFC documents 2630 to 2634 [22–26]) and has been submitted to the Internet standards track.[19] The changes between version 2 and version 3 are not fundamental, and it is generally recommended that S/MIME version 3 implementations should attempt to have the greatest interoperability possible with S/MIME version 2 implementations. The S/MIME version 3 enhanced security services as specified in [26] are taken rather directly from the Message Security Protocol (MSP) that was developed for the Defense Message System during the late 1980s, before the S/MIME work.

Since the very beginning of the standardization effort, many vendors of Internet messaging products (including, for example, Microsoft and Netscape Communications) have actively supported S/MIME. In fact, S/MIME is an integral part of most user agent software packages that are available today. This commitment and strong vendor support have not changed so far and are likely to continue in the future.

In the past, S/MIME has had some difficulties receiving consideration as an Internet standards track protocol because of its use of patented technologies and algorithms. Historically, all standards approved by the IETF must use only public domain technologies and algorithms, so anyone can implement them without paying royalties to patent holders. Unfortunately, this is not the case with some public key algorithms. For example, we mentioned in Chapter 5 that the RSA public key algorithm was protected by U.S. Patent No. 4,405,829, "Cryptographic Communications System and Method," granted to MIT in September 1983. Also, other public key algorithms are protected by patents.[20] As mentioned, S/MIME makes use of PKCS #1, PKCS #7, and PKCS #10. Although the PKCS specifications are freely available, any developer who wants to use the algorithms described therein (e.g., the RSA algorithm), whether he or she uses RSA Security's own toolkits or not, is required to pay RSA Security, Inc., royalties, at least for products created and distributed in the United States.[21] Because of this situation, Internet standardization for S/MIME version 2 has been blocked and the pair of informational RFC documents is historical material being published for the public record. Meanwhile, the situation has improved mainly for two reasons:

---

[19]As of this writing, S/MIME version 3 is a Proposed Standard.

[20]Most public key algorithms are protected by U.S. patents (and not international patents as, for example, some of the earlier secret key algorithms).

[21]Outside the United States, the development and marketing of public key cryptography are not restricted.

1. S/MIME version 3 provides more flexibility with regard to the cryptographic algorithms that must be supported.

2. Most public key patents have expired (e.g., the patent for the Diffie-Hellman key exchange and the RSA algorithms).

Consequently, it is possible and very likely that the situation is going to improve and that Internet standardization for S/MIME version 3 will speed up considerably.

Finally, because S/MIME version 3 has been submitted for possible consideration as an Internet standards track protocol, interoperability has become a major issue. Vendors participate in S/MIME compliance and interoperability testing programs conducted over the Internet. As such, they put their application programs through S/MIME test suites that include on-line certification, digitally signed and digitally enveloped message creation, and verification and decryption of received messages. For example, RSA Security, Inc., runs an S/MIME interoperability center that may serve as a reference.

17.3 CONCLUSIONS

In this chapter, we focused on two exemplary message security protocols, PGP and S/MIME, that are used for secure messaging on the Internet. In spite of their many similarities, there are at least two fundamental differences that lead to a situation in which PGP and S/MIME implementations do not easily interoperate:

1. PGP and S/MIME use different message formats.

2. PGP and S/MIME handle public keys and public key certificates in fundamentally different ways:

   - PGP relies on users to directly or indirectly exchange public keys and establish trust in each other.[22] This informal approach to establish a "web of trust" works well for small workgroups but can become hard to manage for large groups.

   - Contrary to that, S/MIME relies on public key certificates that are issued by official (or at least "official-looking") and hierarchically organized CAs and distributed by corresponding directory services.

---

[22]Indirect public key exchange uses directory services and PGP key servers.

Again, you may refer to Chapters 8 and 13 of [4] for a more comprehensive overview and discussion about the way PGP and S/MIME handle public keys and public key certificates.

The first difference between PGP and S/MIME is minor and similar to the differences between various formats for image files, such as GIF and JPEG. They basically do the same things from a user's point of view, but their formats are different.

The second difference is more severe with regard to a long-term convergence of PGP and S/MIME. Fortunately, newer versions of PGP additionally provide support for X.509v3 public key certificates (in addition to PGP certificates). Consequently, it is possible and very likely that we will see user agents that can handle X.509v3 public key certificates and process messages that conform to either the PGP or S/MIME formats. In the long term, however, it would be preferable that Internet standardization comes up with one unified secure messaging format and corresponding protocol specification(s). Consequently, it would be necessary to merge the IETF OpenPGP and SMIME WGs into one IETF WG dedicated to secure messaging. Unfortunately, there are too many commercial interests involved to make this happen anytime soon.

REFERENCES

[1] D. Eastlake, J. Reagle, and D. Solo, "XML-Signature Syntax and Processing," Request for Comments 3075, March 2001.

[2] J. Reagle, "XML Signature Requirements," Request for Comments 2807, July 2000.

[3] J. Boyer, "Canonical XML Version 1.0," Request for Comments 3076, July 2000.

[4] R. Oppliger, *Secure Messaging with PGP and S/MIME*, Artech House, Norwood, MA, 2001.

[5] P. R. Zimmermann, *The Official PGP User's Guide*, MIT Press, Cambridge, MA, 1995.

[6] P. R. Zimmermann, *PGP Source Code and Internals*, MIT Press, Cambridge, MA, 1995.

[7] S. Garfinkel, *PGP: Pretty Good Privacy*, O'Reilly & Associates, Sebastopol, CA, 1995.

[8] S. T. Kent, "Internet Privacy Enhanced Mail," *Communications of the ACM*, Vol. 36, No. 8, August 1993, pp. 48–60.

[9] J. Linn, "Privacy Enhancement for Internet Electronic Mail: Part I—Message Encryption and Authentication Procedures," Request for Comments 1421, February 1993.

[10] S. T. Kent, "Privacy Enhancement for Internet Electronic Mail: Part II—Certificate-Based Key Management," Request for Comments 1422, February 1993.

[11] D. Balenson, "Privacy Enhancement for Internet Electronic Mail: Part III—Algorithms, Modes, and Identifiers," Request for Comments 1423, February 1993.

[12] B. Kaliski, "Privacy Enhancement for Internet Electronic Mail: Part IV—Key Certification and Related Services," Request for Comments 1424, February 1993.

[13] J. Galvin, et al., "Security Multiparts for MIME: Multipart/Signed and Multipart/Encrypted," Request for Comments 1847, October 1995.

[14] S. Crocker, et al., "MIME Object Security Services," Request for Comments 1848, October 1995.

[15] J. Galvin and M. S. Feldman, "MIME Object Security Services: Issues in a Multi-User Environment," *Proceedings of USENIX UNIX Security V Symposium*, June 1995.

[16] D. Atkins, W. Stallings, and P. R. Zimmermann, "PGP Message Exchange Formats," Request for Comments 1991, August 1996.

[17] M. Elkins, "MIME Security with Pretty Good Privacy (PGP)," Request for Comments 2015, October 1996.

[18] J. Callas, et al., "OpenPGP Message Format," Request for Comments 2440, November 1998.

[19] RSA Data Security, Inc., *S/MIME Implementation Guide*, Interoperability Profile, Version 1, August 1995.

[20] S. Dusse, et al., "S/MIME Version 2 Message Specification," Request for Comments 2311, March 1998.

[21] S. Dusse, et al., "S/MIME Version 2 Certificate Handling," Request for Comments 2312, March 1998.

[22] R. Housley, "Cryptographic Message Syntax," Request for Comments 2630, June 1999.

[23] E. Rescorla, "Diffie-Hellman Key Agreement Method," Request for Comments 2631, June 1999.

[24] B. Ramsdell, "S/MIME Version 3 Certificate Handling," Request for Comments 2632, June 1999.

[25] B. Ramsdell, "S/MIME Version 3 Message Specification," Request for Comments 2633, June 1999.

[26] P. Hoffman, "Enhanced Security Services for S/MIME," Request for Comments 2634, June 1999.

Chapter 18

Conclusions and Outlook

In this part of the book we focus on communication security and address the major cryptographic security protocols that have been proposed, specified, implemented, and deployed for the four layers[1] of the Internet model (i.e., the network access, Internet, transport, and application layers). Finally, we elaborated on some possibilities to provide security services above the application layer (and we called the resulting protocols *message security protocols*).

Given this variety of cryptographic security protocols, we ask at least two questions:

- Which security protocol is the best?

- Which layer is best suited to provide communication security services?

With regard to the first question, we saw in the previous chapters of this part that the cryptographic security protocols have unique and partly incomparable advantages and disadvantages. For example, the IPsec and IKE protocols provide

---

[1]It is very likely and possible that we will see a session layer between the transport and application layers in a future Internet model. In fact, the SSL and TLS protocols as well as the SSH transport layer protocol are session layer security protocols and could also be described under this title.

support for many parameters and options that are negotiable between the communicating peers, whereas the SSL and TLS protocols are rather strict in terms of parameters and options that must be implemented and supported. Given this situation and its diversity, it is very difficult or even impossible to have the protocols compete with each another and to actually decide which one is the best. Fortunately, most security protocols we overviewed and discussed provide a reasonable level of security. In fact, most of them use the same or very similar cryptographic techniques and algorithms (e.g., the HMAC construction for message authentication, DES, 3DES, or AES for bulk data encryption, and RSA for entity authentication and key exchange). Only a few protocols have been shown to be weak and have serious security problems. As an example, we elaborated on MS-PPTP (especially version 1) in Chapter 13. Note, however, that this is only an example and that there are probably more weak than strong protocols in use today. This is particularly true for proprietary and unpublished security protocols that one sometimes finds in commercial security products.

If deciding which security protocol is the best is difficult if not impossible, the next question is related to the layer that is best suited to provide communication security services. This leads us to the second question listed. This question is simpler to answer mainly because it addresses classes of security protocols (instead of individual security protocols). In order to further simplify the discussion (and to reduce the variety of layers that can provide communication security services), one usually distinguishes between lower layers (i.e., the network access and Internet layers) and higher layers (i.e., the transport and application layers, as well as the provision of security services above the application layer). In either case, there are arguments to provide security services at either the lower or higher layers in a given protocol stack:

- In short, the proponents of providing security services at the lower layers argue that lower-layer security can be implemented transparently to users and application programs, effectively killing many birds with a single stone.

- Contrary to that, the proponents of providing security services at the higher layers argue that lower-layer security attempts to do too many things, and that only protocols that work at higher layers can meet application-specific security needs and provide corresponding security services both effectively and efficiently.

Unfortunately, both arguments are true in some sense and there is no generally agreed-upon best layer to provide security services. The best layer actually depends on the security services that are required in a given environment and the application environment in which the services must be implemented and deployed. For example, non-repudiation services are typically provided at the higher layers, whereas data confidentiality services can also be provided at the lower layers. Also, in an application environment where one can assume users to have smartcards and public key certificates the implementation and provision of non-repudiation services is usually simple and straightforward. In either case, the end-to-end argument originally proposed in [1] also applies for security and provides a strong argument for providing security services at the higher layers. In short, the end-to-end argument says that the function in question (e.g., a security function) can completely and correctly be implemented only with the knowledge of the application standing at the endpoints of the communications system. Therefore, providing that function as a feature of the communications system itself is not possible (sometimes an incomplete version of the function provided by the communications system may be useful as a performance enhancement).

From a practical point of view, providing security services at the lower or higher layers has several advantages and disadvantages:

- Providing security services at the lower layers has the big advantage that the applications and application programs must not be modified (i.e., the client and server software can be left as it is). In other words, the security services can be provided transparently to all users and applications, and all applications can be made secure simultaneously. The major disadvantage of lower-layer security protocols is related to the fact that the provision of security services must be implemented inside the networking infrastructure (either at the network access or Internet layer). This is not always possible and sometimes ad hoc solutions must be used instead. For example, we saw that BITS and BITW implementations for the IPsec and IKE protocols are very common and widespread today. Hopefully, the relevant standards will be made mandatory for future releases of the corresponding protocol specifications. For example, support for the IPsec and IKE protocols is mandatory for IPv6 implementations. This will make a large difference in terms of deployment.

- Contrary to that, providing security services at the higher layers has the distinct advantage that the networking infrastructure must not be modified and can be left as it is. This advantage is important, since it allows the provision of security services on an end-to-end basis. The major disadvantage of higher layers security protocols, however, is related to the fact that the applications or application protocols must be modified to provide the security services, and that the client and server software must also be modified accordingly. Sometimes the required modifications are moderate or negligible (e.g., if an application is layered on top of SSL/TLS), but sometimes the required modifications are quite substantial (e.g., if an application protocol is redesigned to additionally provide security services). Not all possibilities equally apply for all applications. For example, if we have to secure a UDP-based application, the use of SSL/TLS or another transport layer security protocol is generally not possible.

An analogy may help us better understand the possibilities to place security services in a communications protocol stack. Let us assume we have some valuable goods to transport from one location to another (e.g., a collection of jewelry). If we want to use a railway system to transport the goods, we have the choice of either securing the railway system as a whole and transporting the goods as they are, or securing the goods (e.g., put them in a safe and put some armed forces in front of the safe) and transporting them on the railway system as it is. In this analogy, the first possibility refers to the possibility of providing security services at the lower layers, whereas the second possibility refers to the possibility of providing security services at the higher layers. For obvious reasons, the second possibility is often more effective and more efficient.

One can also argue that the question of which layer is best suited to provide communication security services depends on and must be answered for each service individually. For example, bulk data cryptographic transformations, such as message authentication, integrity checking, and data encryption, are well suited to be provided at the network access or Internet layer, which is usually tightly coupled with the operating system kernel and thus allows for efficient employment and scheduling of potentially available dedicated hardware, random number generators, and other components. At the same time, security policies that may be defined for a site or corporate intranet may be enforced without individual users being able to circumvent them. This has to be supplemented by an API and other utilities residing in application space. The API and the utilities are to provide applications with information about the level of authenticity a connection actually has, and what algorithms for data encryption and authentication should be used. Other services, however, are better provided at higher layers. Examples include entity authentication and non-repudiation services empowered by the use of digital or electronic signatures.

Against this background, the question of which layers are best suited to provide communication security services is not an "either-or" decision but rather an "and" decision, actually traversing and encompassing multiple layers. In the future, it is possible and very likely that we will see both network and application providers have their duties and care about security requirements and corresponding solutions. From the technologist's point of view, it will be important to provide both of them with appropriate security technologies and solutions.

REFERENCE

[1] J. H. Saltzer, D. P. Reed, and D. D. Clark, "End-to-End Arguments in System Design," *ACM Transactions on Computer Systems*, Vol. 2, No. 4, November 1984, pp. 277–288.

Part IV

DISCUSSION

Chapter 19

Public Key Infrastructures

In Chapter 5, we introduced public key cryptography and the notion of public key certificates. In Part III, we used public key certificates in cryptographic security protocols without addressing the question on how to establish and actually deploy a public key infrastructure (PKI). This question is further addressed in this chapter. More specifically, we introduce the topic in Section 19.1, focus on public key certificates and attribute certificates in Sections 19.2 and 19.3, overview and discuss the work of the relevant IETF working group (i.e., the IETF PKIX WG) in Section 19.4, address certificate revocation in Section 19.5, and conclude with some final remarks in Section 19.6. Parts of this chapter are taken from Chapter 8 of [1] and Chapter 13 of [2]. Further information about public key certificates and PKIs also can be found in [3–5].

19.1 INTRODUCTION

According to RFC 2828, the term *certificate* refers to "a document that attests to the truth of something or the ownership of something" [6]. Historically, the term was coined and first used by Loren M. Kohnfelder to refer to a digitally signed record holding a name and a public key [7]. As such, the certificate attests to the legitimate ownership of a public key and attributes a public key to a principal, such as a person, a hardware device, or any other entity. As discussed in Chapter 5, the resulting certificates are called *public key certificates*.

More generally and in accordance with RFC 2828, a certificate can not only be used to attest to the legitimate ownership of a public key (in the case of a public key certificate), but also to attest to the truth of any property attributed to a specific certificate owner. This more general class of certificates is commonly referred to as *attribute certificates*. Consequently, the major difference between a public key certificate and an attribute certificate is that the former includes a public key (the key that is certified), whereas the latter includes a list of attributes (the attributes that are certified).

In either case, the certificates are issued (and possibly revoked) by an authority that is recognized and trusted by some community of users. Authorities that issue (and possibly revoke) public key certificates and attribute certificates are named differently:

- An authority that issues public key certificates is called a *certification authority* (CA).[1]

- Contrary to that, an authority that issues attribute certificates is called an *attribute authority* (AA).

Against this background, a PKI is "a system of CAs that perform some set of certificate management, archive management, key management, and token management functions for a community of users" that employ public key cryptography [6]. In this definition, the term CA comprises the more specific term AA.

Many standardization bodies have been working in the field of public key certificates and PKIs. The Telecommunication Standardization Sector of the International Telecommunication Union (ITU-T) has released and has been periodically updating a recommendation that is commonly referred to as X.509 [8]. Meanwhile, the ITU-T recommendation X.509 has also been adopted by many other standardization bodies, including, for example, the ISO/IEC JTC1 [9] and the IETF (as further addressed in Section 19.4).

---

[1]In the past, CAs were often called trusted third parties (TTPs). This is particularly true for CAs that are operated by government bodies.

19.2 PUBLIC KEY CERTIFICATES

According to RFC 2828, a public key certificate is "a digital certificate that binds a system entity's identity to a public key value, and possibly to additional data items" [6]. As such, it is a digitally signed data structure that attests to the ownership of a public key.

There are several types and formats of public key certificates, but all of them contain at least the following three pieces of information:

- A public key;

- Some naming information;

- One or more digital signatures.

The public key is the piece of information for which the public key certificate has been issued at first place. Without a public key, a public key certificate does not make a lot of sense (unless it is used to carry some other attributes associated with the certificate owner).

The naming information is used to identify the owner of the public key certificate, such as his or her name (e.g., "Rolf Oppliger"). In the past, there has been some confusion about the naming scheme that is appropriate for the global Internet. For example, the ITU-T recommendation X.500 introduced the notion of a distinguished name (DN) that can be used to uniquely identify an entity (i.e., a public key certificate owner) in a globally unique namespace. There are other examples of globally unique namespaces on the Internet, the most prominent being the DNS. The existence and usefulness of a globally unique namespace, however, has also been challenged in a couple of research papers (e.g., [10]). Most important, the simple distributed security infrastructure (SDSI) architecture and initiative [11] have evolved from the argument that a globally unique namespace is not appropriate for the global Internet, and that logically linked local namespaces provide a simpler and more realistic model [12]. As such, work on SDSI inspired the establishment of a Simple Public Key Infrastructure (SPKI) WG within the IETF. The WG was tasked with producing a certificate infrastructure and operating procedure to meet the needs of the Internet community for trust management in as easy, simple, and extensible a way as possible. It published a pair of experimental RFC documents [13, 14] before its activities were abandoned early in 2001.

Finally, the digital signatures are used to attest to the fact that the other two items (i.e., the public key and the naming information) actually belong together. This part of a public key certificate turns the certificate into something useful.

As of this writing, there are two practically relevant formats for public key certificates[2]: PGP certificates and X.509 certificates. A distinguishing feature of the PGP certificate format is that it allows potentially multiple user identities (user IDs) and signatures per certificate. What this basically means is that a PGP certificate is issued for a public key and that multiple user IDs can be associated with this key. Furthermore, multiple signatures can certify the fact that a specific user ID is associated with the public key. Consequently, there is a one-to-many relationship between the public key of a PGP certificate and its user IDs, and there is another one-to-many relationship for each of these user IDs and the signatures that are associated with it. Contrary to that, the X.509 certificate format is much simpler. In general, it allows only one user ID associated with a public key[3] and one signature that attests to and certifies this association. The situation is illustrated in Figure 19.1. The left side illustrates the structure of a PGP certificate, whereas the right side illustrates the comparably simpler structure of an X.509 certificate. Note that the X.509 certificate format can be considered to be special case of a PGP certificate, namely, one with one user ID and one signature.

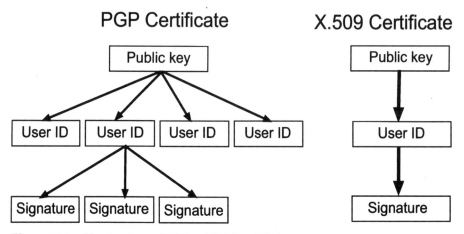

Figure 19.1   The structures of PGP and X.509 certificates.

---

[2]There are also other certificate formats, such as the format for certificates that conform to the wireless transport layer security (WTLS) specifications that is used to secure the wireless application protocol (WAP).

[3]Multiple user IDs can be simulated using the **AltSubjectName** field that can be used to hold alternative naming information related to the subject.

As of this writing, ITU-T X.509 public key certificates are widely deployed on the Internet. In fact, the ITU-T recommendation X.509 specifies both a certificate format and a certificate distribution scheme [8]. It was first published in 1988 as part of the X.500 directory recommendations. The X.509 version 1 (X.509v1) format was extended in 1993 to incorporate two new fields, resulting in the X.509 version 2 (X.509v2) format. In addition, and as a result of attempting to deploy certificates within the global Internet, X.509v2 was revised to allow for additional extension fields. The resulting X.509 version 3 (X.509v3) specification was officially released in June 1996. Meanwhile, the ITU-T recommendation X.509 has been approved by the ISO/IEC JTC1 [9].

The format of an X.509v3 certificate is specified in the abstract syntax notation one (ASN.1) and the resulting certificates are typically encoded according to specific encoding rules[4] to produce a series of bits and bytes suitable for transmission in computer networks and distributed systems. An X.509 public-key certificate contains a sequence of data items and has a digital signature computed by a CA on that sequence. In addition to the signature, all three versions contain items 1 through 7 listed below. Only version 2 and version 3 certificates may additionally contain items 8 and 9, whereas only version 3 may contain item 10:

1. A version number (identifying version 1, version 2, or version 3);

2. A serial number (i.e., a unique integer value assigned by the issuer);

3. An object identifier (OID) that specifies the signature algorithm that is used to sign the public key certificate;

4. The DN of the issuer (i.e., the name of the CA that actually signed the certificate);

5. A validity period specifying an interval in which the certificate is valid;

6. The DN of the subject (i.e., the owner of the certificate);

7. Information related to the public key of the subject (i.e., the key and the OID of the algorithm);

8. Some optional information related to the issuer (defined for versions 2 and 3 only);

9. Some optional information related to the subject (defined for versions 2 and 3 only);

---

[4]There are many encoding rules. Examples include the basic encoding rules (BER) and the distinguished encoding rules (DER).

10. Some optional extensions (defined for version 3 only).

ITU-T X.509 can be used in many ways. Consequently, every nontrivial group of users who want to work with X.509 public key certificates has to produce a profile which nails down many features which are left undefined in X.509. The difference between a specification (i.e., ITU-T X.509) and a profile is that a specification does not generally set any limitations on what combinations can and cannot appear in various certificate types, whereas a profile sets various limitations, for example, by requiring that signing and confidentiality keys be different. Many profiling activities are currently going on with regard to the legislation of digital and electronic signatures.

19.3   ATTRIBUTE CERTIFICATES

For many years, the computer and communications industries have argued that the availability of public key certificates is a prerequisite for the evolution and success of electronic commerce. Against this background, many countries have put in place or are about to draft laws and directives for digital or electronic signatures (refer to Section 5.8.3 to get an overview about the legal situation).

Meanwhile, people have started to realize that public key certificates that can be used to properly authenticate users and customers solve only half of the problems related to electronic commerce. In addition to authentication, electronic commerce providers must also have an opportunity to properly authorize users and customers [15]. In fact, one may argue that an electronic commerce provider is generally not interested in authentication information about his or her customers. The only information that is relevant to him or her is whether the customer is authorized to access and make use of the service.[5] Consequently, the electronic commerce provider must have an opportunity to attain some authorization information about his or her users and customers.

As mentioned in Section 19.2, an X.509v3 public key certificate can also convey authorization information about its owner. The information can, for example, be encoded in one of the X.509v3 standard or extension fields. Note, however, that there are at least two reasons why caution should be taken in using X.509v3 public key certificates for conveying authorization information [3]:

1. The authority that is most appropriate for verifying the identity of a person associated with a public key (i.e., the CA) may not be appropriate for certifying the

---

[5]Note, however, that authorization requires proper authentication most of the times.

corresponding authorization information. For example, in a company the corporate security or human resources departments may be the appropriate authorities for verifying the identities of persons holding public keys, whereas the corporate finance office may be the appropriate authority for certifying permissions to sign on behalf of the company.

2. The dynamics of the two types of certificates may be fundamentally different. For example, the persons authorized to perform a particular function in a company may vary monthly, weekly, or even daily. Contrary to that, public key certificates are typically designed to be valid for a much longer period of time (e.g., 1 or 2 years). If it becomes necessary to revoke and reissue public key certificates frequently because of changing authorizations (that are encoded into the public key certificates), this may have a severe impact on the performance characteristics of the resulting certificate management scheme.

Recognizing that public key certificates are not always the best vehicle to carry authorization information, the U.S. American National Standards Institute (ANSI) X9 committee developed an alternative approach known as *attribute certificates*. Meanwhile, this approach has been incorporated into both the ANSI X9.57 standard and the X.509-related standards and recommendations of the ITU-T, ISO/IEC, and IETF.

According to RFC 2828, an attribute certificate is "a digital certificate that binds a set of descriptive data items, other than a public key, either directly to a subject name or to the identifier of another certificate that is a public-key certificate" [6]. The ITU-T recommendation also specifies X.509 attribute certificates (currently in version 1). An X.509 attribute certificate also has a subject field, but the attribute certificate is a separate data structure from that subject's public key certificate. A subject may have multiple attribute certificates associated with each of its public key certificates, and an attribute certificate may be issued by a different authority (i.e., the AA) than the authority that issued the associated public key certificate (i.e., the CA).

In essence, an attribute certificate binds one or more pieces of additional information to the certificate owner. As such, the attribute certificate may contain group membership, role, clearance, or any other form of authorization or access control-related information associated with its owner. In conjunction with authentication services, attribute certificates may provide the means to securely transport authorization information to applications and application programs. Consequently, attribute certificates are particularly well suited to control access to system resources, and to implement role-based authorization and access controls accordingly

[16]. Note that attribute certificates are conceptually similar to PACs as used in SESAME and Microsoft's Windows 2000 operating system (refer to Section 16.2 for an overview about SESAME and Windows 2000 PACs).

Anyone can define and register attribute types and use them in attribute certificates. The certificate is digitally signed and issued by an AA. AAs, in turn, are assumed to be certified by CAs, so that a single point of trust—namely, a trusted public key of a root CA—can eventually be used to validate the certificates of AAs, other CAs, and end users.

An X.509 attribute certificate contains a sequence of data items and has a digital signature that is computed from that sequence. In addition to the digital signature, an attribute certificate contains the following nine pieces of information:

1. A version number (typically specifying version 1);

2. A subject (either a DN or a serial number of an X.509 public key certificate);

3. An issuer (i.e., the DN of the issuing AA);

4. An object identifier for the algorithm that is used to sign the attribute certificate;

5. A serial number (i.e., a unique integer assigned by the issuer);

6. A validity period specified by a pair of time values (i.e., a start time and an expiration time);

7. A sequence of attributes describing the subject;

8. An optional field that may be used to identify the issuer if a DN is not sufficient;

9. An arbitrary number of optional extensions.

Apart from differences in content, an attribute certificate is managed the same way as a public key certificate. For example, if an organization already runs a directory service for public key certificates and related status information, this service can also be used to distribute attribute certificates.

Also similar to public key certificates, attribute certificates can be used in either the "push" or "pull" model:

• In the "push" model, the certificates are pushed from the client to the server.

- In the "pull" model, the certificates are pulled by the server from an on-line network service (either the certificate issuer or a directory service that is fed by the certificate issuer).

A PKI and attribute certificate infrastructure should support both models, because some applications work best when a client pushes the certificates to the server, whereas for other applications it is more convenient for the client simply to authenticate to the server and for the server to request the client's certificates from a corresponding network service or certificate repository.

19.4   IETF PKIX WG

In 1995, the IETF recognized the importance of public key certificates, and chartered an IETF Public-Key Infrastructure X.509 (PKIX[6]) WG with the intent of developing Internet Standards needed to support an X.509-based PKI for the Internet community. In the past, the PKIX WG has initiated and stimulated a lot of standardization and profiling activities within the IETF. It is closely aligned with the activities within the ITU-T.

The operational model of the IETF PKIX WG consists of subjects and end entities,[7] CAs, and *registration authorities* (RAs).[8] The functions that the RA may carry out will vary from case to case but may include personal authentication, token distribution, certificate revocation reporting, name assignment, key generation, and key archival. In any PKI architecture, RAs are optional components that are transparent to the end entities (when they are not present, the CA is assumed to be able to carry out the RAs' functions so that the PKI management protocols are the same from the end entities' point of view). Finally, the certificates generated by the CAs may be made publicly available in certificate repositories (e.g., network services that are available on-line).

According to this operational model, several informational, experimental, and standards track RFC documents in support of the original goals of the IETF PKIX WG have been approved by the IESG:

---

[6]http://www.ietf.org/html.charters/pkix-charter.html

[7]In the specifications of the IETF PKIX WG, the term *end entity* is used rather than the term *subject* to avoid confusion with the X.509v3 certificate field of the same name.

[8]Other terms are used elsewhere for the functionality of an RA. For example, the term local registration agent (LRA) is used in ANSI X9 standards, local registration authority (also with the acronym LRA) is used in [3], organizational registration agent (ORA) is used in certain U.S. government specifications, and registration agent (RA) has also been used elsewhere.

- Standards track RFC 2459 [17] profiles the format and semantics of X.509v3 certificates and X.509v2 certificate revocation lists (CRLs[9]) for use on the Internet. As such, it describes in detail the X.509v3 certificate format and its standard and Internet-specific extension fields, as well as the X.509v2 CRL format and a required extension set. Finally, the RFC also describes an algorithm for X.509 certificate path validation and provides ASN.1 specifications for all data structures that are used in the profiles.

- Standards track RFC 2510 [18] describes the various certificate management protocols that are supposed to be used in an X.509-based PKI for the Internet.

- More specifically, standards track RFC 2511 [19] specifies the syntax and semantics of the Internet X.509 certificate request message format (CRMF) that is used to convey a request for a certificate to a CA (possibly via an RA) for the purpose of X.509 certificate production. The request typically includes a public key and some related registration information.

- Informational RFC 2527 [20] presents a framework to assist the writers of certificate policies and certificate practice statements (CPS) for CAs and PKIs. More specifically, the framework provides a comprehensive list of topics that potentially need to be covered in a certificate policy definition or CPS. Note that the framework needs to be customized in a particular operational environment.

- Informational RFC 2528 [21] profiles the format and semantics of the field in X.509v3 certificates containing cryptographic keys for the KEA.[10]

- Standards track RFC 2559 [22] addresses requirements to provide access to certificate repositories for the purpose of retrieving PKI information and managing that information. The mechanism is based on the Lightweight Directory Access Protocol (LDAP) as specified in RFC 1777 [23], defining a profile of LDAP for use within the X.509-based PKI for the Internet. In addition, RFC 2587 [24] defines a minimal schema to support PKIX in an LDAPv2 environment, as defined in RFC 2559.

- Standards track RFC 2585 [25] specifies the conventions for using FTP and HTTP to obtain certificates and CRLs from certificate repositories.

---

[9]The notion of a CRL will be introduced and discussed in Section 19.5.1.

[10]The KEA is a key exchange algorithm that was originally proposed by NIST for use together with the Skipjack encryption algorithm in Clipper and Fortezza chips. Refer to http://csrc.nist.gov/encryption/skipjack-kea.htm for a specification of the Skipjack and KEA algorithms.

- Standards track RFC 2560 [26] specifies an *Online Certificate Status Protocol* (OCSP) that is useful in determining the current status of a digital certificate. The OCSP will be briefly addressed in Section 19.5.2.

- Standards track RFC 2797 [27] specifies a certificate management protocol using the cryptographic message syntax (CMS). The resulting protocol has the acronym CMC.

- Standards track RFC 2875 [28] specifies two methods for producing an integrity check value from a Diffie-Hellman key pair.[11]

- Standards track RFC 3039 [29] forms a certificate profile for qualified certificates[12], based on RFC 2459, for Internet use.

- Finally, the experimental RFC 3029 [30] describes a general data validation and certification server (DVCS) and the protocols to be used when communicating with it. In short, the DVCS is a TTP that can be used as one component in building reliable non-repudiation services. It is designed to provide data validation services, asserting correctness of digitally signed documents, validity of public key certificates, and possession or existence of data. As a result of a validation process, the DVCS generates a data validation certificate (DVC).

In summary, the RFC documents itemized above specify an X.509-based PKI for the Internet community. This evolving PKI is sometimes also referred to as *Internet X.509 public key infrastructure* (IPKI). As of this writing, the RFC documents that specify the IPKI refer to Proposed Standards.

The number of RFC documents that specify various aspects of the IPKI will certainly grow in the future, since a lot of work is done to further refine the IPKI and its operational protocols and procedures. In fact, the number of RFC documents specifying the IPKI will certainly have increased by the time you read this book. Refer to the IETF PKIX WG home page to get a complete and more comprehensive overview about the RFC and Internet-Draft documents that are currently available. The current trend in industry is to make commercial PKI products "PKIX compliant," and this trend is likely to continue in the future.

---

[11]This behavior is needed for such operations as creating the signature of a PKCS #10 certification request. These algorithms are designed to provide a proof of possession rather than general-purpose signing.

[12]The term *qualified certificate* is used to describe a certificate with a certain qualified status within applicable governing law.

19.5   CERTIFICATE REVOCATION

According to RFC 2828, certificate revocation refers to "the event that occurs when a CA declares that a previously valid digital certificate issued by that CA has become invalid" [6]. In practice, there are many reasons that may require certificate revocation. For example, a user's or a CA's private key may be compromised, or a user may no longer be registered and certified by a particular CA. In many legislations for digital or electronic signatures, the user may suspend a certificate (in addition to revoking it). This is interesting from a user's point of view, because it allows him or her to temporarily disable a certificate. Note, however, that providing support for certificate suspension is also very difficult to say the least. It requires that the entire history of a certificate (i.e., the validity intervals for the certificate) is maintained and properly managed for a potentially very long period of time. While we are starting to understand certificate revocation, certificate suspension is still largely not understood today. Therefore, we are not going to address the topic in this book.

In general, the certification and revocation of certificates involves three different parties:

- The certificate-issuing authority (i.e., the CA or AA);

- The certificate repository, such as a networked directory service (which may be replicated several times);

- The users of the certificate-issuing authorities and the corresponding certificate repositories.

In this setting, the certificate-issuing authorities do not necessarily provide on-line certificate status information about the certificates they have issued to the users. Instead, they may operate off-line and update the certificate repositories only on a periodic basis. The certificate repositories, in turn, may operate on-line to be permanently available and accessible to the users. In general, it must be assumed that the certificate-issuing authorities are trustworthy and trusted, whereas the certificate repository and the users may not be. A user who contacts the certificate repository does not only want to retrieve a certificate, but may also want to get some kind of proof of validity for the certificates he or she retrieves.

From a theoretical point of view, there are several approaches to address certificate revocation:

1. To have certificates expire automatically after a certain amount of time and to require periodic renewals of certificates;

2. To list all nonrevoked certificates in an on-line certificate repository, and to accept only certificates that are found there;

3. To have all certificate-issuing authorities periodically issue lists that itemize all certificates that have been revoked and should no longer be used;

4. To provide an on-line certificate status checking mechanism that informs users whether a specific certificate has been revoked.

Note that the approaches are not mutually exclusive, but can be combined to develop more efficient or more effective certificate revocation schemes. Also note that all approaches have advantages and disadvantages. For example, the first approach has the advantage of not requiring explicit certificate revocation (because the certificates expire after a certain amount of time). The disadvantages of this approach are due to the fact that certificate expiration only provides a slow revocation mechanism, and that it depends on servers having accurate clocks. Someone who can trick a server into turning back its local clock can still use expired certificates (the security of the certificate revocation mechanism thus depends on the security of the timing service). Similarly, the second approach has the advantage that it is almost immediate, whereas the disadvantages are that the availability of authentication is only as good as the availability of the certificate repository, and that the security of the certificate revocation mechanism as a whole is only as good as the security of the certificate repository. Furthermore, users tend to cache certificates they have retrieved from the directory service for performance reasons, and the use of such a cache actually defeats the original purpose of the certificate repository (i.e., to provide timely status information). The third approach has the advantage that it is simple and straightforward, whereas the disadvantages are that the lists must be retrieved and taken into account and that the revocation of a certificate is enforced only after the publication and distribution of the next list. Finally, the fourth approach is immediate and provides a high level of security, but also reintroduces an on-line component.

For all practical purposes, the first and second approaches are the ones that are being followed for the revocation of attribute certificates, whereas the third and fourth approaches are the ones that are being followed for the revocation of public key certificates. For example, the ITU-T recommendation X.509 follows the third approach for the revocation of public key certificates.[13] More specifically, it recommends that each CA periodically issue a certificate revocation list (CRL) that itemizes all certificates that have been revoked and should no longer be used. The CRLs can be pushed or pulled by the communicating peers:

- If a CRL is pushed, the initiating peer (e.g., the client) provides the currently valid CRL to the responding peer (e.g., the server).

- Contrary to that, if a CRL is pulled, the responding peer retrieves the CRL from the certificate-issuing authority.

Applications that use certificates can either use the push model, the pull model, or both. For example, IKE, SSL/TLS, and S/MIME are protocols that can push CRLs rather than requiring CRL retrieval from a repository.

In addition to the use of CRLs as proposed in the ITU-T recommendation X.509, the IETF PKIX WG is also following the fourth approach and has specified a standards track Online Certificate Status Protocol (OCSP) in RFC 2560 [26] and an experimental DVCS in RFC 3029 [30]. CRLs and OCSP are further addressed in the rest of this section. Afterward, we mention some alternative certificate revocation schemes that are primarily of theoretical interest.

19.5.1   CRLs

The classical and simplest solution to the certificate revocation problem is the use of CRLs. As mentioned, this approach is being followed in the ITU-T recommendation X.509 [8] and ISO/IEC 9594-8 [9]. In this approach, a CA periodically issues and digitally signs a message that lists all certificates that have been revoked and should no longer be used. This message is called a CRL and it is made available through the certificate repository. Users who want to make sure that a particular certificate has not been revoked must query the certificate repository and retrieve the latest CRL. If the CRL does not include the certificate, the user can assume that the certificate has not been revoked (at least until the time the CRL was issued and digitally signed).

If a CRL is becoming too large, the use of delta CRLs may be appropriate. In short, a delta CRL lists all certificates that have been revoked and should no longer be used since the latest break point. Consequently, the set of all revoked certificates

---

[13]The X.509 CRL format is an ITU-T and ISO/IEC standard, first published in 1988 as version 1 (X.509v1 CRL). Similar to the ITU-T X.509 certificate format, the X.509v1 CRL was subsequently modified to allow for extension fields, resulting in X.509 version 2 CRL (X.509v2 CRL) format.

at a given point in time consists of all certificates listed in the most recent CRL plus all certificates listed in the delta CRLs that have been published meanwhile. Furthermore, other mechanisms are included in X.509 to allow a CA to split CRLs into multiple pieces (e.g., using CRL distribution points).

The major advantage of using CRLs (together with delta CRLs) is simplicity. A user of a certificate is required to retrieve the latest CRL from the appropriate CA or the repository and check whether the certificate has been revoked. Only if the certificate is not included in the CRL (and has not been revoked accordingly) is the user authorized to accept and use the certificate. Obviously, the consequence of this scheme is that the user has to periodically retrieve the latest CRLs from all the CAs he or she uses and accepts certificates from. This introduces some communication costs between the CA and the certificate repository, and high communication costs between the repository and the users (as CRLs may be very long). Another disadvantage is that a user does not receive succinct proof for the validity of a particular certificate.

Finally, note that a CRL is a negative statement. It is the digital equivalent of the little paper books of bad checks or bad credit cards that were distributed to cashiers in the 1970s and before. These have been replaced in the retail world by positive statements in the form of on-line validation of a single check, ATM card, or credit card. The digital equivalent to this on-line validation of a certificate is provided by the OCSP (or a similar protocol).

19.5.2 OCSP

Instead of, or as a supplement to, checking against periodically issued CRLs, it may be necessary to obtain timely information regarding a certificate's current status. Examples include high-value funds transfer or large stock trades. Consequently, the IETF PKIX WG has specified and standardized an OCSP in RFC 2560 [26]. In short, the OCSP enables a user to determine the status of an identified certificate. An OCSP client issues a status request to an OCSP responder and suspends acceptance of the certificate in question until the responder provides a response (whether the certificate in question is good, revoked, or is in an unknown state for the responder). A certificate-issuing authority can either respond to OCSP requests directly or have one (or several) delegated OCSP responder(s) providing OCSP responses to the requesting entities on its behalf.

As of this writing, the use of OCSP is not yet widely deployed on the Internet.[14]

---

[14]Note that browsers do not currently check the revocation status of any certificate at all. The only time a browser knows that a site certificate has been revoked is when it eventually

Nevertheless, it is assumed and very likely that future CAs and certificate repositories will provide support for both certificate revocation mechanisms (CRLs and
OCSP queries). It is also possible and very likely that the value of an electronic
commerce transaction will finally determine whether a check in a CRL is sufficient
enough, or whether an OCSP query must be invoked.

Finally, note that for financial transactions the merchant often needs to know
not just whether a certificate is valid, but whether the charge to be made against
the account represented by the certificate is acceptable (e.g., because of credit limit
concerns). Thus, in such circumstances, timeliness of certificate status information
may be irrelevant, because the merchant may need to contact the site responsible
for the account (e.g., a bank for a bank credit-card charge) and that site would have
very timely knowledge of certificate status information, which probably would not
rely on CRLs and OCPS.

19.5.3   Alternative Schemes

We have seen that the use of CRLs introduces some communication costs between
the CA and the certificate repository, and high communication costs between the
repository and the users (as CRLs may be very long), and that by using CRLs, a
user does not receive succinct proof for the validity of a particular certificate. We
have also seen that protocols, such as the OCSP, can be used to address the second
problem.

More recently, some alternative certificate revocation schemes have been proposed that try to address both problems mentioned. Chapter 8 of [2], for example,
overviews and discusses Silvio Micali's certificate revocation system (CRS), Paul
Kocher's certificate revocation trees (CRT), and a certificate revocation and update
scheme proposed by Moni Naor and Kobbi Nissim. These discussions are not repeated in this book. The alternative certificate revocation schemes are interesting
mainly from a theoretical point of view (as of this writing, they are not relevant for
all practical purposes).

19.6   CONCLUSIONS

In this chapter, we elaborated on PKI considerations for the Internet. More specifically, we overviewed and discussed the state of the art related to public key and

---

expires. It is possible and very likely that this behavior will change in the future, and that
certificate revocation checking will be adapted in one way or another. For example, Netscape has
implemented a preliminary and incomplete version of OCSP.

attribute certificates. There exist a number of standards and standardized procedures to issue, manage, and possibly revoke certificates. This is particularly true for public key certificates, but is also becoming true for attribute certificates. With regard to attribute certificates, however, most security protocols must be modified to make use of them. For example, the SSL and TLS protocols are able to handle public key certificates to address authentication and key exchange; they are not yet able to handle attribute certificates to address authorization. Nevertheless, it would be convenient to have an SSL/TLS client submit a list of relevant attribute certificates to access an intranet server. To make this happen, the SSL and TLS protocols must be extended and the extended protocols must be implemented and deployed. Consequently, there is still a long way to go until we will see attribute certificates deployed in practice.

Because of the steadily increasing role of authorization (in addition to authentication), the term PKI is currently being replaced with one of the following terms:

- Privilege management infrastructure (PMI);

- Authentication and authorization infrastructure (AAI).

It is possible and very likely that such a term will become a new buzzword in the future. In either case, the long-term goal of security professionals is to design, implement, and deploy PMIs or AAIs that are both sufficiently secure and scalable to the size of the Internet (or at least to the size of large corporate intranets).

The role of a PKI and some alternative technologies to address authentication and authorization are being reconsidered in a new branch of research that is collectively referred to as "trust management." Trust management is a rather artificial term, and its use is greatly overblown in the PKI arena. In fact, there is a large body of literature that addresses trust management and various aspects thereof [31–37].

Following the line of arguments introduced in [38] and further explored in Chapter 21, one may also argue that trust management is not particularly important and that all that matters is risk management:

"Trust management is surely exciting, but like most exciting ideas it is unimportant. What is important is risk management, the sister, the dual of trust management. And because risk management makes money, it drives the security world from here on out."

To clarify the point, we consider the situation in which a customer wants to order some goods from an on-line merchant. In this situation, there are two possible questions a customer may ask:

- Does he or she trust the merchant (to handle his or her order properly)?

- Does he or she carry the risk of having the merchant not properly handling his or her order?

Obviously, the first question is related to trust management, whereas the second question is related to risk management. In many situations, it is much simpler and more efficient to elaborate on risks that it is to discuss trust. In fact, trust is difficult to address and even more difficult to quantify. In either case, however, it is important to note that trust and risks are not independent, and that the two things basically try to measure the same (or at least closely related) things. For example, if we trust something we usually mean that the risks involved using it are small. Similarly, if we assume high risks we usually do not trust something or somebody.

As of this writing, many companies and organizations face the problem of how to get the X.509v3 certificates they require for emerging technologies, such as IPsec, SSL/TLS, and S/MIME.[15] In general, there are two possibilities:

- The companies and organizations can establish a PKI of their own;

- The companies and organizations can outsource certification services and buy corresponding X.509v3 certificates from one or several commercial certification service providers.

If a company or organization wants to establish a PKI of its own, it can use one of the many commercial PKI solutions and products that are available on the market. Examples include Entrust/PKI[16] from Entrust Technologies or UniCERT[17] from Baltimore Technologies. Refer to the trade press to get a more comprehensive and up-to-date overview about currently available PKI solutions and products.

If a company or organization wants to outsource certification services, it can buy corresponding X.509v3 certificates from one (or several) commercial certification service provider(s). Exemplary certification service providers are VeriSign, Inc.[18] and Entrust.net.[19] In fact, an increasingly large number of commercial certification service providers are offering their services to the general public. Again, this trend is strengthened by legislation initiatives for digital or electronic signatures.

---

[15]Refer to Part II of this book if these acronyms do not mean anything to you.

[16]http://www.entrust.com/entrust/

[17]http://www.baltimore.com/products/unicert/

[18]http://www.verisign.com

[19]http://www.entrust.net

In addition to the two possibilities mentioned, there is a whole range of intermediate possibilities. The general idea is to have the company or organization act as RA for its users and make use of a commercial certification service provider to actually issue certificates. This is interesting mainly because it is simple for the company or organization to register and authenticate its users, and also because almost everything can be batched from the certification service provider's point of view. A corresponding architecture was proposed in [39] and has been implemented and marketed in various offerings, such as VeriSign's OnSite Managed Trust Service.[20]

A more critical word should be said about the overall cost of public key cryptography in general, and PKIs in particular. Note that one of the original claims of public key cryptography was to minimize the initiation cost of a secure communication path between parties that share no prior administrative relationship. It was assumed that this would be the major reason why public key cryptography would dominate electronic commerce applications in the first place. Note, however, that with no shared administrative structure to connect the parties, we must invent many things, such as certificate chaining, certificate revocation, and certificate directory services. In other words, we have to invent the very thing that public key cryptography claimed not to need, namely administrative overhead. This point was made by Aviel D. Rubin, Daniel Geer, and Marcus J. Ranum in [40]. In fact, they do not argue against public key cryptography in general, but they argue that much of the implied cost savings of public key cryptography over secret key cryptography is nothing more than an illusion. To further clarify the point, they argue that the sum of the cost for cryptographic-key issuance and the cost for cryptographic-key revocation is more or less constant (for both public key cryptography and secret key cryptography). Note that this argument is only an assertion and is not yet substantiated by any detailed analysis. Also note that much of the initial motivation for use of public key cryptography was not cost based, but rather security based. For example, the argument was made that there are many more vulnerabilities associated with schemes that make use of secret key cryptography only as compared with schemes that selectively make use of public key cryptography, especially when one crosses organization boundaries. Remember the discussion of the Kerberos authentication system, especially in the case of inter-realm authentication. In spite of the fact that the argument is not substantiated by any detailed analysis and that the initial motivation for the use of public key cryptography and corresponding PKIs was security (not costs), the argument should still be considered with care. Note, for example, the problems we face when we try to establish and operate a PKI

---

[20]http://www.verisign.com/products/onsite/

today. Some of the problems are caused by the need to revoke certificates. This problem makes it necessary to have an on-line component permanently available for an otherwise off-line CA. Ideally, certificate revocation is handled by an on-line component that is physically or logically separated from the off-line CA [41].

Finally, it should be kept in mind that the widespread use of public key certificates that include (or are logically linked to) globally unique names, such as DNs, may also provide the means to build a worldwide tracking system for user transactions. If a user acquires multiple certificates, each of which contains a different subject name with only local significance, he or she will not be able to be tracked. If, however, he or she acquires only one certificate and this certificate is used for multiple (or all) applications, he or she can be tracked very easily. Consequently, the widespread use of a single certificate per person may also contradict his or her privacy requirements. Against this background, Stefan A. Brands developed a technological approach that can be used to replace X.509-based certificates [42]. The resulting certificates can be used to authenticate and authorize their owners; they do not, however, reveal any information that is not necessary to the certificate verifier. This is an example of a privacy enhancing technology (PET), and it is possible and very likely that we will see similar PETs being developed and deployed in the future. You may refer to Chapter 13 of [1] for an overview about PETs for Internet messaging and the WWW.

REFERENCES

[1] R. Oppliger, *Security Technologies for the World Wide Web*, Artech House Publishers, Norwood, MA, 2000.

[2] R. Oppliger, *Secure Messaging with PGP and S/MIME*, Artech House, Norwood, MA, 2001.

[3] W. Ford and M. S. Baum, *Secure Electronic Commerce: Building the Infrastructure for Digital Signatures & Encryption*, 2nd edition, Prentice Hall PTR, Upper Saddle River, NJ, 2000.

[4] J. Feghhi, J. Feghhi, and P. Williams, *Digital Certificates: Applied Internet Security*, Addison-Wesley Longman, Reading, MA, 1999.

[5] C. Adams and S. Lloyd, *Understanding the Public-Key Infrastructure*, New Riders Publishing, Indianapolis, IN, 1999.

[6] R. Shirey, "Internet Security Glossary," Request for Comments 2828, May 2000.

[7] L. M. Kohnfelder, "Towards a Practical Public-Key Cryptosystem," Bachelor's thesis, Massachusetts Institute of Technology, Cambridge, MA, May 1978.

[8] ITU-T, Recommendation X.509: The Directory—Authentication Framework, 1988.

[9] ISO/IEC 9594-8, *Information Technology—Open Systems Interconnection—The Directory Part 8: Authentication Framework*, 1990.

[10] C. Ellison, "Establishing Identity Without Certification Authorities," *Proceedings of USENIX Security Symposium*, July 1996.

[11] R. L. Rivest and B. Lampson, "SDSI—A Simple Distributed Security Infrastructure," April 1996.

[12] M. Abadi, "On SDSI's Linked Local Name Spaces," *Proceedings of 10th IEEE Computer Security Foundations Workshop*, June 1997, pp. 98–108.

[13] C. Ellison, "SPKI Requirements," Request for Comments 2692, September 1999.

[14] C. Ellison, et al., "SPKI Certificate Theory," Request for Comments 2693, September 1999.

[15] J. Feigenbaum, "Towards an Infrastructure for Authorization," position paper, *Proceedings of USENIX Workshop on Electronic Commerce*, 1998.

[16] R. Oppliger, G. Pernul, and C. Strauss, "Using Attribute Certificates to Implement Role-Based Authorization and Access Control Models," *Proceedings of 4. Fachtagung Sicherheit in Informationssystemen (SIS 2000)*, October 2000, pp. 169–184.

[17] R. Housley, et al., "Internet X.509 Public Key Infrastructure Certificate and CRL Profile," Request for Comments 2459, January 1999.

[18] C. Adams, "Internet X.509 Public Key Infrastructure Certificate Management Protocols," Request for Comments 2510, March 1999.

[19] M. Myers, et al., "Internet X.509 Certificate Request Message Format," Request for Comments 2511, March 1999.

[20] S. Chokhani and W. Ford, "Internet X.509 Public Key Infrastructure Certificate Policy and Certification Practices Framework," Request for Comments 2527, March 1999.

[21] R. Housley and W. Polk, "Internet X.509 Public Key Infrastructure Representation of Key Exchange Algorithm (KEA) Keys in Internet X.509 Public Key Infrastructure Certificates," Request for Comments 2528, March 1999.

[22] S. Boeyen, T. Howes, and P. Richard, "Internet X.509 Public Key Infrastructure Operational Protocols—LDAPv2," Request for Comments 2559, April 1999.

[23] Y. Yeong, T. Howes, and S. Kille, "Lightweight Directory Access Protocol," Request for Comments 1777, March 1995.

[24] S. Boeyen, T. Howes, and P. Richard, "Internet X.509 Public Key Infrastructure LDAPv2 Schema," Request for Comments 2587, June 1999.

[25] R. Housley and P. Hoffman, "Internet X.509 Public Key Infrastructure Operational Protocols: FTP and HTTP," Request for Comments 2585, May 1999.

[26] M. Myers, et al., "X.509 Internet Public Key Infrastructure Online Certificate Status Protocol—OCSP," Request for Comments 2560, June 1999.

[27] M. Myers, et al., "Certificate Management Messages over CMS," Request for Comments 2797, April 2000.

[28] H. Prafullchandra and J. Schaad, "Diffie-Hellman Proof-of-Possession Algorithms," Request for Comments 2875, July 2000.

[29] S. Santesson, et al., "Internet X.509 Public Key Infrastructure Qualified Certificates Profile," Request for Comments 3039, January 2001.

[30] C. Adams, et al., "Internet X.509 Public Key Infrastructure Data Validation and Certification Server Protocols," Request for Comments 3029, February 2001.

[31] U. M. Maurer and P. E. Schmid, "A Calculus for Secure Channel Estabishment in Open Networks," *Proceedings of European Symposium on Research in Computer Security (ESORICS)*, 1994, pp. 175–192.

[32] U. M. Maurer, "Modelling a Public-Key Infrastructure," *Proceedings of European Symposium on Research in Computer Security (ESORICS)*, 1996, pp. 325–350.

[33] R. Kohlas and U. M. Maurer, "Reasoning About Public-Key Certification: On Bindings Between Entities and Public Keys," *Proceedings of Financial Cryptography*, 1999.

[34] R. Kohlas and U. M. Maurer, "Confidence Valuation in a Public-Key Infrastructure Based on Uncertain Evidence," *Proceedings of the International Workshop on Practice and Theory in Public-Key Cryptography*, 2000.

[35] M. Blaze, J. Feigenbaum, and J. Lacy, "Decentralized Trust Management," *Proceedings of IEEE Conference on Security and Privacy*, 1996, pp. 164–173.

[36] M. Blaze, J. Feigenbaum, and M. Strauss, "Compliance-Checking in the PolicyMaker Trust-Management System," *Proceedings of Financial Cryptography*, 1998, pp. 251–265.

[37] M. Blaze, et al., "The KeyNote Trust-Management System Version 2," Request for Comments 2704, September 1999.

[38] D. Geer, "Risk Management Is Where the Money Is," November 1998, electronic version available at **http://catless.ncl.ac.uk/Risks/20.06.html#subj1**.

[39] R. Oppliger, A. Greulich, and P. Trachsel, "A Distributed Certificate Management System (DCMS) Supporting Group-Based Access Controls," *Proceedings of Annual Computer Security Applications Conference (ACSAC '99)*, 1999, pp. 241–248.

[40] A. D. Rubin, D. Geer, and M. J. Ranum, *Web Security Sourcebook*, John Wiley & Sons, Inc., New York, 1997.

[41] M. Lomas, "Untrusted Third Parties: Key Management for the Prudent," *Report on DIMACS Workshop on Trust Management*, 1996.

[42] S. A. Brands, *Rethinking Public Key Infrastructures and Digital Certificates: Building in Privacy*, MIT Press, Cambridge, MA, 2000.

Chapter 20

Electronic Commerce

This book is about technologies that can be used to provide Internet and intranet security. While most of these technologies are interesting from a theoretical point of view, they need a better and more practical reason to be used and deployed on a large scale. Electronic commerce (e-commerce) is commonly considered to be such a reason and to be one of the major driving forces for the use and further deployment of security technologies, mechanisms, and services on the Internet.

According to RFC 2828, the term *e-commerce* refers to any kind of "business conducted through paperless exchanges of information, using electronic data interchange, electronic funds transfer (EFT), electronic mail, computer bulletin boards, facsimile, and other paperless technologies " [1]. There are several other buzzwords that also refer to similar ideas:

- Electronic business (e-business);

- Electronic government (e-government);

- Mobile commerce (m-commerce).

The term *e-business* is often used to refer to the integration of systems, processes, organizations, value chains, and entire markets using Internet-based and related technologies and concepts. As such, e-commerce is merely a part of e-business and is limited essentially to marketing and sales processes. Similarly, the term *e-government* refers to the use of information technologies to deliver government services directly to the customer (i.e., a citizen, a business, or even another government entity). E-government delivers services in a manner that is most convenient for the customer, while at the same time allowing government to provide those services at a significantly lower cost. Finally, the term *m-commerce* is used for something similar to e-commerce with the additional requirement that clients are mobile and not necessarily bound to a specific location.

In this book, we use the term e-commerce to collectively refer to all the terms itemized and briefly explained here. In either case, the aim is to use an open and public network, such as the Internet, to electronically market goods and services without having to be physically present at the point of sale [2]. As such, there are many security requirements related to e-commerce. A comprehensive overview is given in [3].

In e-commerce, the Internet may serve several purposes, including, for example, marketing, services, sales, and payments.

- Internet marketing includes advertising and providing information about an organization (i.e., a company) and its current offerings. Compared to advertising with print media, advertising on the Internet is attractive, given its low cost and easy access to a potentially very large audience. In the recent past, however, Internet marketing investments have slowed down considerably.

- There are many forms of services that can be provided over the Internet. Many of these services are just electronic counterparts of the services we know and are familiar with in the physical world. Examples include on-line shopping in virtual malls, on-line gambling in virtual casinos, and on-line banking in virtual banks. Other services are inherently new and must be explored with regard to user acceptance first. For example, Federal Express (FedEx) and United Parcel Service (UPS) provide customer access to their databases to check the current status of their postal deliveries. This kind of service is new and has no counterpart in the physical world. It is possible and very likely that we will see many such services evolve in the future. Some of them will be successful, whereas others will not succeed and disappear after a short period of time. In either case, it is very important to be first with a new service.

- The Internet can also be used for sales. Material goods must still be delivered with conventional delivery services (e.g., FedEx and UPS), whereas many nonmaterial goods may be delivered directly over the Internet. Note that more and more goods that have been offered in material form in the past are now being offered in nonmaterial form. Examples include all forms of print media, such as newspapers, magazines, journals, and books. We are familiar with all forms of electronic newspapers, magazines, and journals. Furthermore, publishing companies and book resellers are strongly pushing electronic books (e-books) to market. With the proliferation of high-speed Internet access, it has even become possible to deliver voice and video recordings in nonmaterial and electronic form. Also note that the Internet is still seldom used for sales. An Internet storefront simply enhances the sales at the real-world retail outlet. It may take a couple of years for merchants to determine the optimal ways to sell effectively on-line, as well as to find and maintain corresponding customers. Retailers still need to demonstrate the advantages of virtual malls, such as timeliness, convenience, ease of use, and potentially lower prices.

- Finally, the Internet can also be used to handle payments. In fact, there is a wide range of electronic payment systems available today, including, for example, digital cash, electronic checks, electronic credit card payments, and micropayments. Refer to Chapter 7 of [4] or [5–7] for a more comprehensive and up-to-date picture about currently available electronic payment systems.

In general, there are many reasons why an organization (i.e., a company) would like to establish a presence on the Internet. Probably the first and foremost reason is access to a potentially very large audience. Globalization is another issue. Through the Internet, a organization can reach customers in almost every country of the world. Establishing a presence on the Internet is particularly cheap compared with the alternative of opening physical shops and advertising in various countries. Another important reason is potential savings in sales costs. Note that it costs an organization a considerable amount of money to establish a physical shop in a mall, as well as to pay bills, salaries, and commission fees to the corresponding sales staff. Many of these expenses can be reduced by establishing a presence on the Internet. These savings can in turn help reduce the costs of goods or services and make them more competitive as a whole. Finally, organizations can also provide instant updates to the announcements of their goods or services. Note that an organization can easily insert an update that reaches on-line customers almost instantly. The availability of such a rapid update mechanism is particularly interesting for selling goods or services that expire in a relatively short amount of time. For example, on-line updates are attractive for selling vacant seats on airline flights as well as tickets for evening theater shows and plays. Another example in which on-line updates are particularly interesting and important is the distribution of antivirus software.

However, there are also benefits from an e-commerce customer's point of view. Perhaps the most important benefit is the potential savings in time. By logging on to the Internet and accessing information on-line, customers can browse through shops and merchandise from their home at any time. Alternatively, in the real world a customer usually spends hours on a shopping trip, including travel to and from the shopping mall.[1] A related benefit is convenient access to a wide variety of shops and merchandise. For example, a physical shopping mall may provide clothing and some other merchandise, but it may not include a car dealership, an airline ticket office, or an Asian food store. Consequently, a customer must travel to several places if he or she has specific needs. This is arguably not the case in a virtual shopping trip to the Internet. A customer may also like to shop in a virtual mall simply to compare instantly the quality and price of a product from different shops. This may help make shopping decisions easier and faster.

Against this background, a lot has been said about the future of mobile code and agent-based systems. In such a system, a user can send out a (software) agent that autonomously roams through the Internet and acts on his or her behalf. For example, the agent travels to the relevant Web sites, compares the current offerings, and eventually signs a contract on the user's behalf. Obviously, there also are some serious security problems related to the use of mobile code and agent-based systems. How do you, for example, hide the function implemented by the agent? And how do you protect the collected information or the private key the agent must use to digitally sign documents on the user's behalf? The problems are further explored in [8] and Chapter 11 of [4]. In short, there are two core problems:

1. How to protect an execution environment against potentially malicious mobile code;

2. How to protect the mobile code against potentially malicious hosts and execution environments.

The first problem can be addressed with a couple of technologies, such as sandboxing or digital signatures to authenticate the software developer. Contrary to that, the second problem is very difficult (if not impossible) to address. The intrinsic difficulty of the second problem was first pointed out by Bennet S. Yee [9]:

---

[1]Note, however, that sometimes a shopping trip is also considered to be a social event.

"In agent-based computing, most researchers have been concentrating on one side of the security issue: protecting the server from potentially malicious agents (...) The converse side of the agent security problem, however, is largely neglected and needs to be addressed: how do we protect agents from potentially malicious servers?"

This statement is still true. In fact, there are only a few preliminary results and largely insufficient technologies to address the second problem. To make things worse, the two problems seem to be dependent, meaning that a solution for the second problem is very likely going to make it more difficult to find an appropriate solution for the first problem. For example, if one partly solves the second problem by hiding the agent's function from a potentially malicious host and execution environment (i.e., the execution environment is not able to "see inside" the agent), one also loses the possibility to decide whether the agent is malicious or not. In this case, it becomes very difficult—if not impossible—to make intelligent decisions with regard to the protection of the execution environment. Consequently, at least some technical solutions to address the second problem will be contradictory to the possibility of finding appropriate solutions for the first problem. It is not clear whether other solutions exist at all. This is a very bad situation and it severely limits the likelihood that we will see mobile code and agent-based systems being used for financially relevant applications in the future.

In Part III, we introduced and discussed technologies that can be used to provide communication security on the Internet (i.e., cryptographic security protocols). It is, however, important to note that secure communications do not satisfy all security needs for e-commerce. For example, a customer willing to purchase goods or services from an Internet merchant must still trust the Web server's administrator with his or her credit card information, even if the communication channel is securely encrypted. Note that communication security, in general, protects only the communication channels; it does not protect against disreputable or careless people who may induce careless customers into entering a transaction with them. In a sense, this is similar to the mode of business conducted over switched networks, such as the PSTN or the ISDN. It is common practice today to order goods or services over the telephone network with credit card information, such as the credit card brand, the card number, and the expiration date. More precisely, a customer telephones the merchant, orders some items, and gives out his or her credit card information to accomplish the purchase. The merchant, in turn, verifies the credit card information with the corresponding credit card company. If the credit card is valid, the merchant delivers the items and has the customer's credit card account charged for the corresponding amount of money. The customer gives out his or her credit card information because he or she feels secure that nobody is eavesdropping on the telephone line, and because he or she trusts the merchant to use the information only in reference to the business being conducted and for nothing else. One thing that should be considered with care is that credit card information is stored locally at the merchant's site for later reuse or marketing purposes. Let us assume the very likely scenario in which a customer who has used his or her credit card to buy something in the past and who wants to buy some additional items, is kindly asked at the checkout counter of a shop whether he or she wants to charge the same credit card as the previous time. It is very obvious in this case that the customer's credit card information has been stored at the merchant' site, and that the customer has implicitly trusted the merchant to protect the credit card information against misuse and other security-related threats. This level of trust may not always be justified.

Following this line of argumentation, the credit card number problem that has driven the Internet security discussion in the past is not particularly an Internet security problem; it is rather a problem of how we carelessly use credit card information in the real world. The credit card information that is generally used to order goods or services today should simply not be sufficient to place such an order. In addition to the credit card information, a customer should also be able to provide some additional information that would be used to strongly authenticate him or her and to prove his or her identity or creditworthiness accordingly. This is where cryptography and cryptographic techniques come into play. Many electronic payment systems that are available today address these issues (again, you many refer to the references given above for a more comprehensive overview about currently available electronic payment systems). Note, for example, that one specific feature of the secure electronic transaction (SET) standard for credit card payment over the Internet is that the merchant does not necessarily learn the credit card information of its customers.

REFERENCES

[1] R. Shirey, "Internet Security Glossary," Request for Comments 2828, May 2000.

[2] V. Ahuja, *Secure Commerce on the Internet*, Academic Press, Inc., Orlando, FL, 1997.

[3] V. Hassler, *Security Fundamentals for E-Commerce*, Artech House, Norwood, MA, 2001.

[4] R. Oppliger, *Security Technologies for the World Wide Web*, Artech House, Norwood, MA, 2000.

[5] D. O'Mahony, M. Peirce, and H. Tewari, *Electronic Payment Systems for E-Commerce*, 2nd Edition, Artech House, Norwood, MA, 2001.

[6] V. Hassler, et al., *Java Card for E-Payment*, Artech House, Norwood, MA, 2001.

[7] C. Radu, *Deploying Electronic Payment Systems*, Artech House, Norwood, MA, scheduled to be published in 2002.

[8] R. Oppliger, "Security Issues Related to Mobile Code and Agent-Based Systems," *Computer Communications*, Vol. 22, No. 12, July 1999, pp. 1165–1170.

[9] B. S. Yee, "A Sanctuary for Mobile Agents," *DARPA Foundations for Secure Mobile Code Workshop*, Monterey, CA, March 1997.

Chapter 21

Risk Management

In this chapter, we elaborate on risk management and how the Internet has changed (or is about to change) the way we think about risk management in the IT world. More specifically, we introduce the topic in Section 21.1, elaborate on formal risk analysis in Section 21.2, address some alternative approaches and technologies for risk management in Section 21.3, and draw some conclusions in Section 21.4.

21.1 INTRODUCTION

In practice, it is often important to know the risks one faces when entering a new technology. This is particularly true for the Internet and Internet-based technologies and applications. A company or organization that considers establishing a presence on the Internet or the WWW is very likely (and well advised) to question the vulnerabilities, threats, and related risks.

Recall from Chapter 1 that a *vulnerability* refers to "a flaw or weakness in a system's design, implementation, or operation and management that could be exploited to violate the system's security policy," and that a *threat* refers to "a potential for violation of security, which exists when there is a circumstance, capability, action, or event that could breach security and cause harm" [1].

369

Also referring to RFC 2828, the term *risk* refers to "an expectation of loss expressed as the probability that a particular threat will exploit a particular vulnerability with a particular harmful result" [1]. Similarly, the term *risk analysis* (or *risk assessment*) refers to "a process that systematically identifies valuable system resources and threats to those resources, quantifies loss exposures (i.e., loss potential) based on estimated frequencies and costs of occurrence, and (optionally) recommends how to allocate resources to countermeasures so as to minimize total exposure," and the term *risk management* refers to "the process of identifying, controlling, and eliminating or minimizing uncertain events that may affect system resources" [1].

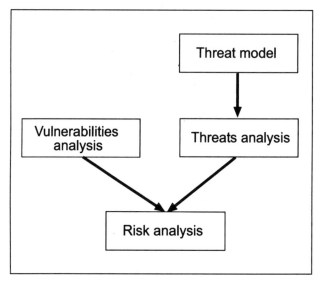

Figure 21.1   The individual steps in a risk management process.

The individual steps in a risk management process are illustrated in Figure 21.1. On the left side, a vulnerabilities analysis must be performed. This analysis has to reveal the vulnerabilities that are relevant for a given situation (i.e., a given IT environment). On the right side, a threats analysis must be performed. A threats analysis, in turn, requires an explicit threat model; that is, a model that elaborates on who is capable and motivated to attack the system in question. In the absence of such a model, one cannot hope to estimate the threats and the corresponding risks. Note that it is something completely different to secure a corporate intranet against foreign intelligence services than it is to secure a corporate intranet against casual attacks. Based on the results of a vulnerabilities analysis and a threats analysis, a risk analysis can finally be performed. The risk analysis quantifies loss exposures based on estimated frequencies and costs of occurrence.

From a more general point of view, everything we do in daily life—either professionally or privately—is driven by risk management considerations. If there is no vulnerability or threat (and, consequently, no risk), we generally do not spend any time or money in security and safety. If, however, there are risks and these risks are severe or appear severe to us in terms of expected losses, we are generally willing to spend large amounts of time or money in security and safety. The point is that we are not always aware that some risk management considerations are performed in our heads. For example, if somebody tells you to jump from a building, the expected loss (i.e., the loss of your life) is generally too high to be tolerable. Consequently, you are not going to jump (at least we hope so). If, however, someone asks you for the current time, there is no loss to expect.[1] Consequently, you would tell this person the current time. All these risk management considerations are done automatically and we may not always be aware of them.

In the IT world, we are not yet accustomed to making risk management considerations. This is because the field is still new, dynamically changing, and not well understood. Also, there are hardly any statistical investigations we can use to make some long-term claims about the relevant risks. Consequently, we have to consider each risk individually. This is usually done in a labor-intensive process called *formal risk analysis*.

21.2 FORMAL RISK ANALYSIS

In the past, several frameworks, models, methods, and methodologies to formally perform risk analyses have been developed and proposed [2, 3]. For example, the British Central Computer and Telecommunications Agency (CCTA) came up with a methodology called *CCTA Risk Analysis and Management Methodology* (CRAMM) and a tool of the same name. The tool is being marketed by Logica.[2] Similarly, a methodology called MARION—an acronym derived from the French term *méthodologie d'analyse des risques informatiques et d'optimation par niveau*—was developed by the French *club de la sécurité informatique francais* (CLUSIF[3]).

---

[1]There may still be a loss to expect, namely, if the question for the current time only wants to distract you so you can be robbed more easily.

[2]http://www.logica.com

[3]https://www.clusif.asso.fr/

Unfortunately, the performance of a formal risk analysis has turned out to be difficult in practice. There are mainly two reasons:

1. A formal risk analysis process requires the establishment of an inventory for all assets (e.g., to decide whether they are valuable). Unfortunately, this is a very difficult and labor-intensive task. To make things worse, the inventory is a moving target that changes permanently and must be periodically updated.

2. A formal risk analysis always requires the quantification of loss exposures based on estimated frequencies and costs of occurrence. Either value—the estimated frequencies and the costs of occurrence—is hard to quantify. How do you, for example, quantify the estimated frequency for a system being hacked? Does this value depend on the operating system in use? Does it depend on the actual configuration? Does is depend on software patches being installed or not installed? Similarly, how do you quantify the costs of occurrence? Note that no system or network resource must be damaged during the system hack. Nevertheless, the loss of reputation and customer confidence may still be large and worrisome. It turns out that probability theory is an inappropriate approach to quantify loss exposures in the IT world. Unfortunately, we do not have an alternative approach so far.

Because of these difficulties, it is common today to perform only qualitative risk analyses. A *qualitative risk analysis*, in turn, differs from a (quantitative or formal) risk analysis in the quantification step. In fact, a qualitative risk analysis only addresses risks that are existent (independent from potential loss exposures). For example, if a Web site is connected to the Internet, a qualitative risk analysis would only identify the risk of being hacked (possibly specifying the risk to be low, medium, or high), whereas a (quantitative or formal) risk analysis would additionally try to quantify the estimated frequency and the costs of occurrence to eventually compute a quantitative value for the risk under consideration. In either case, risk analysis must start with an analysis of vulnerabilities and threats.

In many companies and organizations it is not even possible to perform a qualitative risk analysis, and some simpler risk management approaches and technologies must be used instead. Some alternative approaches and technologies are addressed next.

21.3   ALTERNATIVE APPROACHES AND TECHNOLOGIES

Given the difficulties of performing formal risk analyses, IT security professionals are looking into alternative approaches and technologies to manage the relevant risks. The two most promising approaches and technologies are security scanning to perform vulnerability analyses, and intrusion detection to identify and respond to potentially malicious activities. One major difference between security scanning and intrusion detection is related to the temporal use. A security scanner is running in real time when it is started (i.e., it is rarely run all of the time). Contrary to that, intrusion detection tools and products are designed to run in real time and to constantly monitor systems and networks for possible attacks [4]. Security scanning and intrusion detection are overviewed and briefly discussed next.

21.3.1   Security Scanning

The term *security scanning* refers to the process of performing vulnerability analyses, whereas the term *security scanner* refers to a tool that can be used to automatically perform such analyses. In essence, a security scanner holds a database that includes known vulnerabilities of operating systems and corresponding configurations. Each system can be compared against this database to detect and identify the vulnerabilities that are relevant.

Security scanning tools and security scanners can be partitioned into host-based scanners and network-based scanners:

- A *host-based scanner* runs on a system and looks into the configuration of the system from the inside. For example, a host-based scanner can check whether files that contain user authentication information (e.g., user passwords) can be read by nonprivileged processes.

- Contrary to that, a *network-based scanner* runs on a system and looks into the configurations of systems from the outside. For example, a network-based scanner can check what systems are accessible and what services are running on the ports of these systems.

Ideally, a scanner is host-based and network-based, meaning that it can investigate on and take into account information that is available on either side. As of this writing, there are many security scanners commercially or freely available on the Internet. The most widely used and deployed security scanners on the Internet are developed and marketed by Internet Security Systems, Inc.[4] In addition, there are

---

[4]http://www.iss.net/

many security scanners publicly and freely available on the Internet. For example, the Nessus security scanner was developed in an open source project of the same name.[5]

21.3.2   Intrusion Detection

According to [5], an *intrusion* refers to "a sequence of related actions by a malicious adversary that results in the occurrence of unauthorized security threats to a target computing or networking domain," and the term *intrusion detection* refers to the process of identifying and responding to intrusions.

There are many tools that can be used to automate intrusion detection. These tools are commonly referred to as *intrusion detection systems* (IDSs). Although the research community has been actively designing, developing, and testing IDSs for more than a decade, corresponding products have only recently received wider market interest. Furthermore, the IETF has chartered an Intrusion Detection Exchange Format (IDWG) WG "to define data formats and exchange procedures for sharing information of interest to intrusion detection and response systems, and to management systems which may need to interact with them." Refer to the IDWG's home page[6] to get more information about the relevant Internet-Drafts and RFC documents.

There are basically two technologies that can be used to implement an IDS: attack signature recognition and anomaly detection.

- Using attack signature recognition, an IDS uses a database with known attack patterns (or attack signatures) and an engine that uses this database to detect and recognize attacks. The database can either be local or remote. In either case, the quality of the IDS is as good as the database and its attack patterns as well as the engine that makes use of this database. The situation is similar and quite comparable to the antivirus software (i.e., the database must be updated on a regular basis).

- Using anomaly detection, an IDS uses a database with a formal representation of "normal" (or "normal-looking") user activities and an engine that makes use of this database to detect and recognize attacks. For example, if a user almost always starts up his or her e-mail user agent after having successfully logged onto a system, the IDS's engine may get suspicious if he or she starts a Telnet session

---

[5]http://www.nessus.org/
[6]http://www.ietf.org/html.charters/idwg-charter.html

to a trusted host first. The reason for this activity may be an attacker misusing the account to gain illegitimate access to a remote system. Again, the database can either be local or remote, and the quality of the IDS is as good as the database and its statistical material.

Again, it is possible to combine both technologies in an IDS. More information about intrusion detection technologies and IDSs that employ these technologies and are commercially available can be found in [5–9].

21.4 CONCLUSIONS

More often than not, security people elaborate on and argue about the importance, usefulness, and suitability of specific security technologies without having the relevant vulnerabilities, threats, and corresponding risks in mind. For example, using a secure messaging scheme, such as PGP or S/MIME, is almost useless if you have nothing to lose and all you want to do is forward electronic versions of the latest jokes to a friend. The use of a secure messaging scheme, however, is very useful if you want to transfer an electronic order to an e-commerce service provider. Consequently, all we do in terms of security should be driven by risk management considerations. Remember, for example, the discussion we briefly started toward the end of Chapter 19 regarding the relationship of trust management and risk management.

Historically, the usual way to manage risks in the IT world started with a formal risk analysis. This has changed and we start seeing two trends:

1. Formal risk analyses are being replaced with alternative approaches and technologies (e.g., security scanners and IDSs).

2. Preventive security mechanisms are being complemented by detective and reactive security mechanisms.

The first trend occurs simply because formal risk analyses are difficult and labor-intensive and because they poorly scale to large corporate intranets. Contrary to that, the second trend occurs because preventive security mechanisms, such as firewalls and the use of cryptographic security protocols, have turned out to be incomplete, meaning that they do not patch all vulnerabilities and do not protect against all possible threats. As an approximation of the first degree, you may think of all systems and applications to be vulnerable and exploitable by specific attacks. This is true even if the systems and applications use sophisticated preventive security mechanisms. In fact, it is possible and likely that security breaches and vulnerability exploits will always occur and compromise the security of our systems and applications. The role of the preventive security mechanisms is only to lower the likelihood that a serious exploit will happen.

Against this background, we have to think about detection and response. How do you, for example, make sure that exploits and attacks are detected in the first place? Note that, contrary to the real world, a victim must not necessarily be aware of the fact that he or she has become a victim in the digital world. Data can be copied electronically without leaving any traces. Similarly, what do you do if an exploit or attack is actually detected? How do you respond to exploits and attacks? In either case, you need detective and reactive security mechanisms. One may argue that detective and reactive security mechanisms are becoming more important because of the incomplete nature of the preventive security mechanisms we have in place today. In his latest book [10], Bruce Schneier provides some strong arguments about the importance of detection and response and why they are important in the insecure IT world in which we live today. When you are designing security for an intranet environment, you should carefully think about the role of detection and response. These components are in fact becoming increasingly important.

REFERENCES

[1] R. Shirey, "Internet Security Glossary," Request for Comments 2828, May 2000.

[2] D. B. Parker, *Fighting Computer Crime: A New Framework for Protecting Information*, John Wiley & Sons, New York, 1998.

[3] T. R. Peltier, *Information Security Risk Analysis*, CRC Press, Boca Raton, FL, 2001.

[4] T. Escamilla, *Intrusion Detection: Network Security Beyond the Firewall*, John Wiley & Sons, New York, 1998.

[5] E. Amoroso, *Intrusion Detection: An Introduction to Internet Surveillance, Correlation, Trace Back, Traps, and Response*, Intrusion.Net Books, Sparta, NJ, 1999.

[6] S. Northcutt, D. McLachlan, and J. Novak, *Network Intrusion Detection: An Analyst's Handbook*, 2nd Edition, New Riders Publishing, Indianapolis, IN, 2000.

[7] M. Cooper, et al., *Intrusion Signatures and Analysis*, New Riders Publishing, Indianapolis, IN, 2001.

[8] P. E. Proctor, *Practical Intrusion Detection Handbook*, Prentice Hall, Englewood Cliffs, NJ, 2000.

[9] R. G. Bace, *Intrusion Detection*, New Riders Publishing, Indianapolis, IN, 1999.

[10] B. Schneier, *Secrets and Lies: Digital Security in a Networked World*, John Wiley & Sons, New York, 2000.

Epilogue

As mentioned in Chapter 21, every new technology offers new possibilities but also introduces new vulnerabilities, threats, and corresponding risks. This is particularly true for TCP/IP networking and the Internet as a whole. In fact, we overviewed and briefly discussed many risks as well as security technologies, mechanisms, and services to counteract on these risks in the previous parts of this book.

No security technology, mechanism, or service is complete in the sense that it can be used to solve all security problems. This is true for the real world, but it is also true for the digital world. In the real world, we typically use a portfolio of very diverse technologies, mechanisms, and services to provide a good (i.e., safe and secure) feeling to the users. In this sense, the Internet is very comparable to other infrastructures, such as the highway system, the railway system, or even the airway system.

Referring to the highway system comparison (or analogy), for example, a TCP/IP communication problem is something similar to a pothole, a bridge failure, or a closed road. Similarly, a protocol problem is something like a wrongly marked exit sign or a failure of slower traffic to stay in the proper lane, and a network administration problem is something like a lack of emergency vehicle access or notification and response procedures for accidents. Finally, a host problem is something like a store proprietor along the highway leaving the doors open and the store unoccupied. The problem is not the proximity of the highway, but the carelessness of the corresponding store proprietor. Similar examples can be found for the other mentioned infrastructures.

Taking the highway system analogy one step further, it is interesting to have a closer look at the way we attempt to provide safety and security. In particular, we use and deploy several technical, legal, and organizational measures to achieve safe and secure traffic:

- On the technical side, we (or, at least, the manufacturers) attempt to design and build cars that are safe in the sense that the risks of serious injury in an accident are minimized. Similarly, we build highways in a way that minimizes the risks of careless drivers being able to cause serious accidents (e.g., we separate the lines in opposite directions with physical obstacles).

- On the legal side, we have traffic laws that define proper behavior on the street. Furthermore, many laws require drivers to have a license and vehicles (e.g., cars and motorbikes) to pass an emissions test.

- On the organizational side, we have many educational programs and we teach children how to properly behave on the highway. Furthermore, we have police to enforce the traffic laws.

A similar portfolio of technical, legal, and organizational measures should be compiled to provide Internet security. As a matter of fact, several technical measures are currently under consideration for being deployed on the Internet. For example, it is always a good idea to design and develop communication protocols that minimize vulnerabilities and corresponding risks. If a connection-oriented transport layer protocol (e.g., TCP) is designed in a way that state information is maintained only after a connection has successfully been established, the protocol is generally less exposed to DoS attacks. Also, there are people who demand of Internet users some basic education with regard to the proper use of the Internet, and there are people who think that it would be a good idea to require Internet hosts to meet some baseline security requirements. The discussion is even more specific with regard to legal and organizational measures.

Last, but not least, the entire discussion about privacy and (pseudo-)anonymity on the Internet still remains to be held. Referring to the highway system analogy, we have established a system that supports the notion of pseudonyms in reality. In fact, every car license plate lists a unique number, and this number can be used to eventually trace an individual car owner. In the digital world of the Internet, the idea of using pseudonyms is not yet widespread and well understood. Instead, we generally use our real identities (e.g., user IDs and IP addresses) to interact with our peers. This is likely to change in the future. It is possible and very likely that we will see the development and wide proliferation of PETs for the Internet as we already mentioned at the end of Chapter 19. You may refer to [1], Chapter 13 of [2], or [3] for a more comprehensive overview about privacy issues and anonymity services related to the Internet and the WWW. In fact, it is possible and very likely that privacy will become more and more important in a world that is making more and more use of information technologies.

REFERENCES

[1] R. Oppliger, "Privacy Protection and Anonymity Services for the World Wide Web (WWW)," *Future Generation Computer Systems*, Vol. 16, Issue 4, February 2000, pp. 379–391.

[2] R. Oppliger, *Security Technologies for the World Wide Web*, Artech House, Norwood, MA, 2000.

[3] M. Caloyannides, *Computer Forensics and Privacy*, Artech House, Norwood, MA, 2001.

Abbreviations and Acronyms

AA	attribute authority
AAI	authentication and authorization infrastructure
ACL	access control list
ACM	Association for Computing Machinery
ACT	anticlogging token
AES	Advanced Encryption Standard
AFS	Andrew file system
AFT	authenticated firewall traversal
AH	authentication header
ANSI	American National Standards Institute
API	application programming interface
ARPA	Advanced Research Projects Agency
AS	authentication server
ASN.1	abstract syntax notation 1
ATM	asynchronous transfer mode
	automatic teller machine
BAN	Burrows, Abadi, and Needham
BBN	Bolt Beranek and Newman, Inc.
BCP	best current practice
BER	basic encoding rules

BIND	Berkeley Internet name daemon
BXA	Bureau of Export Administration
CA	certification authority
CAT	common authentication technology
CBC	cipher block chaining
CC	common criteria
CCI	common client interface
CCITT	Consultative Committee on International Telegraphy and Telephony (now ITU-T)
CCP	Compression Control Protocol
CCTA	Central Computer and Telecommunications Agency
CD	compact disc
	committee draft
CDP	Certificate Discovery Protocol
CEC	Commission of the European Communities
CERT	computer emergency response team
CERT/CC	CERT coordination center
CFB	cipher feedback
CHAP	Challenge Handshake Authentication Protocol
CLI	command line interface
CLNP	Connectionless Network Protocol
CLUSIF	club de la sécurité informatique francais
CMIP	Common Management Information Protocol
CMS	cryptographic message syntax
COAST	computer operations, audit, and security technology
CORBA	common object request broker architecture
COTS	commercial off-the-shelf
CRAMM	CCTA risk analysis and management methodology
CRC	cyclic redundancy checksum
CRHF	collision resistant hash function
CRL	certificate revocation list
CRMF	certificate request message format
CRS	certificate revocation system
CRT	certificate revocation tree
CSI	Computer Security Institute
CSRG	Computer Systems Research Group
CV	control value

DAC	discretionary access control
DAP	Directory Access Protocol
DARPA	Defense Advanced Research Projects Agency
DCA	Defense Communications Agency
DCE	Distributed Computing Environment
DCMS	distributed certificate management system
DDoS	distributed denial of service
DEC	Digital Equipment Corporation
DER	distinguished encoding rules
DES	Data Encryption Standard
DFA	differential fault analysis
DIS	draft international standard
DISA	Defense Information Systems Agency
DIT	directory information tree
DMZ	demilitarized zone
DN	distinguished name
DNS	domain name system
DoC	U.S. Department of Commerce
DoD	U.S. Department of Defense
DOI	domain of interpretation
DoS	U.S. Department of State
	denial of service
DOS	disk operating system
DPA	differential power analysis
DSA	digital signature algorithm
DSS	Digital Signature Standard
DVC	data validation certificate
DVCS	data validation and certification server
E-cash	electronic cash
ECB	electronic code book
E-commerce	electronic commerce
ECP	Encryption Control Protocol
EDI	electronic data interchange
EFS	encrypting file system
EFT	electronic funds transfer
EGP	Exterior Gateway Protocol
EIT	Enterprise Integration Technologies

E-mail	electronic mail
ESM	encrypted session manager
ESP	encapsulating security payload
EU	European Union
FAQ	frequently asked question
FDDI	fiber distributed data interface
FIPS	Federal Information Processing Standard
FIRST	Forum of Incident Response and Security Teams
FNC	Federal Networking Council
FQDN	fully qualified domain name
FSUIT	Swiss Federal Strategy Unit for Information Technology
FTP	File Transfer Protocol
FWPD	Firewall Product Developers Consortium
FWTK	firewall toolkit
GII	global information infrastructure
GIK	group interchange key
GPS	global positioning system
GSS-API	generic security service API
GUI	graphical user interface
HP	Hewlett-Packard
HTML	Hypertext Markup Language
HTTP	Hypertext Transfer Protocol
IAB	Internet Architecture Board
IAM	Institute for Computer Science and Applied Mathematics
IANA	Internet Assigned Numbers Authority
IBM	International Business Machines Corporation
ICANN	Internet Corporation for Assigned Names and Numbers
ICMP	Internet Control Message Protocol
ICSA	International Computer Security Association
ICSI	International Computer Science Institute
IDEA	international data encryption algorithm
IDS	intrusion detection system
IDWG	intrusion detection exchange format
IEC	International Electrotechnical Committee

IEEE	Institute of Electrical and Electronic Engineers
IESG	Internet Engineering Steering Group
IETF	Internet Engineering Task Force
IFIP	International Federation for Information Processing
IGP	Interior Gateway Protocol
IIOP	Internet Inter-ORB Protocol
IKE	Internet key exchange
IKMP	Internet Key Management Protocol
IMAP	Internet Message Access Protocol
IP	Internet Protocol
IPC	interprocess communications facility
IPng	IP next generation
IPPCP	IP Payload Compression Protocol
IPRA	Internet Policy Registration Authority
IPsec	IP security
IPSP	IP security policy
IPSRA	IP security remote access
IPST	IP Secure Tunnel Protocol
IRSG	Internet Research Steering Group
IRTF	Internet Research Task Force
IS	international standard
ISDN	integrated switched digital network
ISO	International Organization for Standardization
ISOC	Internet Society
IT	information technology
ITSEC	information technology security evaluation criteria
ITU-T	International Telecommunication Union – Telecommunication Standardization Sector
IV	initialization vector
JTC1	Joint Technical Committee 1
Kbps	kilobit per second
KDC	key distribution center
KDS	key distribution server
KEA	key exchange algorithm
KEK	key encryption key
KTC	key translation center

LAN	local area network
LDAP	Lightweight Directory Access Protocol
LLC	logical link control
MAC	message authentication code
MAN	metropolitan area network
MARION	méthodologie d'analyse des risques informatiques et d'optimation par niveau
MBone	multicast backbone
MD	message digest
MDC	modification detection code
MHS	message handling system
MIB	management information base
MIC	message integrity check
MIME	multipurpose Internet mail extensions
MIT	Massachusetts Institute of Technology
MKMP	Modular Key Management Protocol
MLS	multilevel security
MOSS	MIME object security services
MPLS	multi-protocol label switching
MSP	Message Security Protocol
MTA	message transfer agent
MTS	message transfer system
NAS	network access server
NASA	National Aeronautics and Space Agency
NBS	National Bureau of Standards
NCP	Network Control Protocol
NCSA	National Computer Security Association
NetSP	Network Security Program
NII	national information infrastructure
NIST	National Institute of Standards and Technology
NLSP	Network Layer Security Protocol
NMS	network management station
NNTP	Network News Transfer Protocol
NRL	U.S. Naval Research Laboratory
NSA	National Security Agency
NSF	National Science Foundation

NSP	Network Security Policy
NTP	Network Time Protocol
OCSP	Online Certificate Status Protocol
OFB	output feedback
OPIE	one-time passwords in everything
OPSEC	open platform for security
ORB	Object Request Broker
OSF	Open Software Foundation
OSI	open systems interconnection
OSI-RM	OSI reference model
OWHF	one-way hash function
PAC	proxy auto-configuration
PAP	Password Authentication Protocol
PARC	Palo Alto Research Center
PC	personal computer
PCA	policy certification authority
PCT	private communication technology
PDA	personal digital assistant
PEM	privacy enhanced mail
PEP	Protocol Extension Protocol
PET	privacy enhancing technology
PFS	perfect forward secrecy
PGP	Pretty Good Privacy
PIN	personal identification number
PKCS	public key cryptography standard
PKI	public key infrastructure
PKIX	Public Key Infrastructure X.509
PKP	Public Key Partners
PMI	privilege management infrastructure
POP	Post Office Protocol
PPP	Point-to-Point Protocol
PSRG	Privacy and Security Research Group
PSTN	public-switched telephone network
QoS	quality of service
RA	registration authority

RACF	resource access control facility
RADIUS	remote authentication dial-in user service
RFC	request for comment
RIP	Routing Information Protocol
ROM	read-only memory
RPC	remote procedure call
RR	resource record
RSA	Rivest, Shamir, and Adleman
RSVP	Resource Reservation Protocol
SA	security association
SAID	secure association identifier
SALS	simple authentication and security layer
SDNS	secure data network system
SDSI	simple distributed security infrastructure
SECSH	Secure Shell
SESAME	secure European system for applications in a multi-vendor environment
SET	secure electronic transaction
SHA	secure hash algorithm
SHS	secure hash standard
S-HTTP	secure HTTP
SID	security identifier
SILS	standards for interoperable LAN/MAN security
SKIP	simple key-management for Internet protocols
SLIP	serial line IP
S/MIME	Secure MIME
SMS	service management system
SMTP	Simple Mail Transfer Protocol
SNMP	Simple Network Management Protocol
SP3	Security Protocol 3
SP4	Security Protocol 4
SPI	security parameters index
SPKI	simple public key infrastructure
SRA	secure RPC authentication
SRI	Stanford Research Institute
SSH	Secure Shell
	site security handbook

SSL	secure sockets layer
SSR	secure socket relay
STD	Internet Standard
STEL	secure telnet
STS	station-to-station
TACAS	terminal access controller access system
TAMU	Texas A&M University
TAN	transaction authentication number
TCB	trusted computing base
TCP	Transport Control Protocol
TCSEC	trusted computer system evaluation criteria
TEK	token enryption key
TESS	the exponential security system
	trusted entry security server
TFTP	trivial FTP
TIS	Trusted Information Systems, Inc.
TLI	transport layer interface
TLS	transport layer security
TLSP	Transport Layer Security Protocol
TOS	type of service
TTL	time to live
TTP	trusted third party
UC	University of California
UCB	University of California at Berkeley
UCLA	University of California at Los Angeles
UCSB	University of California at Santa Barbara
UDP	User Datagram Protocol
UID	user identification
U.K.	United Kingdom
UPS	United Parcel Service
URL	uniform resource locator
U.S.	United States
UUCP	UNIX-UNIX Copy Protocol
VPN	virtual private network
VTP	Virtual Tunneling Protocol

WAIS	wide area information service
WAN	wide area network
WAP	Wireless Application Protocol
WEF	World Economic Forum
WG	working group
WTLS	wireless transport layer security
WWW	World Wide Web
W3C	World Wide Web Consortium
XML	Extensible Markup Language

About the Author

Rolf Oppliger received M.Sc. and Ph.D. degrees in computer science from the University of Berne, Switzerland, in 1991 and 1993, respectively. After spending one year as a postdoctoral researcher at the International Computer Science Institute (ICSI) in Berkeley, California, he joined the Swiss Federal Strategy Unit for Information Technology (FSUIT) in 1995, and continued his research and teaching activities at several universities and polytechnics in Switzerland and Germany. In 1999, he received the venia legendi from the University of Zürich, Switzerland, became the Artech House series editor for computer security, and founded eSECURITY Technologies Rolf Oppliger (http://www.esecurity.ch) to provide scientific and state-of-the-art consulting, education, and engineering services related to information technology (IT) security. He has published numerous scientific papers, articles, and books, mainly on security-related topics. He is a member of the Swiss Informaticians Society (SI) and its working group on security, the Association for Computing Machinery (ACM), the IEEE Computer Society, and the International Federation for Information Processing (IFIP) Technical Committee 11 (TC11) Working Group 4 (WG4) on Network Security.

Index

Recent Titles in the Artech House Computing Library

Secure Messaging with PGP and S/MIME, Rolf Oppliger

Software Fault Tolerance Techniques and Implementation,
Laura L. Pullum

*Software Verification and Validation for Practitioners and
Managers, Second Edition,* Steven R. Rakitin

Strategic Software Production with Domain-Oriented Reuse,
Paolo Predonzani, Giancarlo Succi, and Tullio Vernazza

Systems Modeling for Business Process Improvement, David
Bustard, Peter Kawalek, and Mark Norris, editors

*User-Centered Information Design for Improved Software
Usability,* Pradeep Henry

*Workflow Modeling: Tools for Process Improvement and
Application Development,* Alec Sharp and Patrick McDermott

For further information on these and other Artech House titles,
including previously considered out-of-print books now available
through our In-Print-Forever® (IPF®) program, contact:

Artech House   Artech House
685 Canton Street   46 Gillingham Street
Norwood, MA 02062   London SW1V 1AH UK
Phone: 781-769-9750   Phone: +44 (0)20 7596-8750
Fax: 781-769-6334   Fax: +44 (0)20 7630-0166
e-mail: artech@artechhouse.com   e-mail: artech-uk@artechhouse.com

Find us on the World Wide Web at:
www.artechhouse.com